FOR MY TOO SAKE...

I saw a bunch of elementary school kids the other day standing around a *Bleach* card game machine. As I got nearer, one of the bigger, bossier kids said, "Don't you know?! This is Genryûsai's Bankai—Kikô Oh, the Firebird King!"

I thought to myself, I've got to work harder.

-Tite Kubo

BLEACH is author Tite Kubo's second title. Kubo made his debut with *ZOMBIEPOWDER.*, a four-volume series for *WEEKLY SHONEN JUMP*. To date, *BLEACH* has been translated into numerous languages and has also inspired an animated TV series that began airing in the U.S. in 2006. Beginning its serialization in 2001, *BLEACH* is still a mainstay in the pages of *WEEKLY SHONEN JUMP*. In 2005, *BLEACH* was awarded the prestigious Shogakukan Manga Award in the *shonen* (boys) category.

D0059400

BLEACH
Vol. 30: THERE IS NO HEART WITHOUT YOU
SHONEN JUMP Manga Edition
This volume contains material that was originally published in English
in SHONEN JUMP #84–86. Artwork in the magazine may have been
altered slightly from what is presented in this volume.

STORY AND ART BY
TITE KUBO

English Adaptation/Lance Caselman
Translation/Joe Yamazaki
Touch-Up Art & Lettering/Mark McMurray
Design/Sean Lee
Editors/Pancha Diaz and Yuki Takagaki

VP, Production/Alvin Lu
VP, Sales & Product Marketing/Gonzalo Ferreyra
VP, Creative/Linda Espinosa
Publisher/Hyoe Narita

BLEACH © 2001 by Tite Kubo. All rights reserved. First published
in Japan in 2001 by SHUEISHA Inc., Tokyo. English translation rights
arranged by SHUEISHA Inc.

The rights of the author(s) of the work(s) in this publication to be so
identified have been asserted in accordance with Copyright, Designs and
Patents Act 1988. A CIP catalogue record for this book is available from
the British Library.

The stories, characters and incidents mentioned in this publication are
entirely fictional.

No portion of this book may be reproduced or transmitted in any form
or by any means without written permission from the copyright holders.

Printed in the U.S.A.

Published by VIZ Media, LLC
P.O. Box 77010
San Francisco, CA 94107

10 9 8 7 6 5 4 3 2 1
First printing, March 2010

PARENTAL ADVISORY
BLEACH is rated T for Teen and is recommended
for ages 13 and up. This volume contains
fantasy violence.
RATED
FOR
TEEN
ratings.viz.com

www.viz.com

THE WORLD'S
MOST POPULAR MANGA
www.shonenjump.com

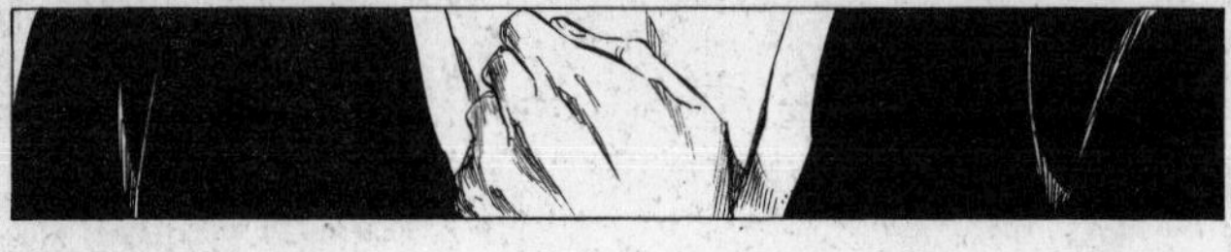

The wound lies deep, like the ocean floor.
The sin is red, growing paler in death.

BLEACH 30

THERE IS NO HEART WITHOUT YOU

Shonen Jump Manga

STARS AND

Rukia Kuchiki

Chad Sado

Ichigo Kurosaki

plot

When high school student Ichigo Kurosaki meets Soul Reaper Rukia Kuchiki his life is changed forever. Soon Ichigo is a soul-cleansing Soul Reaper too, and he finds himself having adventures—and problems—he never could have imagined. Now Ichigo and his friends must stop renegade Soul Reaper Aizen and his army of Arrancars from destroying the Soul Society and wiping out Karakura town in the process.

When the Arrancars abduct Orihime, Ichigo and his friends travel to Hueco Mundo to rescue her. But soon they are forced to separate and take different routes to Aizen's stronghold. Now, locked in combat with a deadly Espada, Chad awakens his true power, the Brazo Izquierda del Diablo!

BLEACH ALL

ノイトラ

Nnoitora

アーロニーロ

Aaroniero

Szayelaporro

ザエルアポロ

STORIES

BLEACH 30

THERE IS NO HEART WITHOUT YOU

Contents

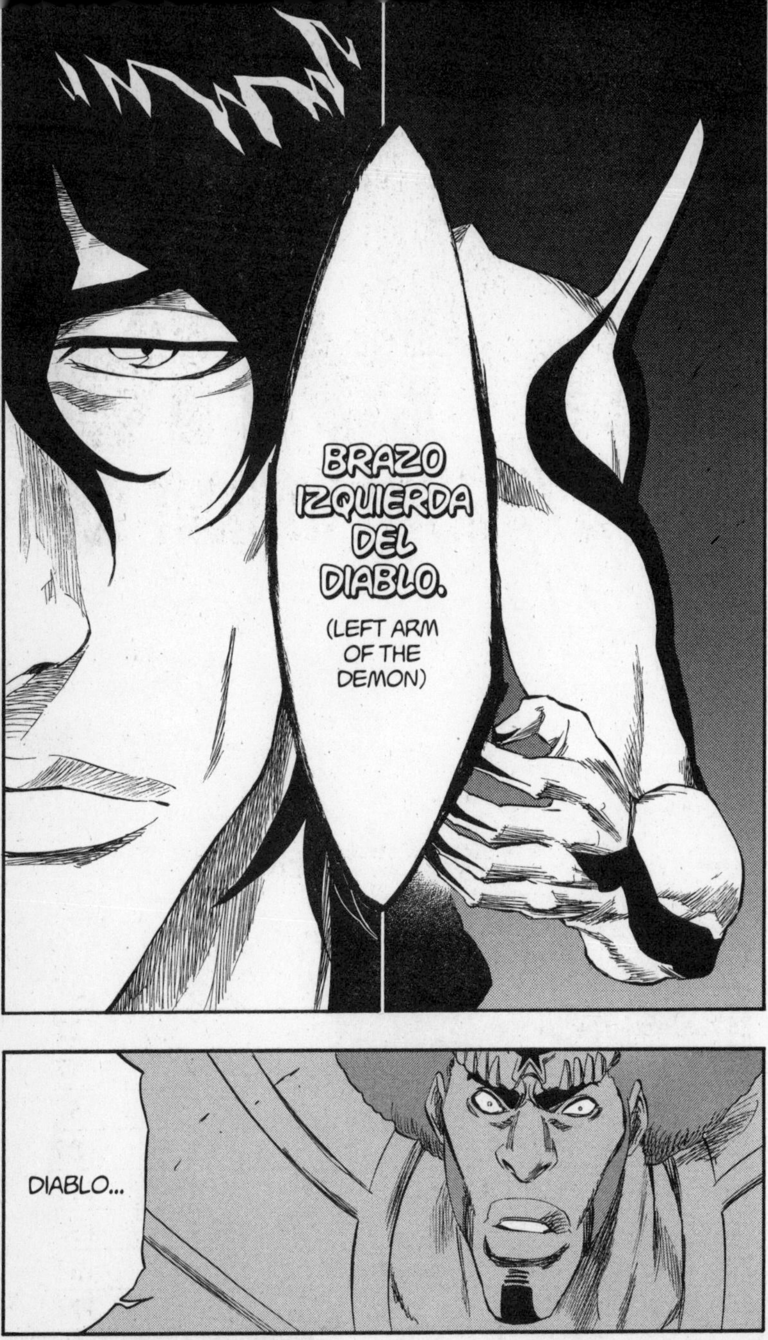
BRAZO IZQUIERDA DEL DIABLO.
(LEFT ARM OF THE DEMON)
DIABLO...

261. LEFT ARM OF THE DEMON

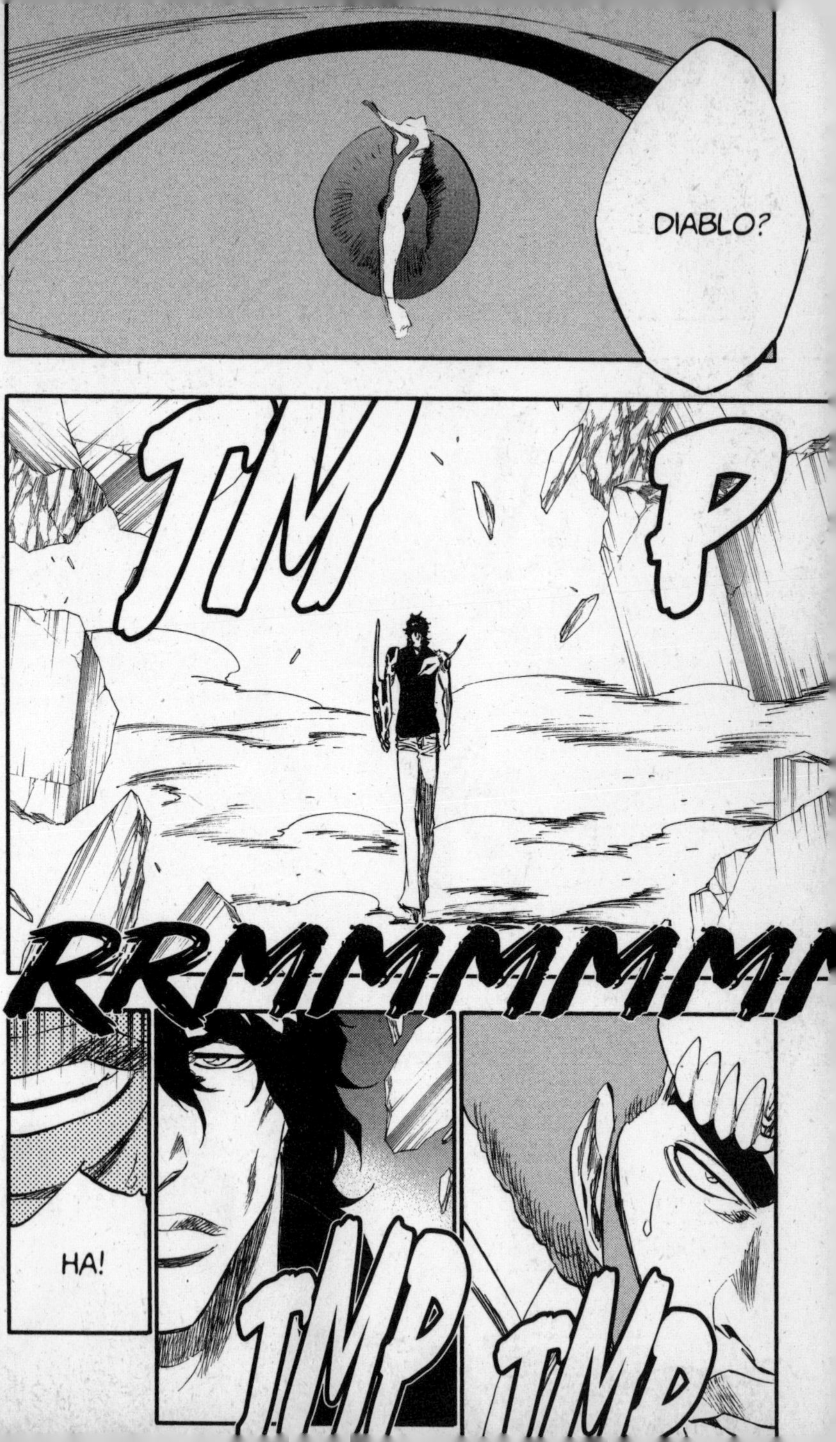
DIABLO?
TMP
RRMMMMMM
TMP
HA!
TMP

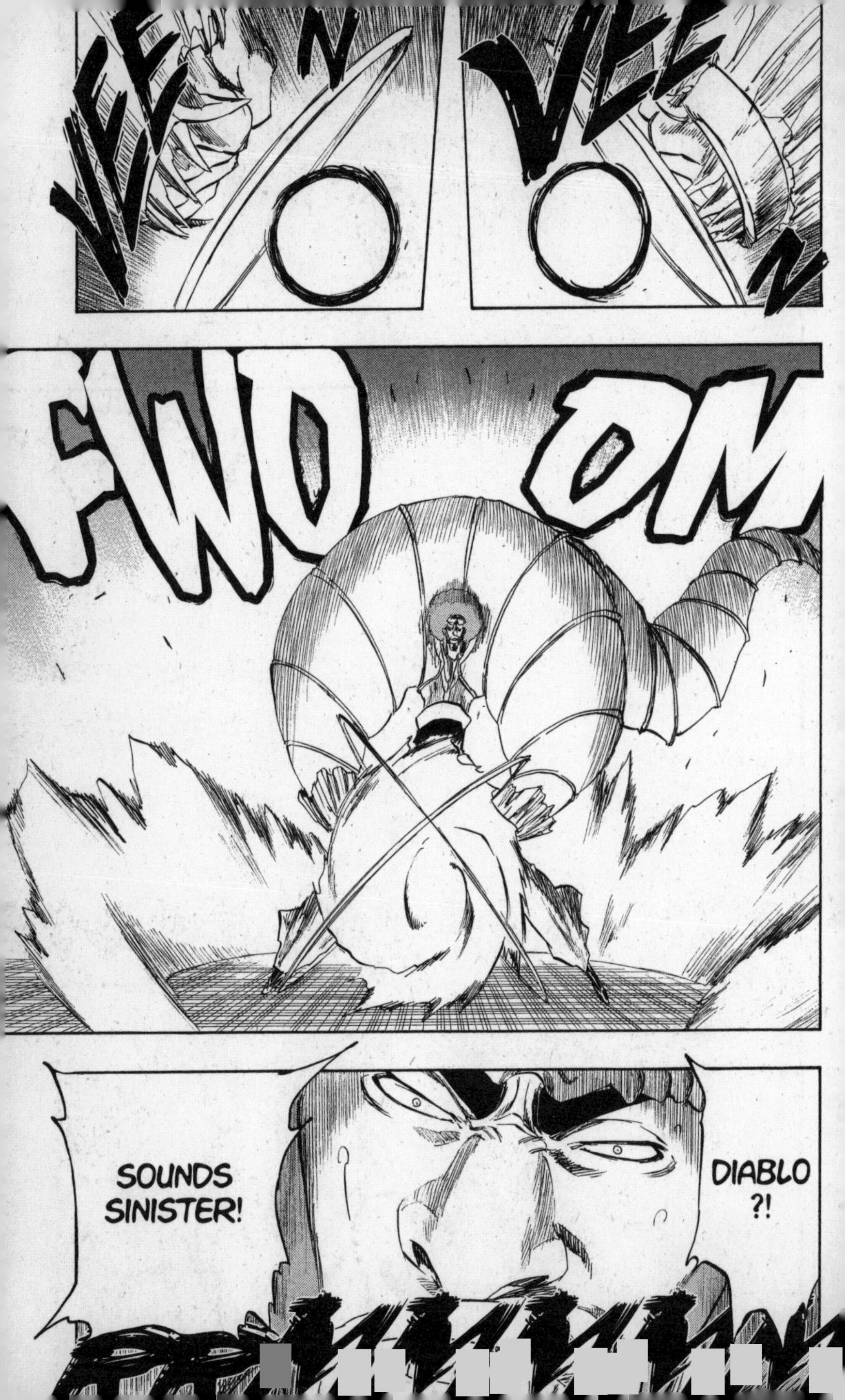
FWOOM
DIABLO ?!
SOUNDS SINISTER!

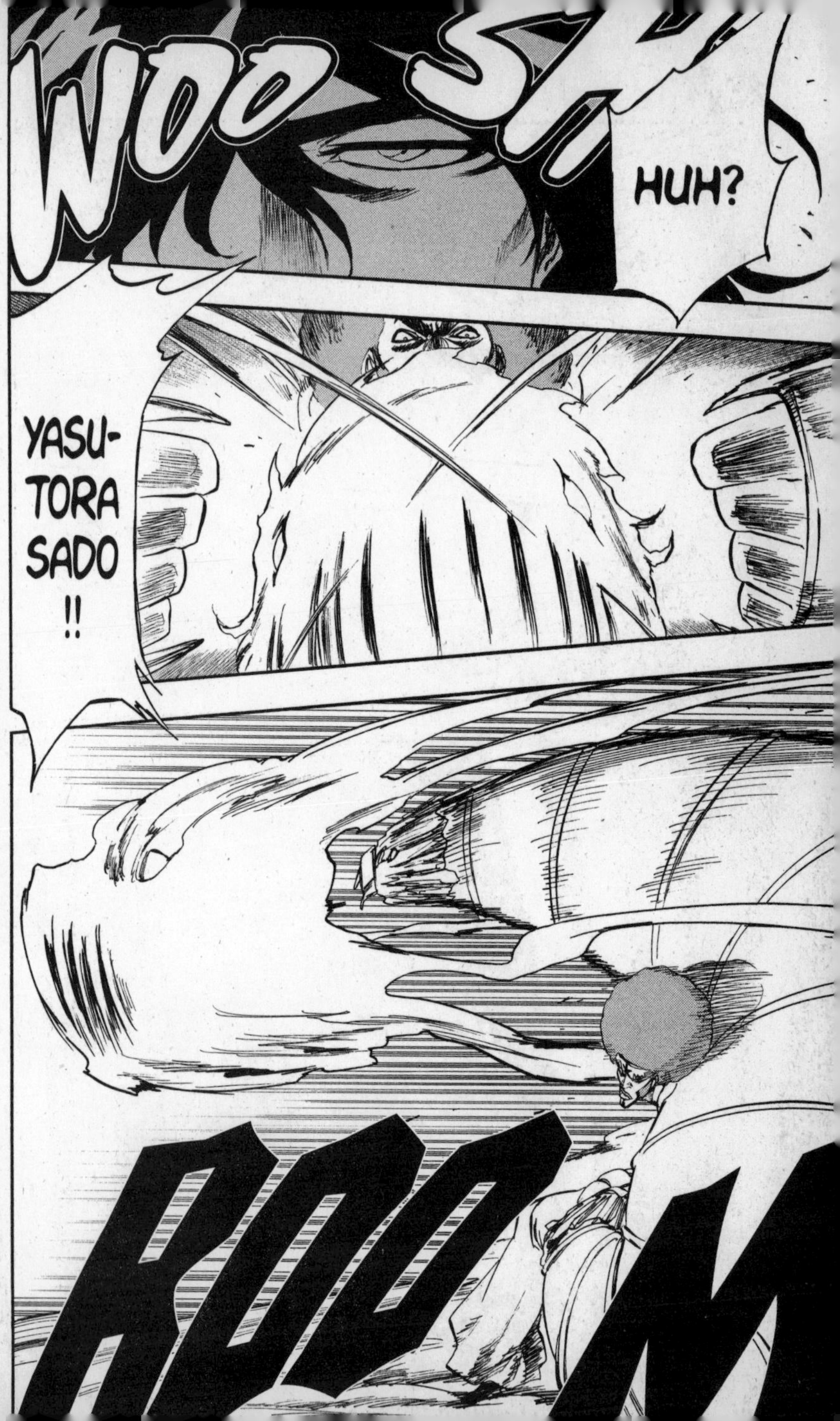
HUH?
YASU-
TORA
SADO
!!

READ THIS WAY

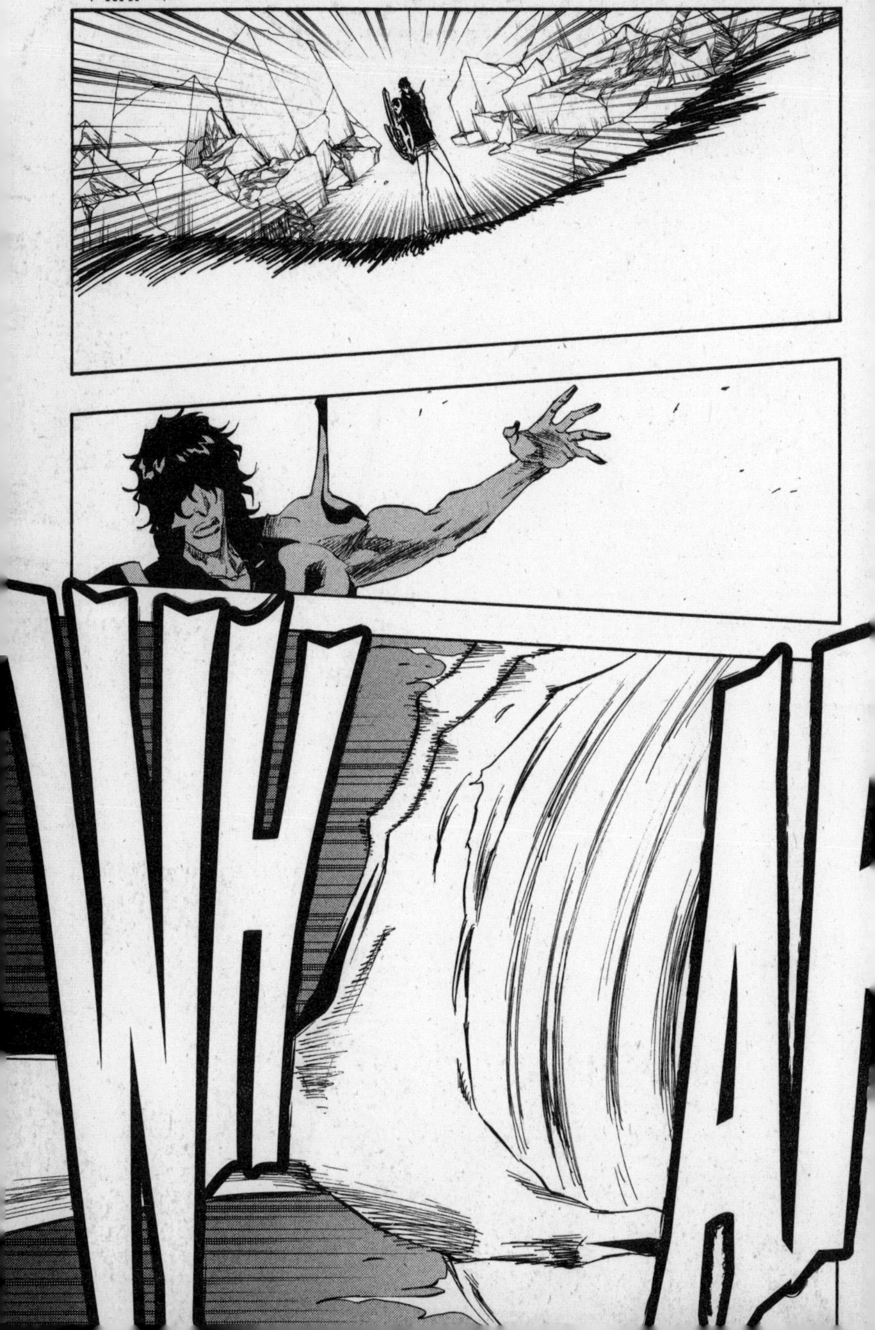

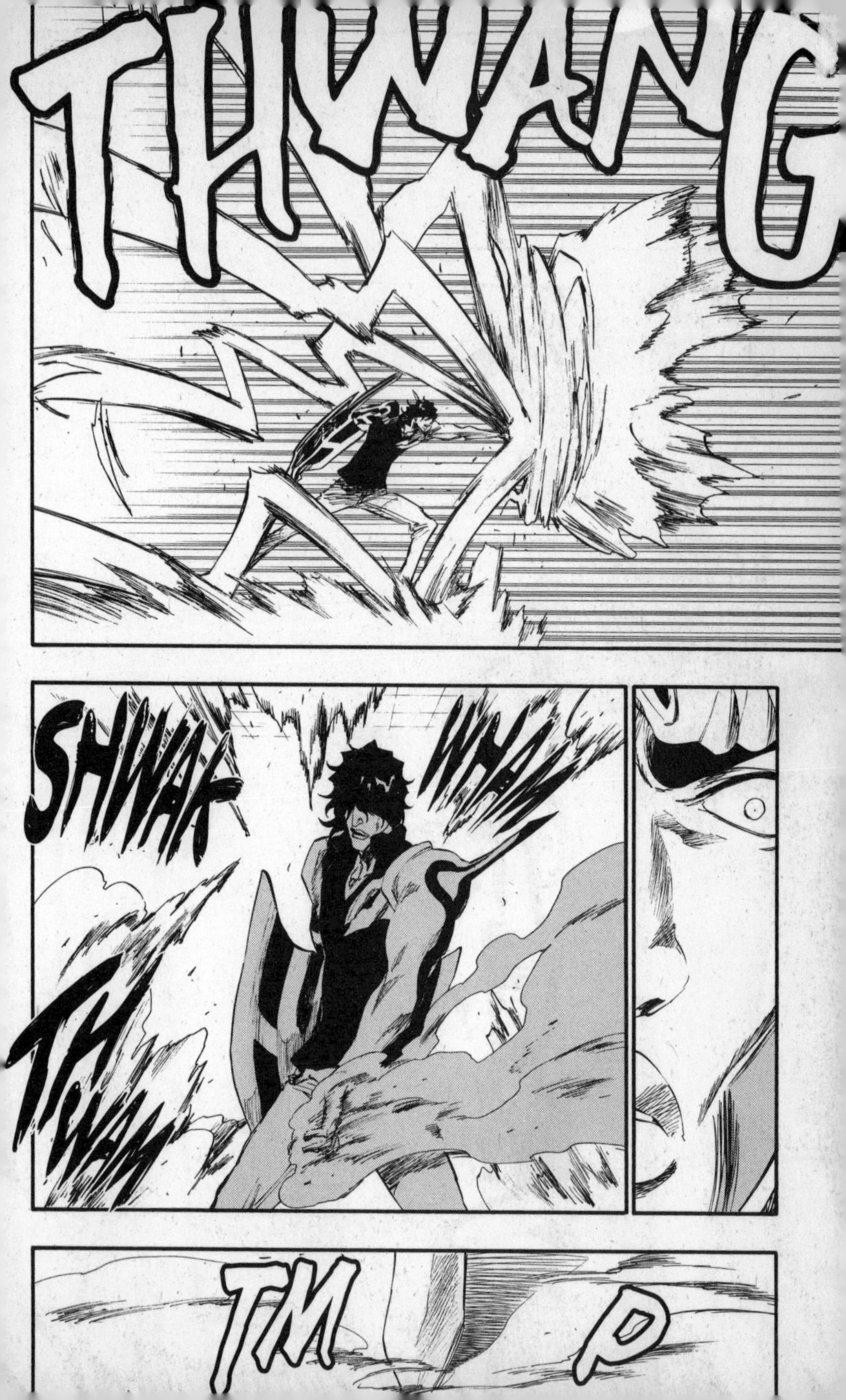
THWANG
WHAK
SHWAK
THWAM
TM P

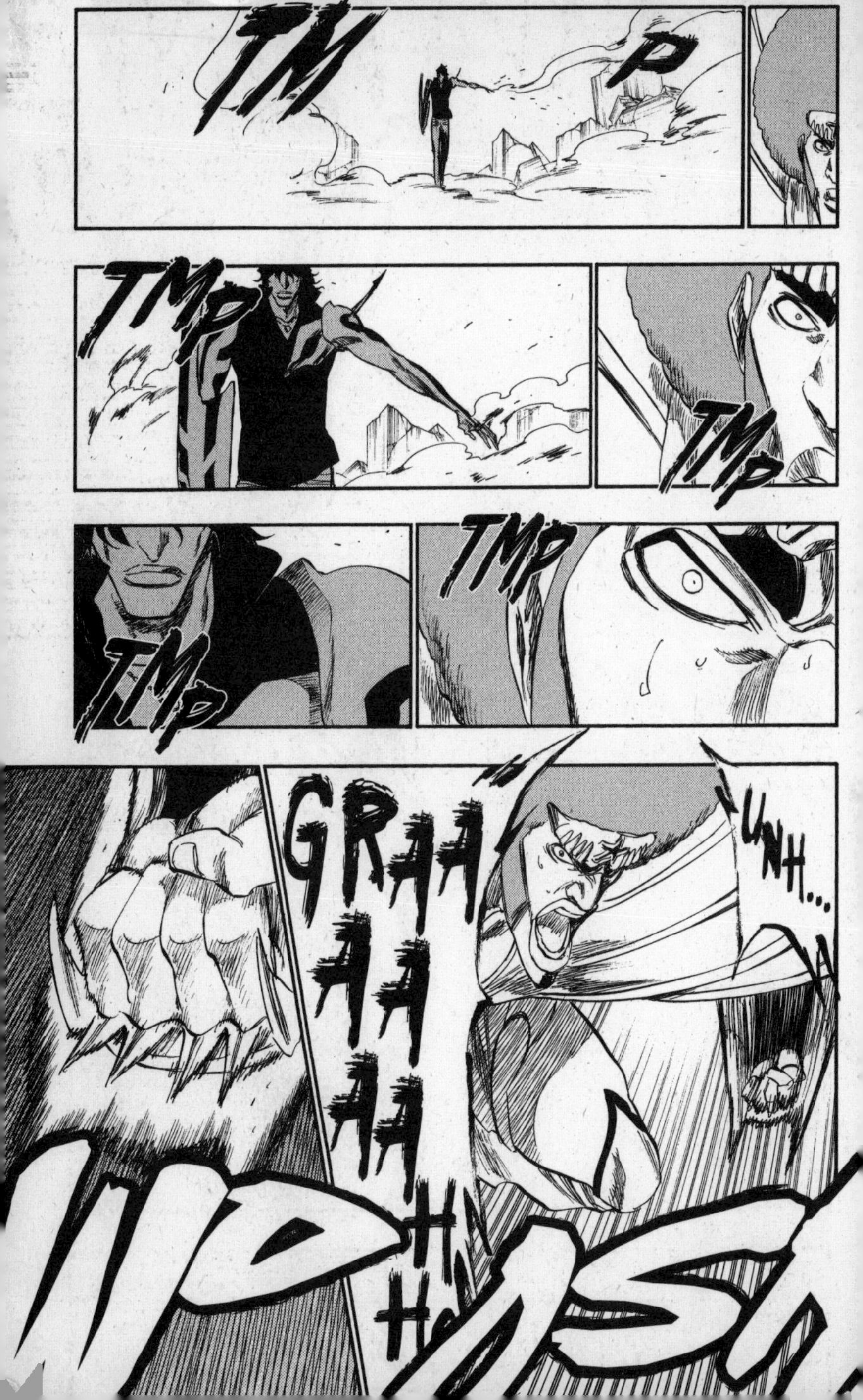
TMP
TMP
TMP
TMP
TMP
UNH...
GRAAAAAAAHH
WHOOSH

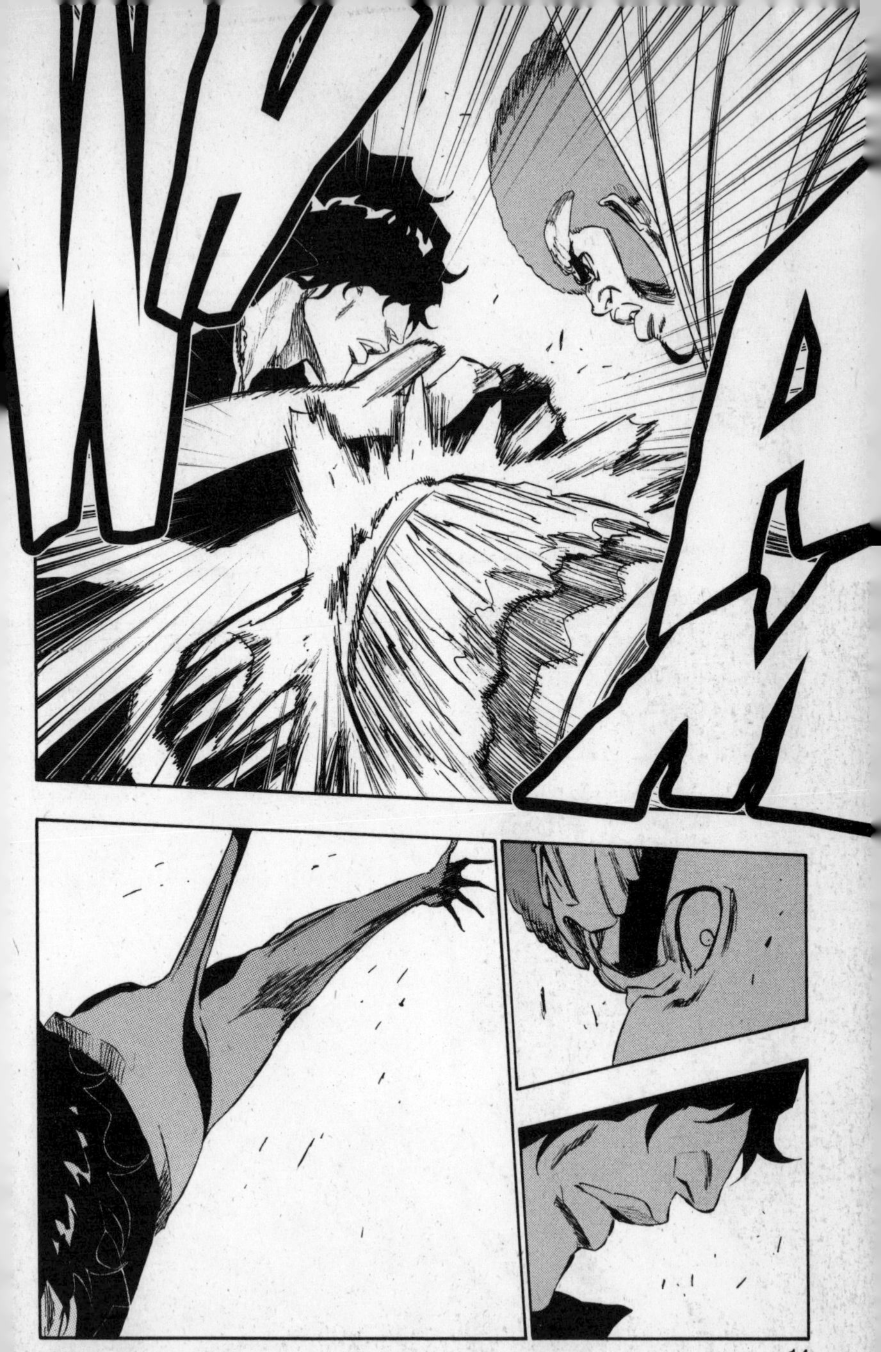
WHAM

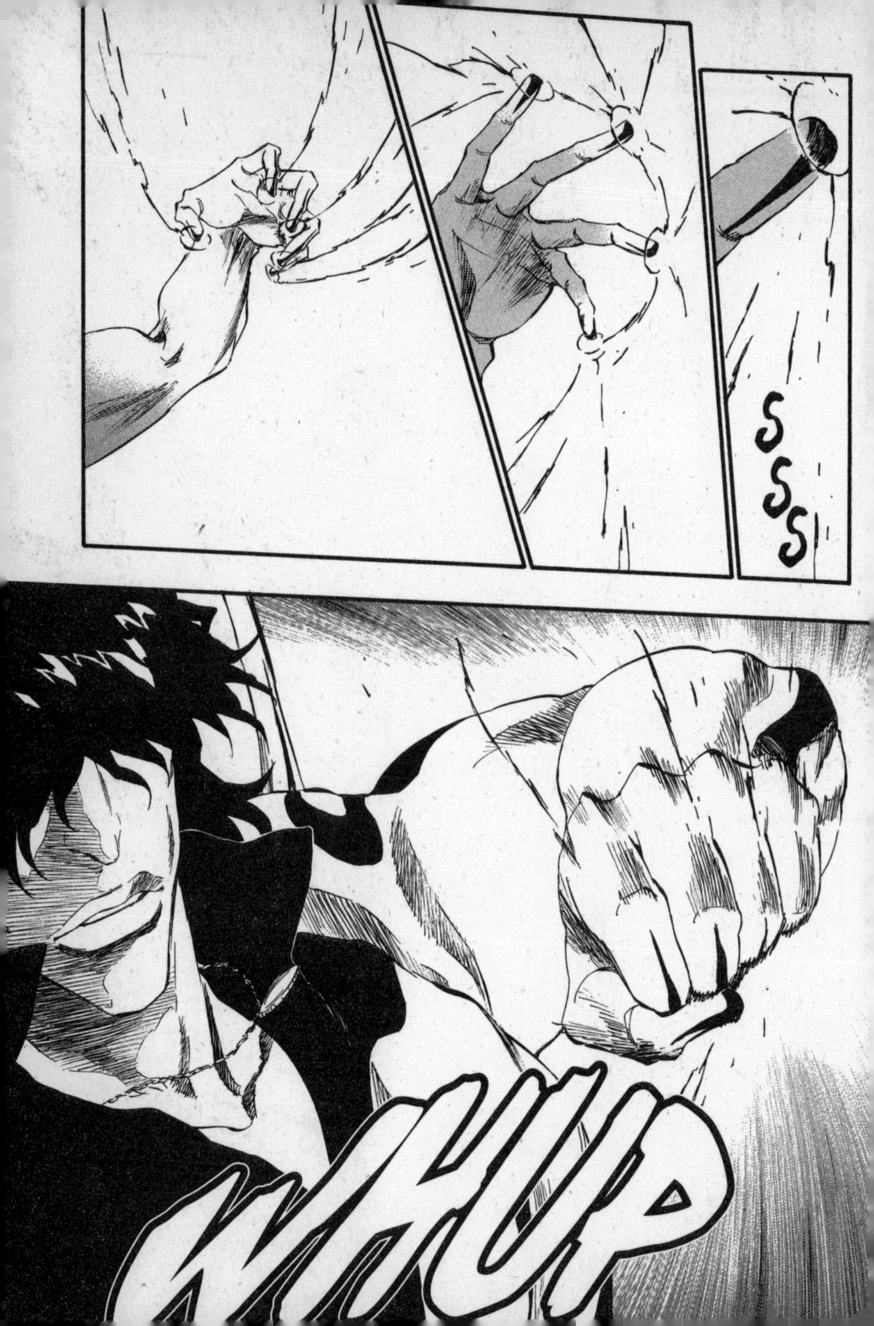
SSS
WHUP

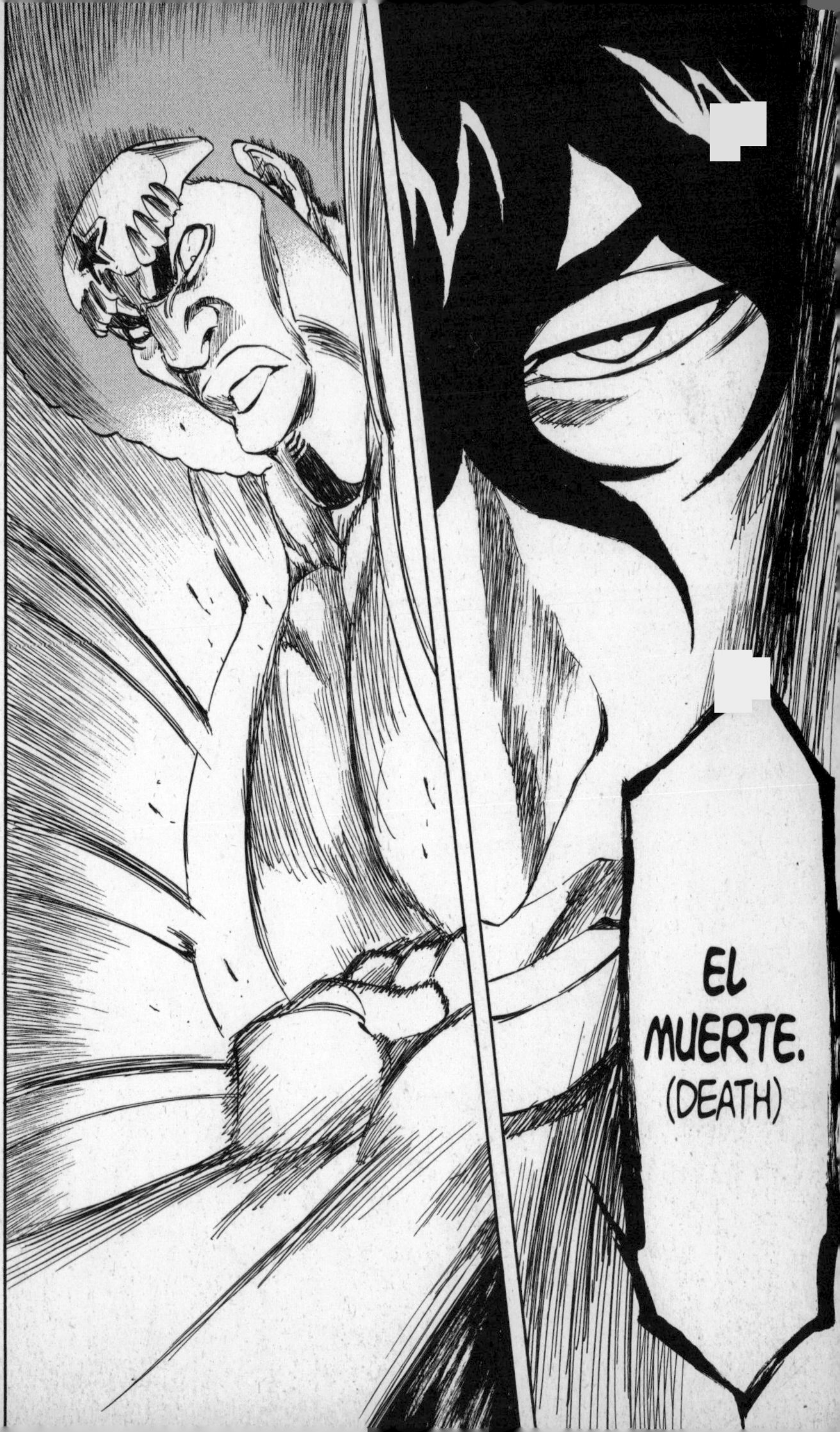
EL MUERTE.
(DEATH)

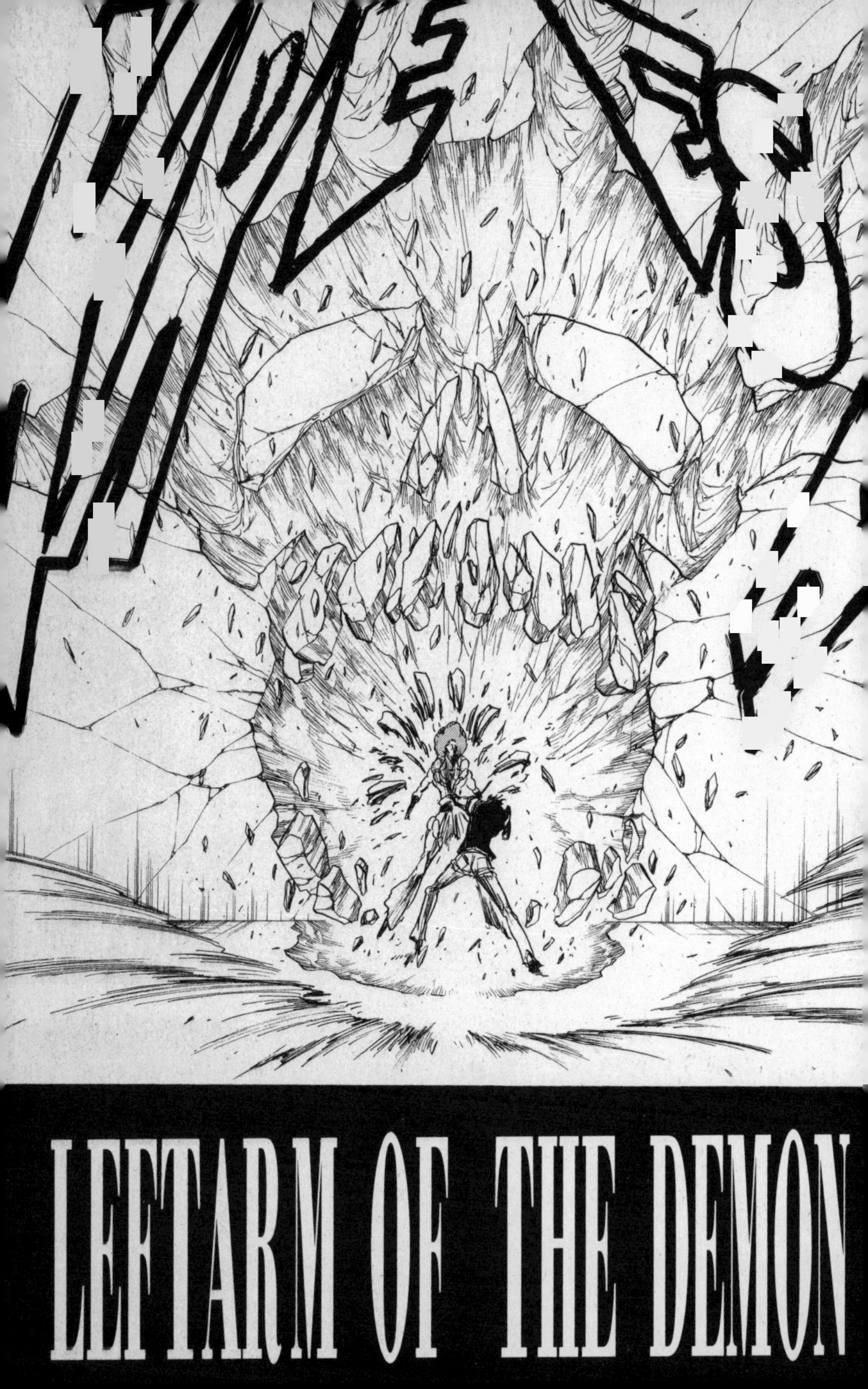

LEFTARM OF THE DEMON

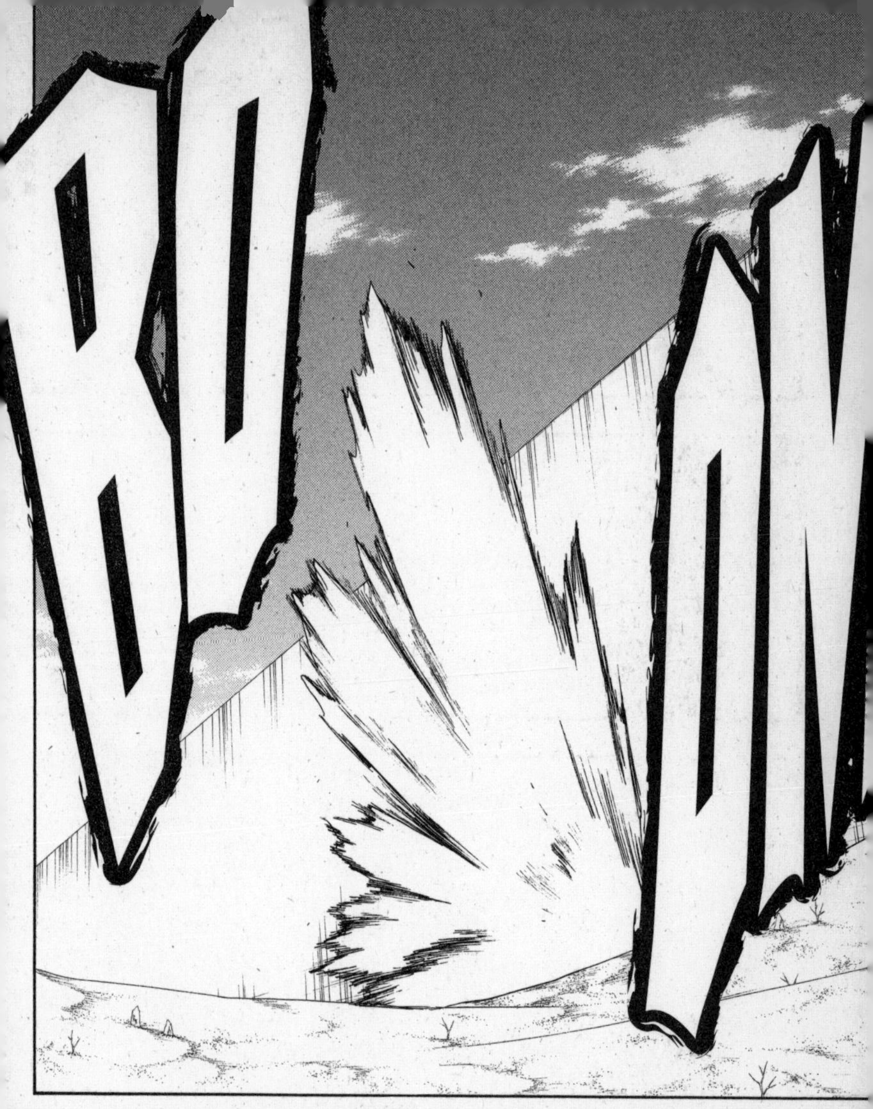
BOOM
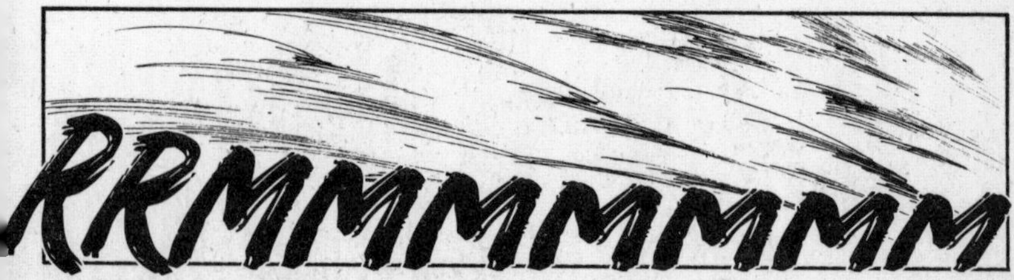
RRMMMMMMM

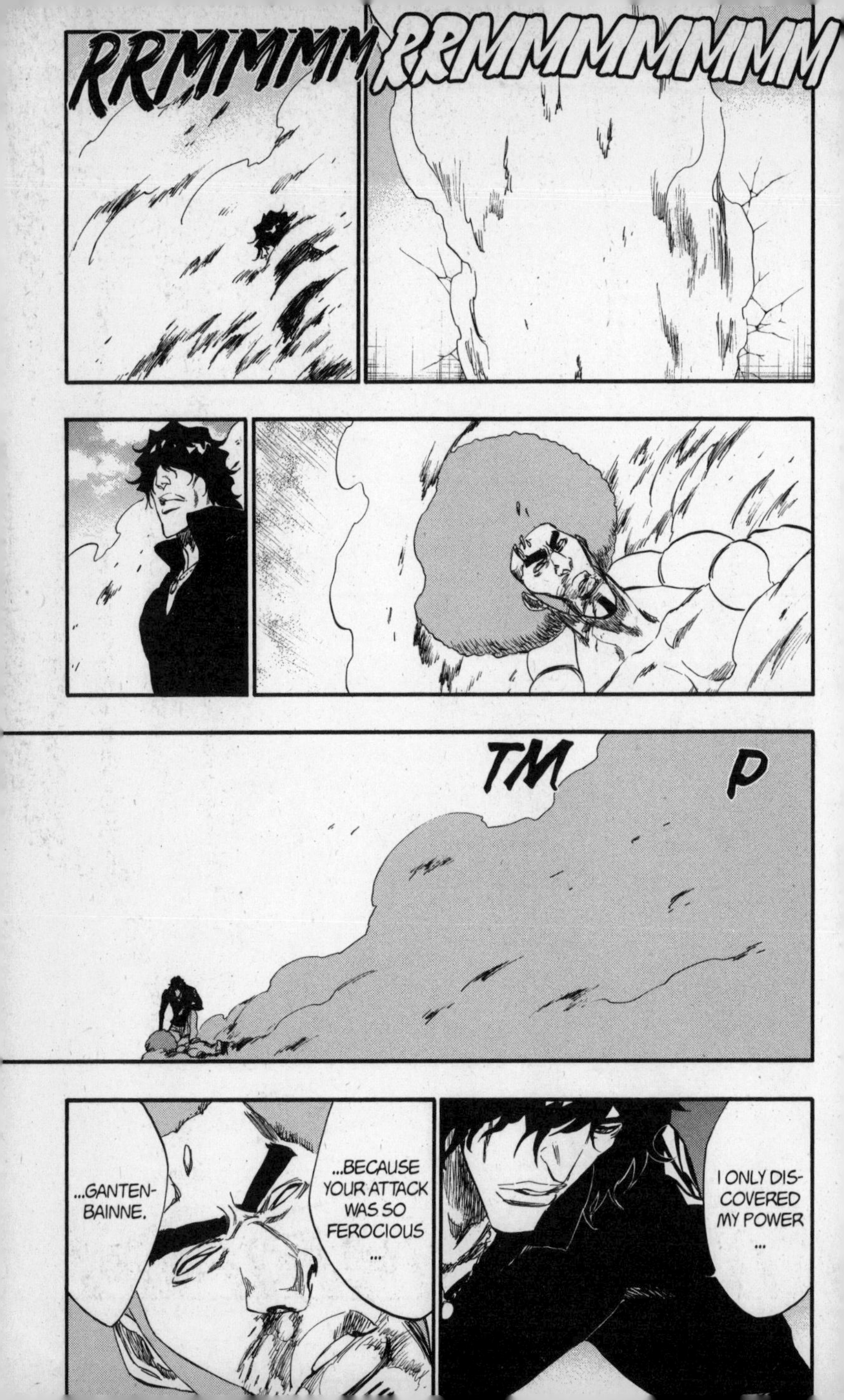

RRMMMMM RRMMMMMMMMMM
TM P
I ONLY DIS-COVERED MY POWER ...
...BECAUSE YOUR ATTACK WAS SO FEROCIOUS ...
...GANTEN-BAINNE.

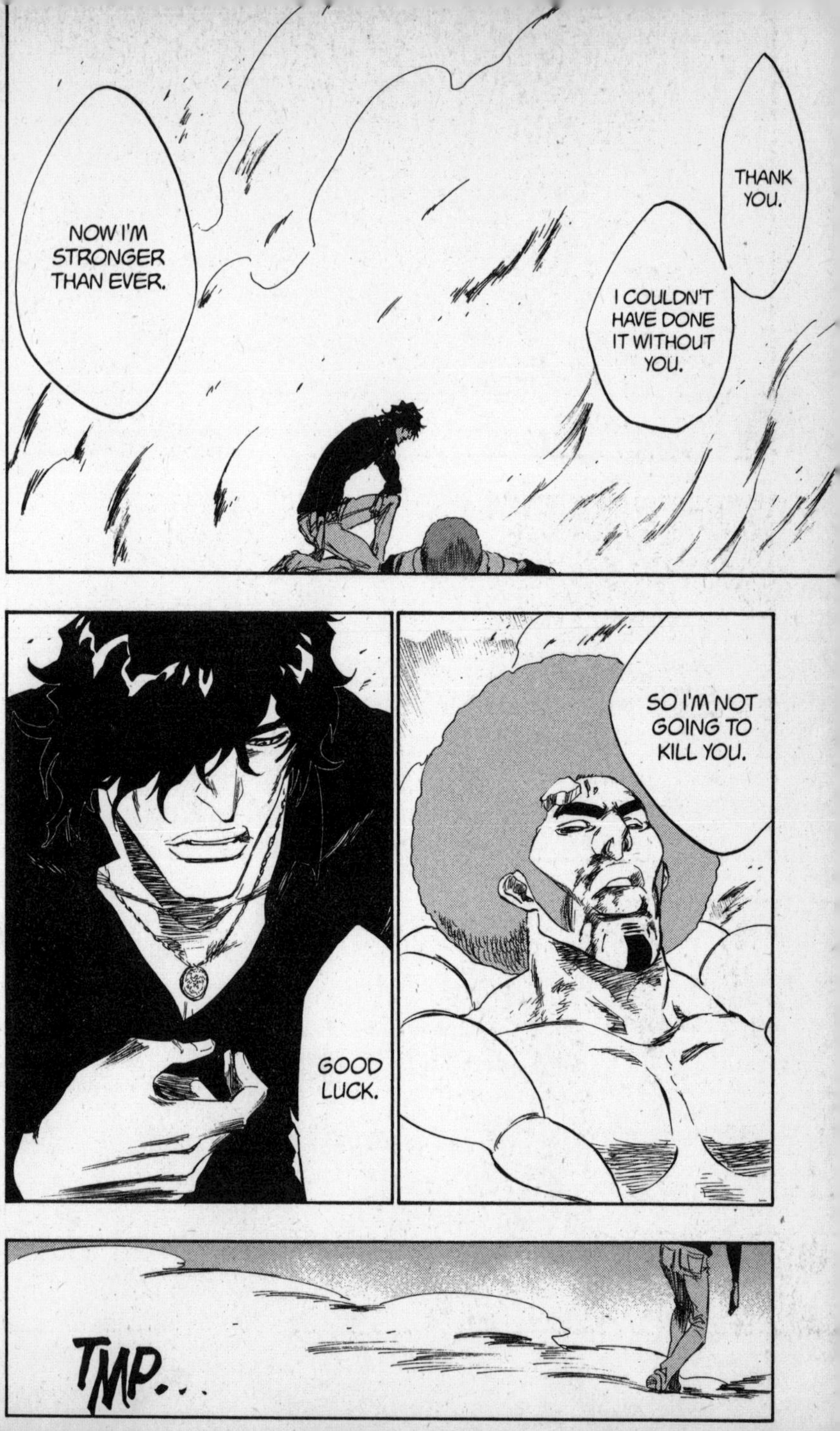
THANK YOU.
I COULDN'T HAVE DONE IT WITHOUT YOU.
NOW I'M STRONGER THAN EVER.
SO I'M NOT GOING TO KILL YOU.
GOOD LUCK.
TMP...

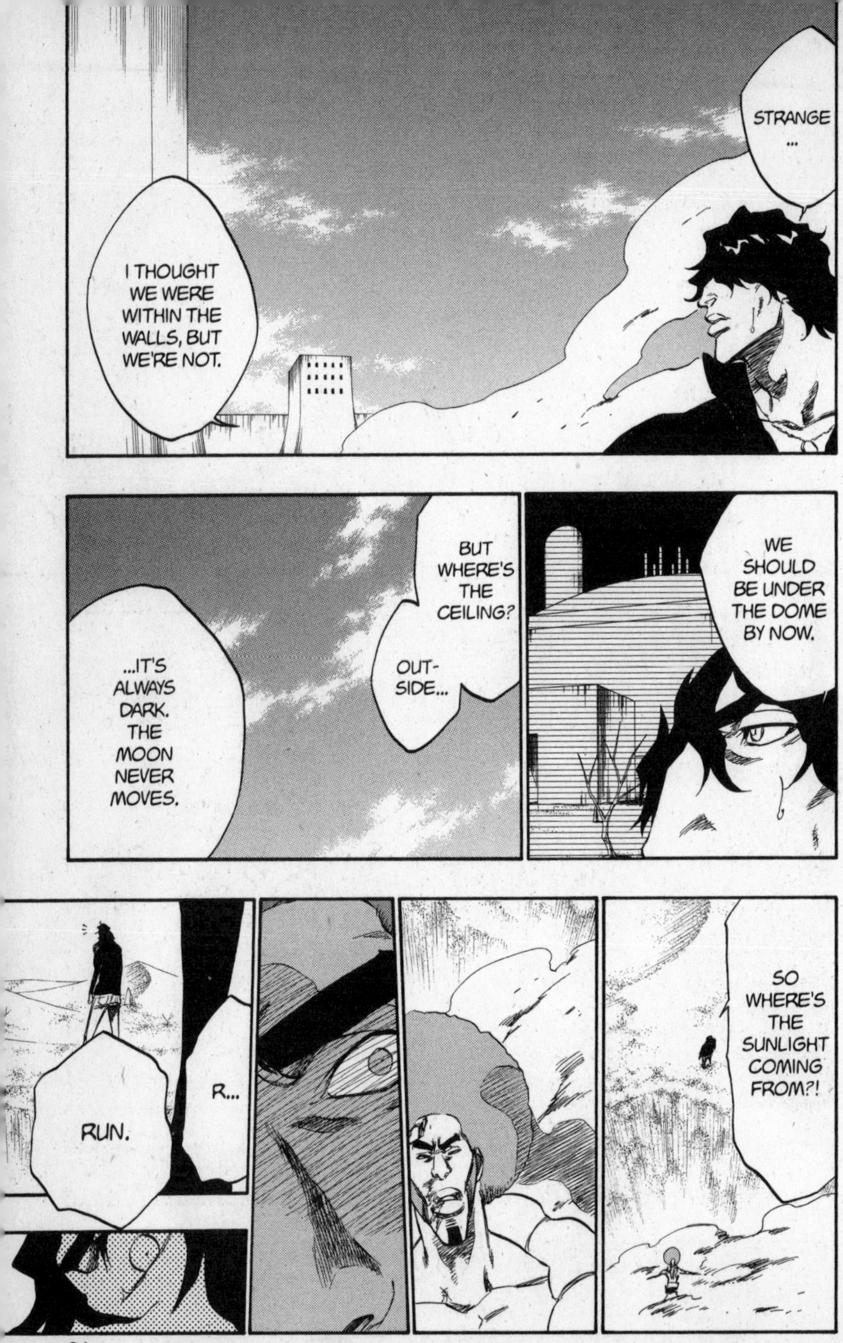
STRANGE ...
I THOUGHT WE WERE WITHIN THE WALLS, BUT WE'RE NOT.
WE SHOULD BE UNDER THE DOME BY NOW.
BUT WHERE'S THE CEILING?
OUT-SIDE...
...IT'S ALWAYS DARK. THE MOON NEVER MOVES.
SO WHERE'S THE SUNLIGHT COMING FROM?!
R...
RUN.

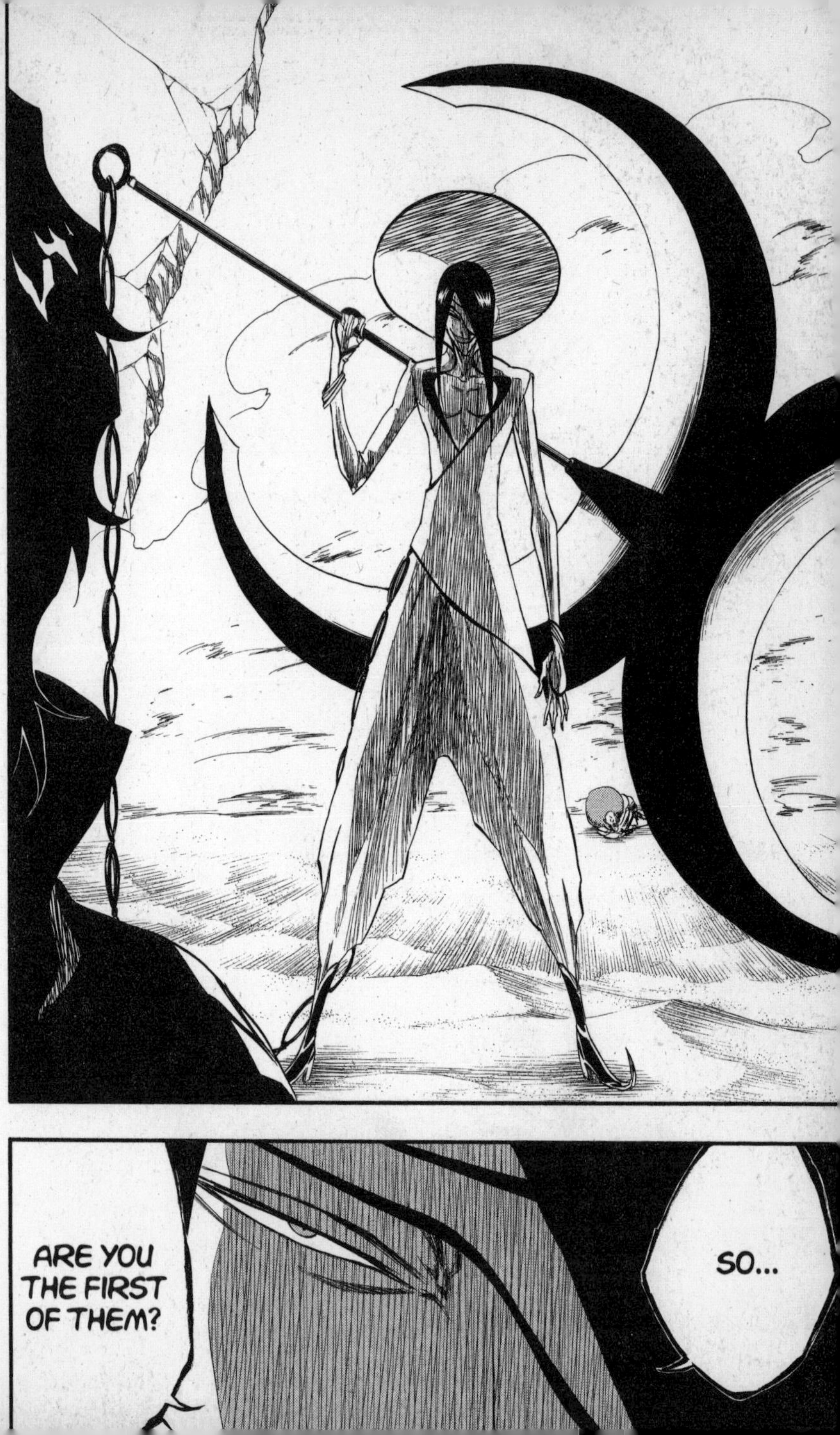
SO...
ARE YOU THE FIRST OF THEM?

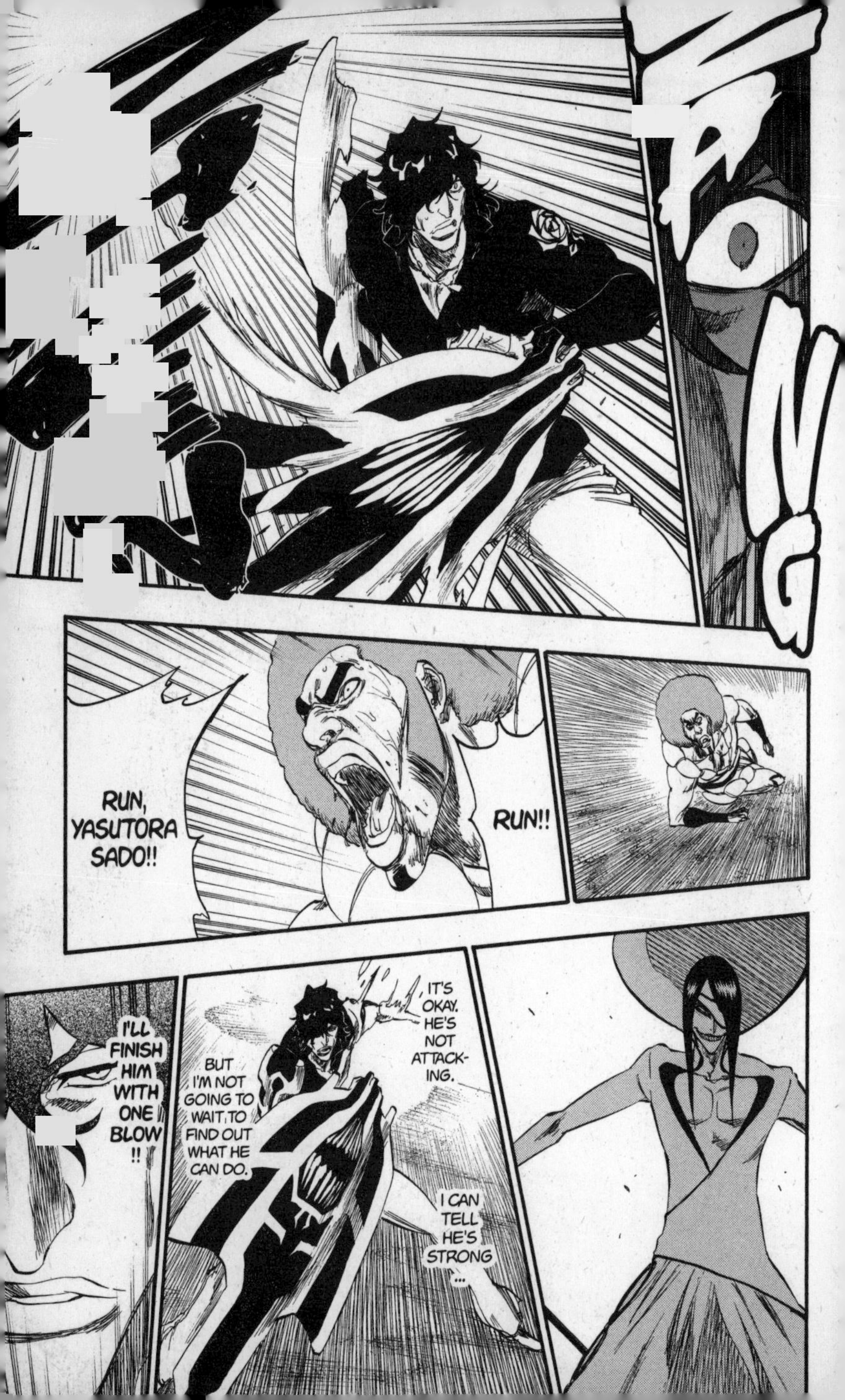
RUN!!
RUN, YASUTORA SADO!!
IT'S OKAY. HE'S NOT ATTACKING.
I CAN TELL HE'S STRONG...
BUT I'M NOT GOING TO WAIT TO FIND OUT WHAT HE CAN DO.
I'LL FINISH HIM WITH ONE BLOW!!

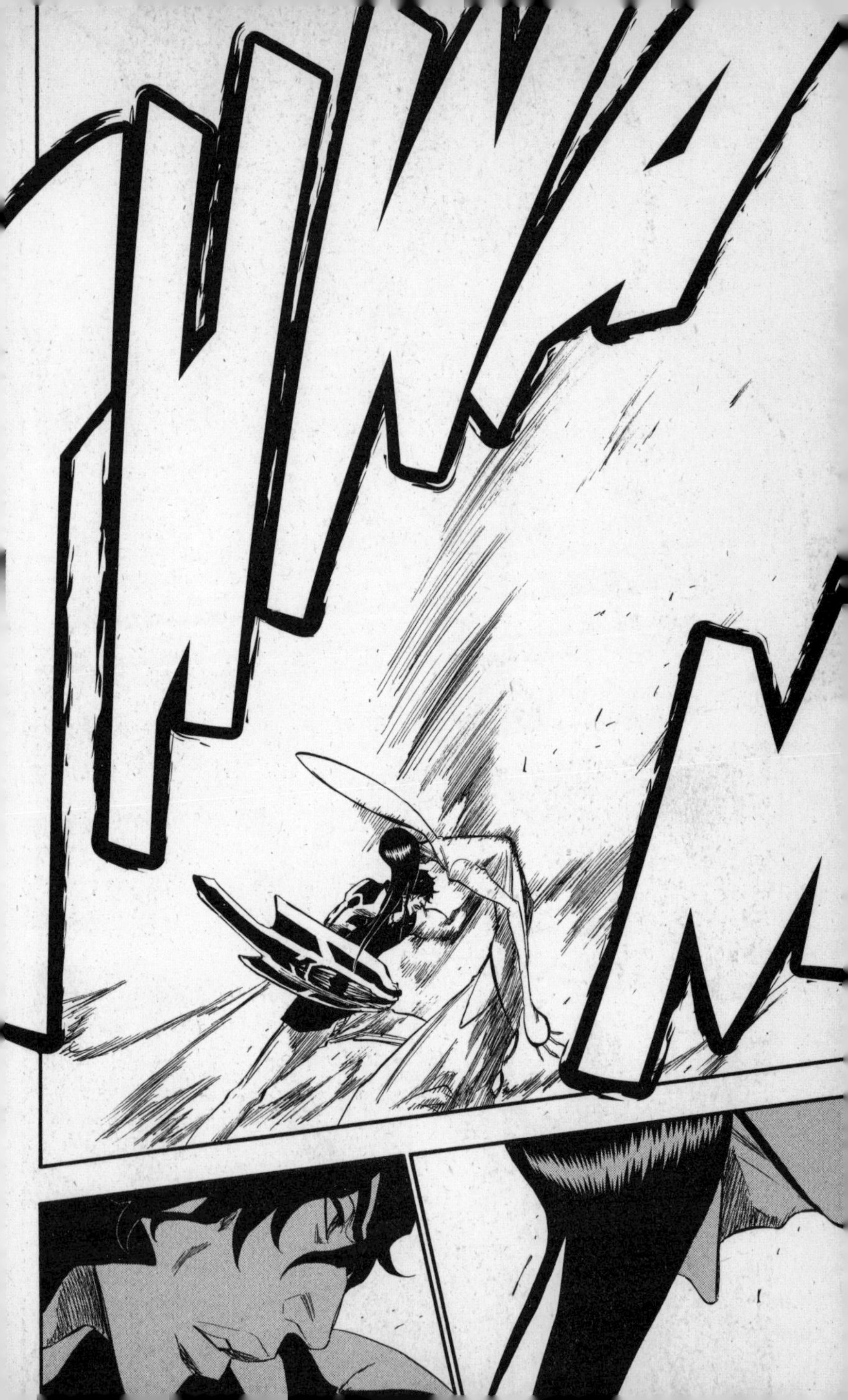

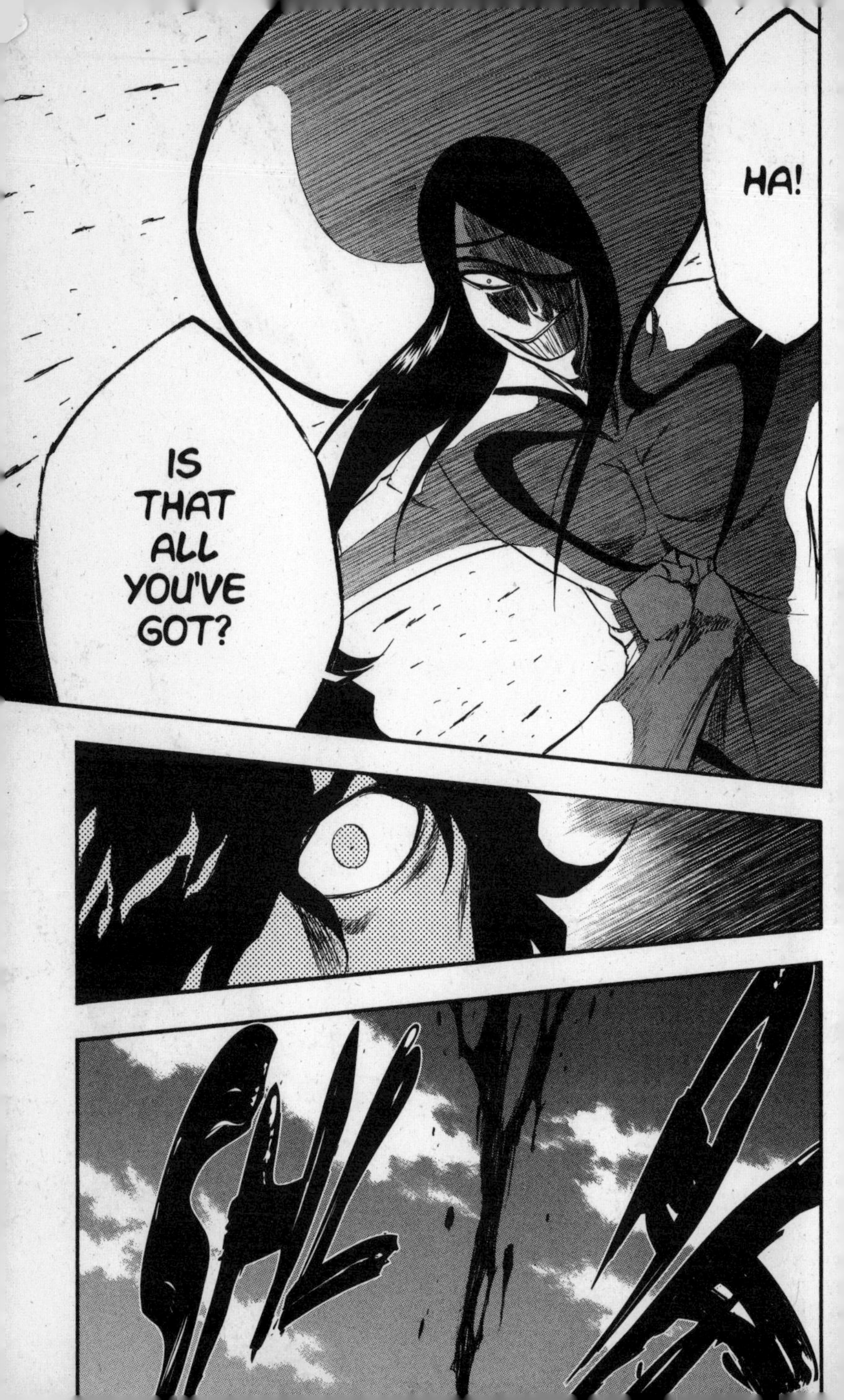
HA!
IS THAT ALL YOU'VE GOT?

Dear Diablo.

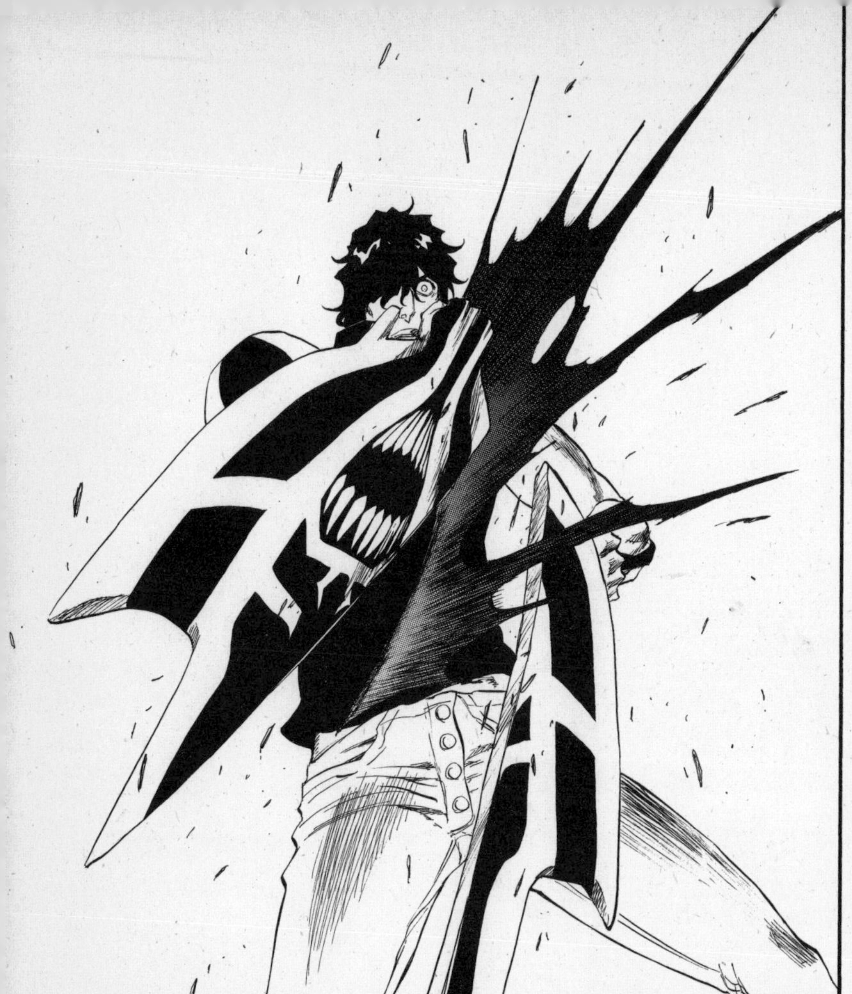

262. Unblendable

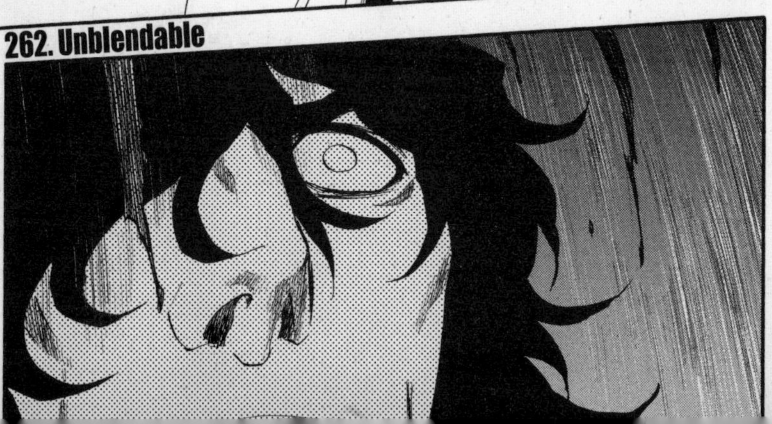

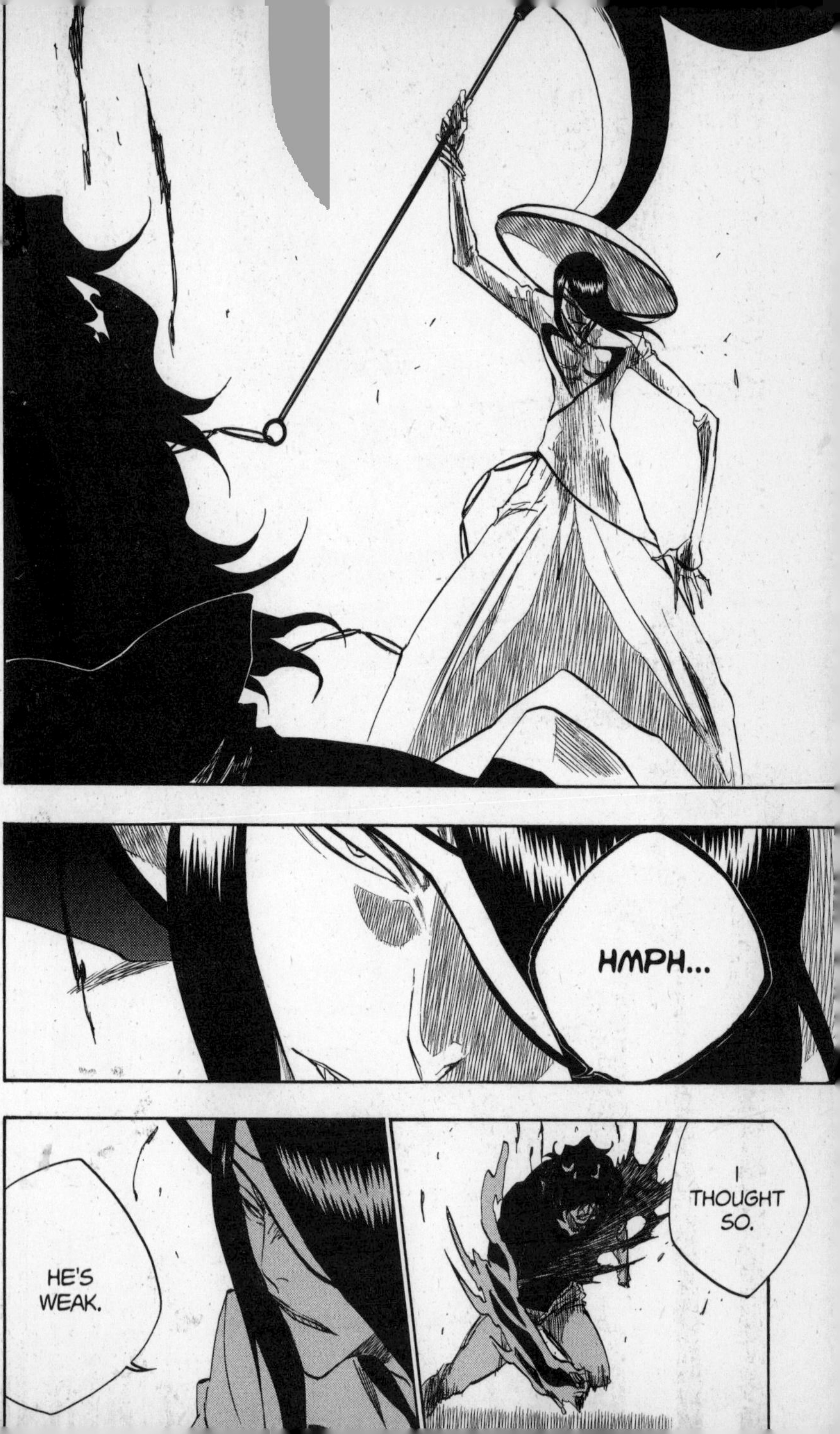
HMPH...
I THOUGHT SO.
HE'S WEAK.

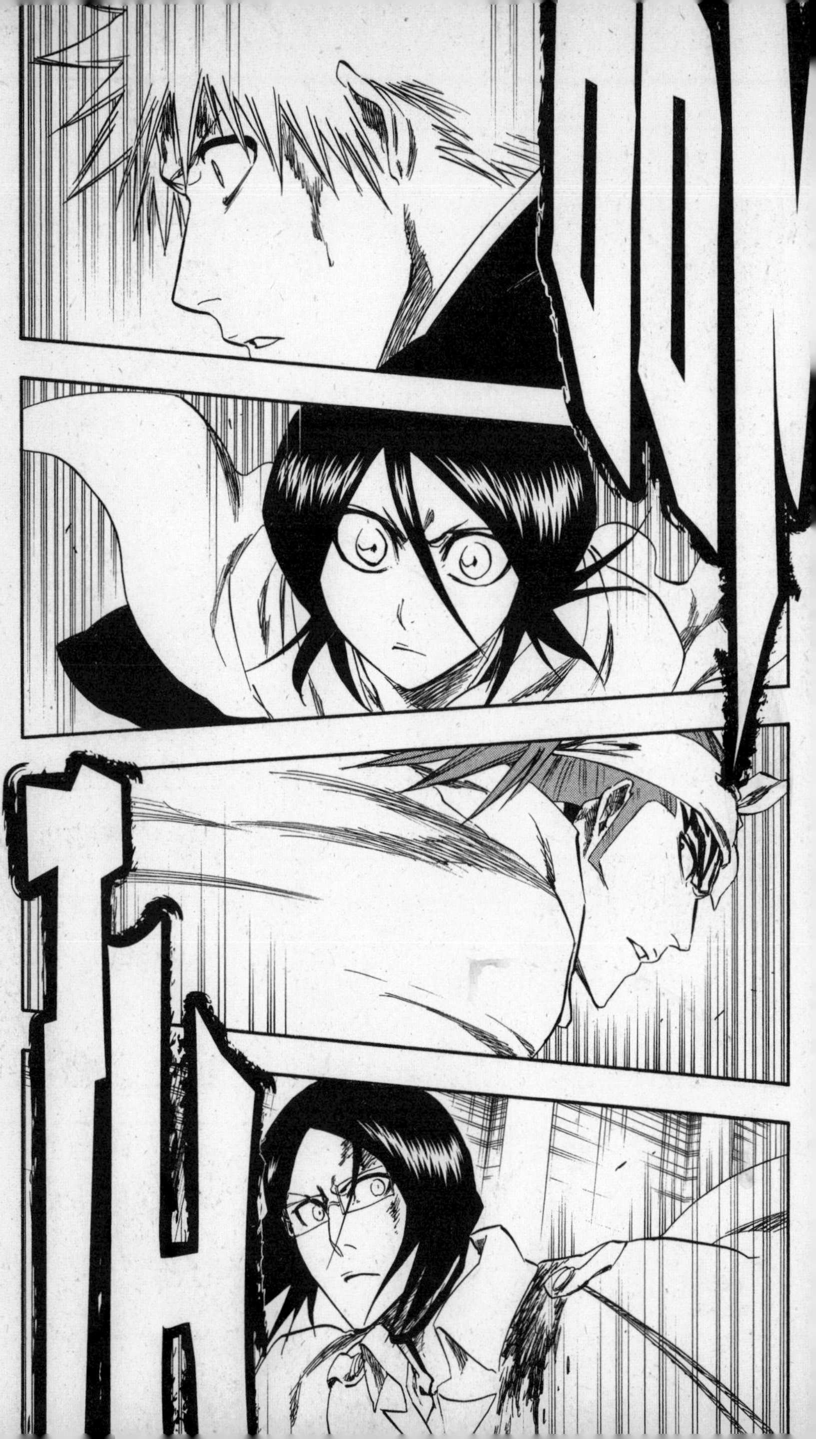

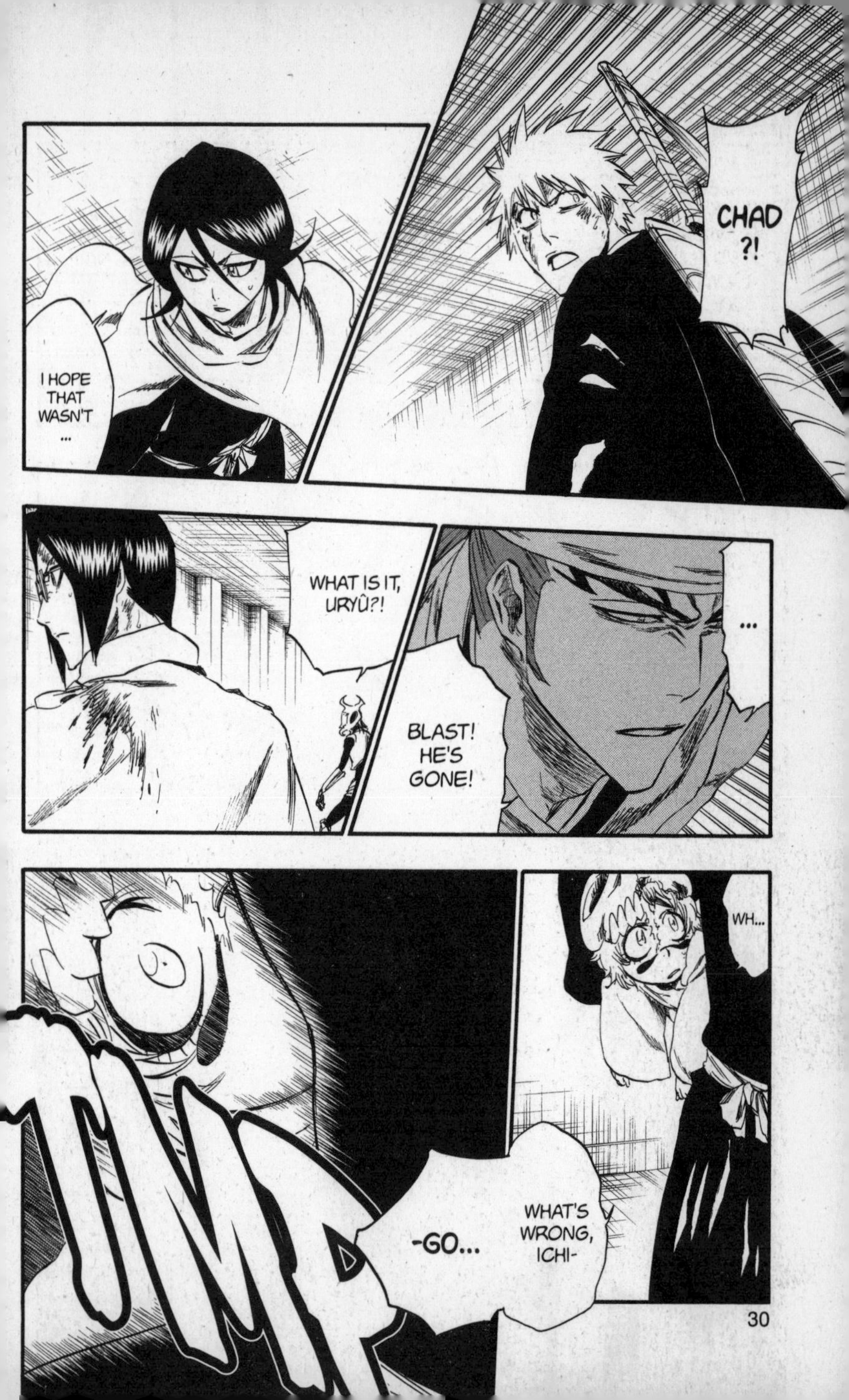
CHAD ?!
I HOPE THAT WASN'T ...
...
BLAST! HE'S GONE!
WHAT IS IT, URYÛ?!
WH...
WHAT'S WRONG, ICHI-
-GO...

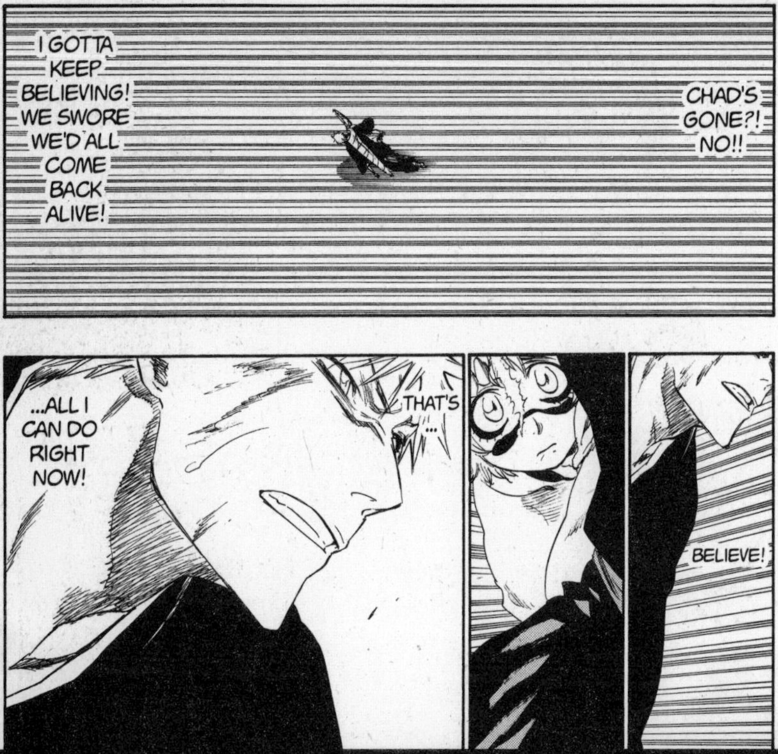
CHAD'S GONE?! NO!!
I GOTTA KEEP BELIEVING! WE SWORE WE'D ALL COME BACK ALIVE!
BELIEVE!
THAT'S ...
...ALL I CAN DO RIGHT NOW!

BLEACH

262. Unblendable

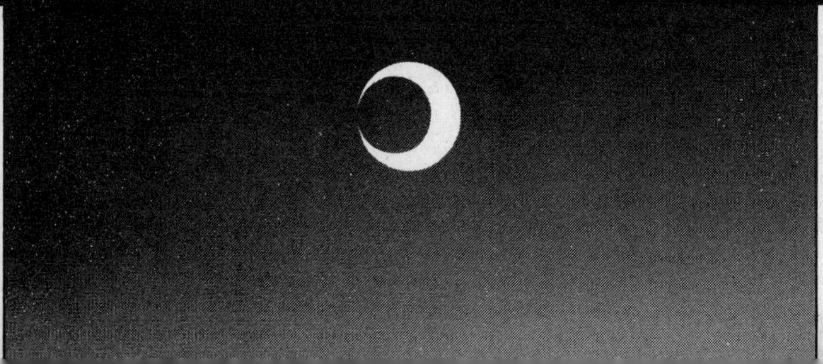

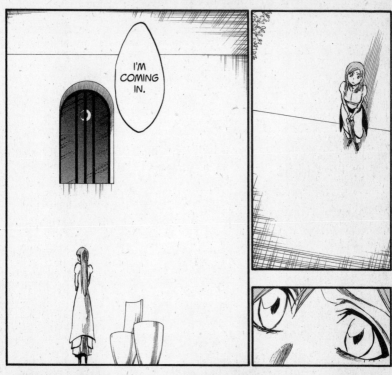

I'M COMING IN.

KREE-˙˙ ̄ ̄ ̄K

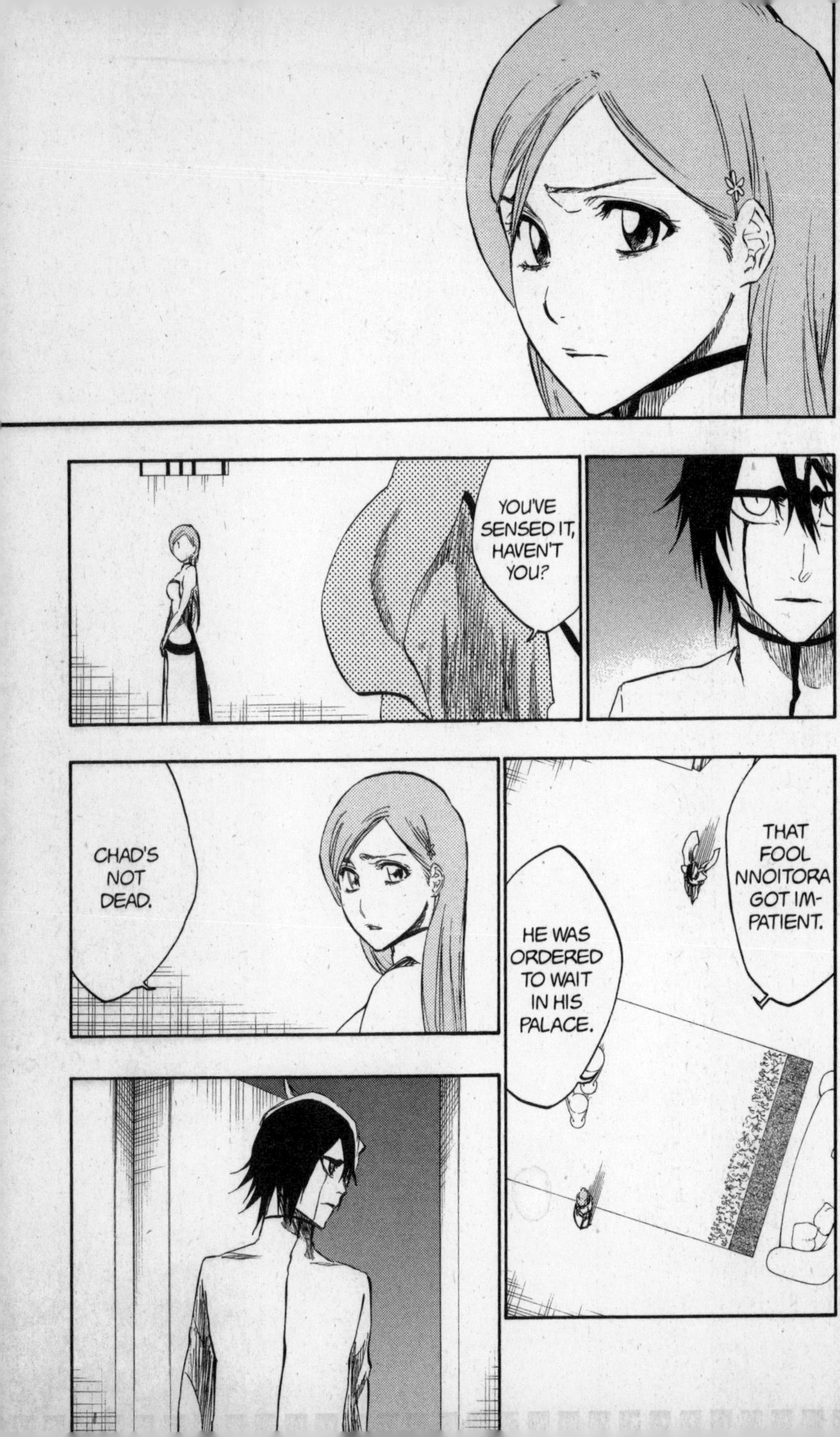
YOU'VE SENSED IT, HAVEN'T YOU?
THAT FOOL NNOITORA GOT IM-PATIENT.
HE WAS ORDERED TO WAIT IN HIS PALACE.
CHAD'S NOT DEAD.

HE'S NOT.

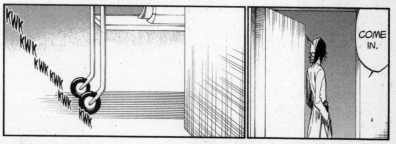

KWK KWK KWK KWK KWK KWK KWK

COME IN.

...

IT'S FOOD.

I'M NOT HUN-GRY.

EAT IT.

READ THIS WAY

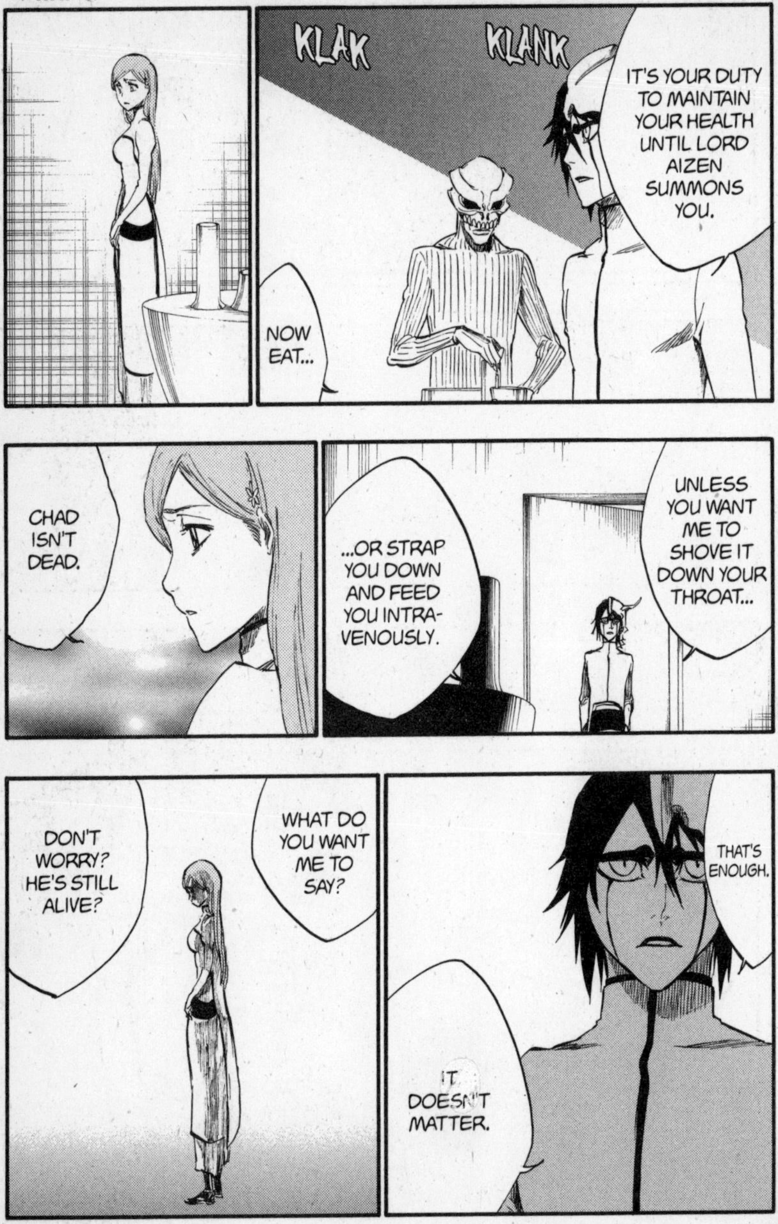
IT'S YOUR DUTY TO MAINTAIN YOUR HEALTH UNTIL LORD AIZEN SUMMONS YOU.
KLANK
KLAK
NOW EAT...
UNLESS YOU WANT ME TO SHOVE IT DOWN YOUR THROAT...
...OR STRAP YOU DOWN AND FEED YOU INTRA-VENOUSLY.
CHAD ISN'T DEAD.
THAT'S ENOUGH.
IT DOESN'T MATTER.
WHAT DO YOU WANT ME TO SAY?
DON'T WORRY? HE'S STILL ALIVE?

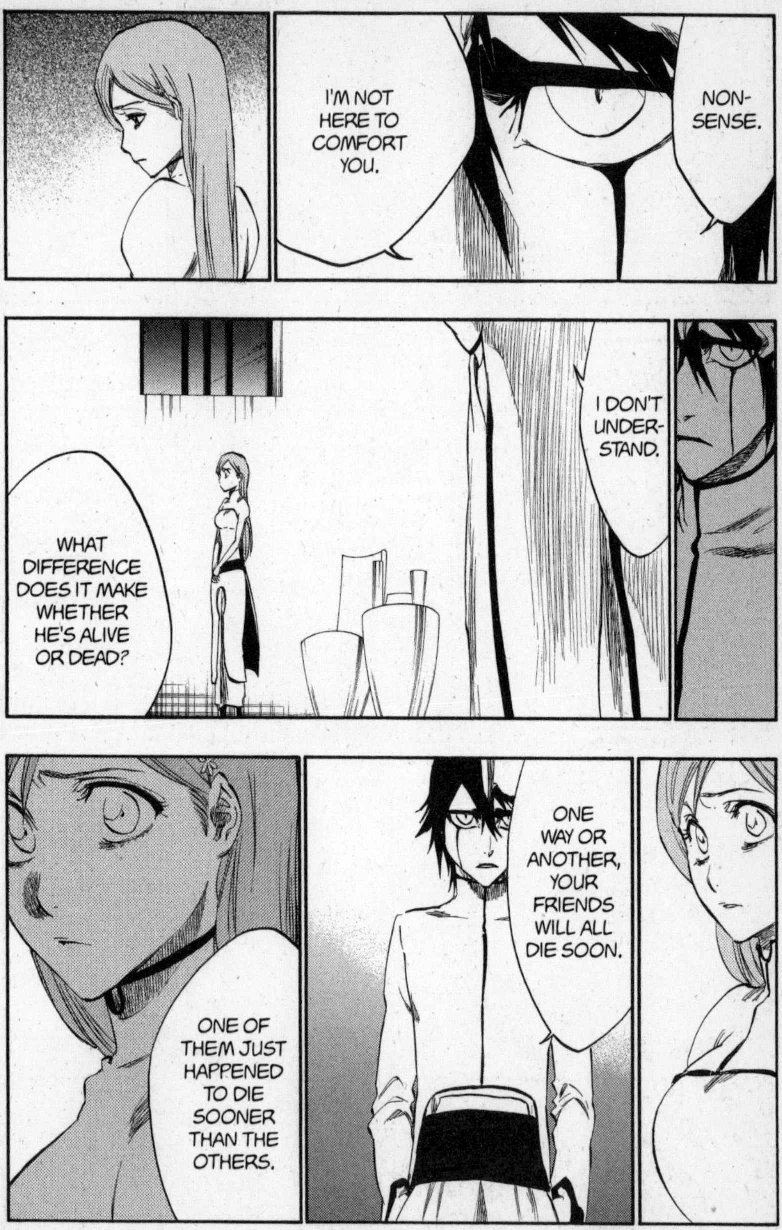
NON-SENSE.
I'M NOT HERE TO COMFORT YOU.
I DON'T UNDER-STAND.
WHAT DIFFERENCE DOES IT MAKE WHETHER HE'S ALIVE OR DEAD?
ONE WAY OR ANOTHER, YOUR FRIENDS WILL ALL DIE SOON.
ONE OF THEM JUST HAPPENED TO DIE SOONER THAN THE OTHERS.

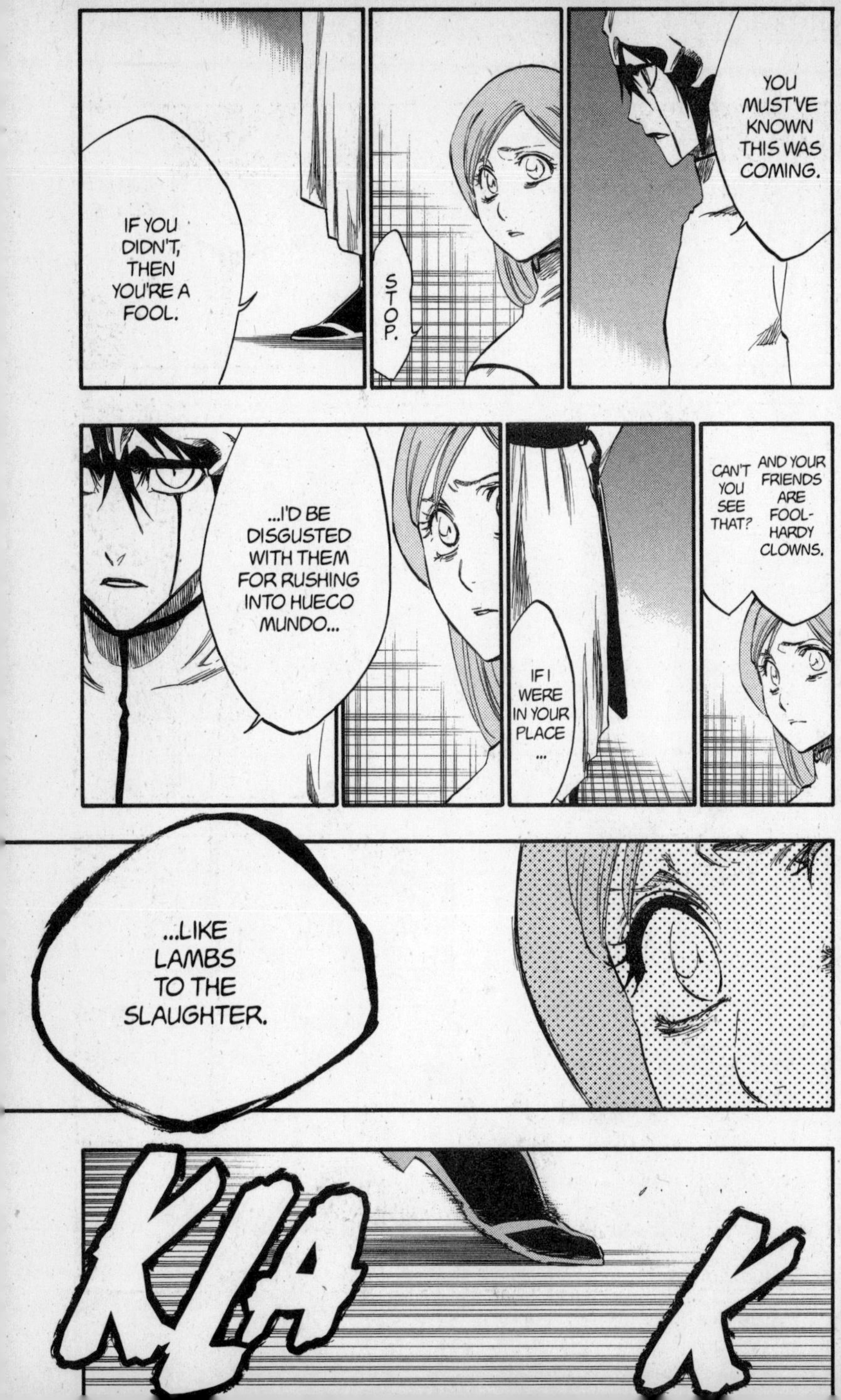

YOU MUST'VE KNOWN THIS WAS COMING.
STOP.
IF YOU DIDN'T, THEN YOU'RE A FOOL.
AND YOUR FRIENDS ARE FOOL-HARDY CLOWNS.
CAN'T YOU SEE THAT?
IF I WERE IN YOUR PLACE...
...I'D BE DISGUSTED WITH THEM FOR RUSHING INTO HUECO MUNDO...
...LIKE LAMBS TO THE SLAUGHTER.
KLAK

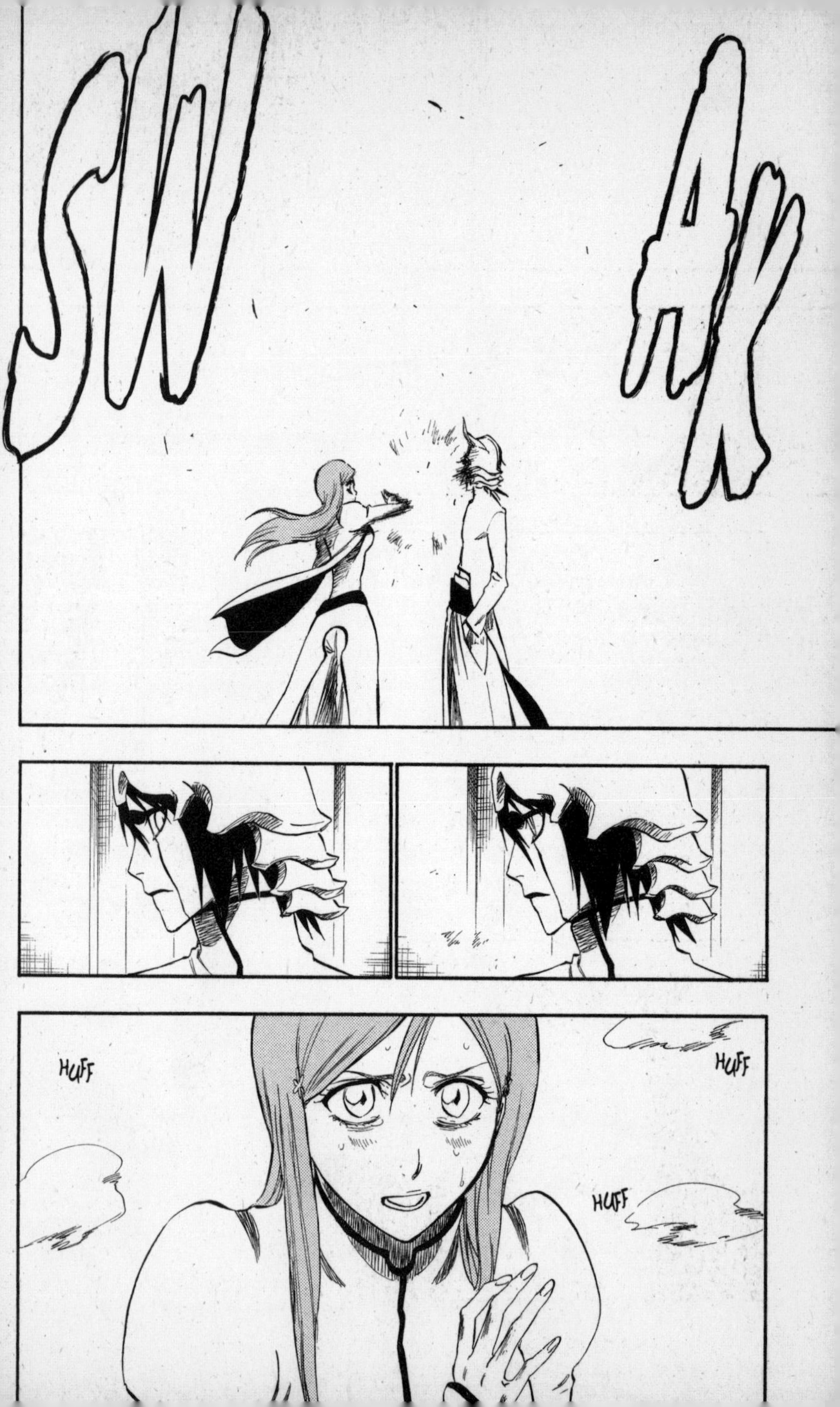
SWAK
HUFF
HUFF
HUFF

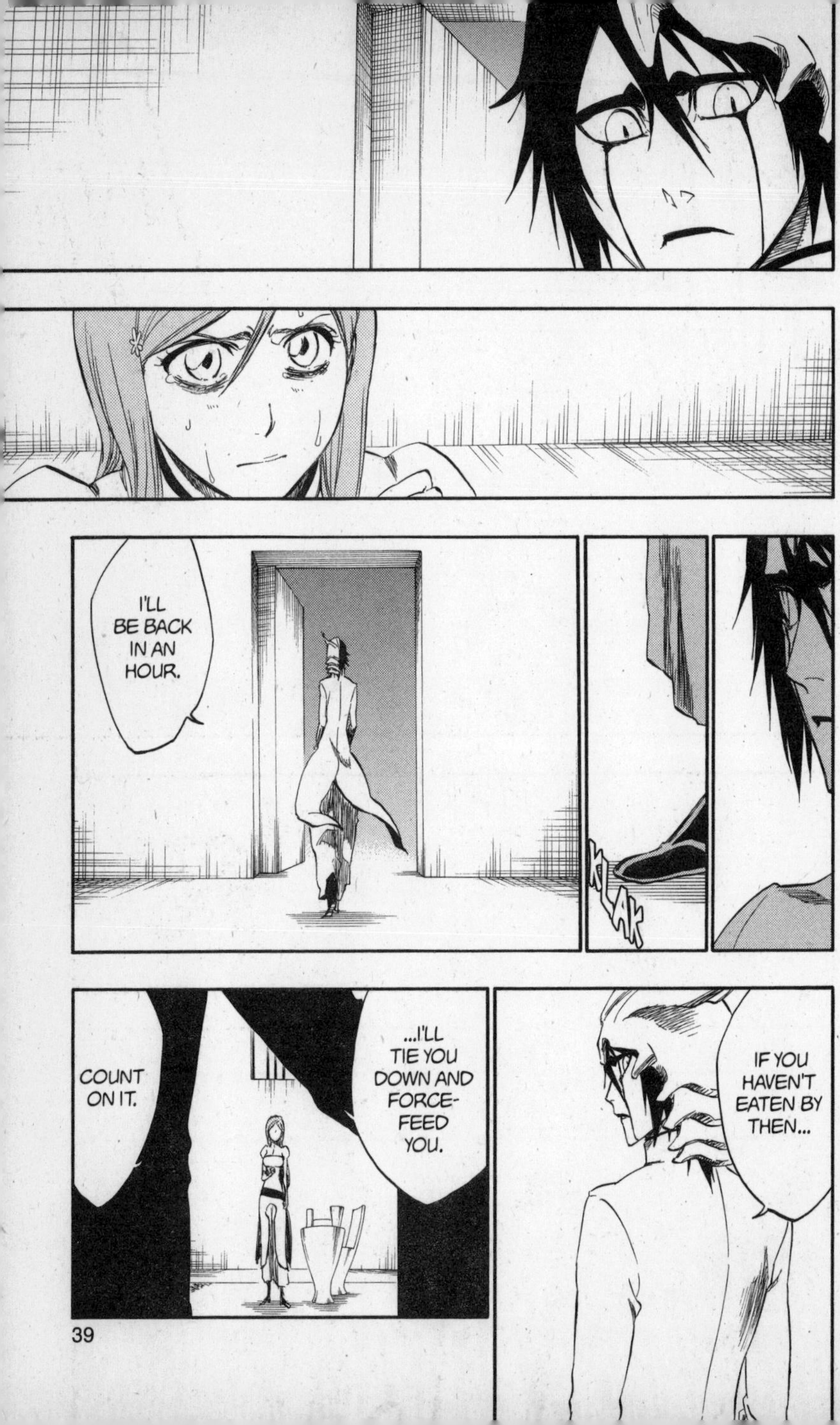
KLAK
I'LL BE BACK IN AN HOUR.
IF YOU HAVEN'T EATEN BY THEN...
...I'LL TIE YOU DOWN AND FORCE-FEED YOU.
COUNT ON IT.

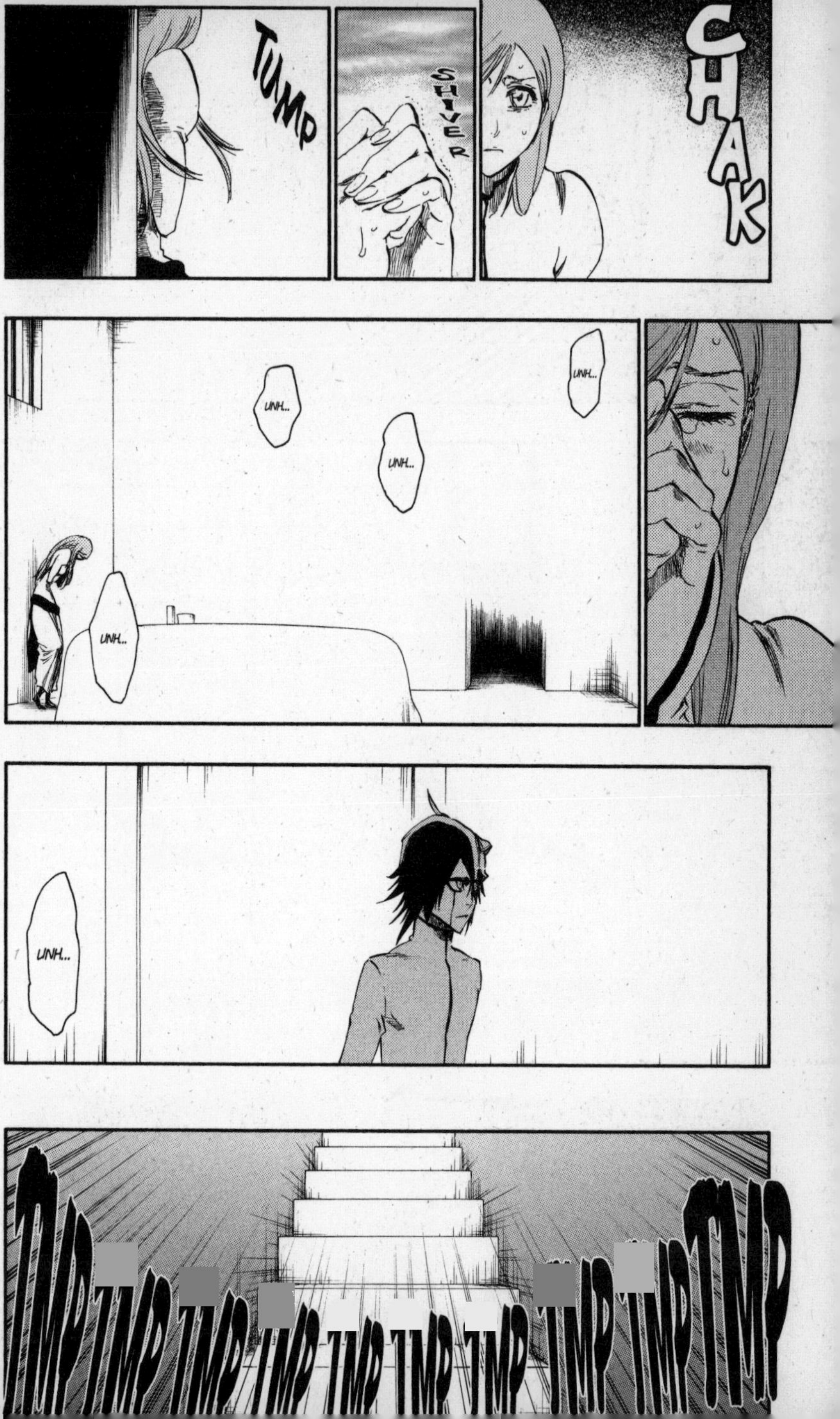
CHAK
SHIVER
TUMP
UNH...
UNH...
UNH...
UNH...
UNH...
TMP TMP TMP TMP TMP TMP TMP TMP TMP TMP

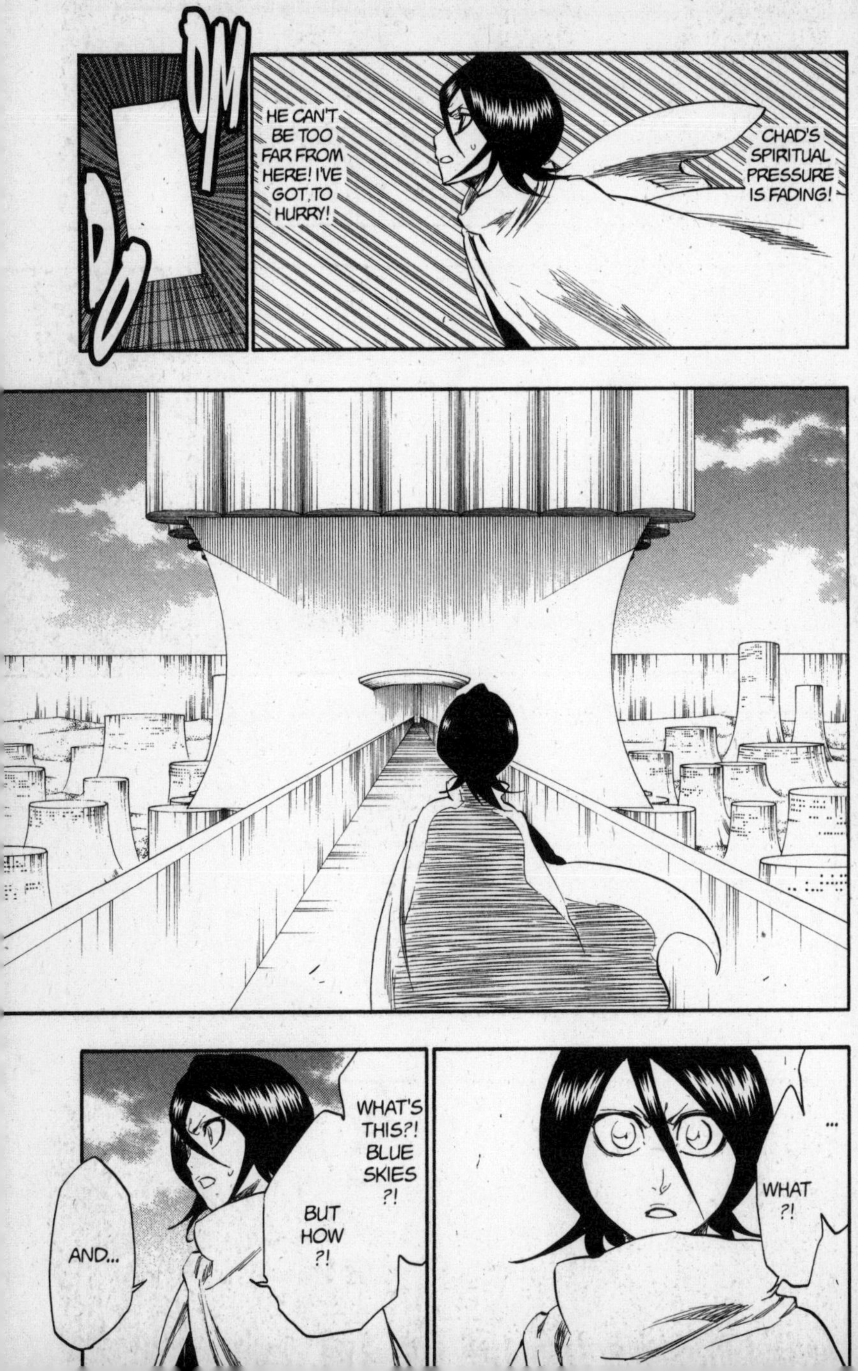
CHAD'S SPIRITUAL PRESSURE IS FADING!
HE CAN'T BE TOO FAR FROM HERE! I'VE GOT TO HURRY!
DOOM
...
WHAT?!
WHAT'S THIS?! BLUE SKIES?!
BUT HOW?!
AND...

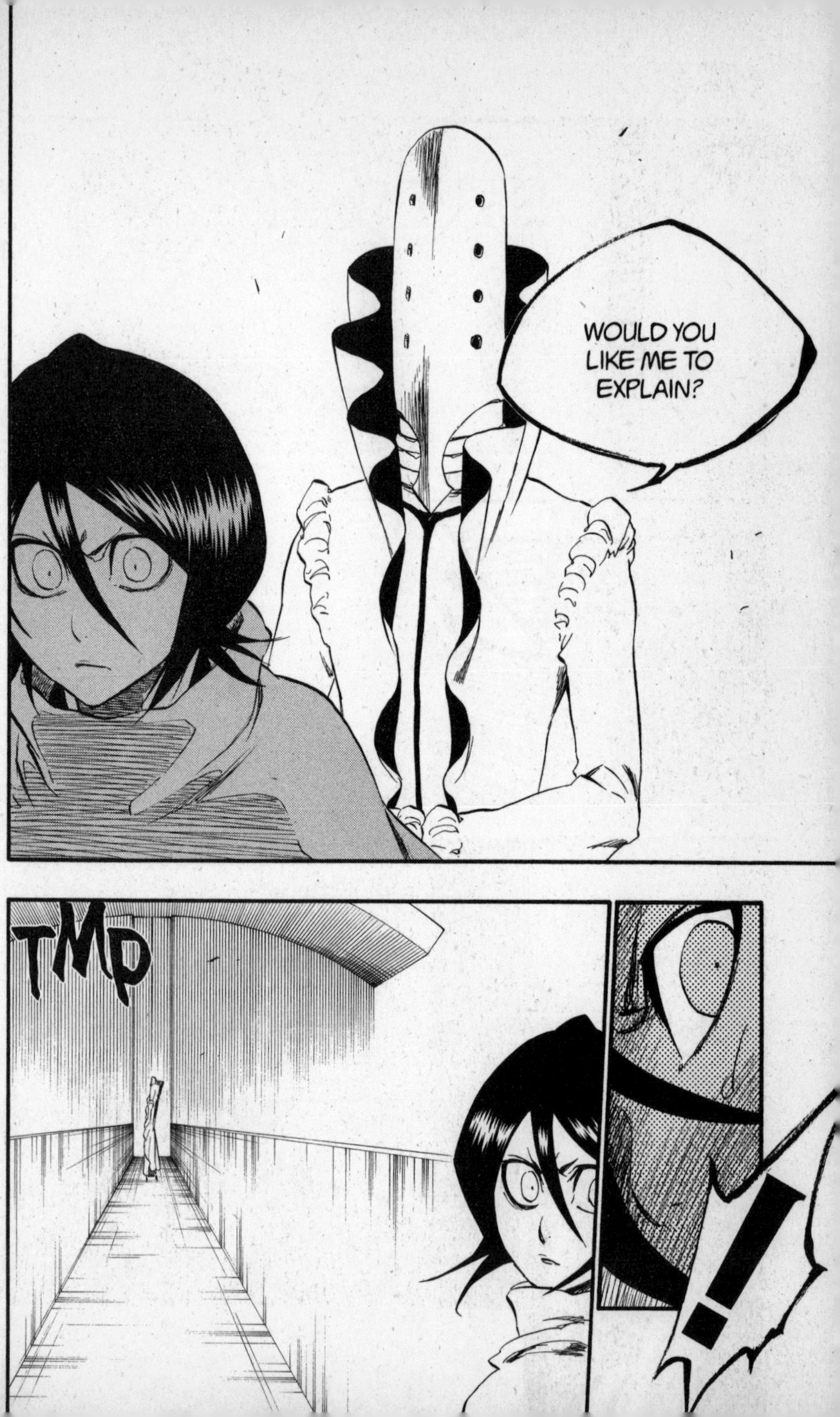
WOULD YOU LIKE ME TO EXPLAIN?
!
TMP

READ THIS WAY

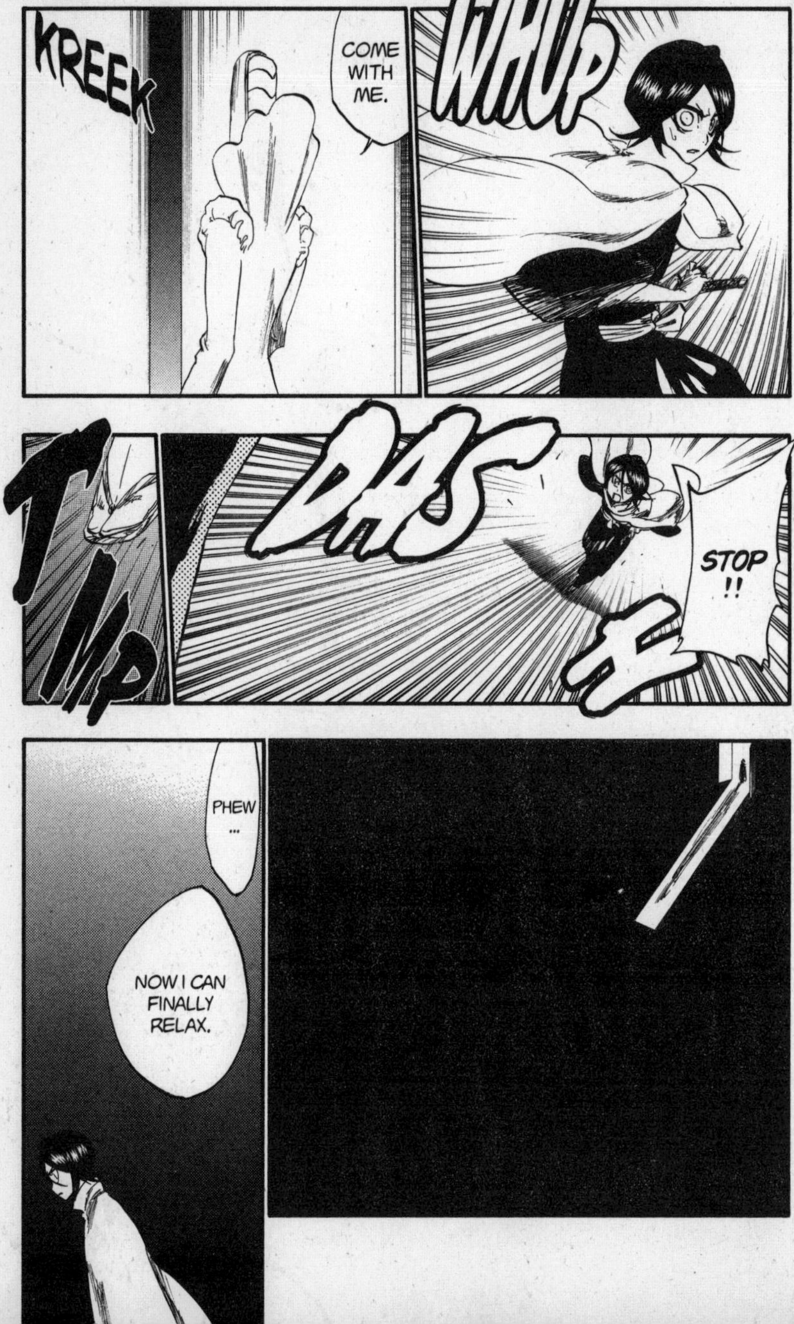
WHUP
KREEK
COME WITH ME.
DASH
STOP!!
TMP
PHEW...
NOW I CAN FINALLY RELAX.

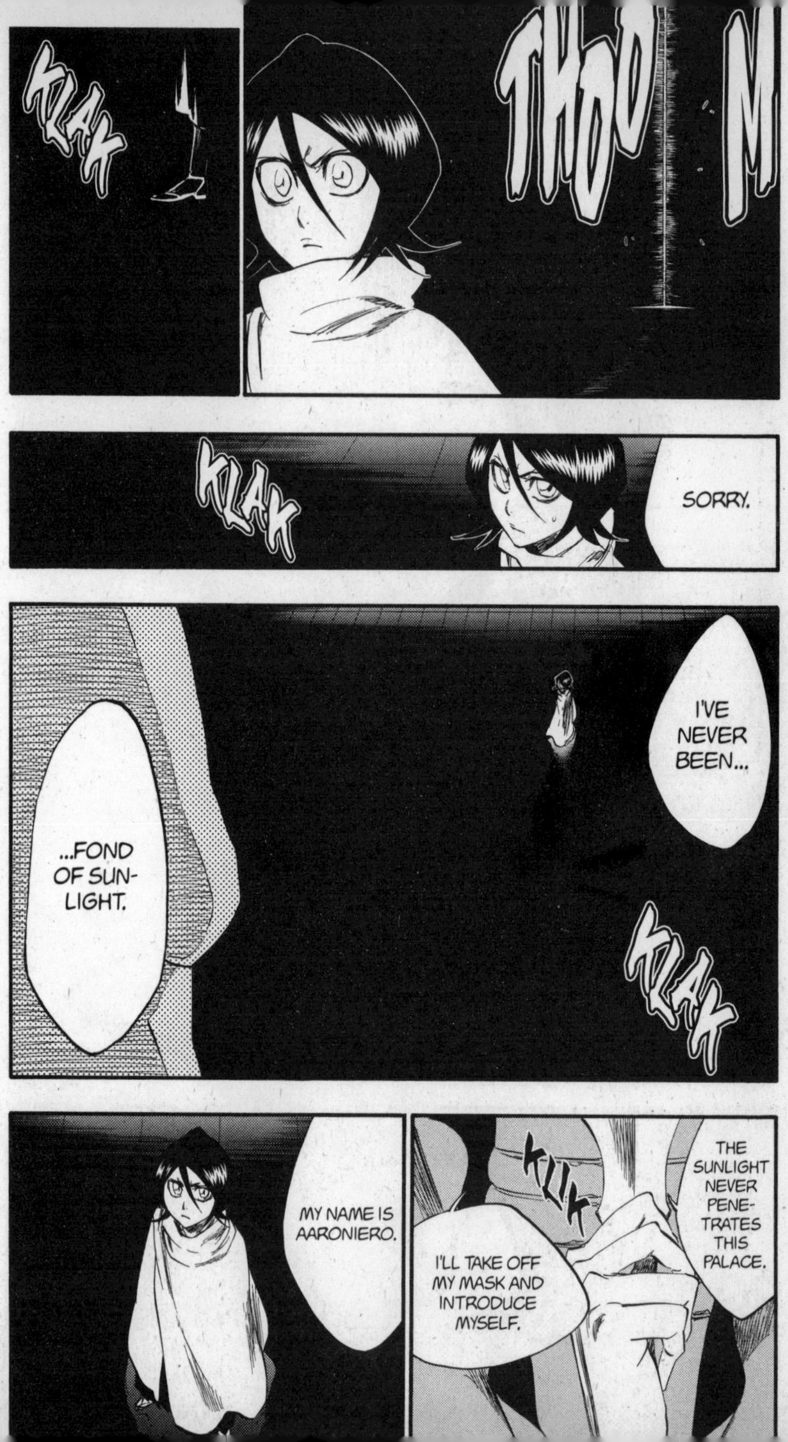
THOOM
KLAK
SORRY.
KLAK
I'VE NEVER BEEN...
KLAK
...FOND OF SUN-LIGHT.
THE SUNLIGHT NEVER PENE-TRATES THIS PALACE.
KLIK
I'LL TAKE OFF MY MASK AND INTRODUCE MYSELF.
MY NAME IS AARONIERO.

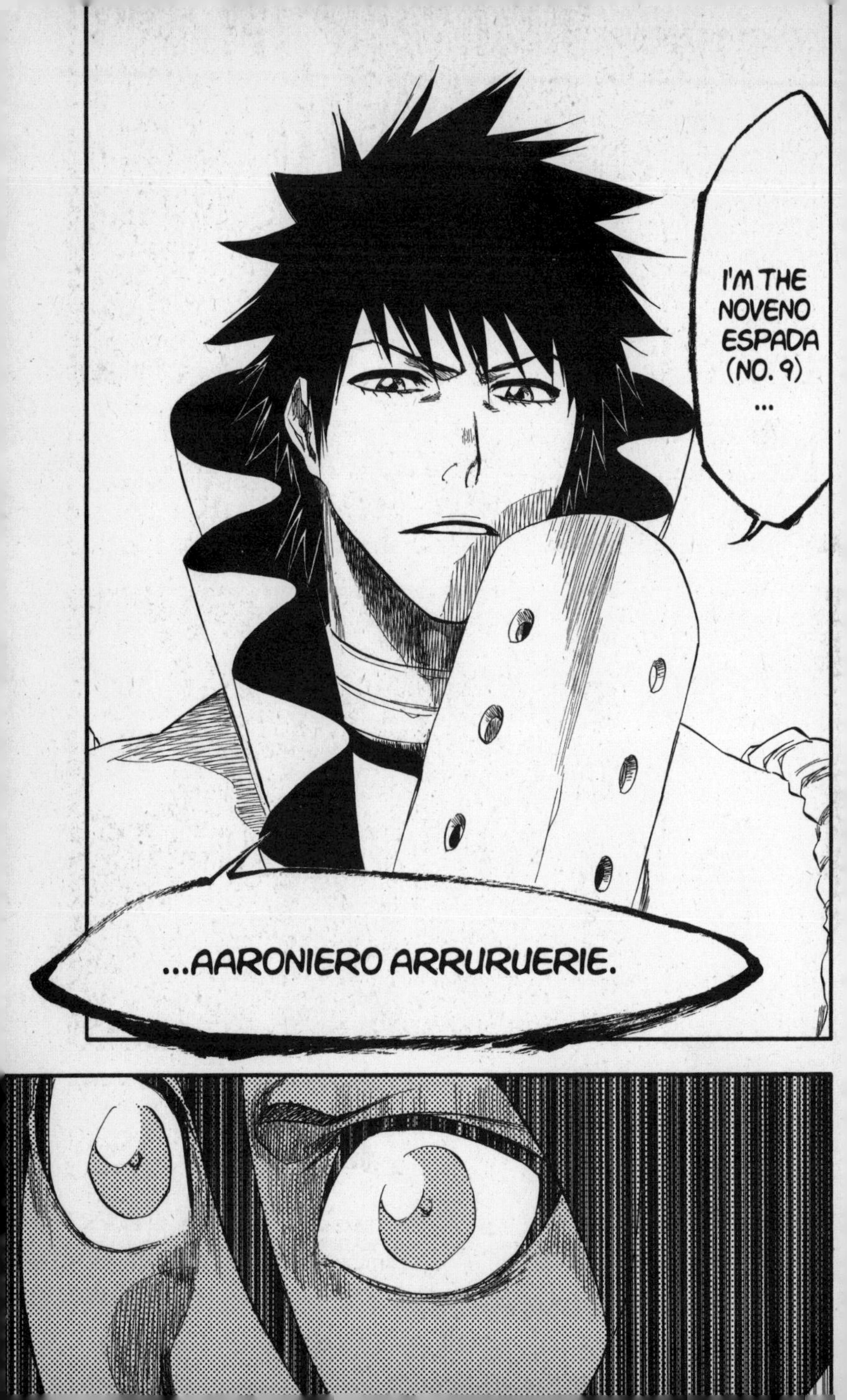
I'M THE NOVENO ESPADA (NO. 9) ...
...AARONIERO ARRURUERIE.

everything divide us.

263. Unexpected

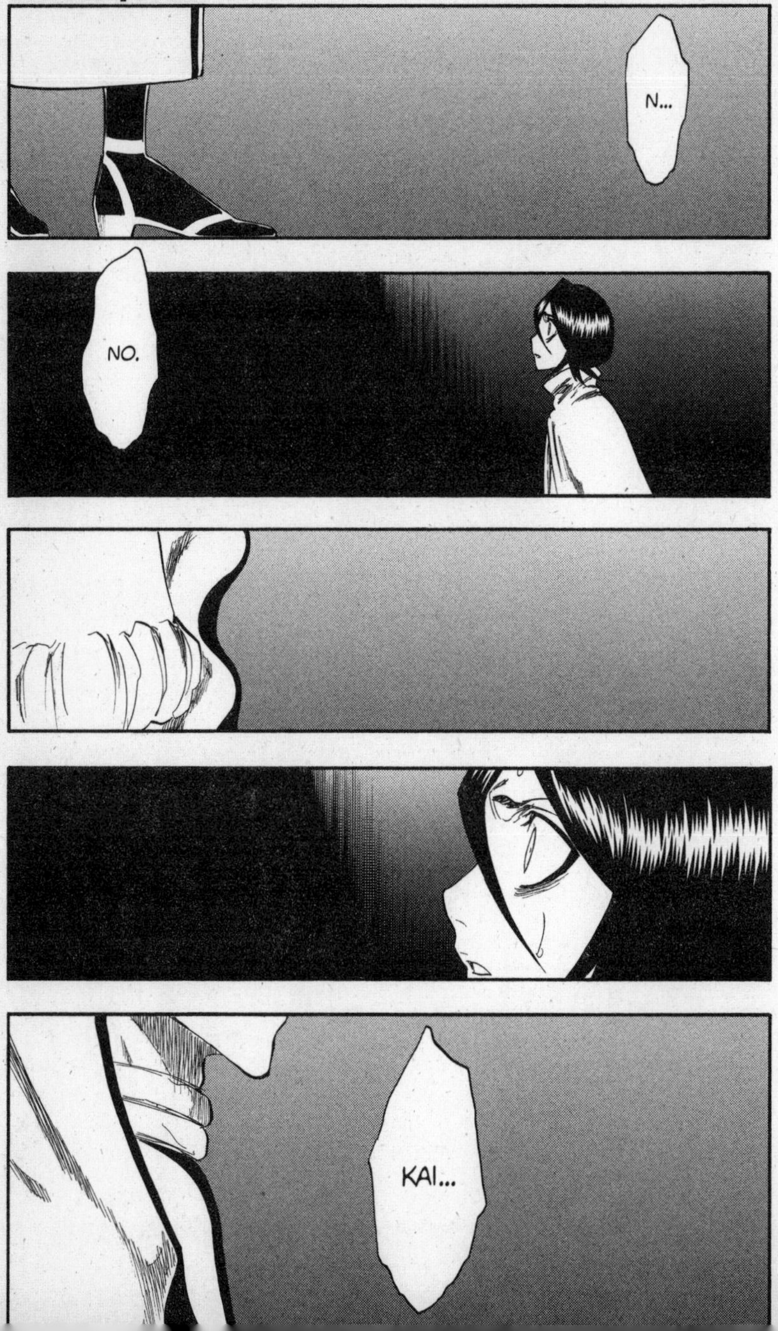
N...
NO.
KAI...

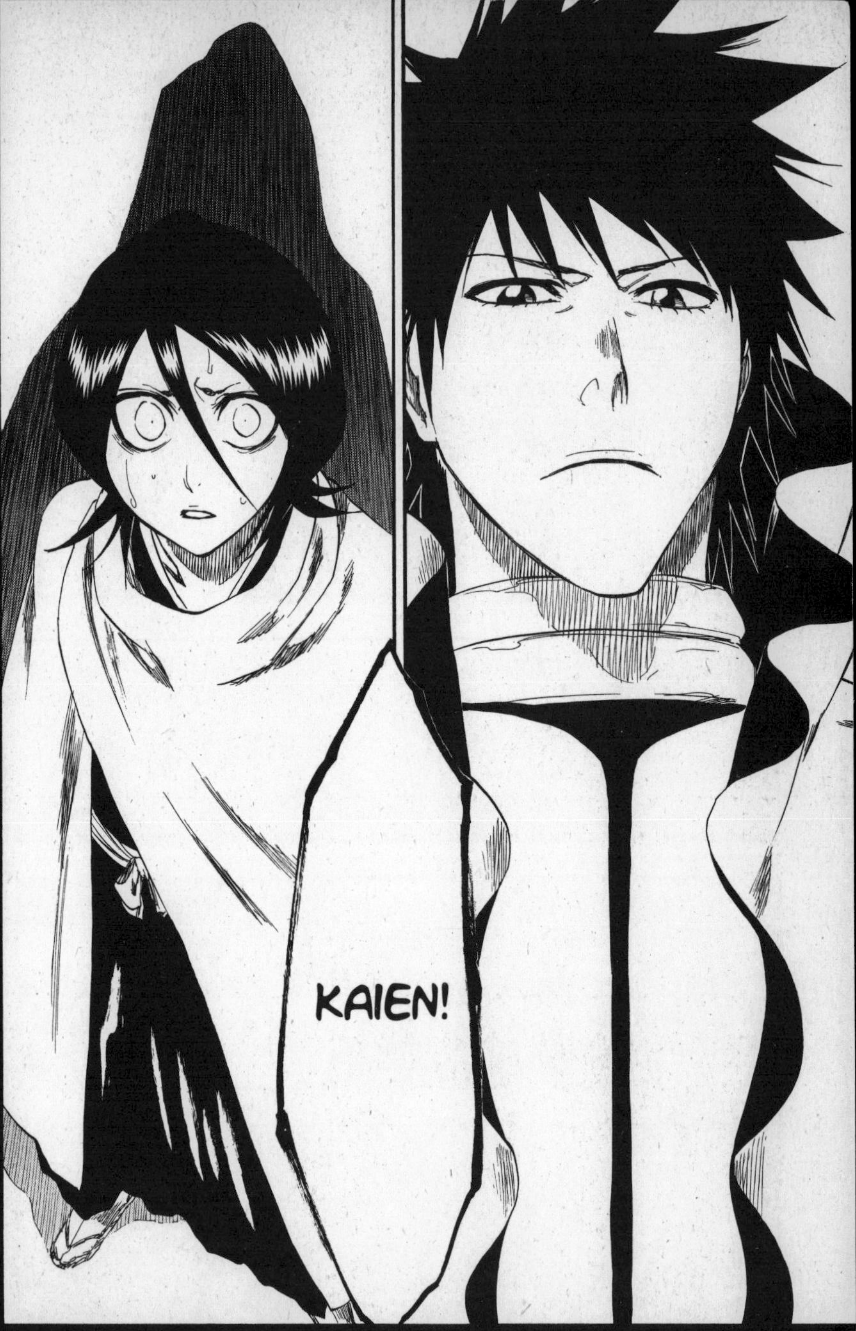
KAIEN!

BLEACH

263. Unexpected

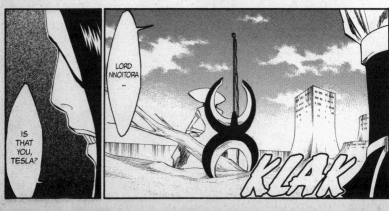

LORD NNOITORA...

IS THAT YOU, TESLA?

KLAK

YES,
SIR.

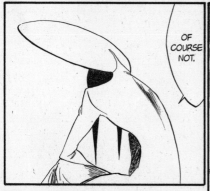

OF
COURSE
NOT.

YOU
HAVEN'T
...

...FIN-
ISHED
HIM
YET.

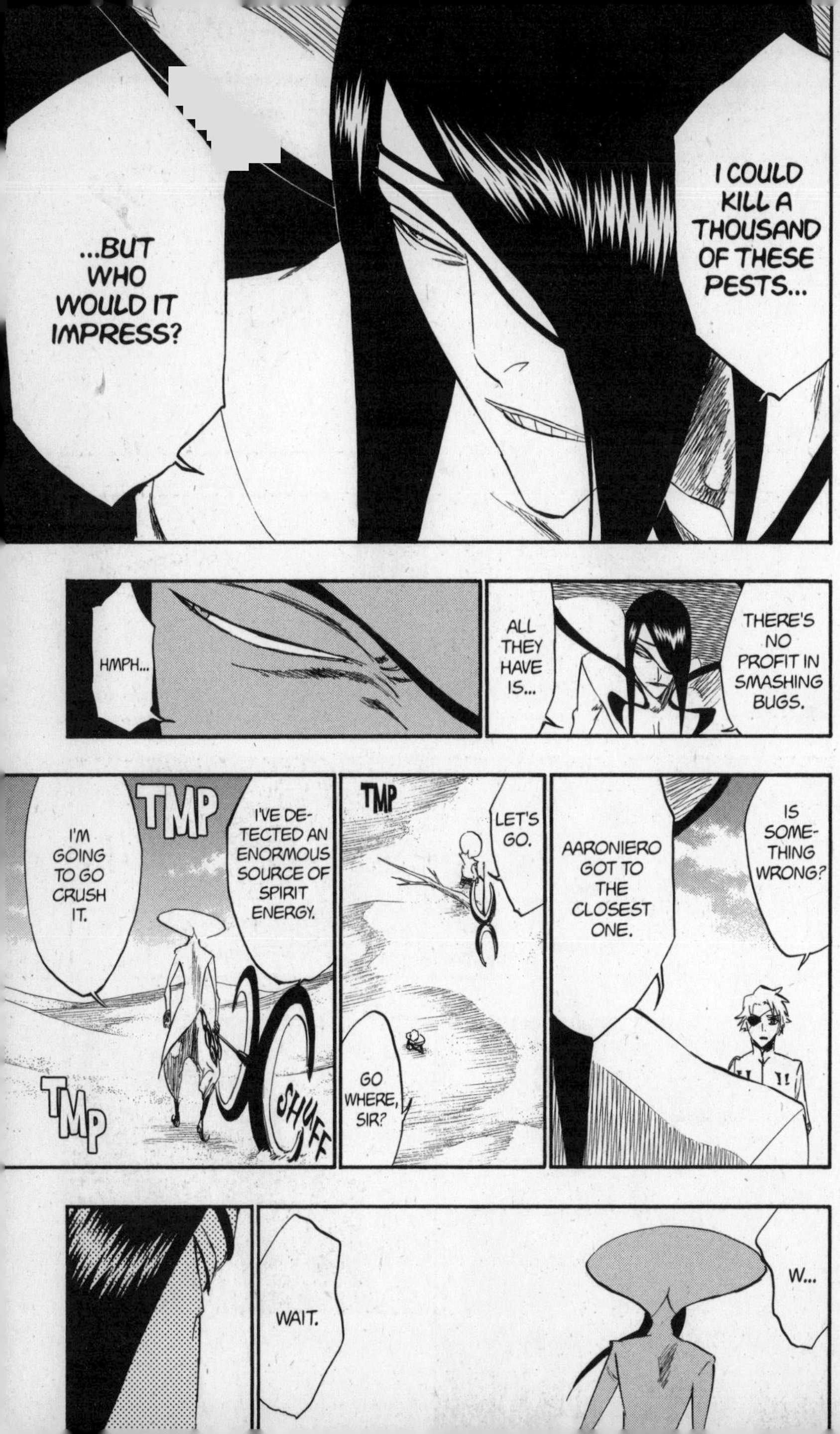
I COULD KILL A THOUSAND OF THESE PESTS...
...BUT WHO WOULD IT IMPRESS?
THERE'S NO PROFIT IN SMASHING BUGS.
ALL THEY HAVE IS...
HMPH...
IS SOME-THING WRONG?
AARONIERO GOT TO THE CLOSEST ONE.
TMP
LET'S GO.
GO WHERE, SIR?
TMP
I'VE DE-TECTED AN ENORMOUS SOURCE OF SPIRIT ENERGY.
I'M GOING TO GO CRUSH IT.
TMP
SHUFF
W...
WAIT.

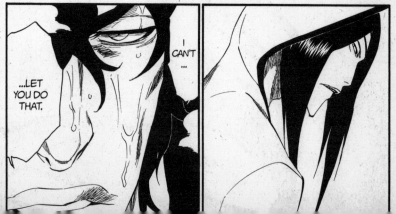

...LET YOU DO THAT.

I CAN'T...

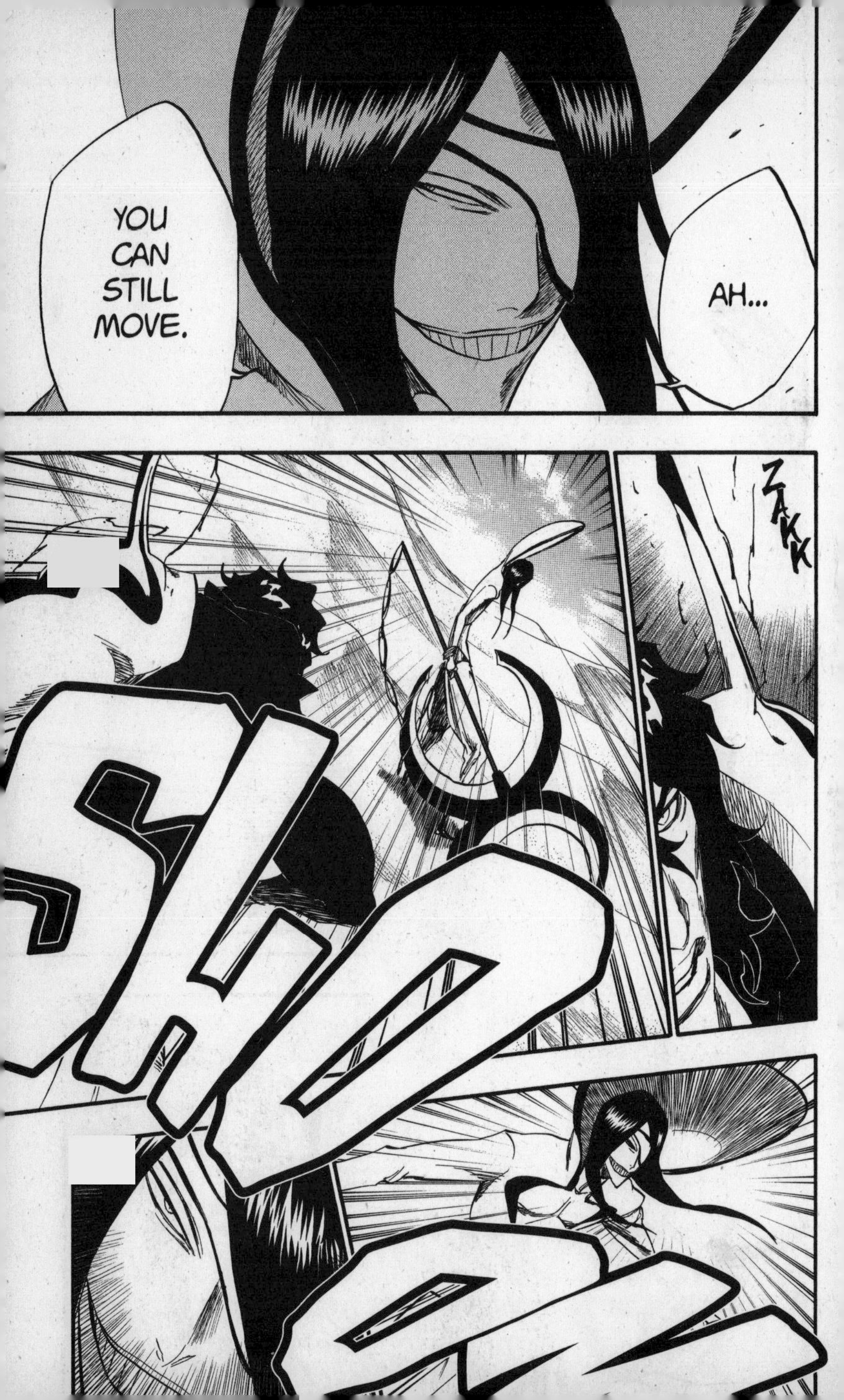
AH...
YOU CAN STILL MOVE.
ZAKK

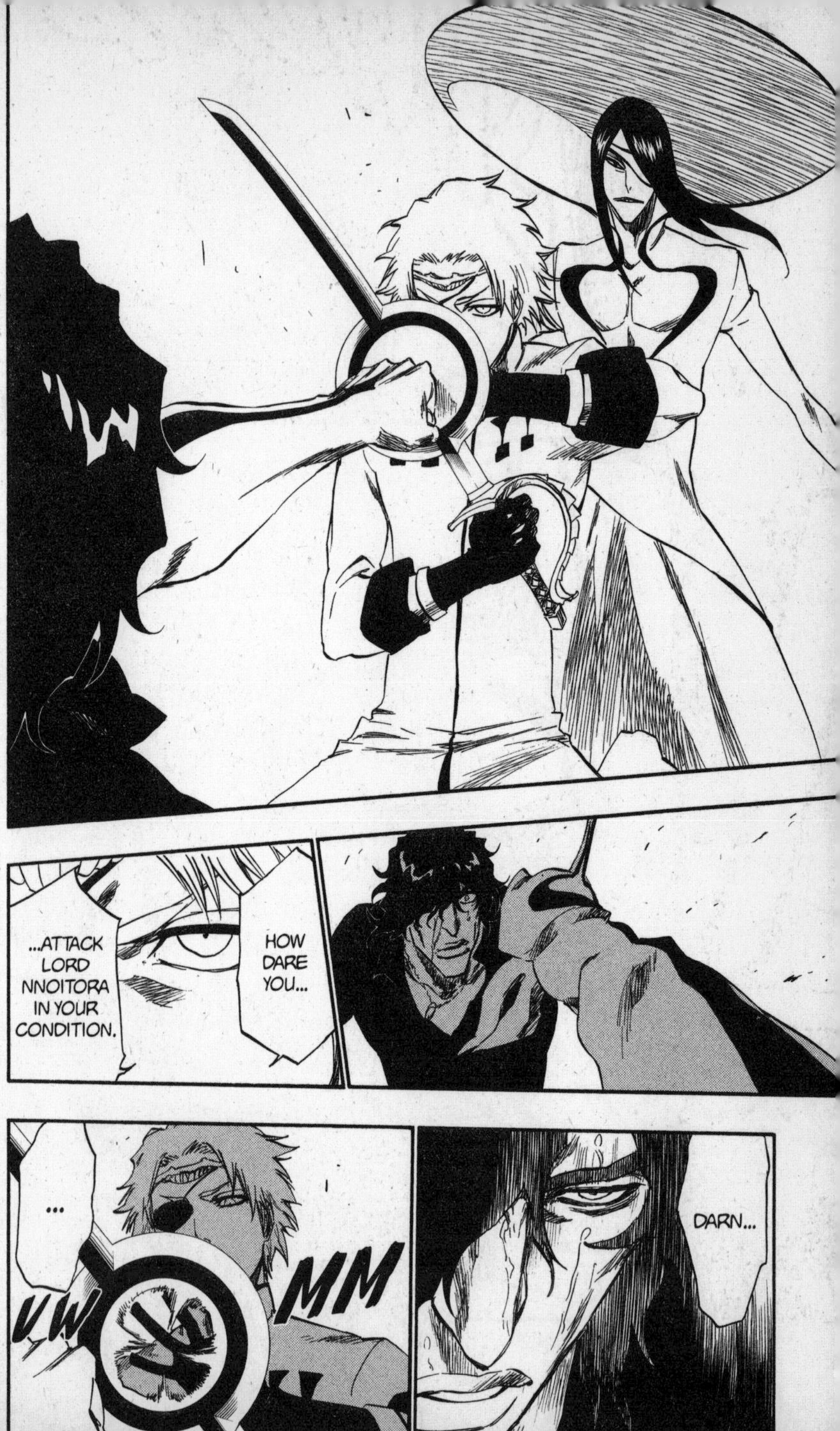
HOW DARE YOU...
...ATTACK LORD NNOITORA IN YOUR CONDITION.
DARN...
...

SIR...

SHALL WE?

SHWWP

KLANK

IF IT HAD LANDED...

I'M SORRY, SIR...

BUT ALL OF HIS REMAINING STRENGTH WAS IN THAT BLOW.

WHAT MADE YOU THINK I NEEDED YOUR HELP?

55

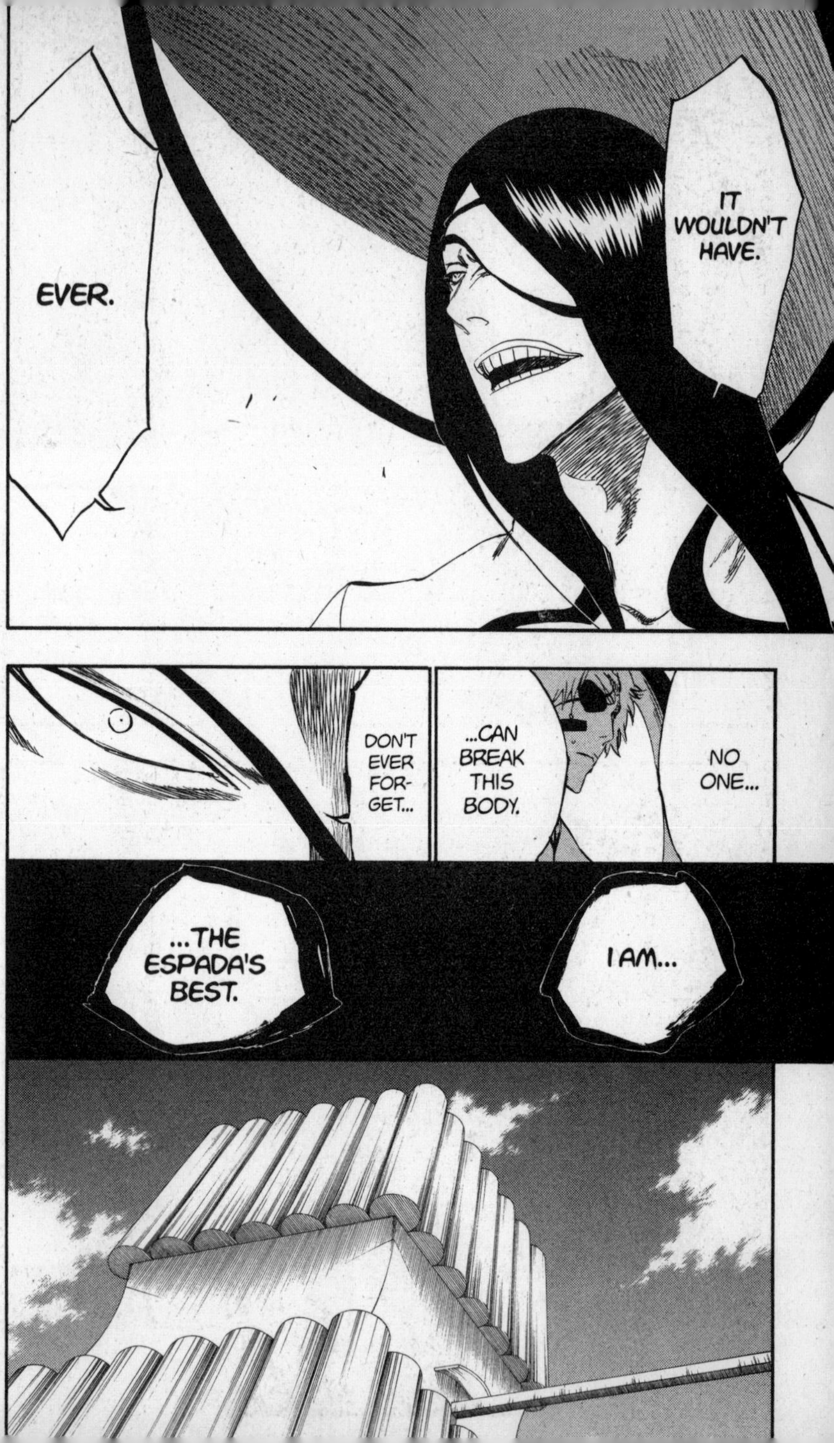
IT WOULDN'T HAVE.
EVER.
NO ONE...
...CAN BREAK THIS BODY.
DON'T EVER FOR-GET...
I AM...
...THE ESPADA'S BEST.

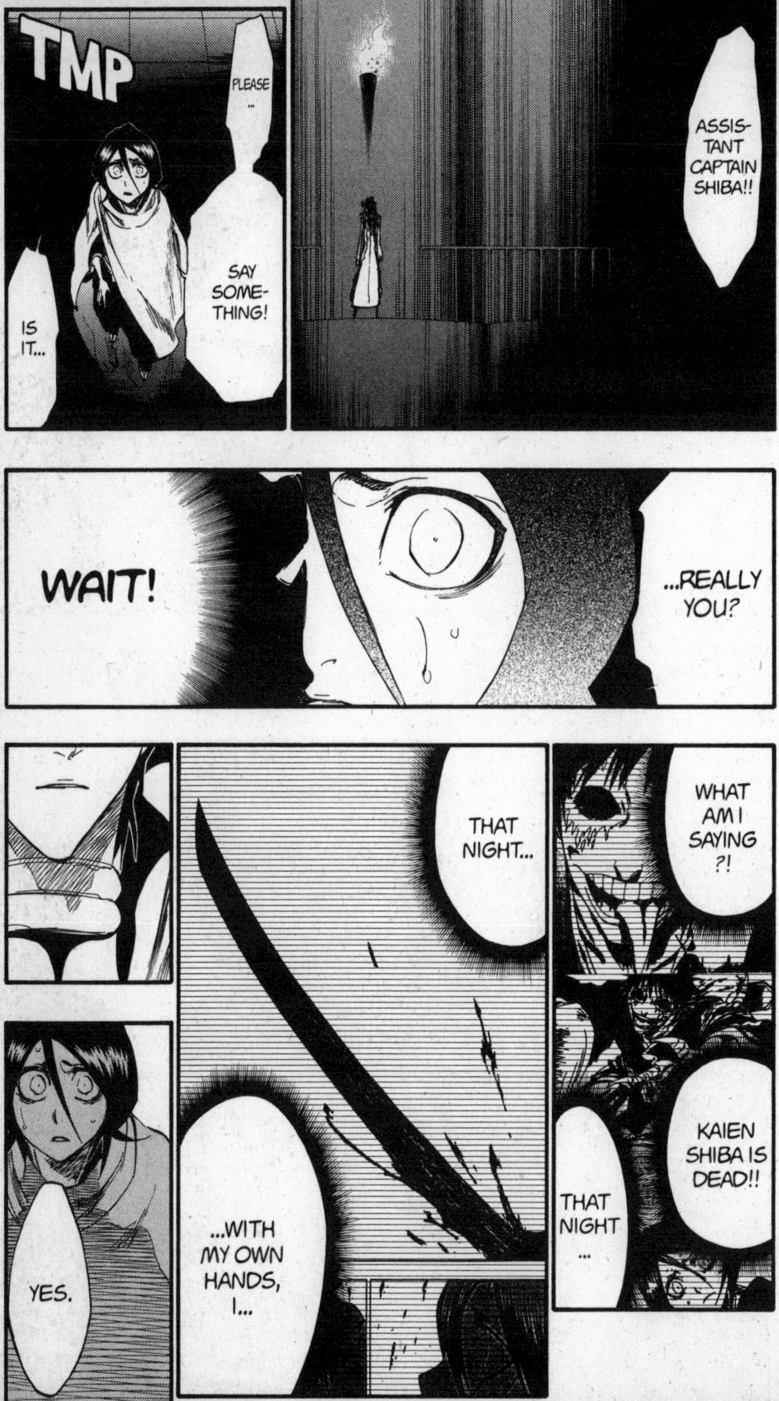
ASSISTANT CAPTAIN SHIBA!!
TMP
PLEASE...
SAY SOMETHING!
IS IT...
...REALLY YOU?
WAIT!
WHAT AM I SAYING?!
KAIEN SHIBA IS DEAD!!
THAT NIGHT...
THAT NIGHT...
...WITH MY OWN HANDS, I...
YES.

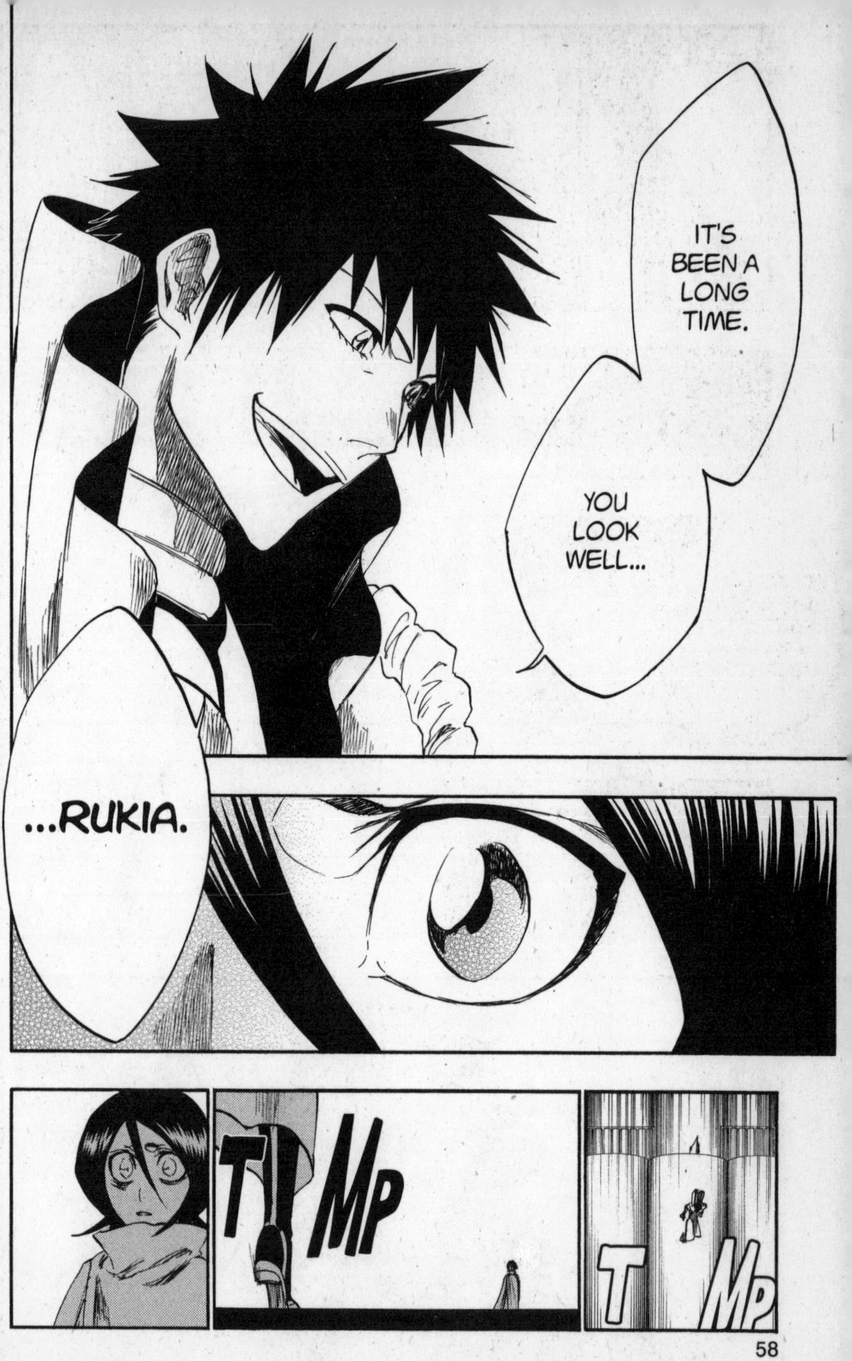
IT'S BEEN A LONG TIME.
YOU LOOK WELL...
...RUKIA.
TMP
TMP

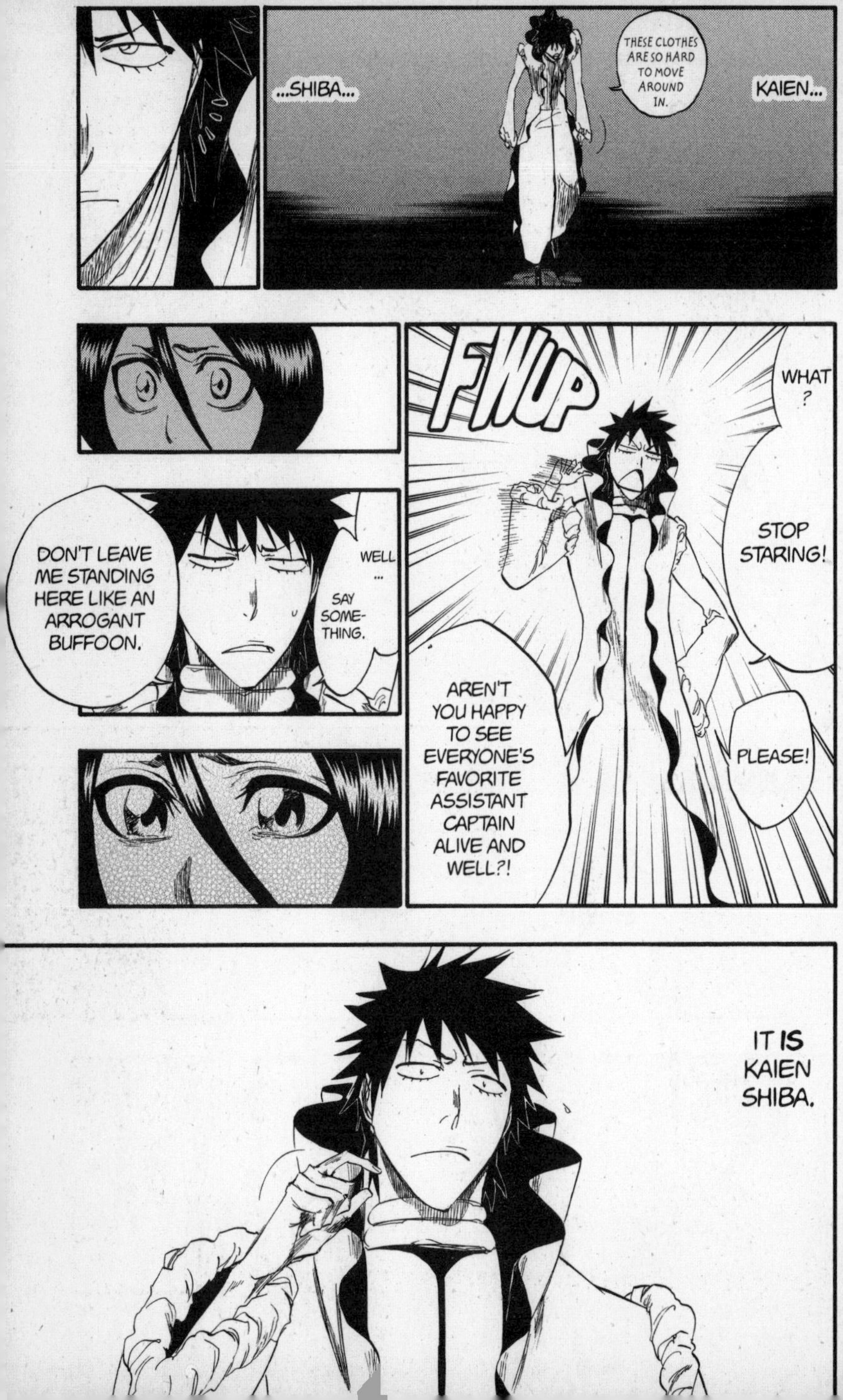
KAIEN...
THESE CLOTHES ARE SO HARD TO MOVE AROUND IN.
...SHIBA...
FWUP
WHAT?
STOP STARING!
PLEASE!
AREN'T YOU HAPPY TO SEE EVERYONE'S FAVORITE ASSISTANT CAPTAIN ALIVE AND WELL?!
WELL...
SAY SOME-THING.
DON'T LEAVE ME STANDING HERE LIKE AN ARROGANT BUFFOON.
IT IS KAIEN SHIBA.

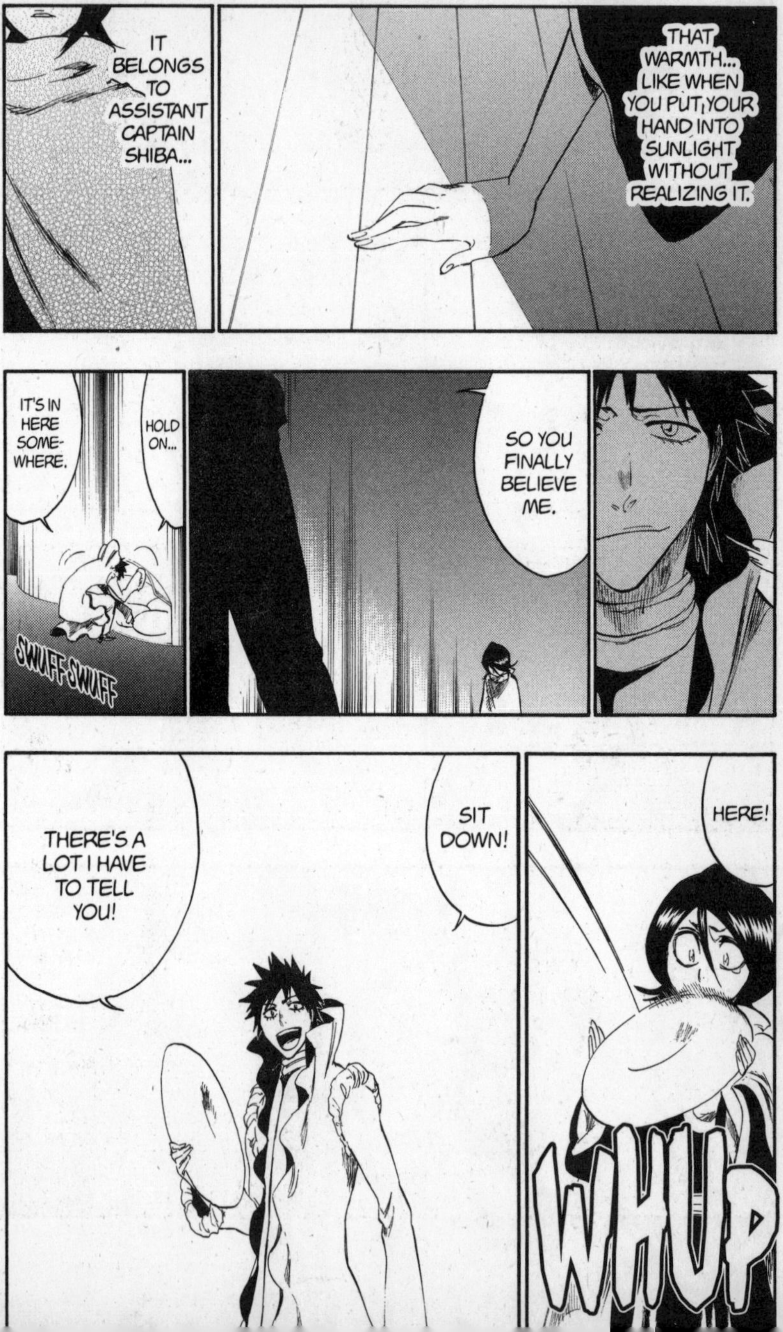
THAT WARMTH... LIKE WHEN YOU PUT YOUR HAND INTO SUNLIGHT WITHOUT REALIZING IT.
IT BELONGS TO ASSISTANT CAPTAIN SHIBA...
SO YOU FINALLY BELIEVE ME.
HOLD ON...
IT'S IN HERE SOME-WHERE.
SWUFF SWUFF
HERE!
WHUP
SIT DOWN!
THERE'S A LOT I HAVE TO TELL YOU!

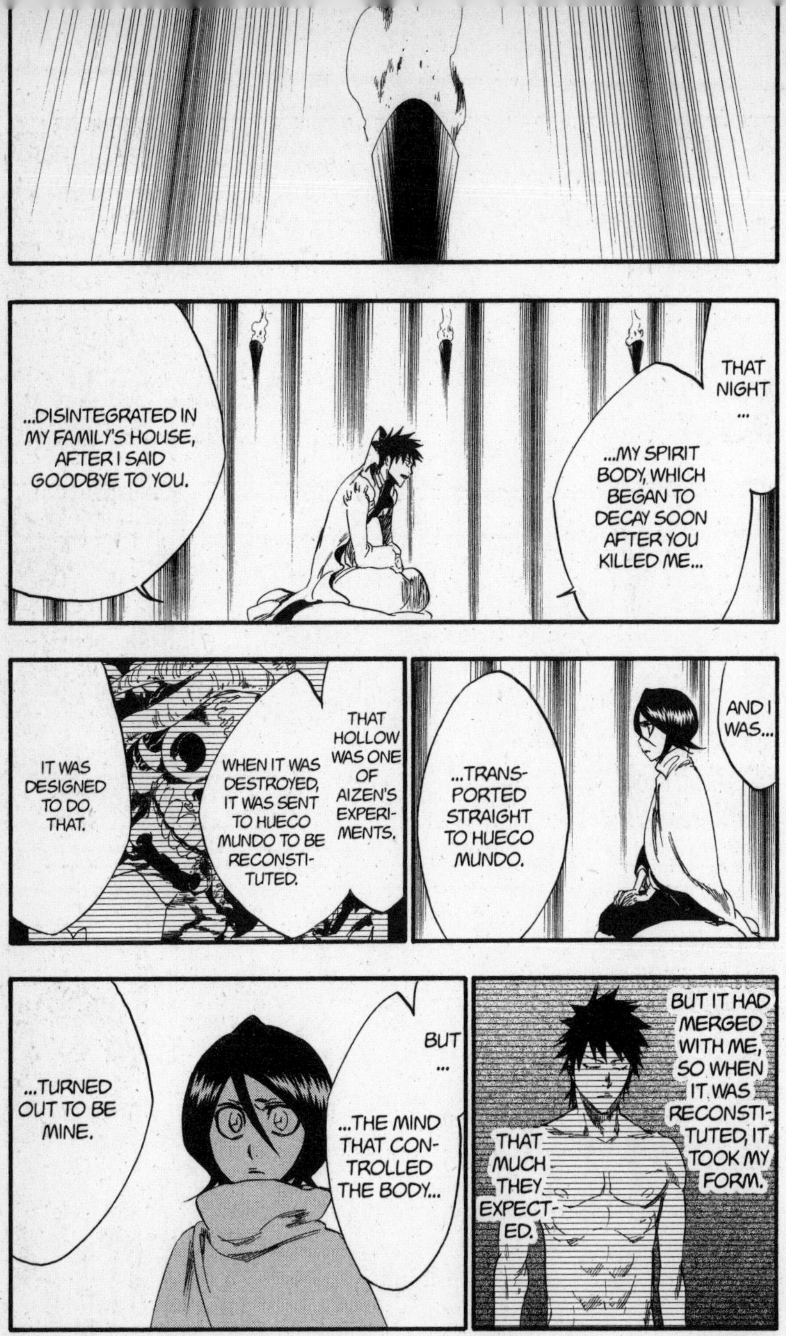
THAT NIGHT ...
...MY SPIRIT BODY, WHICH BEGAN TO DECAY SOON AFTER YOU KILLED ME...
...DISINTEGRATED IN MY FAMILY'S HOUSE, AFTER I SAID GOODBYE TO YOU.
AND I WAS...
...TRANSPORTED STRAIGHT TO HUECO MUNDO.
THAT HOLLOW WAS ONE OF AIZEN'S EXPERIMENTS.
WHEN IT WAS DESTROYED, IT WAS SENT TO HUECO MUNDO TO BE RECONSTITUTED.
IT WAS DESIGNED TO DO THAT.
BUT IT HAD MERGED WITH ME, SO WHEN IT WAS RECONSTITUTED, IT TOOK MY FORM.
THAT MUCH THEY EXPECTED.
BUT ...
...THE MIND THAT CONTROLLED THE BODY...
...TURNED OUT TO BE MINE.

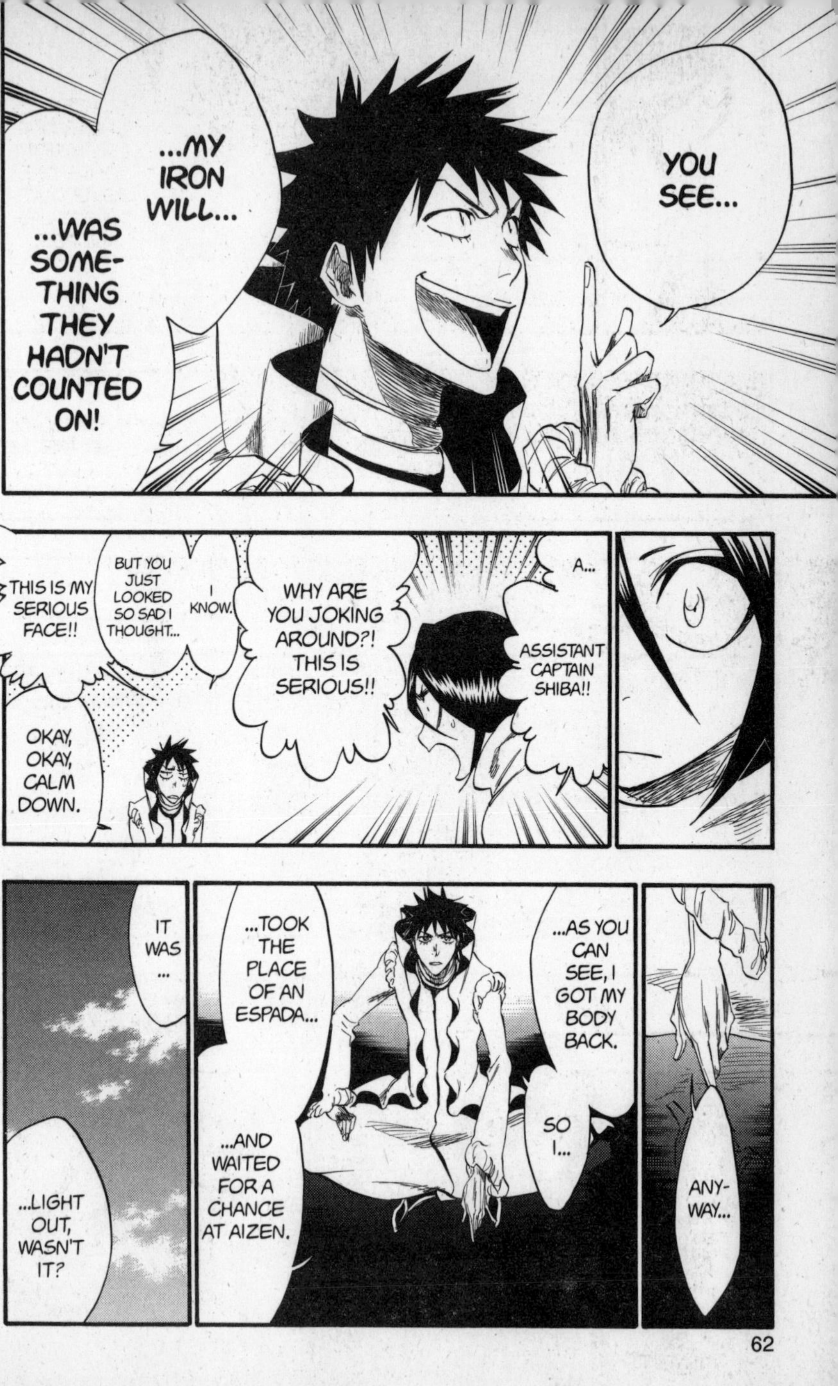
YOU SEE...
...MY IRON WILL...
...WAS SOME-THING THEY HADN'T COUNTED ON!
A... ASSISTANT CAPTAIN SHIBA!!
WHY ARE YOU JOKING AROUND?! THIS IS SERIOUS!!
I KNOW.
BUT YOU JUST LOOKED SO SAD I THOUGHT...
THIS IS MY SERIOUS FACE!!
OKAY, OKAY, CALM DOWN.
ANY-WAY...
...AS YOU CAN SEE, I GOT MY BODY BACK.
SO I...
...TOOK THE PLACE OF AN ESPADA...
...AND WAITED FOR A CHANCE AT AIZEN.
IT WAS...
...LIGHT OUT, WASN'T IT?

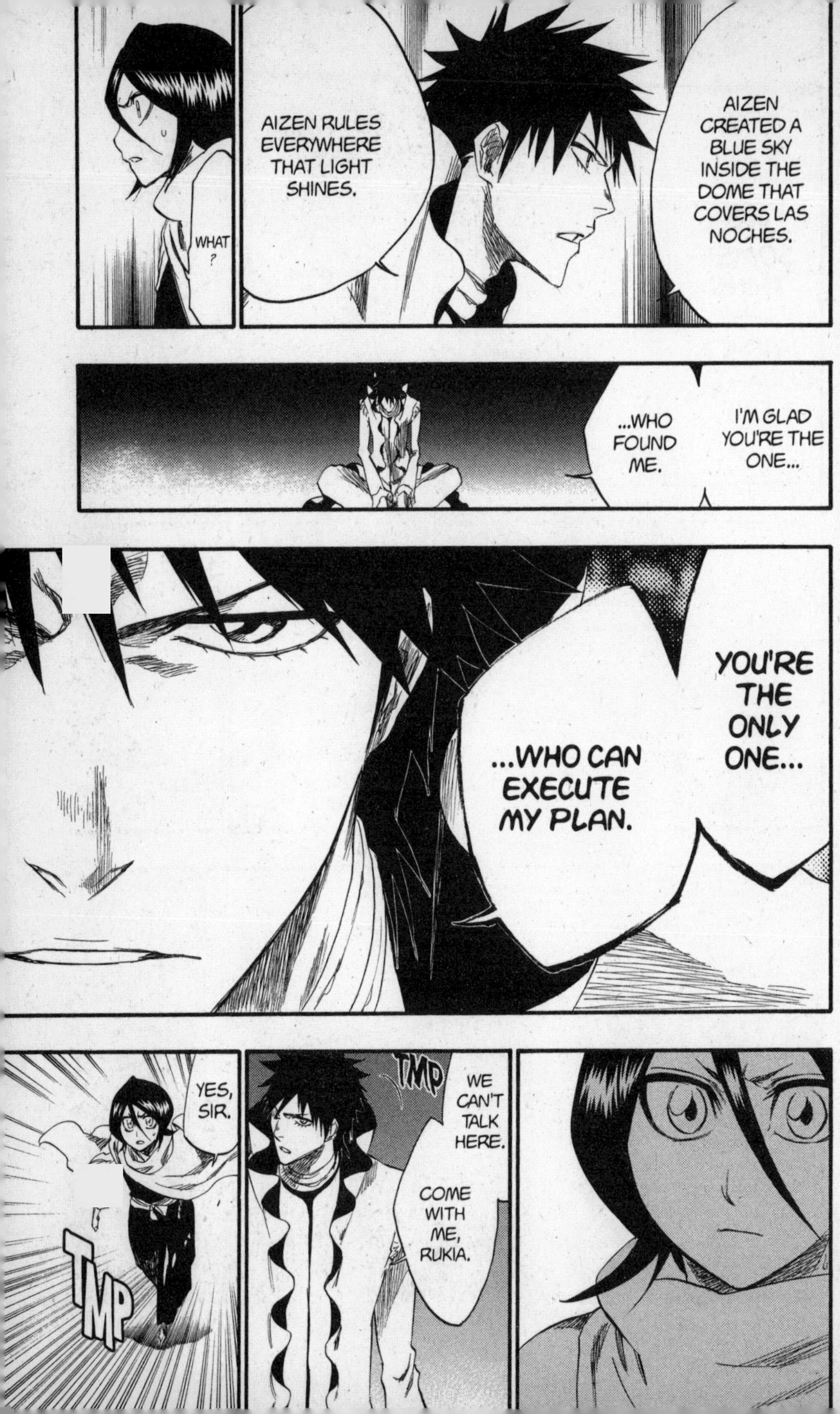
AIZEN CREATED A BLUE SKY INSIDE THE DOME THAT COVERS LAS NOCHES.
AIZEN RULES EVERYWHERE THAT LIGHT SHINES.
WHAT?
I'M GLAD YOU'RE THE ONE...
...WHO FOUND ME.
YOU'RE THE ONLY ONE...
...WHO CAN EXECUTE MY PLAN.
TMP
WE CAN'T TALK HERE.
COME WITH ME, RUKIA.
YES, SIR.
TMP

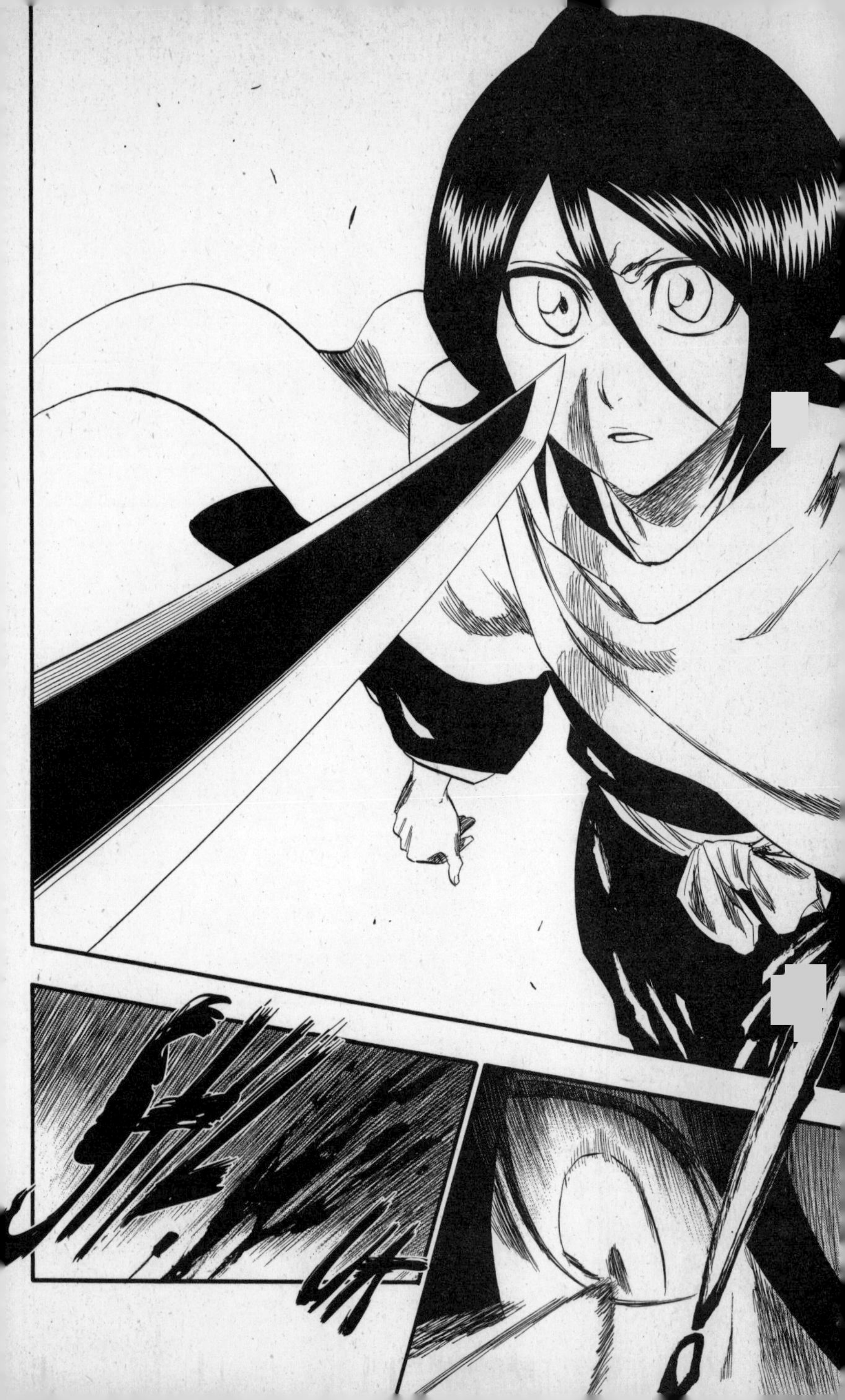

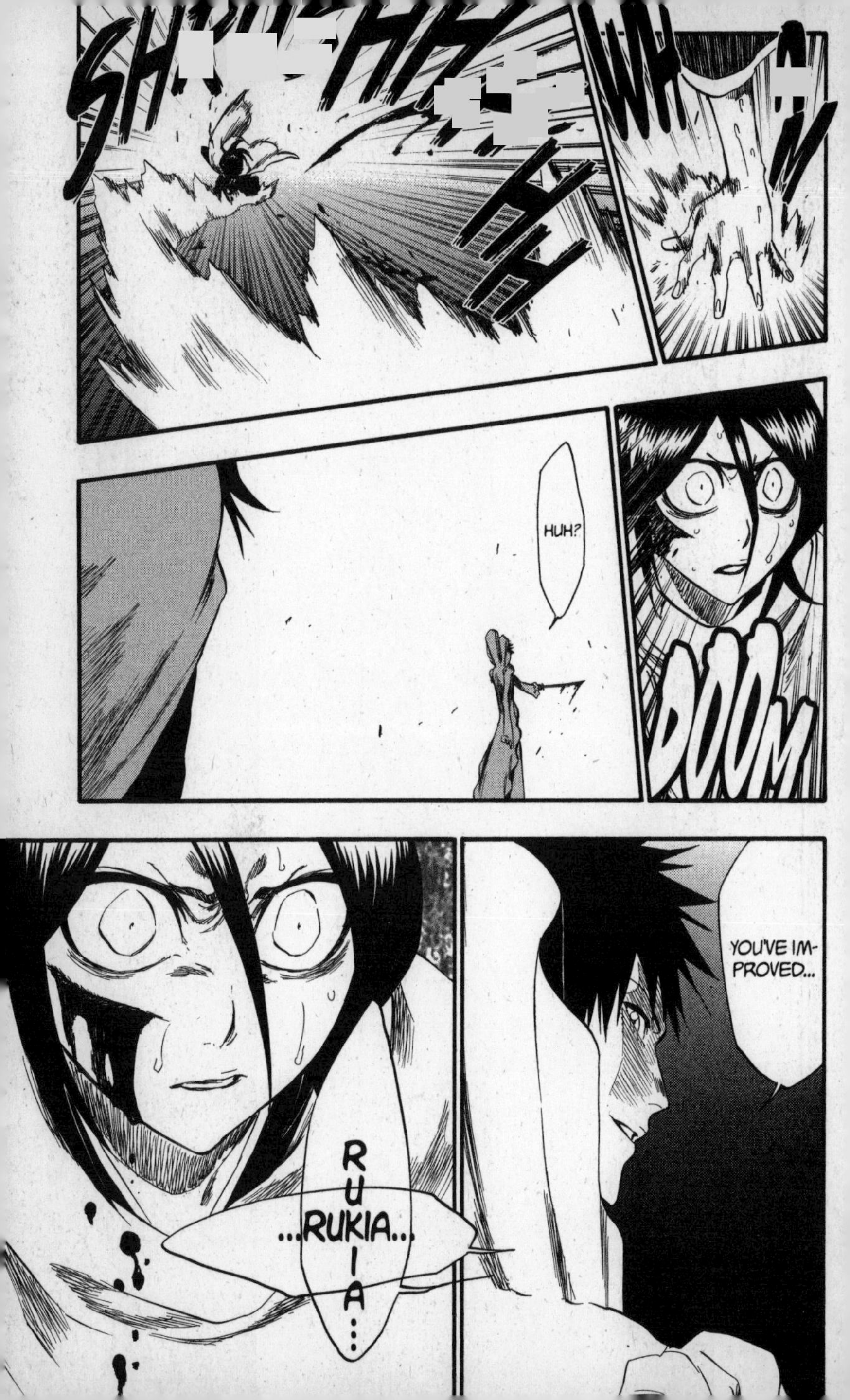
DOOM
HUH?
YOU'VE IM-PROVED...
RUKIA...
...RUKIA...

unexpected.
unexplained.
unexposed.

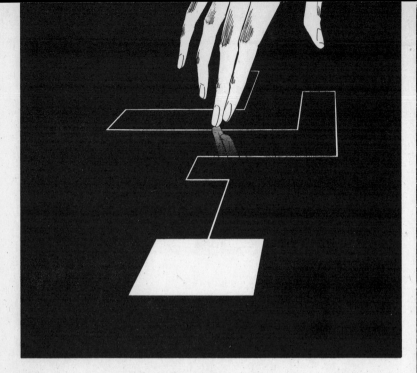

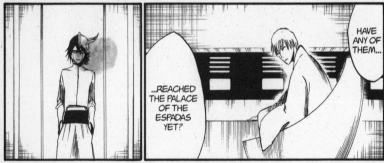

HAVE ANY OF THEM...
...REACHED THE PALACE OF THE ESPADAS YET?
HOW UNUSUAL.
YOU'RE STARTING A CONVER-SATION WITH ME.
I THOUGHT YOU HATED ME.
PLEASE.

264. Don't Say That Name Again

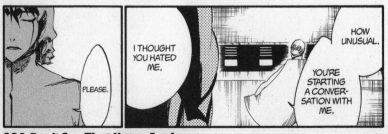

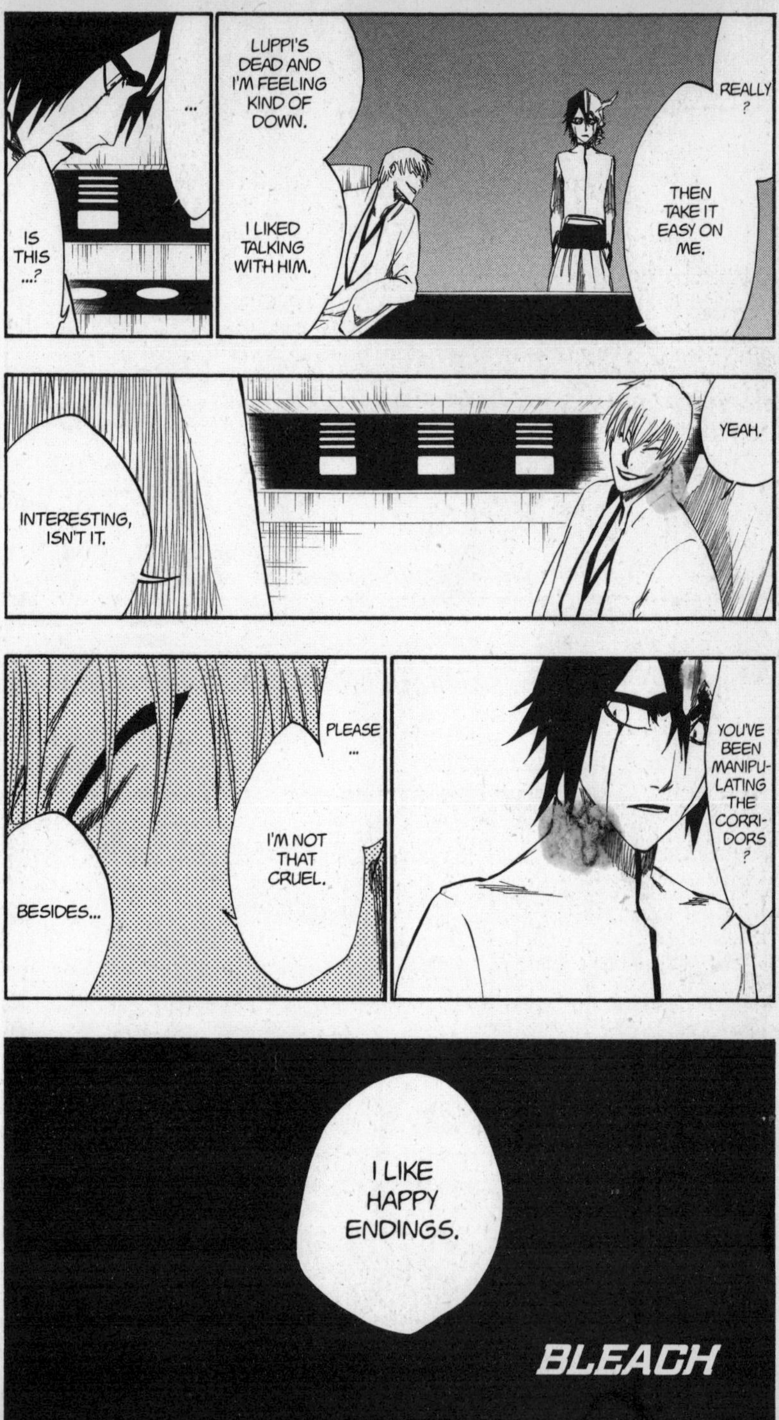
REALLY?
LUPPI'S DEAD AND I'M FEELING KIND OF DOWN.
THEN TAKE IT EASY ON ME.
I LIKED TALKING WITH HIM.
...
IS THIS ...?
YEAH.
INTERESTING, ISN'T IT.
YOU'VE BEEN MANIPULATING THE CORRIDORS?
PLEASE...
I'M NOT THAT CRUEL.
BESIDES...
I LIKE HAPPY ENDINGS.
BLEACH

264. Don't Say That Name Again

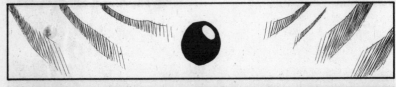

WHAT'S WRONG?

...CONFUSED.

YOU LOOK...

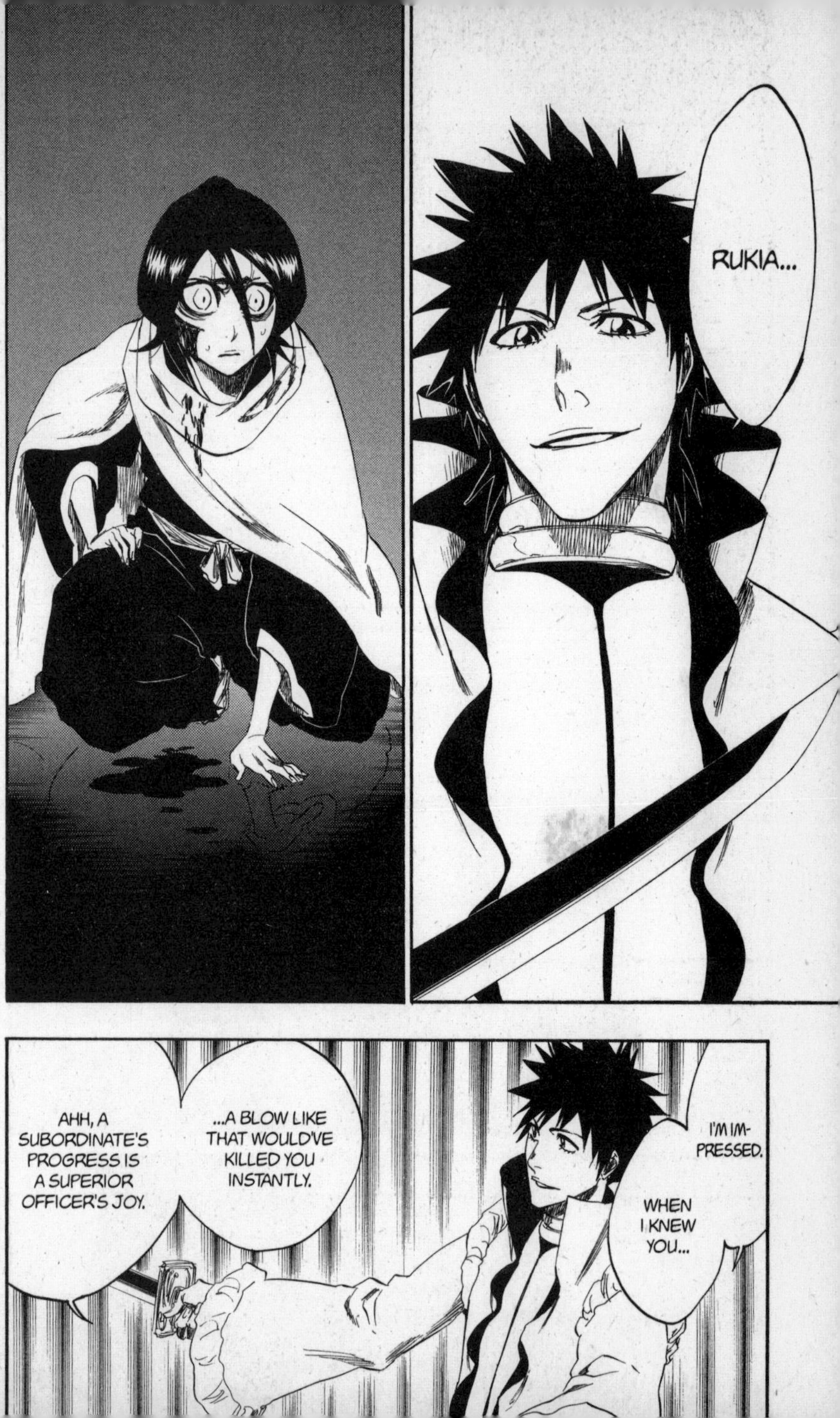
RUKIA...
I'M IM-PRESSED.
WHEN I KNEW YOU...
...A BLOW LIKE THAT WOULD'VE KILLED YOU INSTANTLY.
AHH, A SUBORDINATE'S PROGRESS IS A SUPERIOR OFFICER'S JOY.

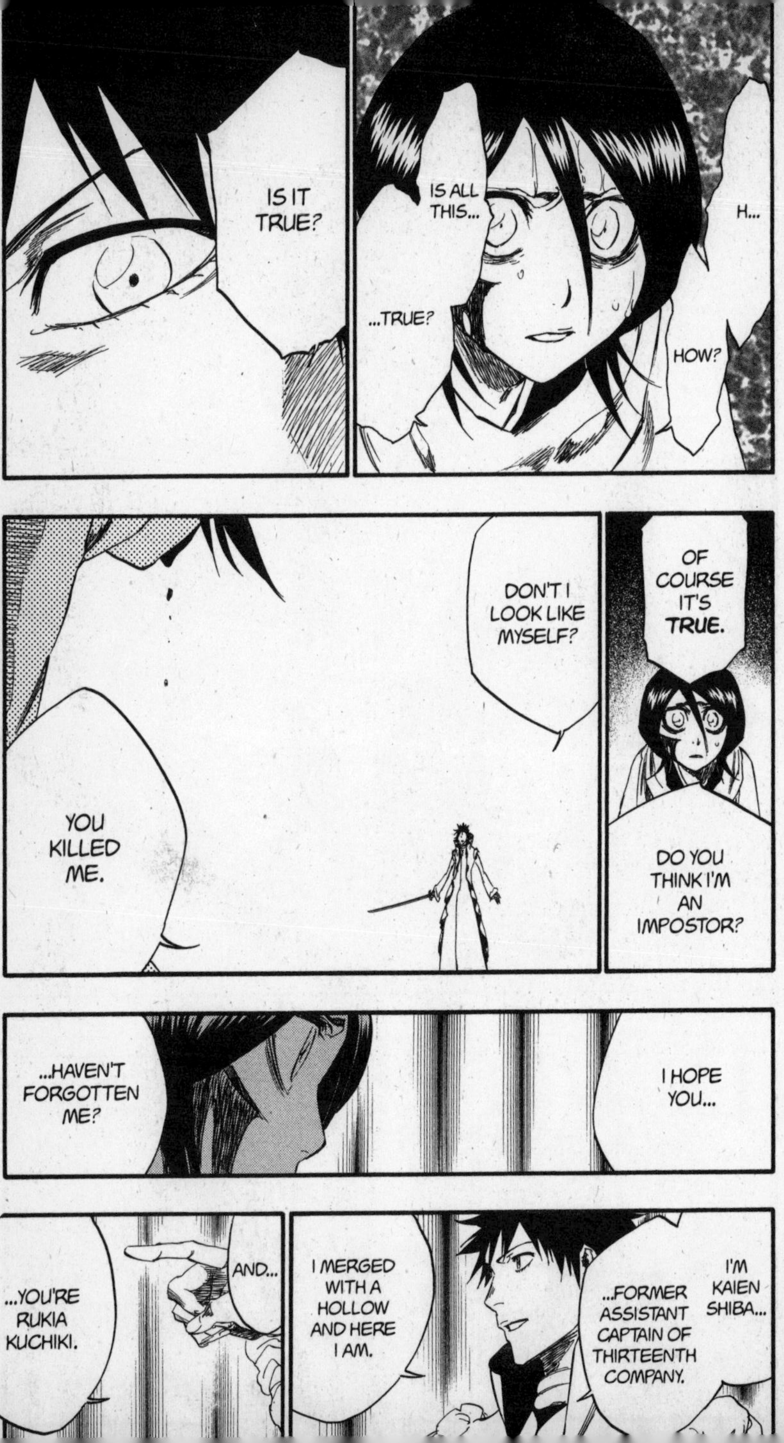
H...
HOW?
IS ALL THIS...
...TRUE?
IS IT TRUE?
OF COURSE IT'S TRUE.
DO YOU THINK I'M AN IMPOSTOR?
DON'T I LOOK LIKE MYSELF?
YOU KILLED ME.
I HOPE YOU...
...HAVEN'T FORGOTTEN ME?
I'M KAIEN SHIBA...
...FORMER ASSISTANT CAPTAIN OF THIRTEENTH COMPANY.
I MERGED WITH A HOLLOW AND HERE I AM.
AND...
...YOU'RE RUKIA KUCHIKI.

THE WOMAN...

...WHO TOOK MY LIFE.

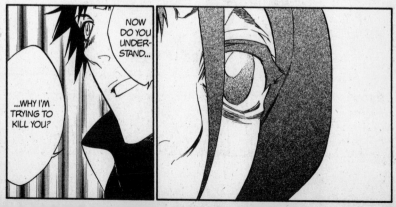

NOW DO YOU UNDERSTAND...

...WHY I'M TRYING TO KILL YOU?

READ THIS WAY

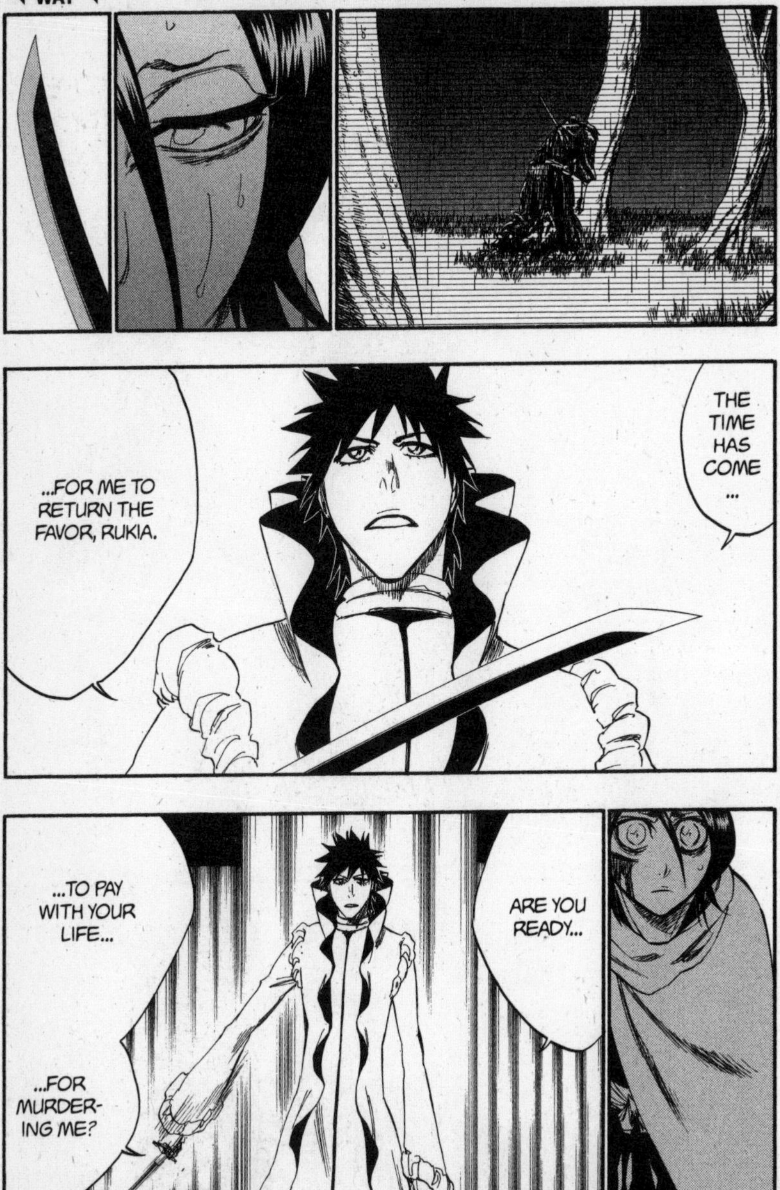
THE TIME HAS COME...
...FOR ME TO RETURN THE FAVOR, RUKIA.
ARE YOU READY...
...TO PAY WITH YOUR LIFE...
...FOR MURDERING ME?

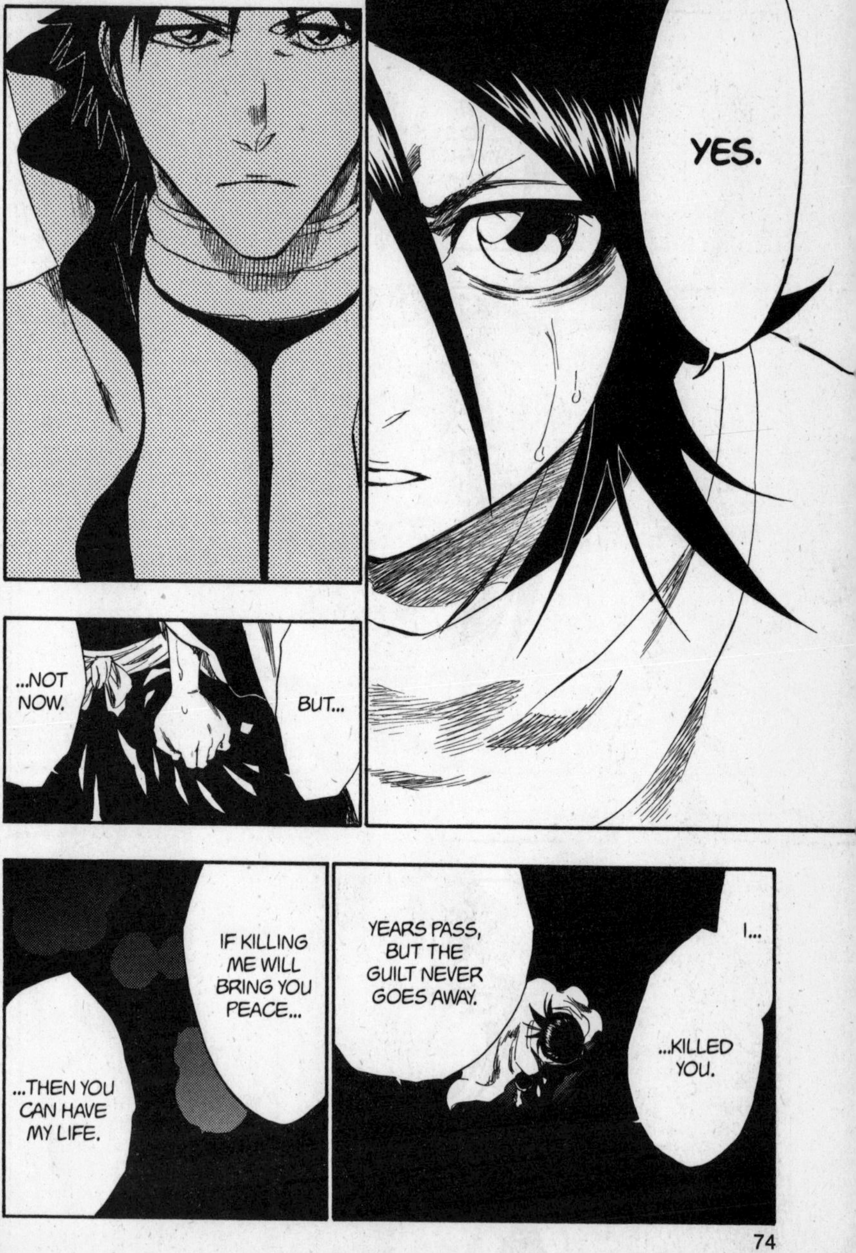
YES.
BUT...
...NOT NOW.
I...
...KILLED YOU.
YEARS PASS, BUT THE GUILT NEVER GOES AWAY.
IF KILLING ME WILL BRING YOU PEACE...
...THEN YOU CAN HAVE MY LIFE.

READ THIS WAY

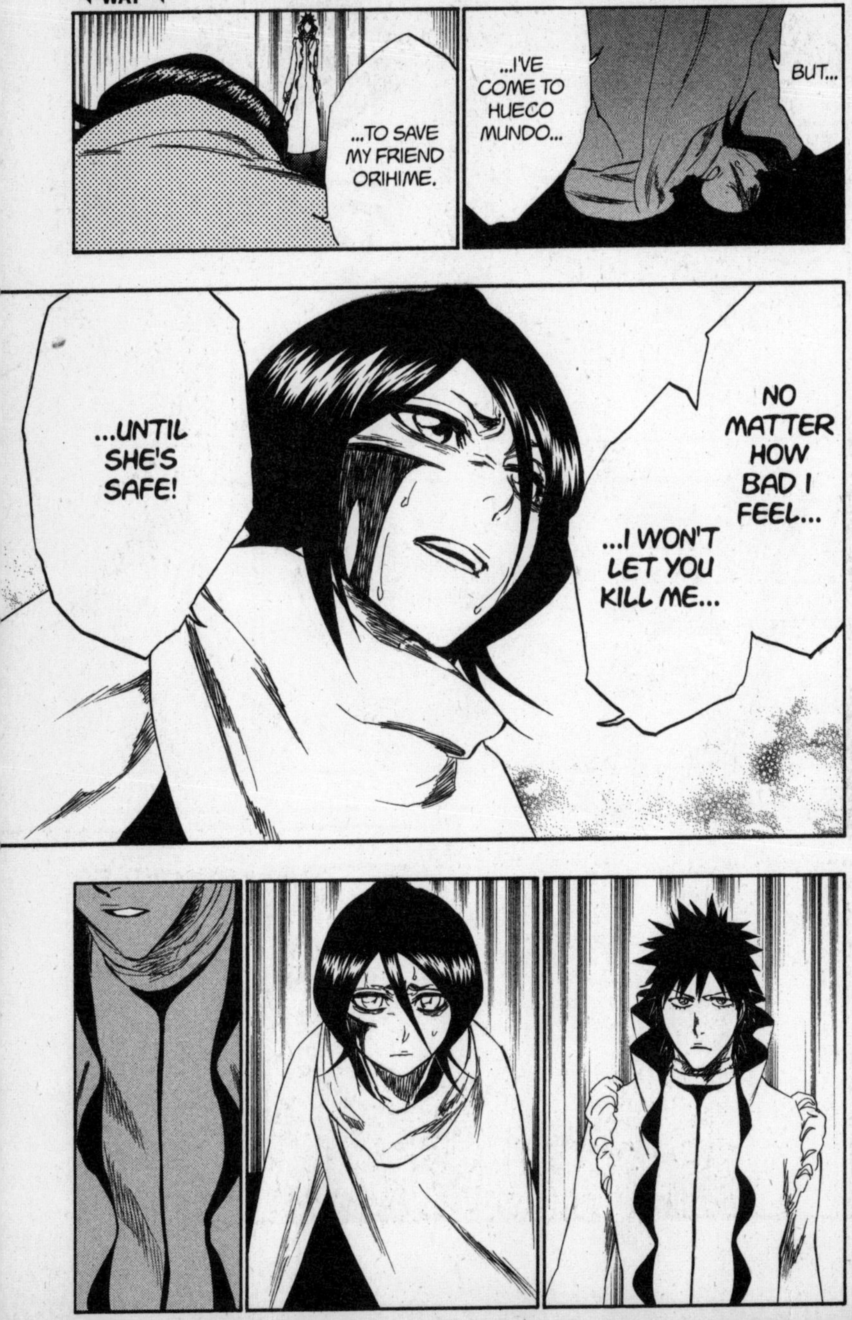

BUT...
...I'VE COME TO HUECO MUNDO...
...TO SAVE MY FRIEND ORIHIME.
NO MATTER HOW BAD I FEEL...
...I WON'T LET YOU KILL ME...
...UNTIL SHE'S SAFE!

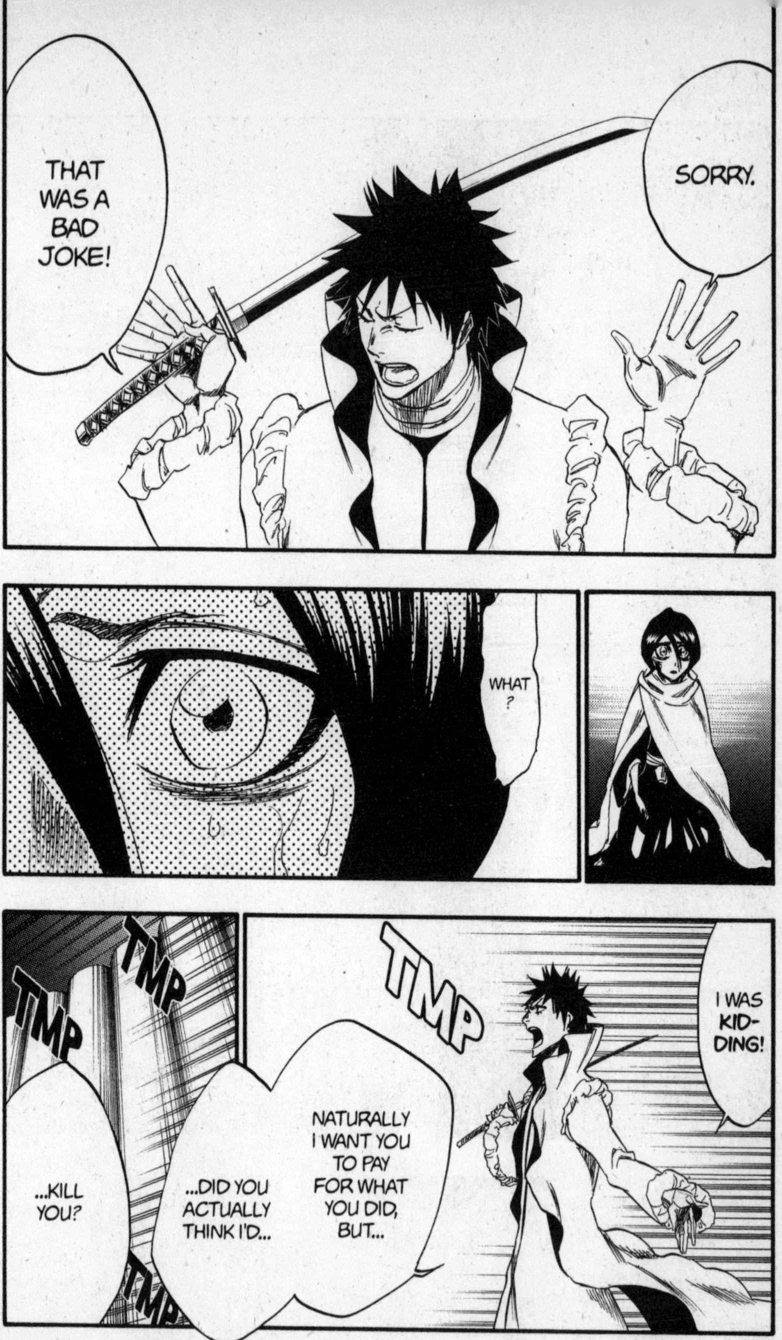

THAT WAS A BAD JOKE!
SORRY.
WHAT?
I WAS KID-DING!
TMP
NATURALLY I WANT YOU TO PAY FOR WHAT YOU DID, BUT...
...DID YOU ACTUALLY THINK I'D...
TMP
TMP
...KILL YOU?
TMP

READ THIS WAY

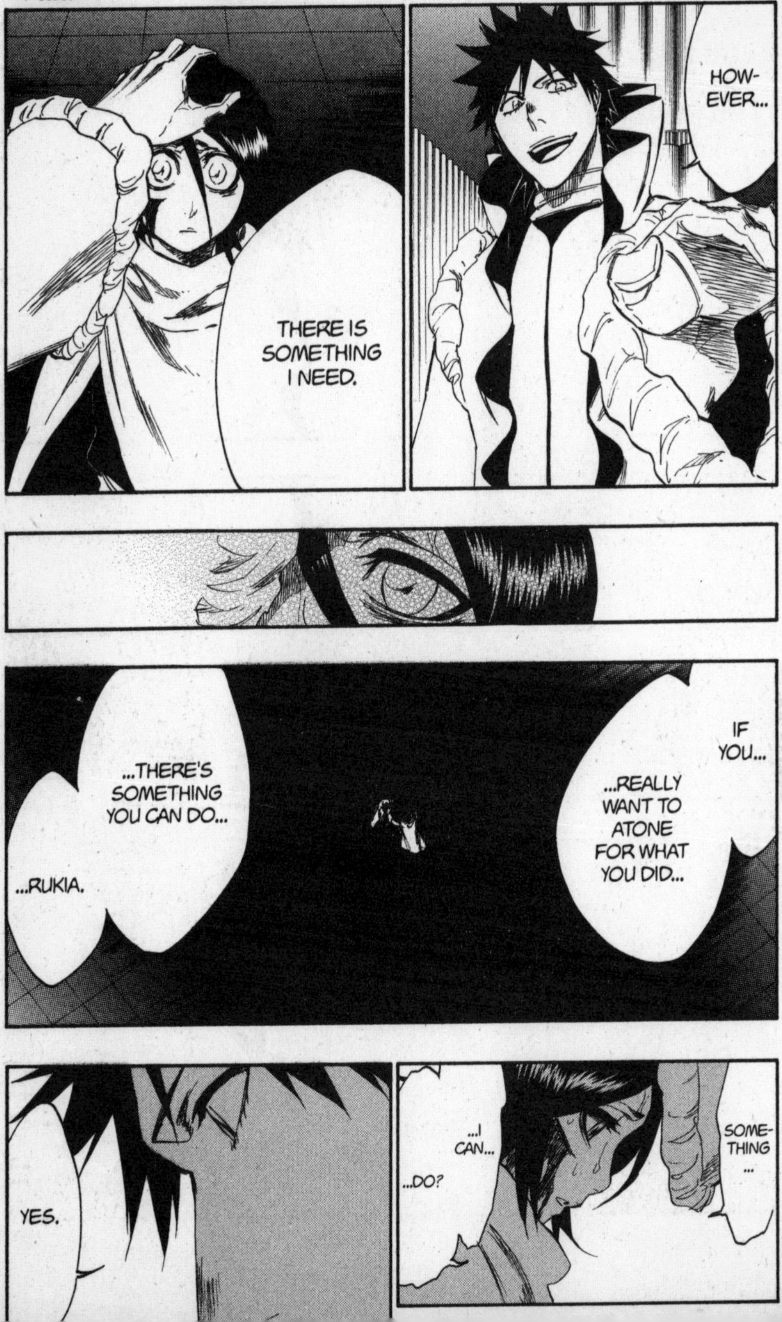
HOW-EVER...
THERE IS SOMETHING I NEED.
IF YOU...
...REALLY WANT TO ATONE FOR WHAT YOU DID...
...THERE'S SOMETHING YOU CAN DO...
...RUKIA.
SOME-THING...
...I CAN...
...DO?
YES.

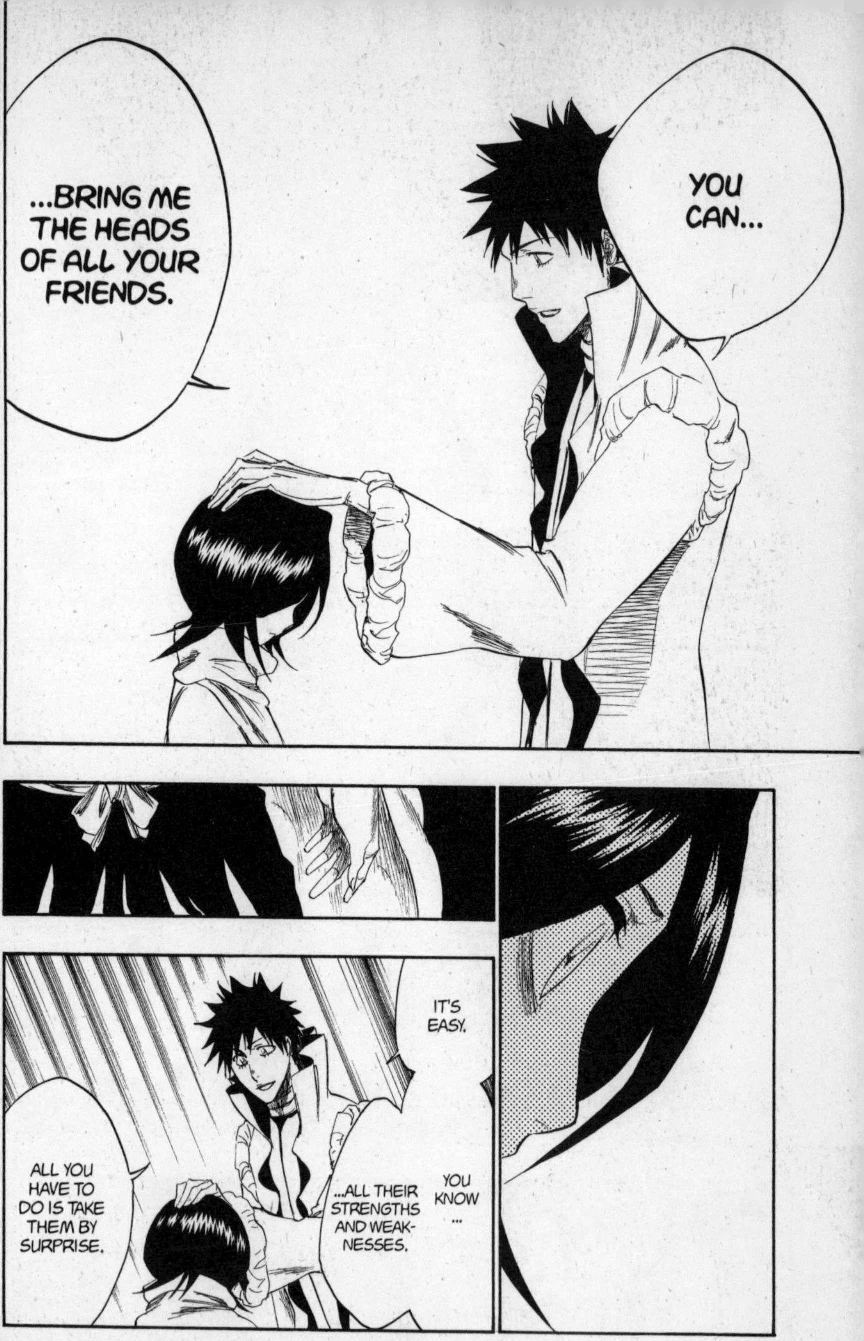
YOU CAN...
...BRING ME THE HEADS OF ALL YOUR FRIENDS.
IT'S EASY.
YOU KNOW ...
...ALL THEIR STRENGTHS AND WEAK-NESSES.
ALL YOU HAVE TO DO IS TAKE THEM BY SURPRISE.

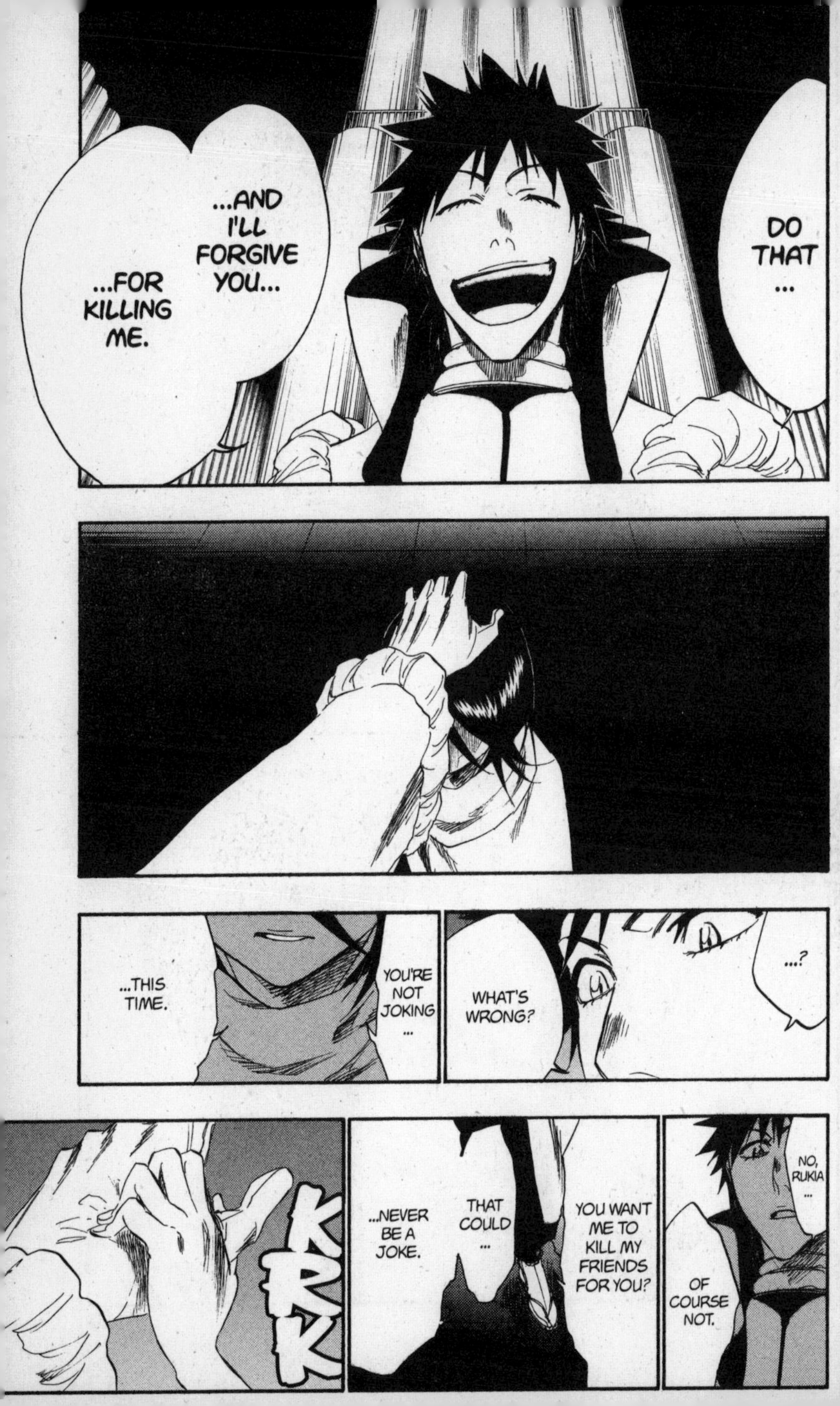
DO THAT ...
...AND I'LL FORGIVE YOU...
...FOR KILLING ME.
...?
WHAT'S WRONG?
YOU'RE NOT JOKING ...
...THIS TIME.
NO, RUKIA ...
OF COURSE NOT.
YOU WANT ME TO KILL MY FRIENDS FOR YOU?
THAT COULD ...
...NEVER BE A JOKE.
KRK

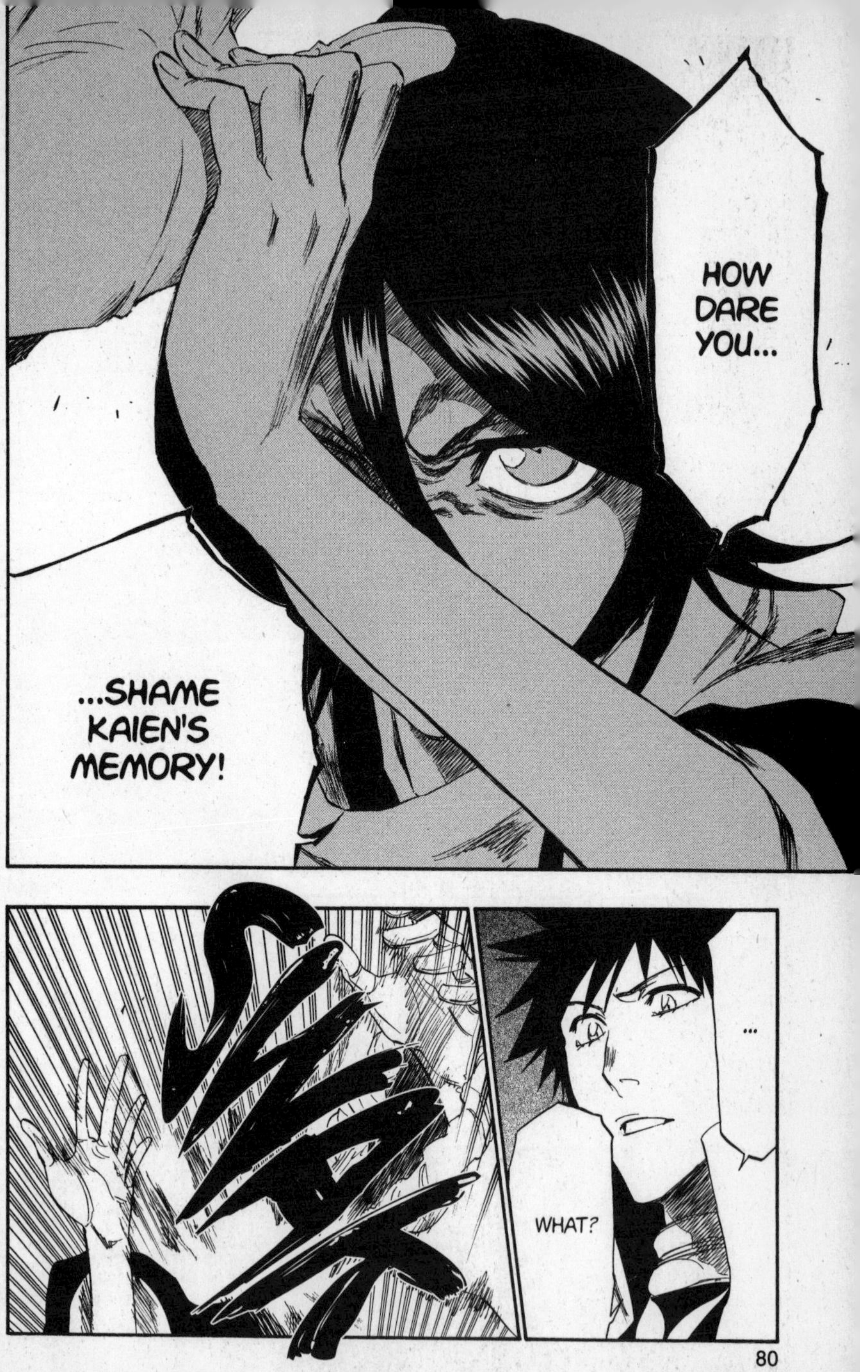
HOW DARE YOU...
...SHAME KAIEN'S MEMORY!
...
WHAT?

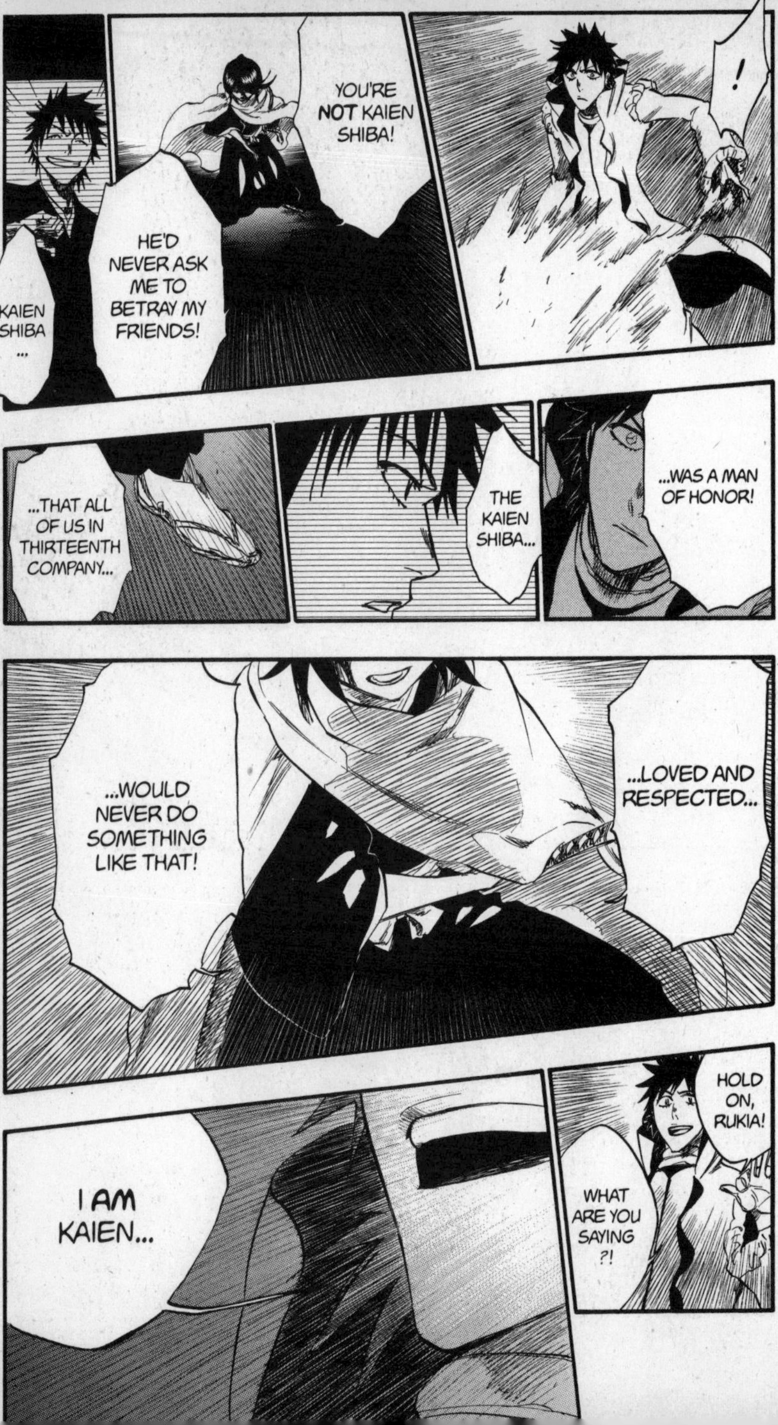
!
YOU'RE **NOT** KAIEN SHIBA!
HE'D NEVER ASK ME TO BETRAY MY FRIENDS!
KAIEN SHIBA ...
...WAS A MAN OF HONOR!
THE KAIEN SHIBA...
...THAT ALL OF US IN THIRTEENTH COMPANY...
...LOVED AND RESPECTED...
...WOULD NEVER DO SOMETHING LIKE THAT!
HOLD ON, RUKIA!
WHAT ARE YOU SAYING ?!
I **AM** KAIEN...

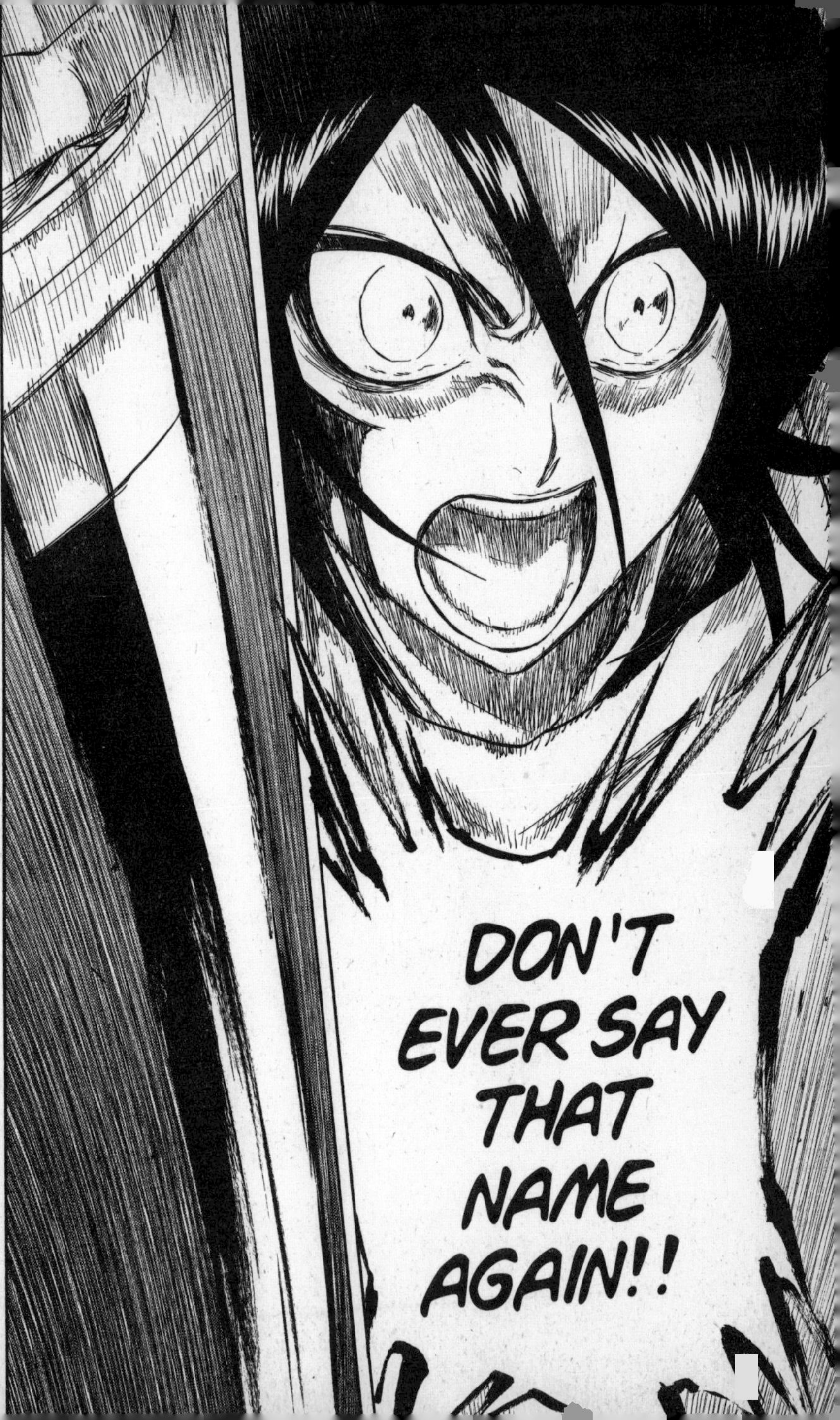
DON'T EVER SAY THAT NAME AGAIN!!

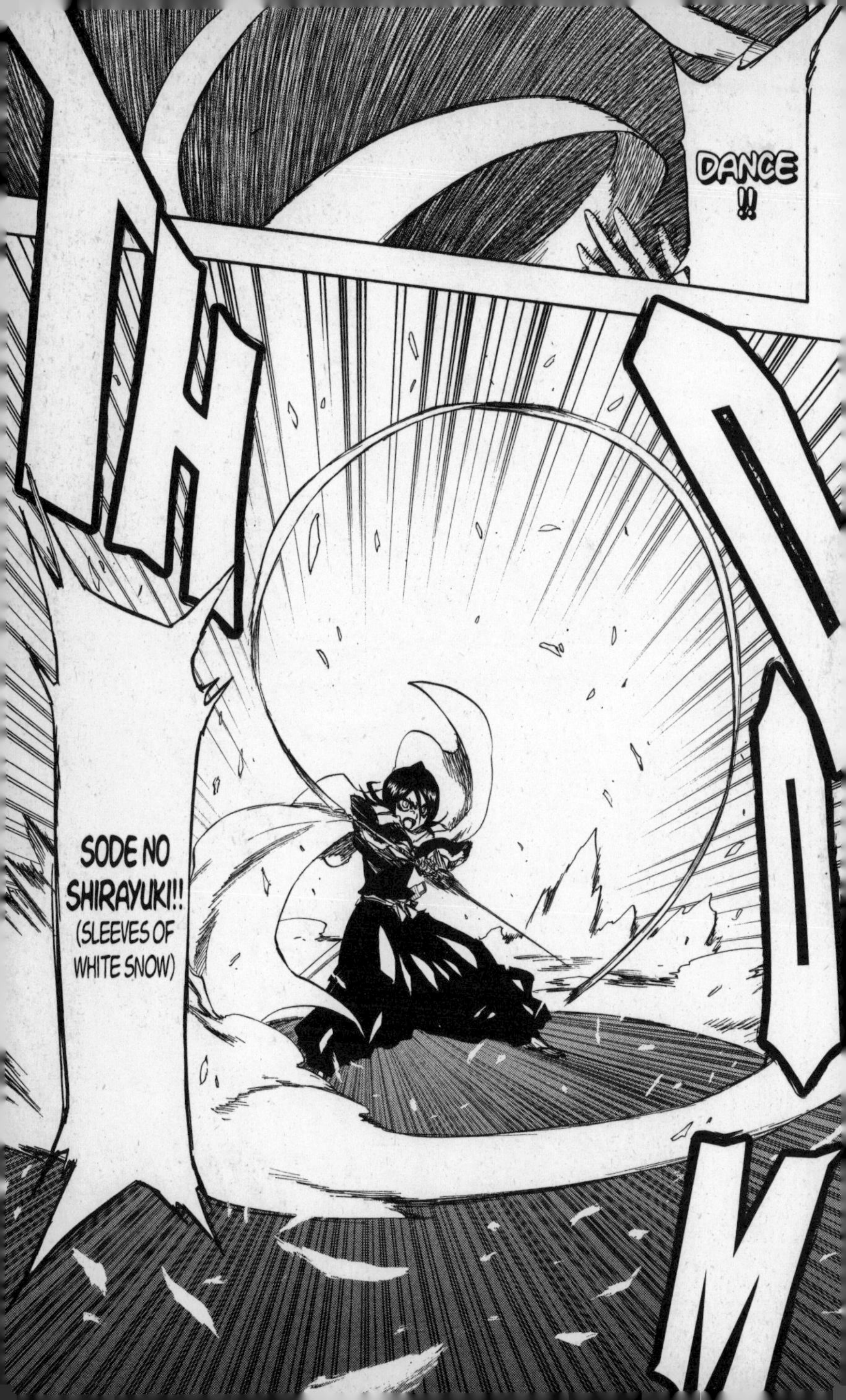
DANCE!!
SODE NO SHIRAYUKI!!
(SLEEVES OF WHITE SNOW)

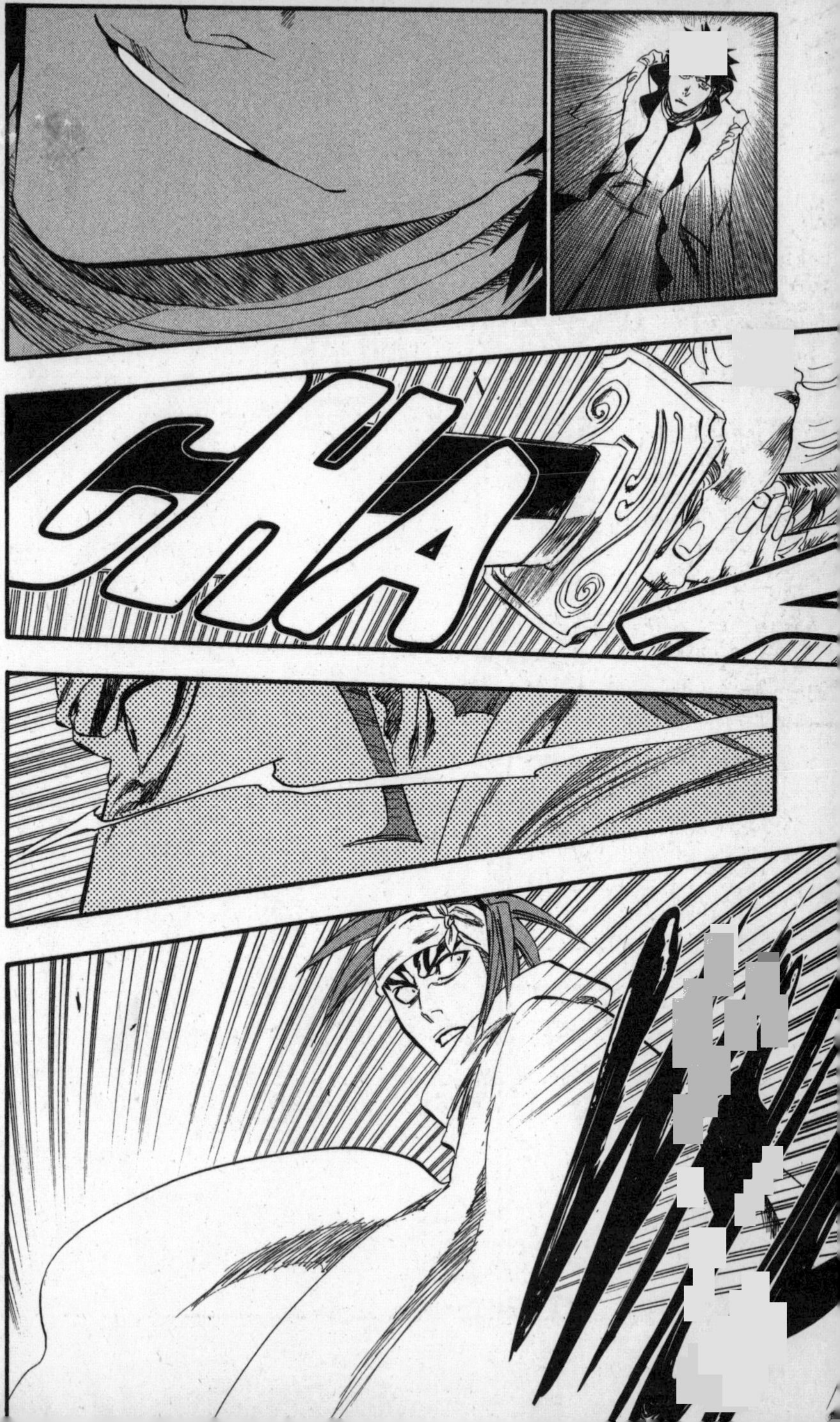
CHA

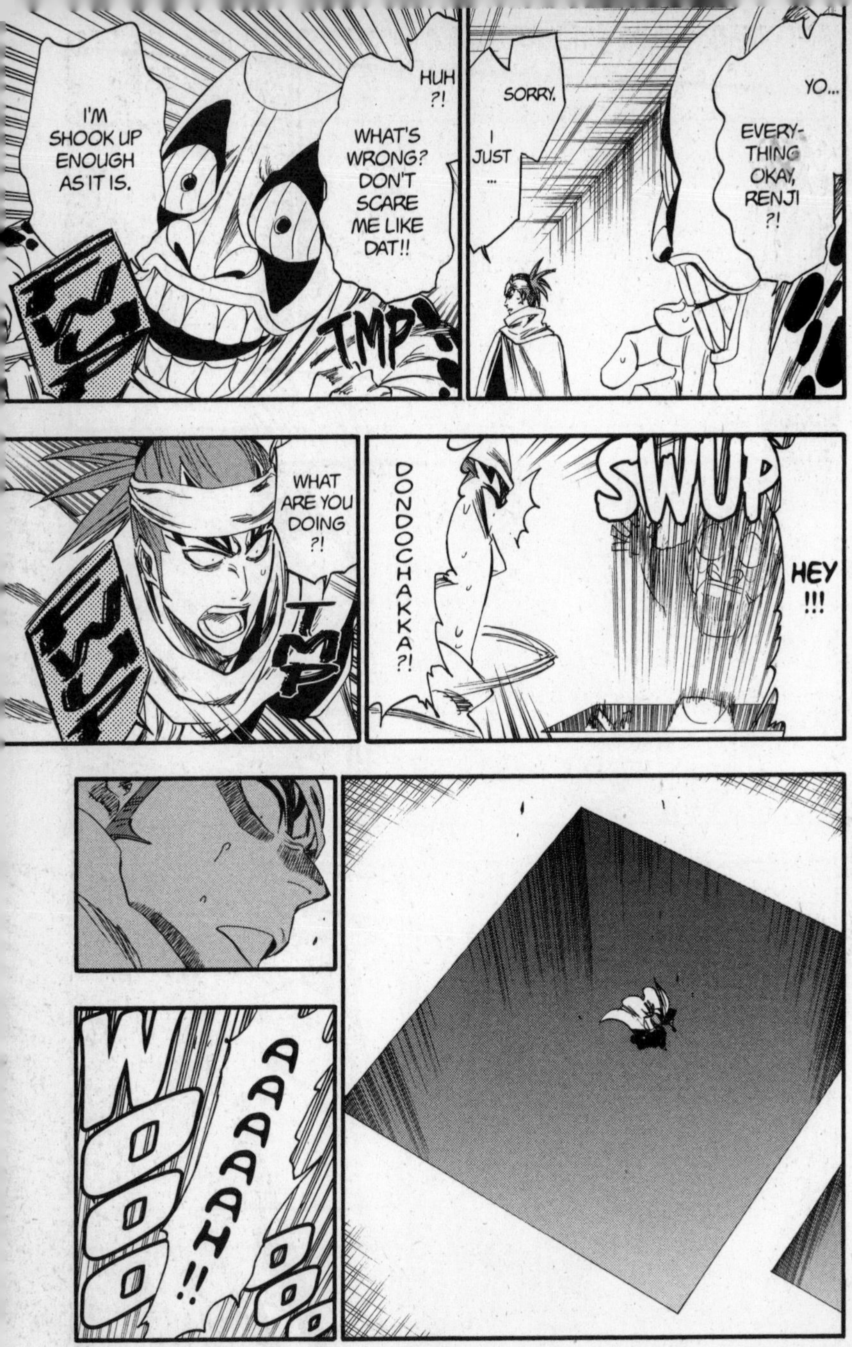
YO...
EVERYTHING OKAY, RENJI?!
SORRY.
I JUST ...
HUH?!
WHAT'S WRONG? DON'T SCARE ME LIKE DAT!!
TMP
I'M SHOOK UP ENOUGH AS IT IS.
SWUP
HEY!!!
DONDOCHAKKA?!
WHAT ARE YOU DOING?!
TMP
WOOOO
AAAAAAH!!
OOO

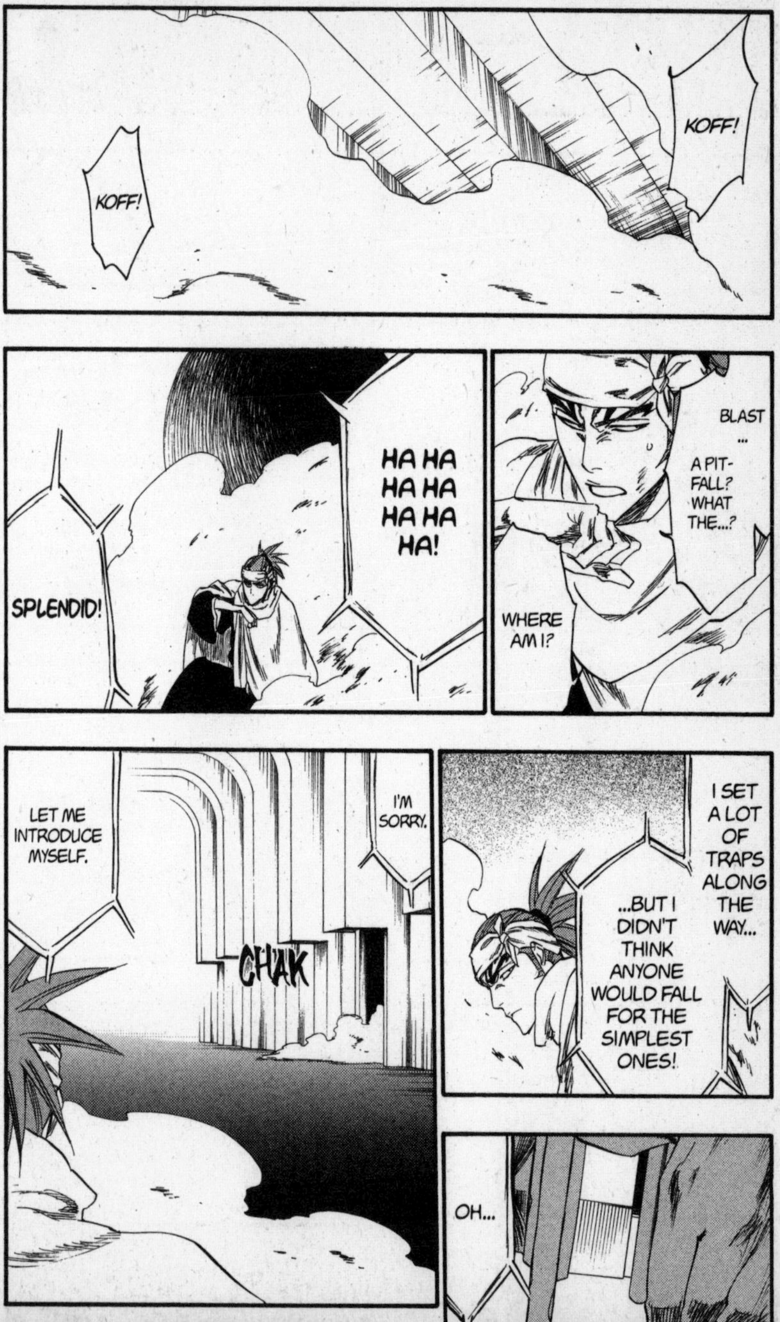
KOFF!
KOFF!
BLAST ... A PIT-FALL? WHAT THE...?
WHERE AM I?
HA HA HA HA HA HA HA!
SPLENDID!
I SET A LOT OF TRAPS ALONG THE WAY...
...BUT I DIDN'T THINK ANYONE WOULD FALL FOR THE SIMPLEST ONES!
OH...
I'M SORRY.
CHAK
LET ME INTRODUCE MYSELF.

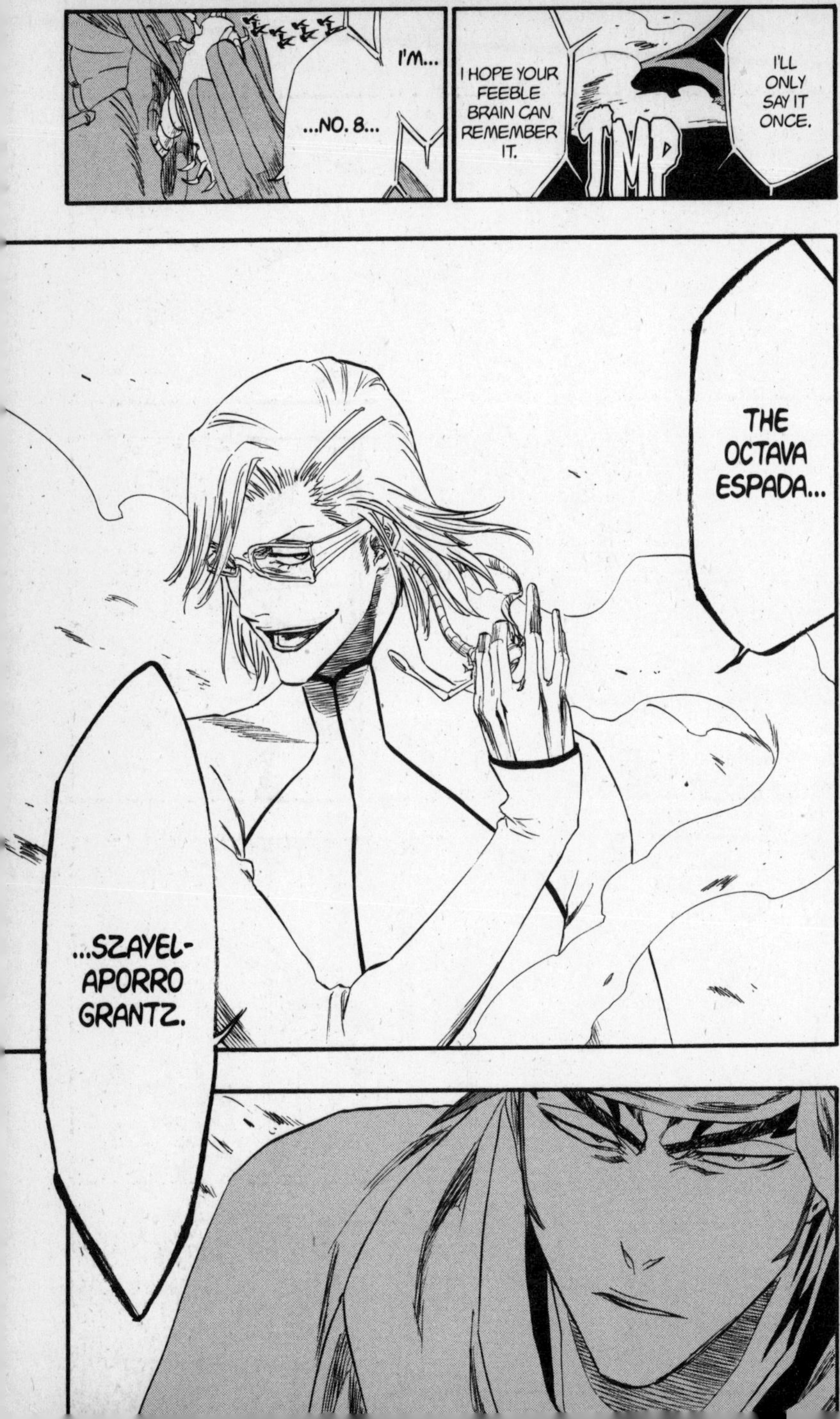
I'LL ONLY SAY IT ONCE.
I HOPE YOUR FEEBLE BRAIN CAN REMEMBER IT.
TMP
I'M...
...NO. 8...
THE OCTAVA ESPADA...
...SZAYEL-APORRO GRANTZ.

(EN)

don't say that name
anymore.

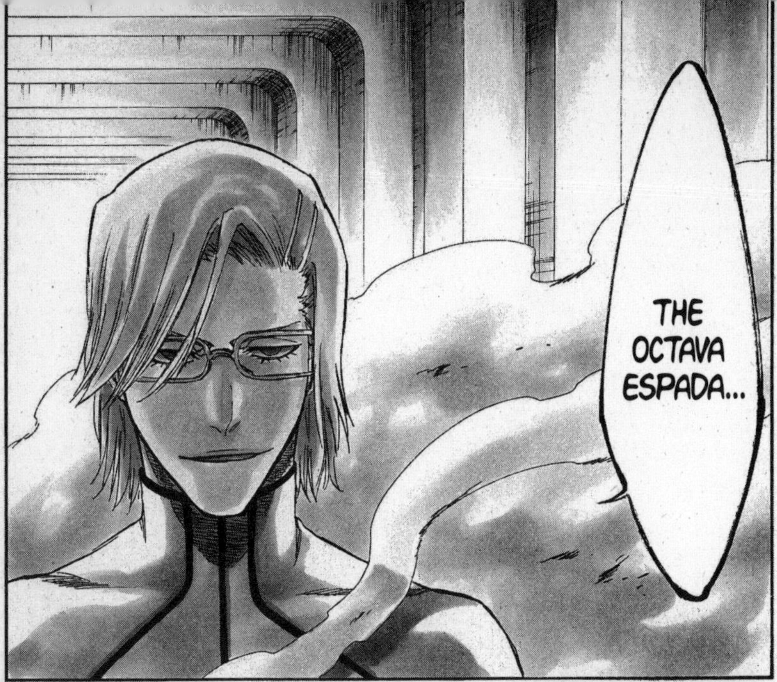
THE OCTAVA ESPADA...

265. Bang the Bore

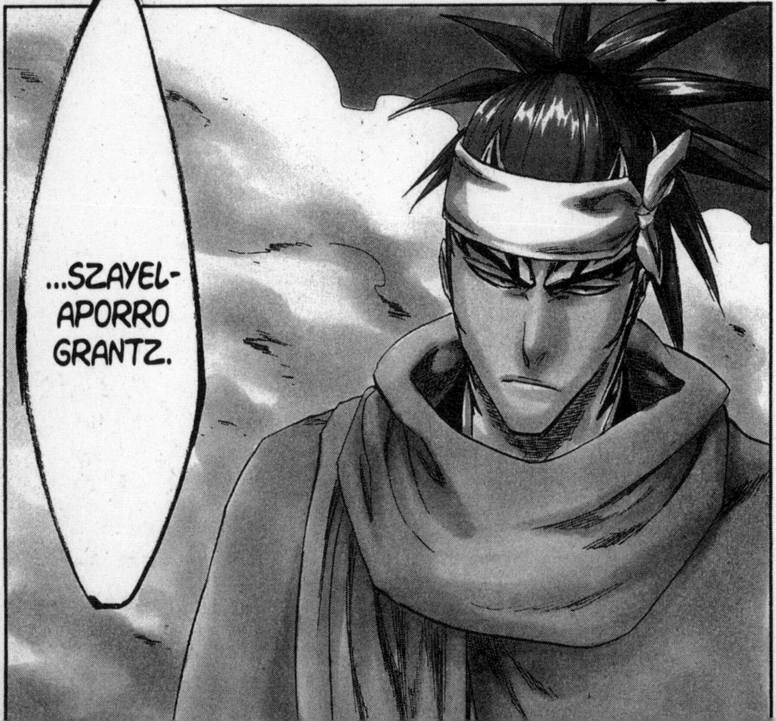
...SZAYEL-APORRO GRANTZ.

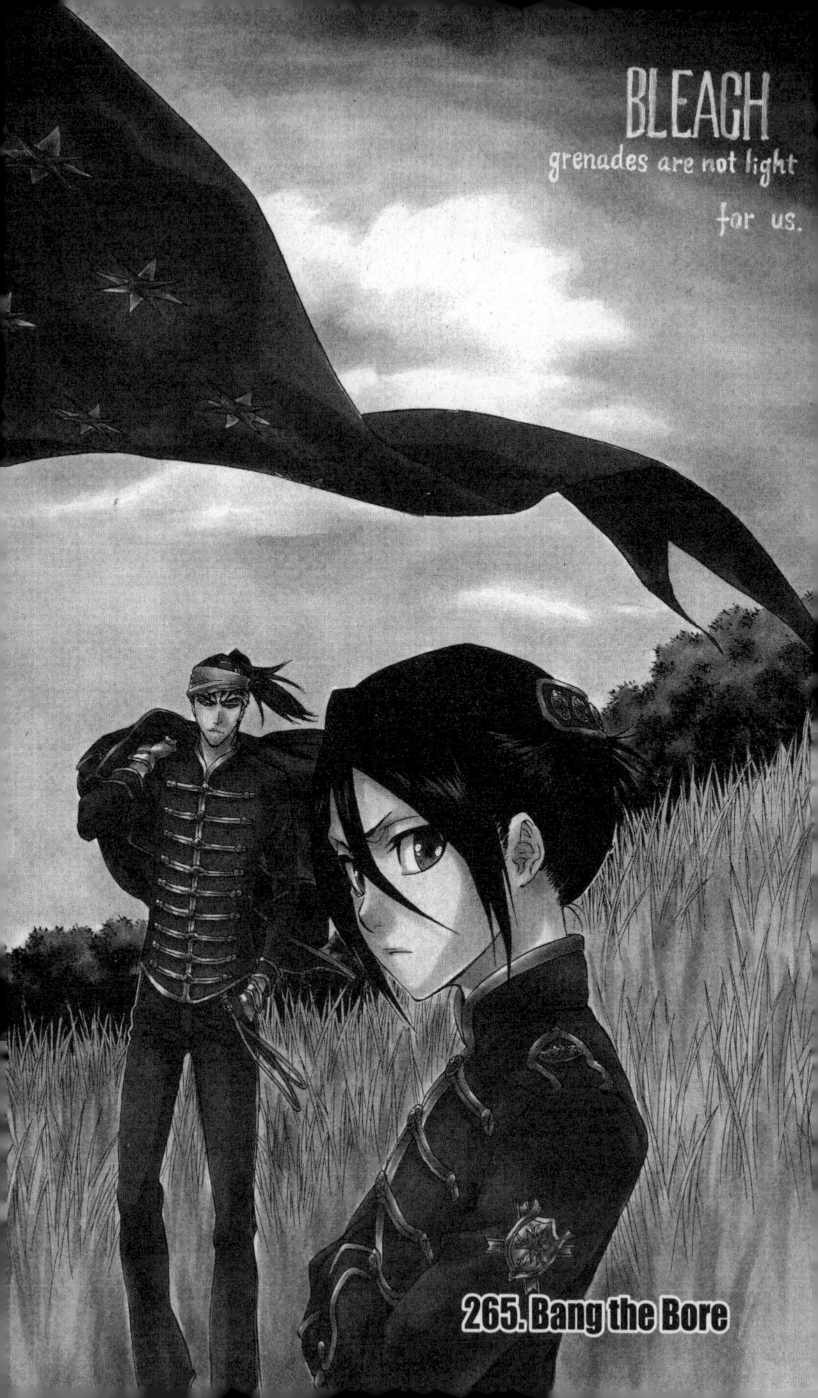

BLEACH
grenades are not light
for us.
265. Bang the Bore

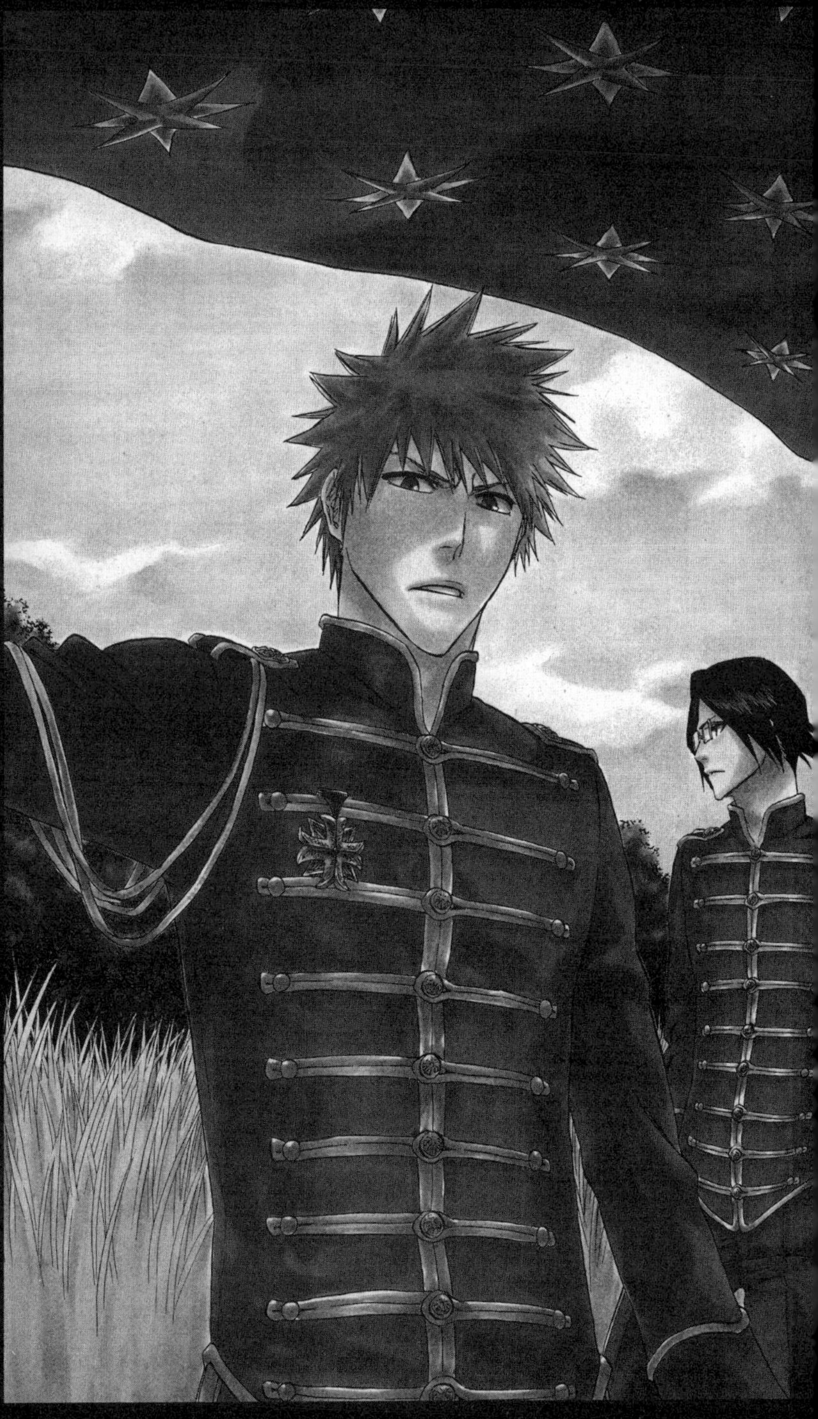

BLEACH
ブリーチ

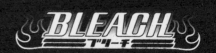

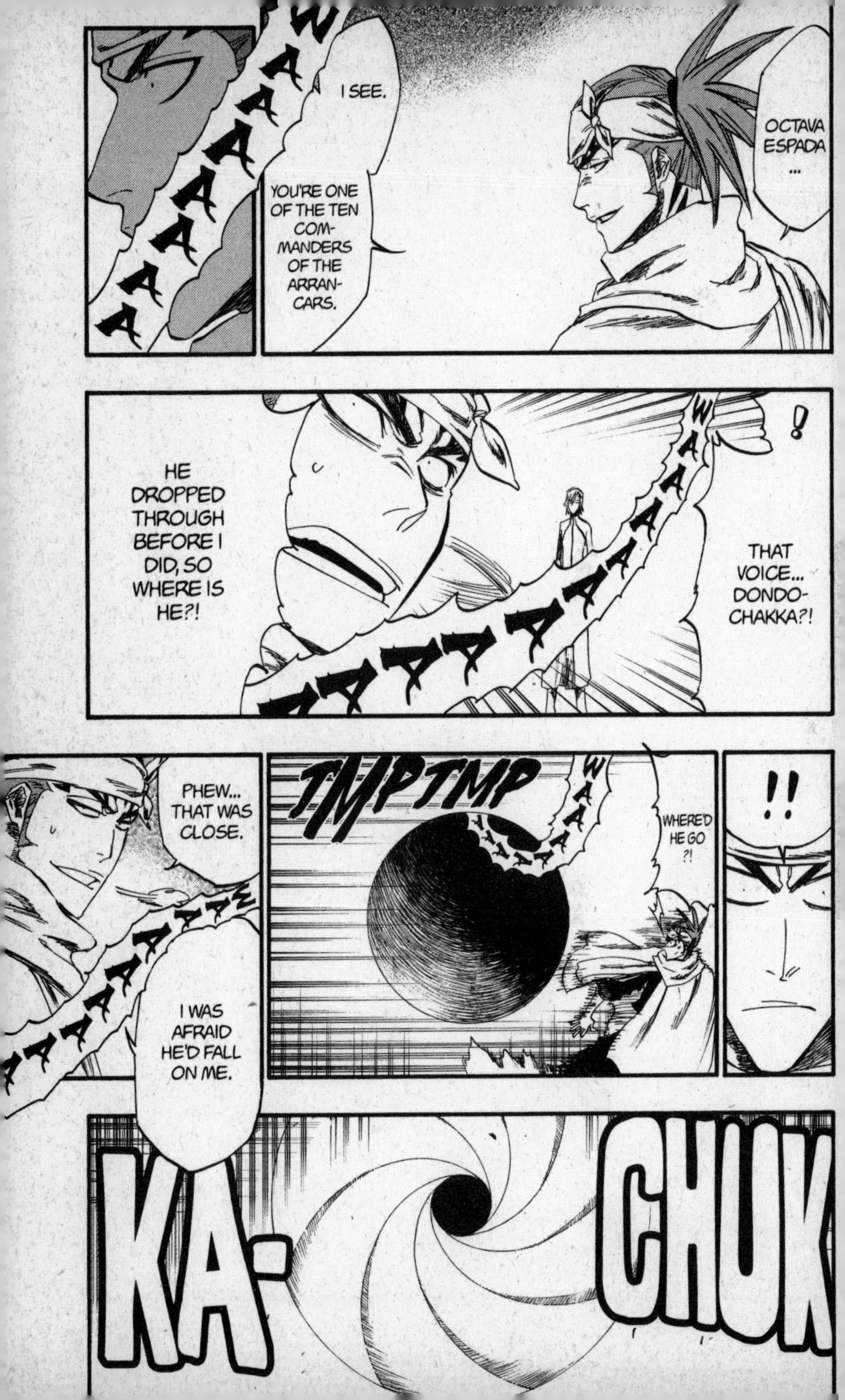

OCTAVA ESPADA ...
I SEE.
YOU'RE ONE OF THE TEN COM-MANDERS OF THE ARRAN-CARS.
WAAAAAAAA
!
THAT VOICE... DONDO-CHAKKA?!
WAAAAAAAAAA
HE DROPPED THROUGH BEFORE I DID, SO WHERE IS HE?!
!!
WHERE'D HE GO ?!
WAAAA
TMPTMP
PHEW... THAT WAS CLOSE.
I WAS AFRAID HE'D FALL ON ME.
WAAAAAAAA
KA-CHUK

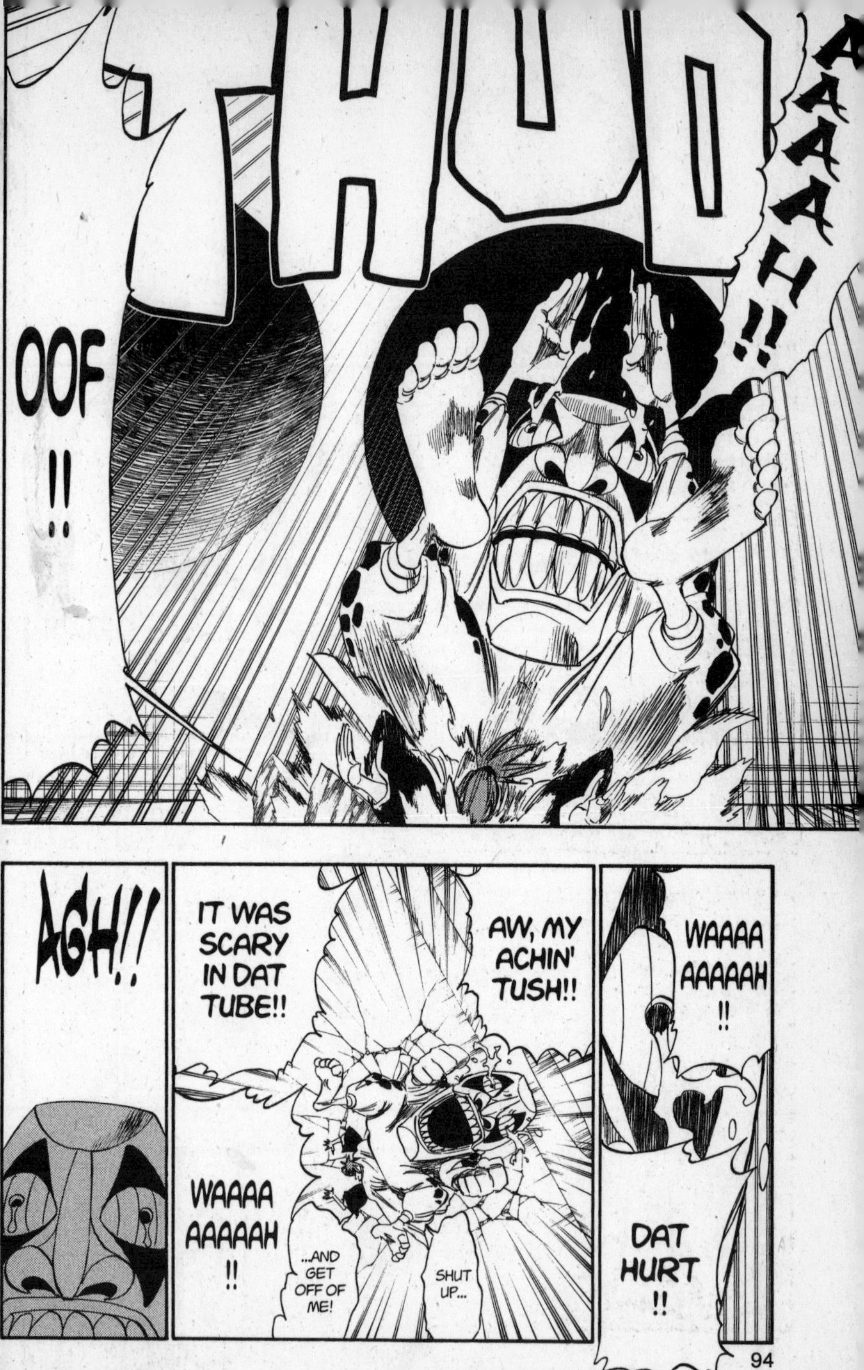
AAAAH!!
THUD
OOF!!
WAAAAAAAAAH!!
DAT HURT!!
AW, MY ACHIN' TUSH!!
IT WAS SCARY IN DAT TUBE!!
SHUT UP...
...AND GET OFF OF ME!
WAAAAAAAAAH!!
AGH!!

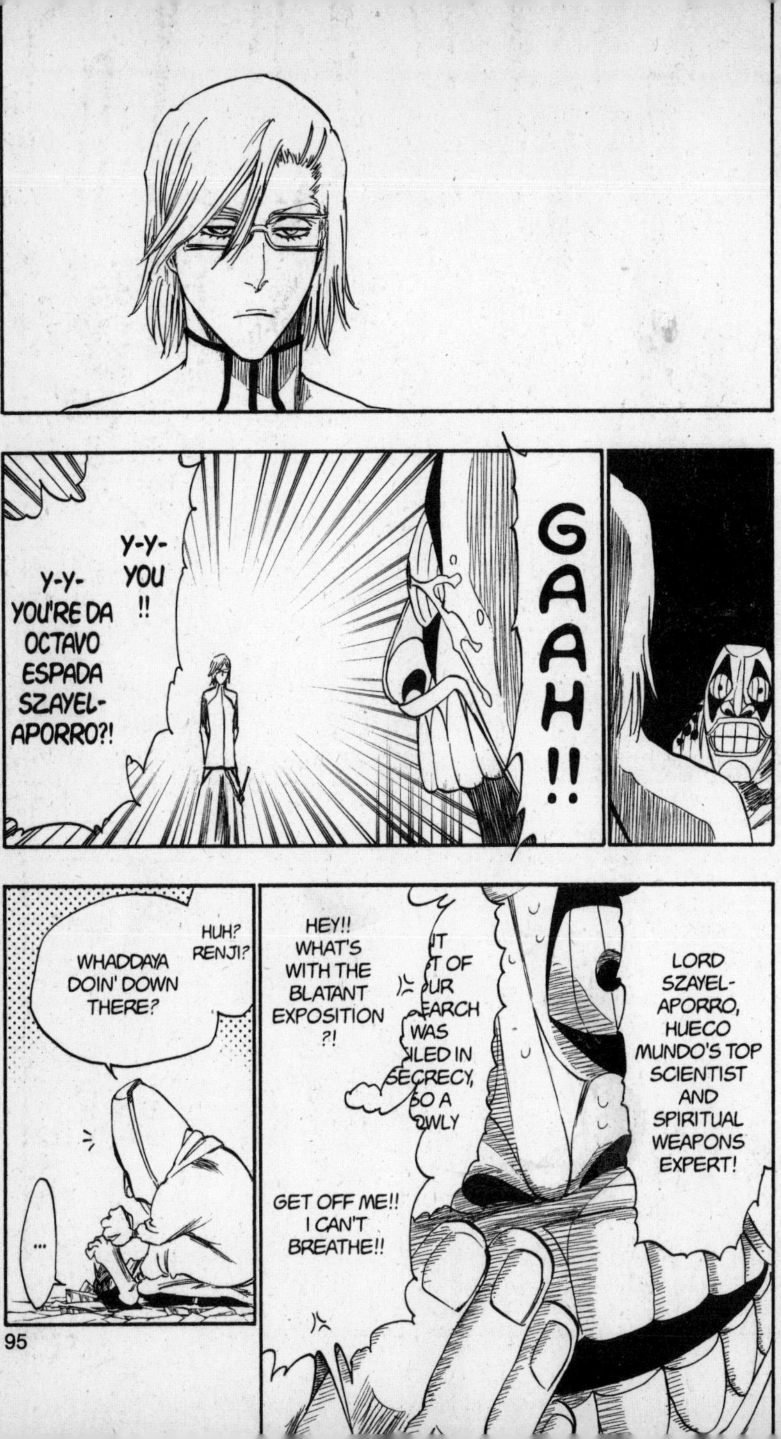
GAAH!!
Y-Y-YOU!!
Y-Y-YOU'RE DA OCTAVO ESPADA SZAYEL-APORRO?!
LORD SZAYEL-APORRO, HUECO MUNDO'S TOP SCIENTIST AND SPIRITUAL WEAPONS EXPERT!
HEY!! WHAT'S WITH THE BLATANT EXPOSITION?!
GET OFF ME!! I CAN'T BREATHE!!
HUH? RENJI?
WHADDAYA DOIN' DOWN THERE?
...

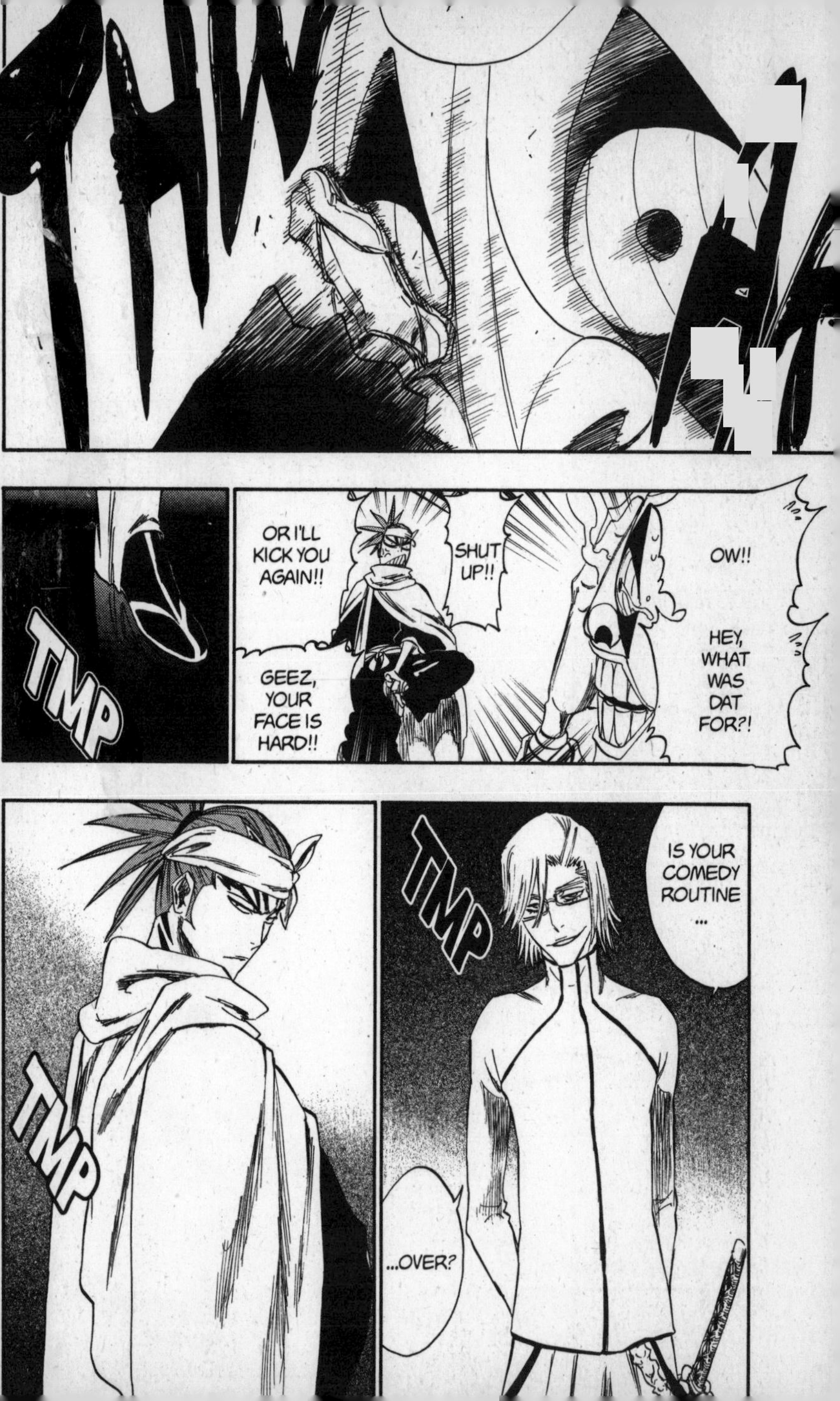
THW
OW!!
HEY, WHAT WAS DAT FOR?!
SHUT UP!!
OR I'LL KICK YOU AGAIN!!
GEEZ, YOUR FACE IS HARD!!
TMP
TMP
IS YOUR COMEDY ROUTINE ...
...OVER?
TMP

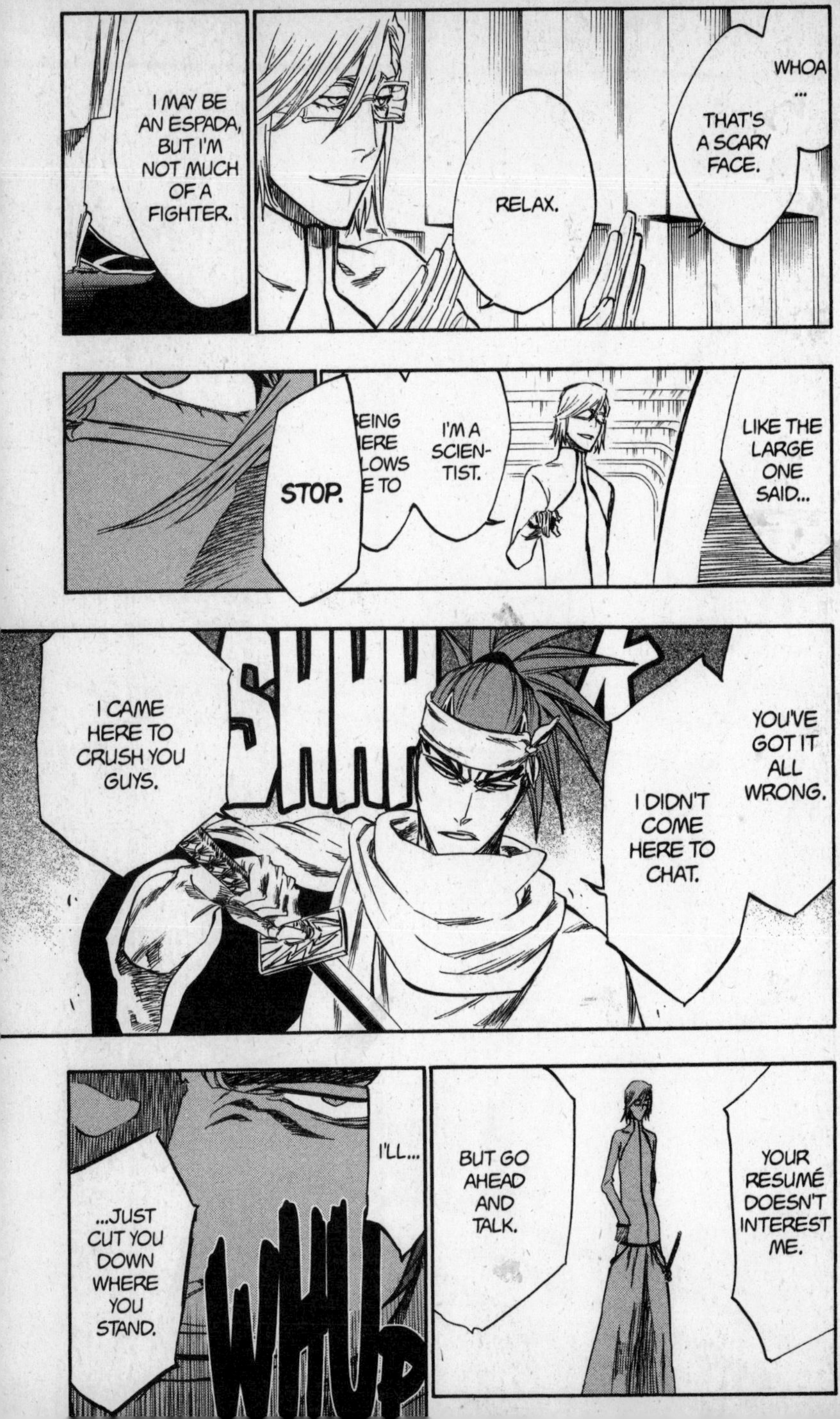
WHOA ... THAT'S A SCARY FACE.
RELAX.
I MAY BE AN ESPADA, BUT I'M NOT MUCH OF A FIGHTER.
LIKE THE LARGE ONE SAID...
I'M A SCIEN- TIST.
EING ERE LOWS E TO
STOP.
YOU'VE GOT IT ALL WRONG.
I DIDN'T COME HERE TO CHAT.
I CAME HERE TO CRUSH YOU GUYS.
YOUR RESUMÉ DOESN'T INTEREST ME.
BUT GO AHEAD AND TALK.
I'LL...
...JUST CUT YOU DOWN WHERE YOU STAND.
WHUP

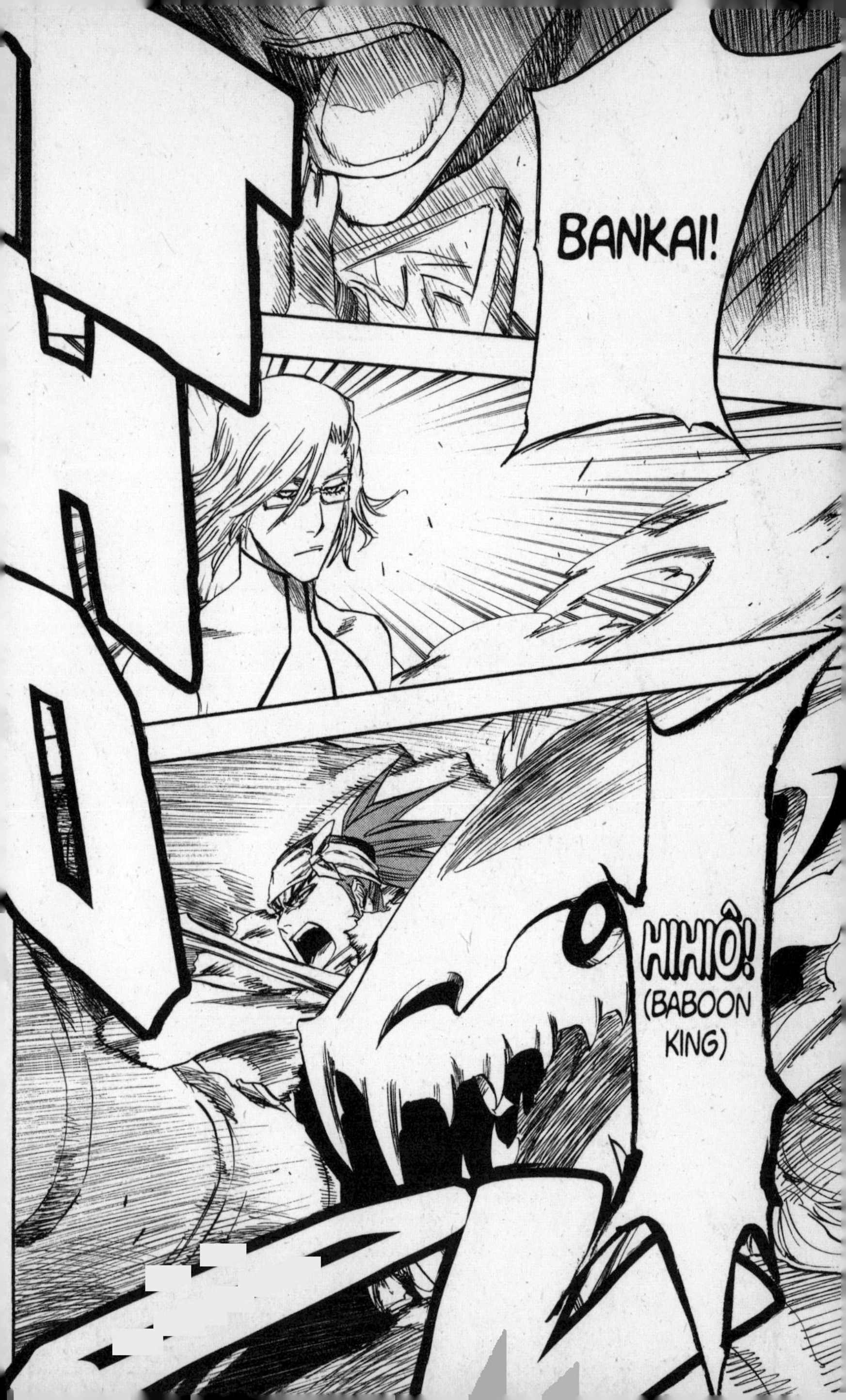
BANKAI!
HIHIÔ!
(BABOON KING)

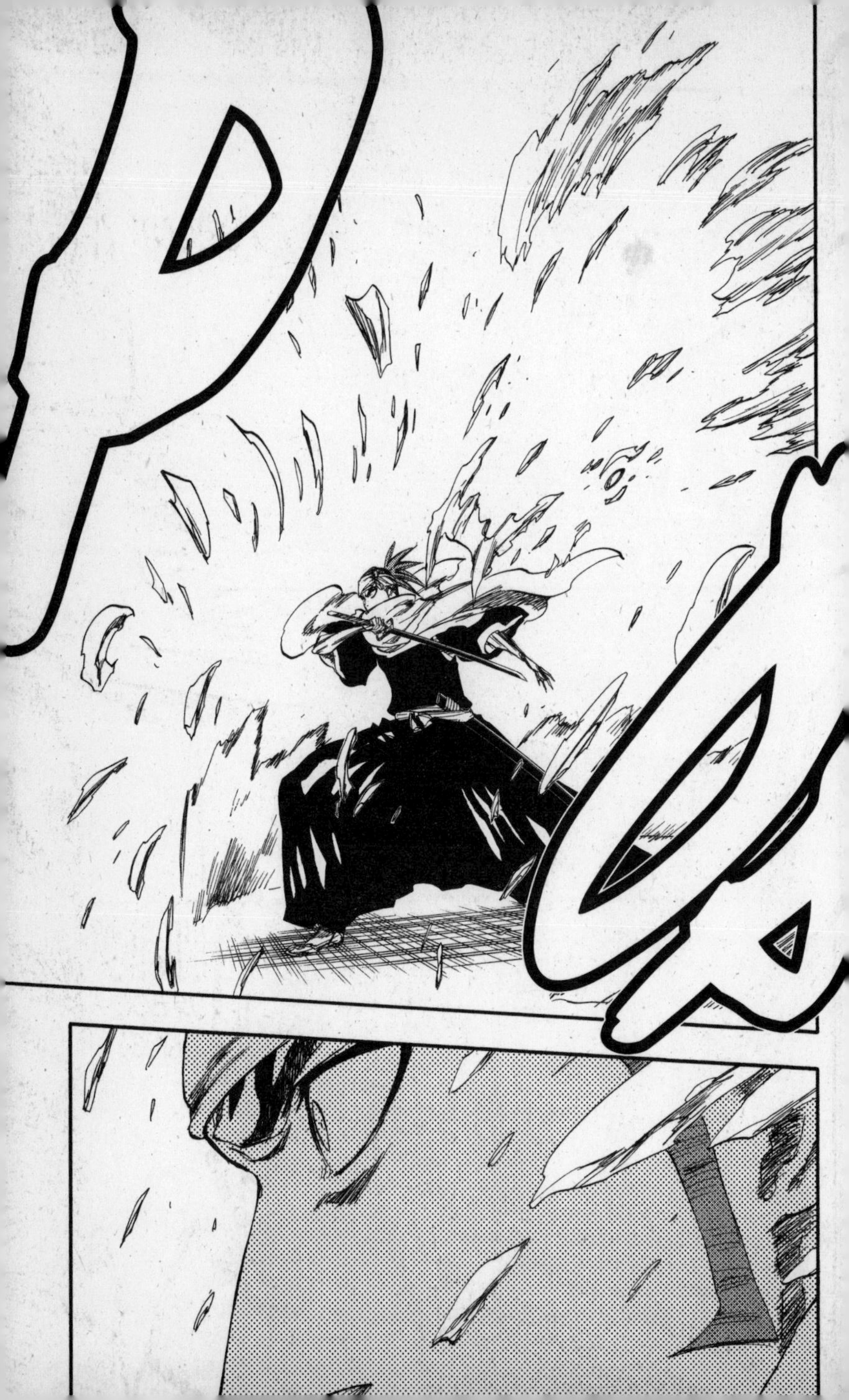

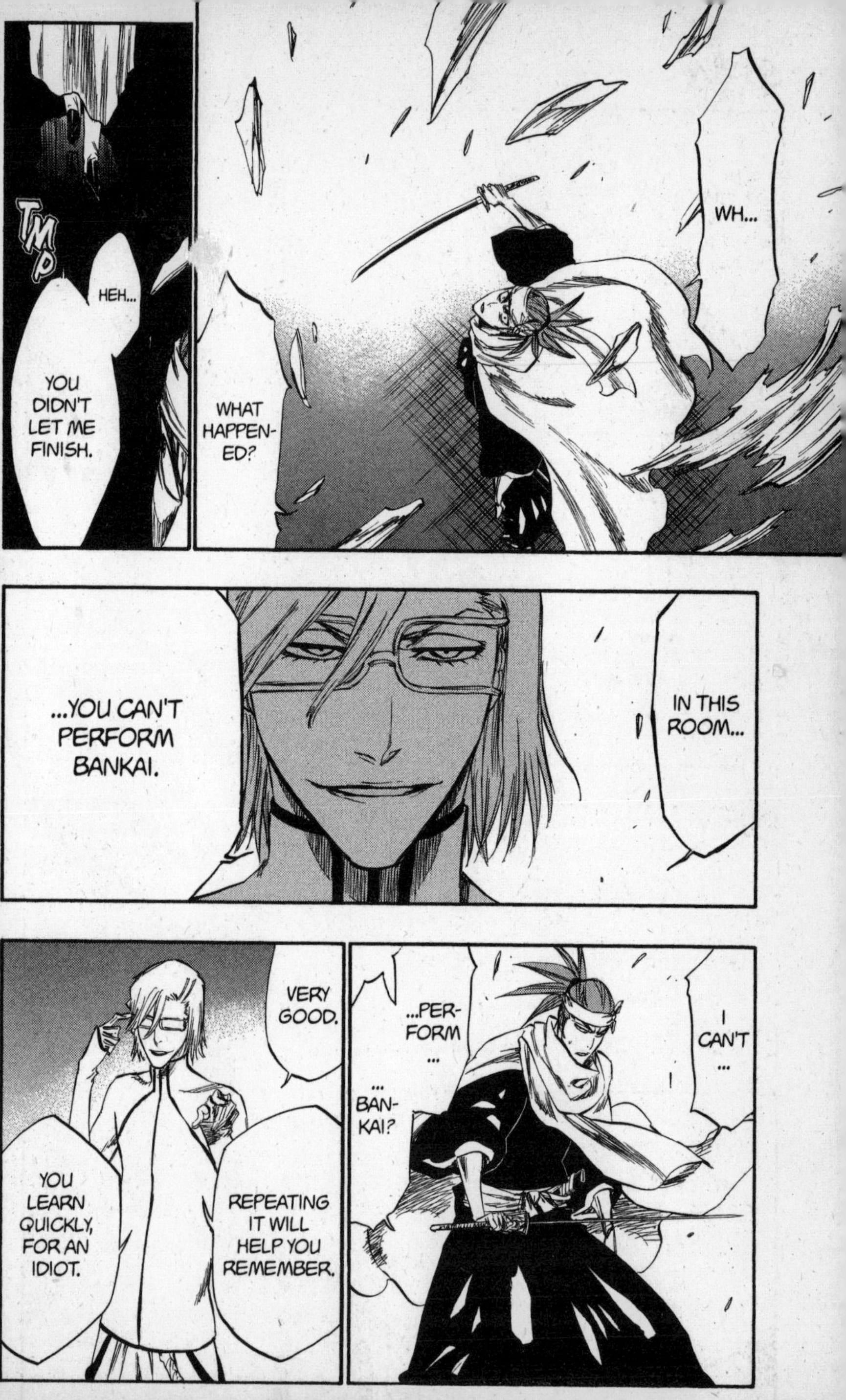
WH...
WHAT HAPPENED?
TMP
HEH...
YOU DIDN'T LET ME FINISH.
IN THIS ROOM...
...YOU CAN'T PERFORM BANKAI.
I CAN'T ...
...PERFORM ...
... BANKAI?
VERY GOOD.
REPEATING IT WILL HELP YOU REMEMBER.
YOU LEARN QUICKLY, FOR AN IDIOT.

READ THIS WAY

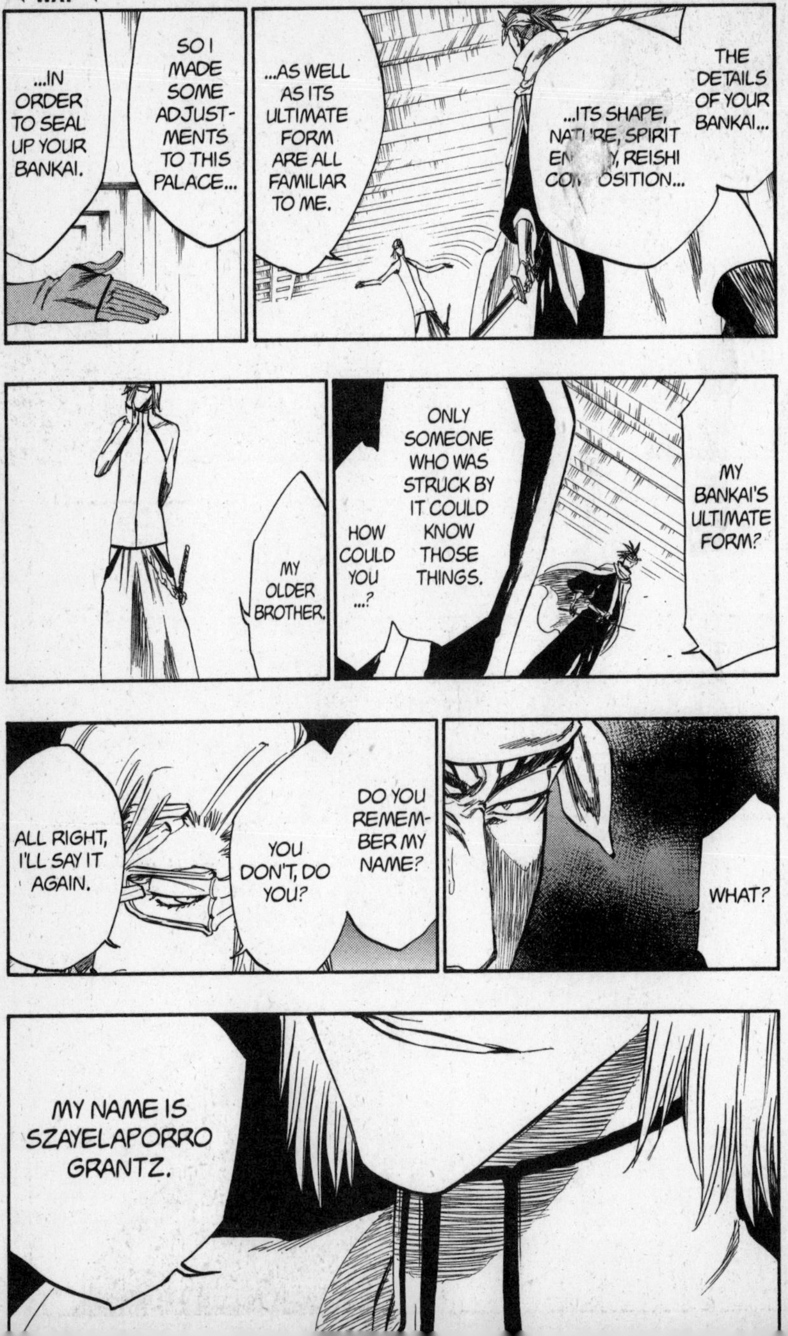

THE DETAILS OF YOUR BANKAI...
...ITS SHAPE, NATURE, SPIRIT ENERGY, REISHI COMPOSITION...
...AS WELL AS ITS ULTIMATE FORM ARE ALL FAMILIAR TO ME.
SO I MADE SOME ADJUSTMENTS TO THIS PALACE...
...IN ORDER TO SEAL UP YOUR BANKAI.
MY BANKAI'S ULTIMATE FORM?
ONLY SOMEONE WHO WAS STRUCK BY IT COULD KNOW THOSE THINGS.
HOW COULD YOU ...?
MY OLDER BROTHER.
WHAT?
DO YOU REMEMBER MY NAME?
YOU DON'T, DO YOU?
ALL RIGHT, I'LL SAY IT AGAIN.
MY NAME IS SZAYELAPORRO GRANTZ.

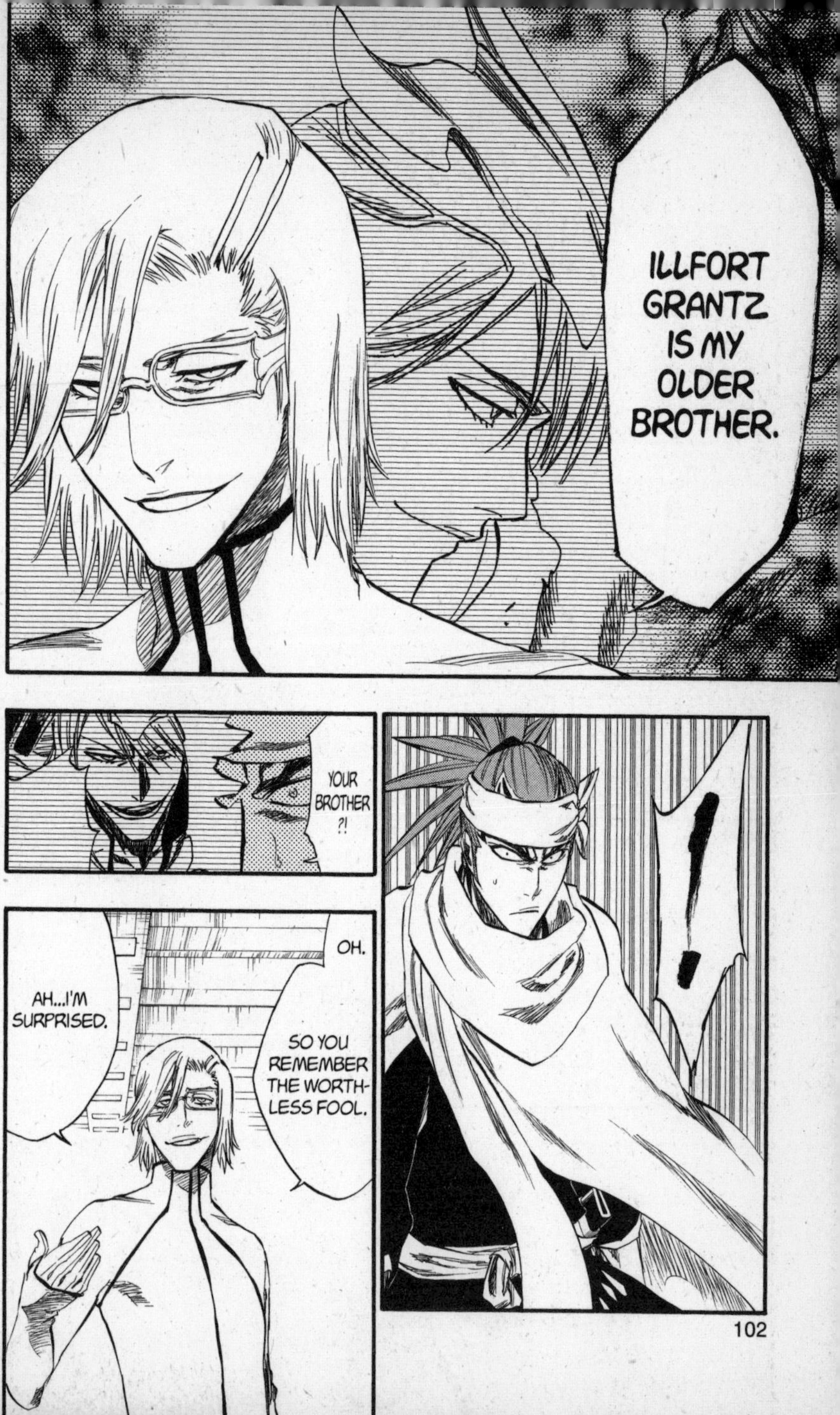
ILLFORT GRANTZ IS MY OLDER BROTHER.
!
YOUR BROTHER ?!
OH.
SO YOU REMEMBER THE WORTH-LESS FOOL.
AH...I'M SURPRISED.

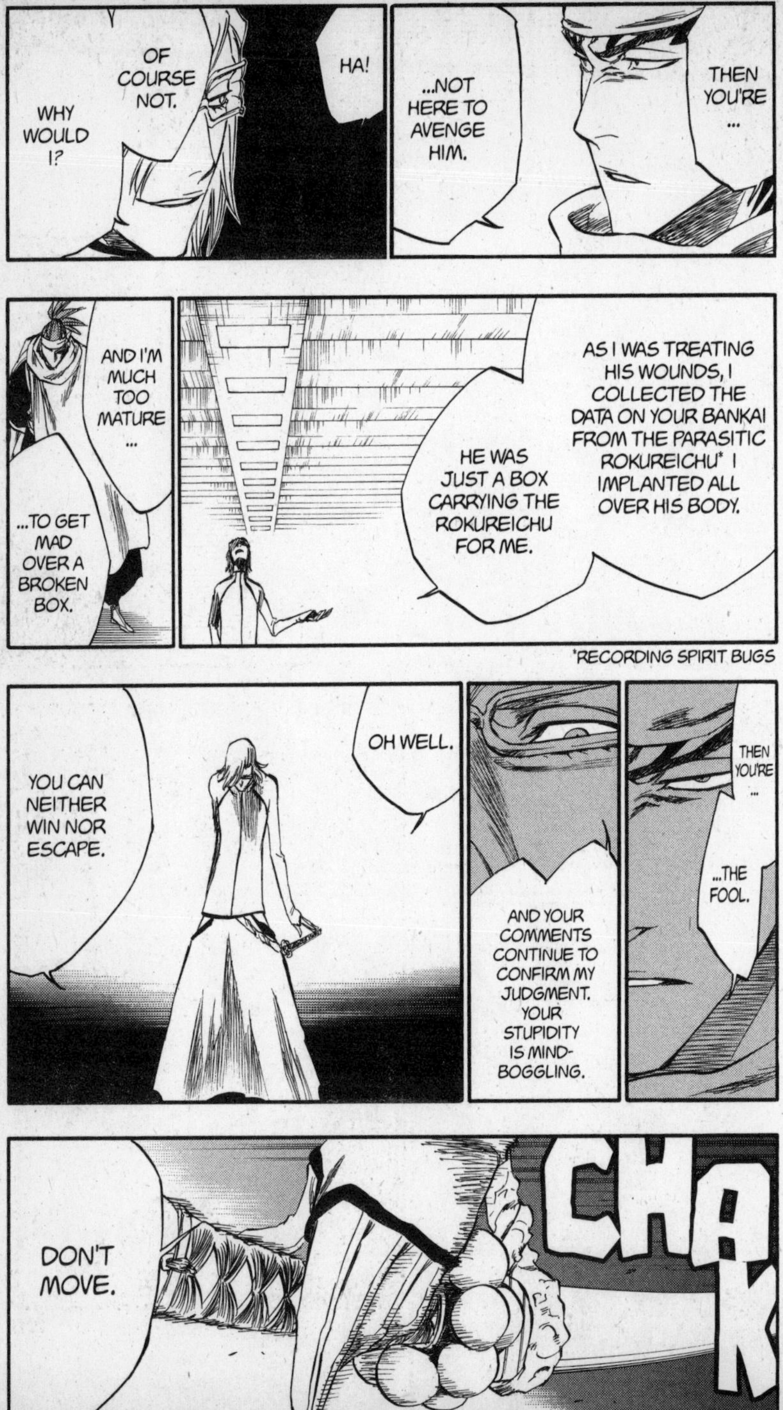
THEN YOU'RE ...
...NOT HERE TO AVENGE HIM.
HA!
OF COURSE NOT.
WHY WOULD I?
AS I WAS TREATING HIS WOUNDS, I COLLECTED THE DATA ON YOUR BANKAI FROM THE PARASITIC ROKUREICHU* I IMPLANTED ALL OVER HIS BODY.
HE WAS JUST A BOX CARRYING THE ROKUREICHU FOR ME.
AND I'M MUCH TOO MATURE ...
...TO GET MAD OVER A BROKEN BOX.
*RECORDING SPIRIT BUGS
THEN YOU'RE ...
...THE FOOL.
AND YOUR COMMENTS CONTINUE TO CONFIRM MY JUDGMENT. YOUR STUPIDITY IS MIND-BOGGLING.
OH WELL.
YOU CAN NEITHER WIN NOR ESCAPE.
CHAK
DON'T MOVE.

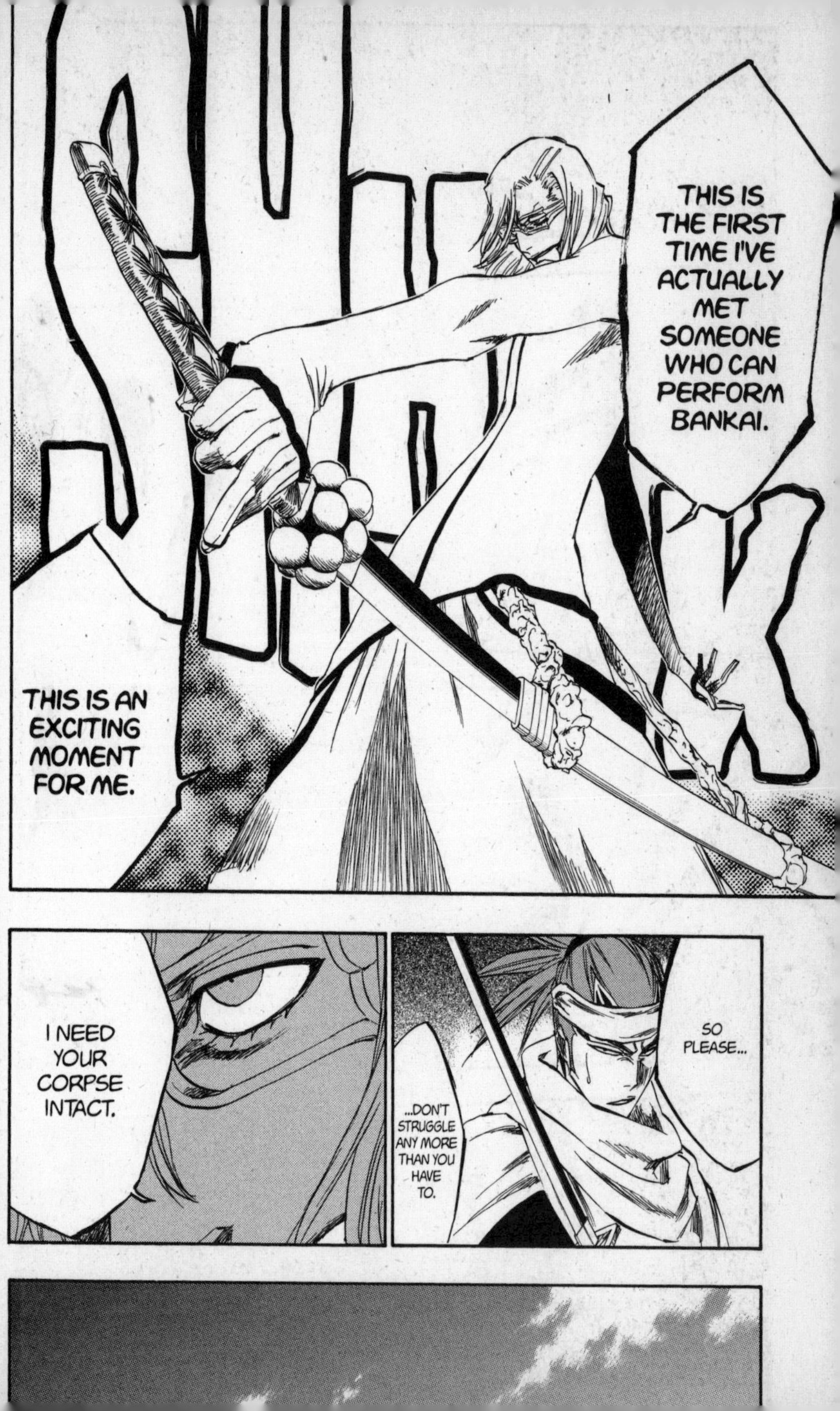
THIS IS THE FIRST TIME I'VE ACTUALLY MET SOMEONE WHO CAN PERFORM BANKAI.
THIS IS AN EXCITING MOMENT FOR ME.
SO PLEASE...
...DON'T STRUGGLE ANY MORE THAN YOU HAVE TO.
I NEED YOUR CORPSE INTACT.

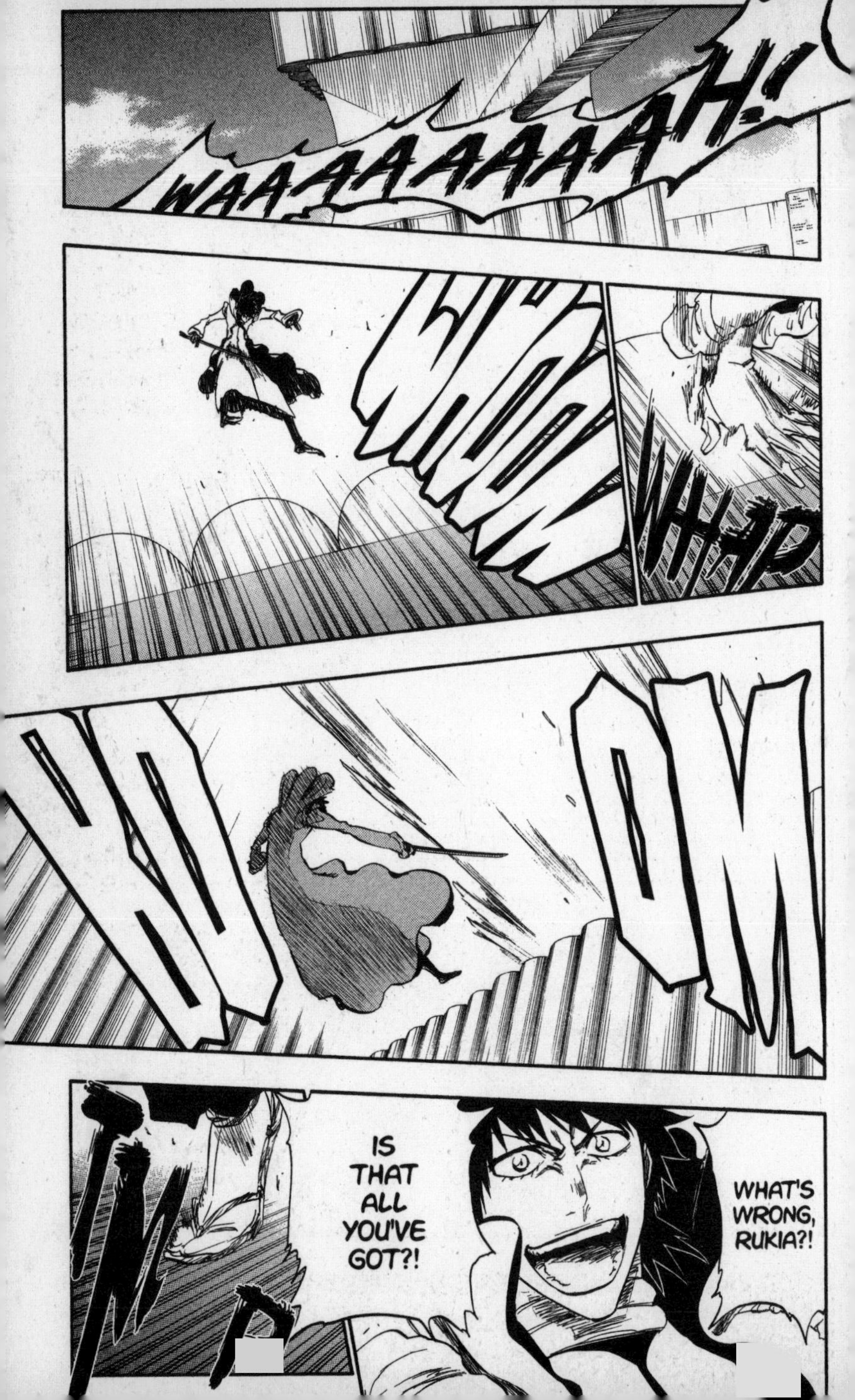
WAAAAAAAAH!
WHAP
WHAT'S WRONG, RUKIA?!
IS THAT ALL YOU'VE GOT?!

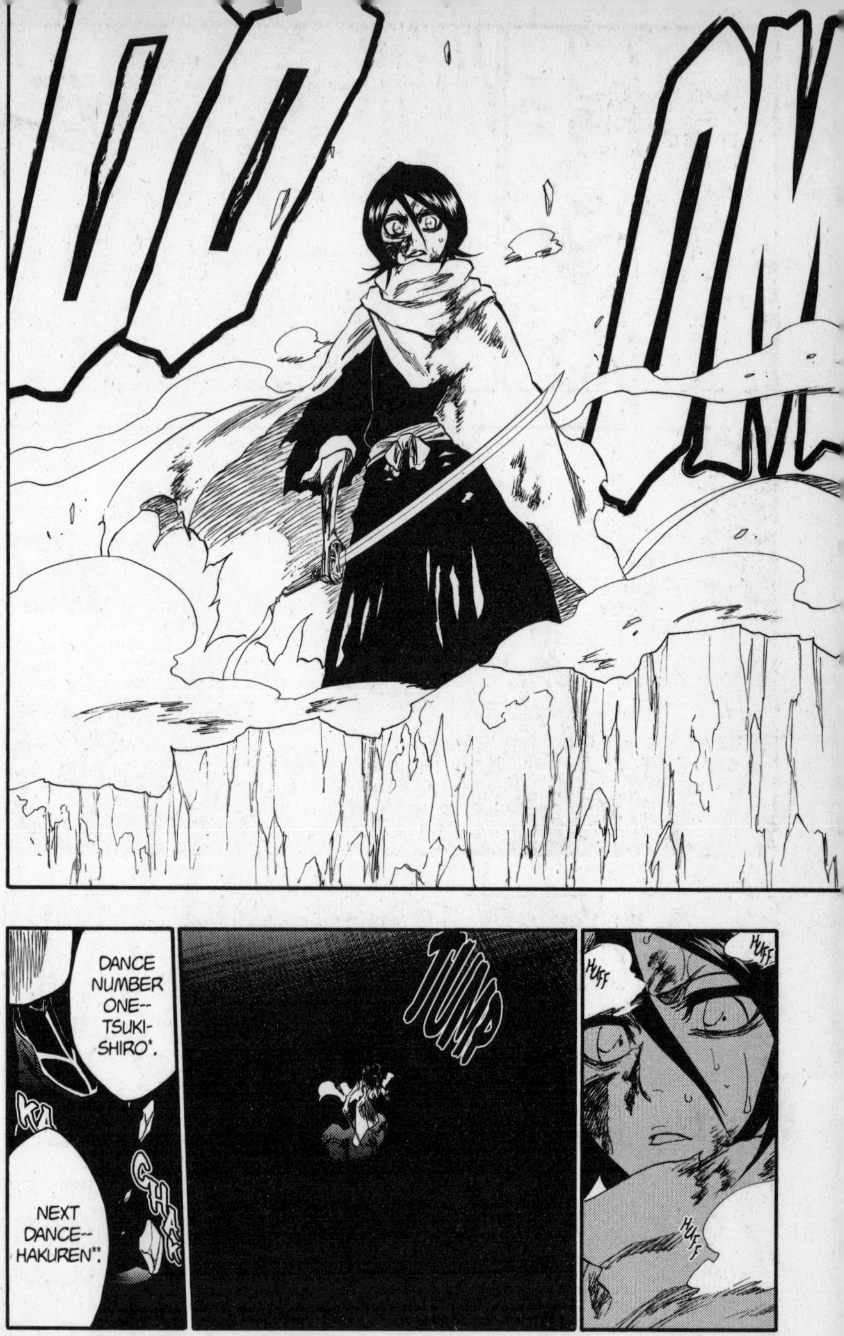
HUFF
HUFF
HUFF
TUMP
DANCE NUMBER ONE-- TSUKI-SHIRO*.
KA
CHAK
NEXT DANCE-- HAKUREN**.

*WHITE MOON
**WHITE WAVE

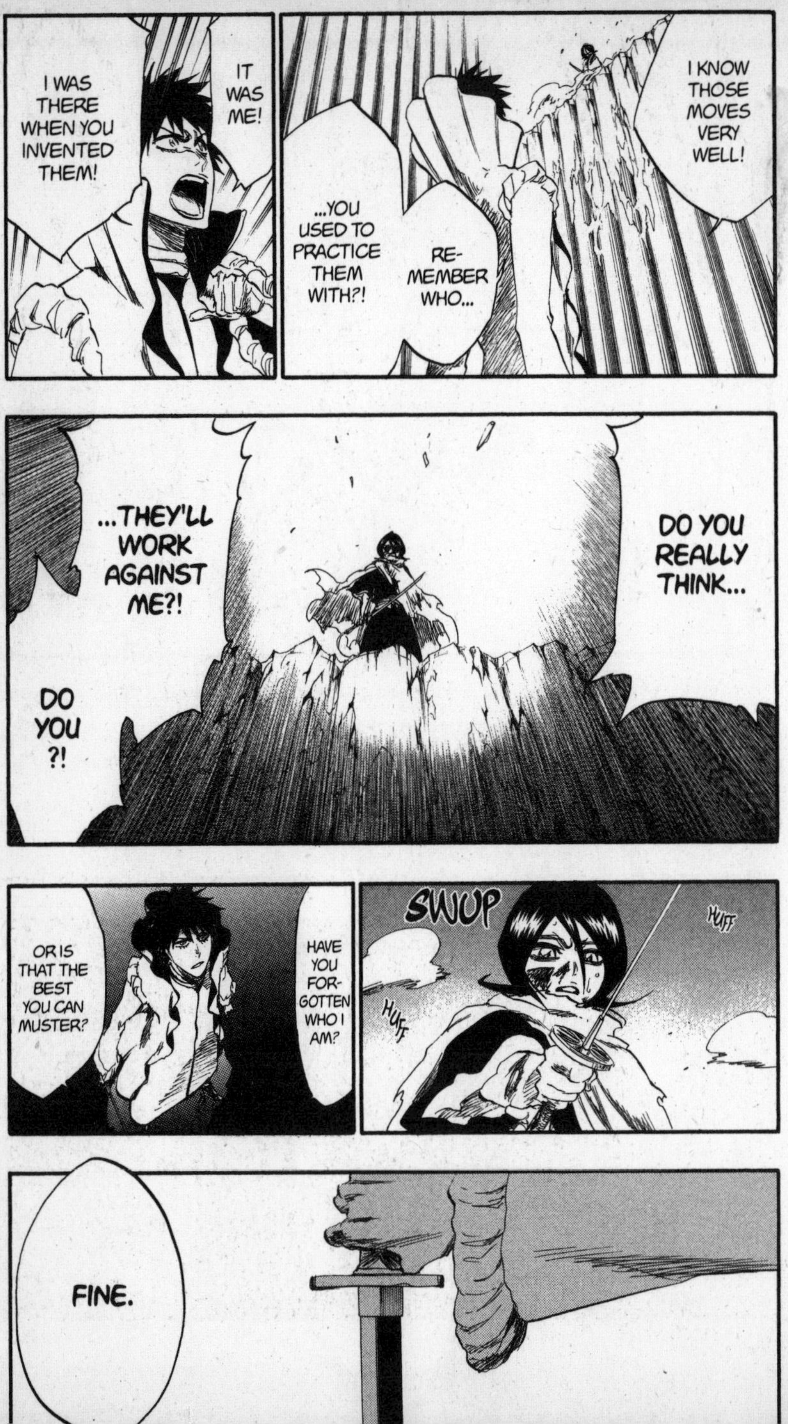
I KNOW THOSE MOVES VERY WELL!
RE-MEMBER WHO...
...YOU USED TO PRACTICE THEM WITH?!
IT WAS ME!
I WAS THERE WHEN YOU INVENTED THEM!
DO YOU REALLY THINK...
...THEY'LL WORK AGAINST ME?!
DO YOU ?!
SWUP
HUFF
HUFF
HAVE YOU FOR-GOTTEN WHO I AM?
OR IS THAT THE BEST YOU CAN MUSTER?
FINE.

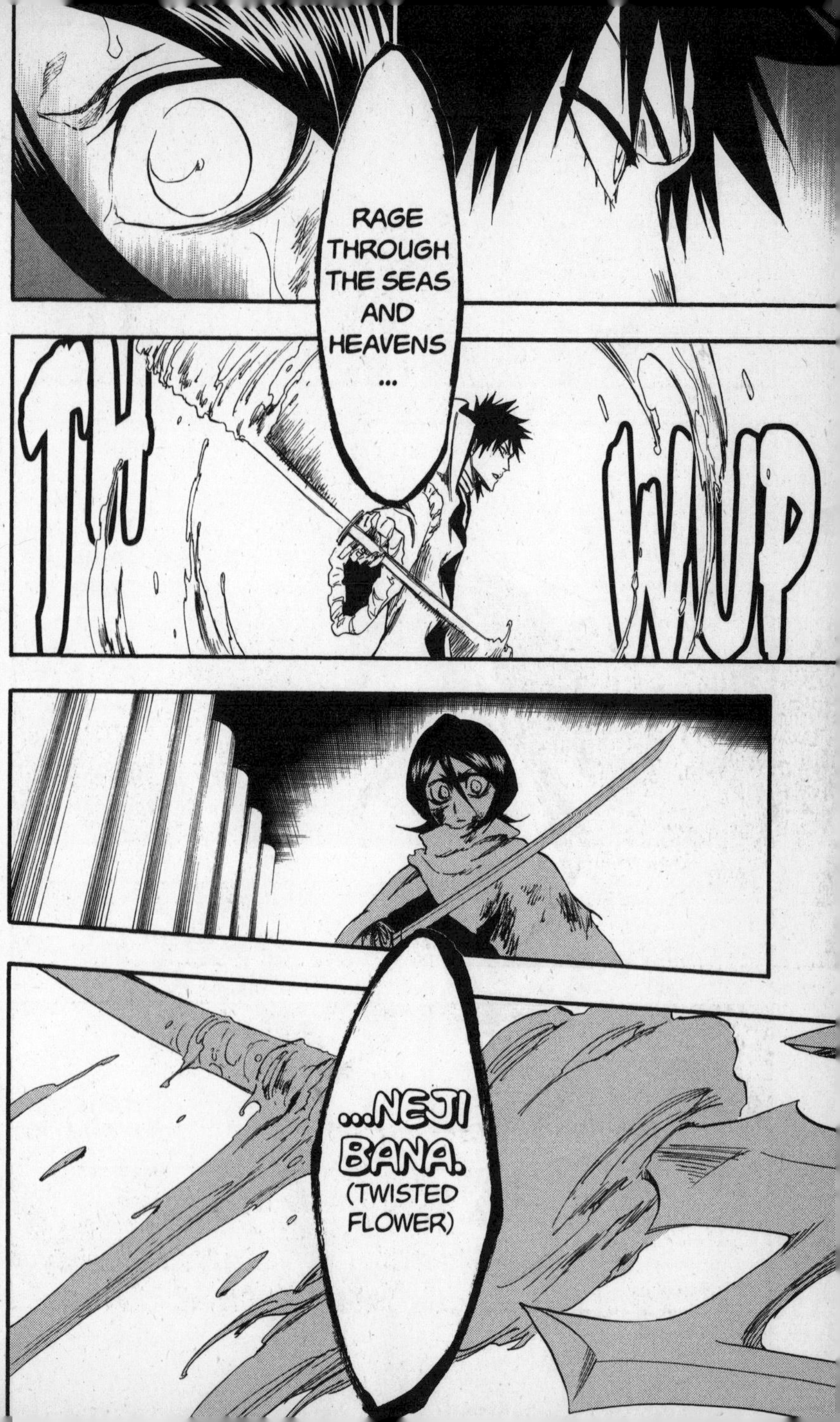
RAGE THROUGH THE SEAS AND HEAVENS ...
TH
WUP
...NEJI BANA. (TWISTED FLOWER)

The Bore kills The Boreas.

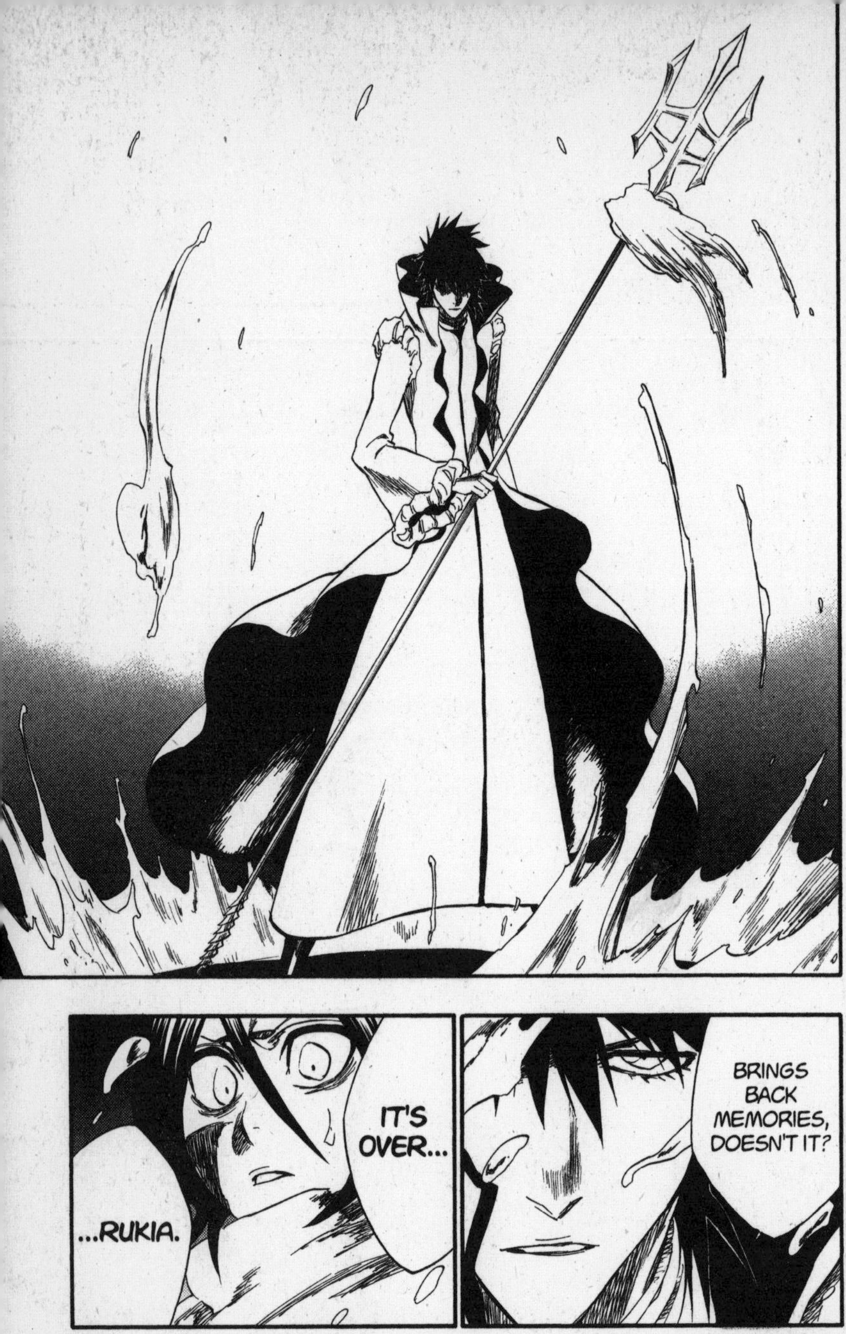
BRINGS BACK MEMORIES, DOESN'T IT?
IT'S OVER...
...RUKIA.

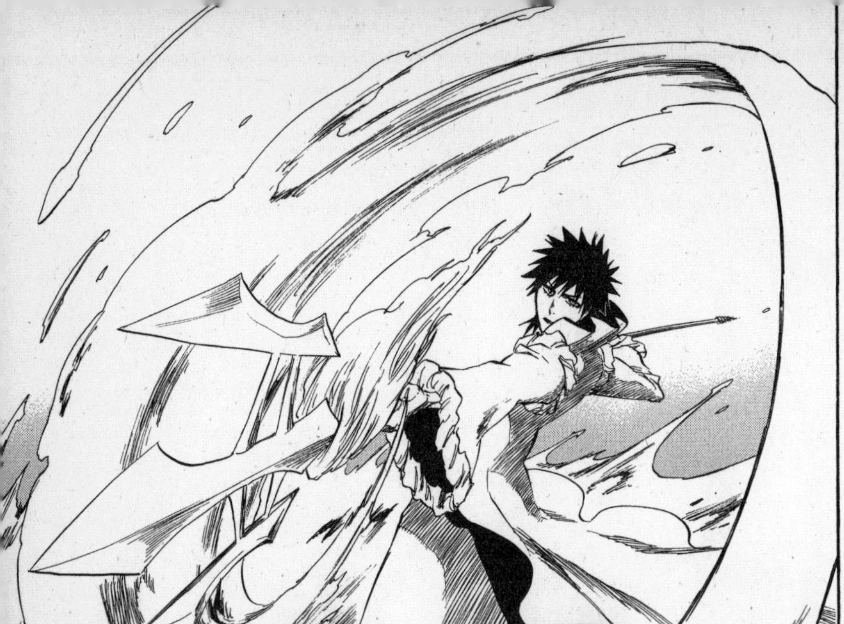
READY?

266. Hide Away From the Sun

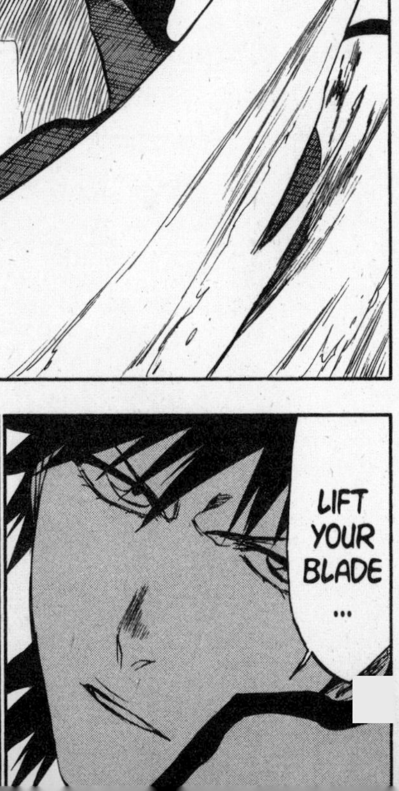
LIFT YOUR BLADE ...

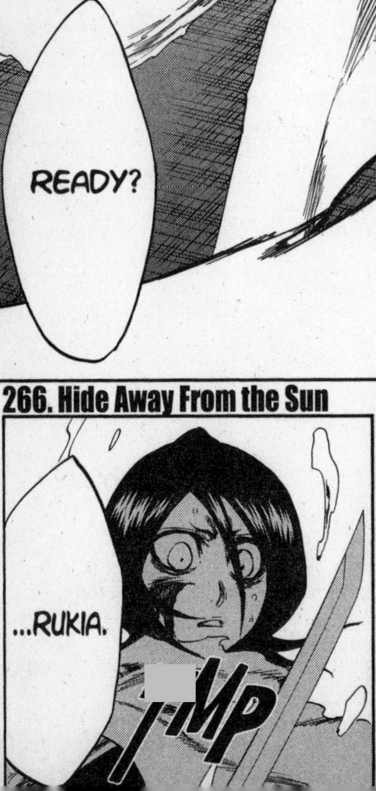
...RUKIA.

Bleach 266. Hide Away From the Sun

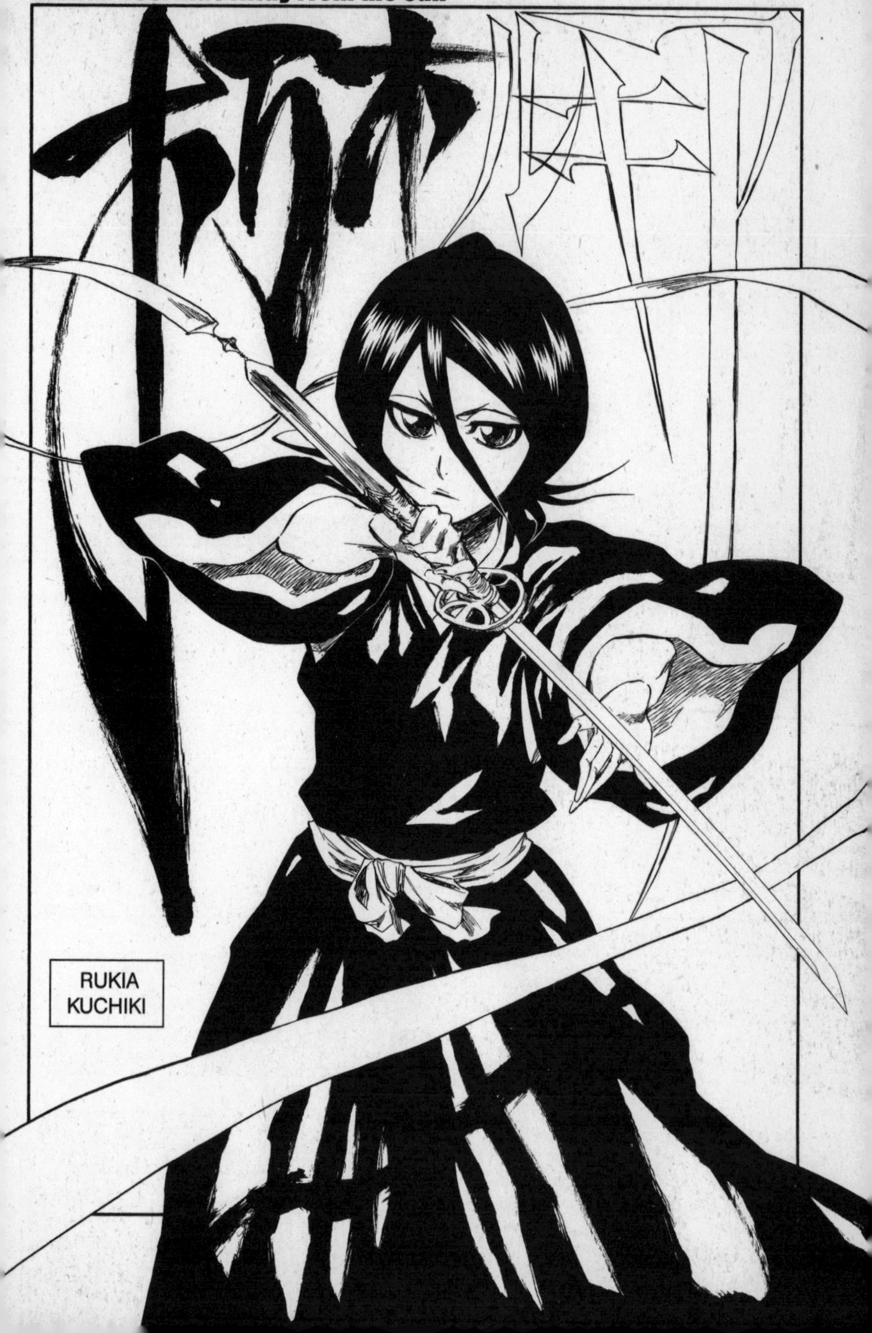
RUKIA
KUCHIKI

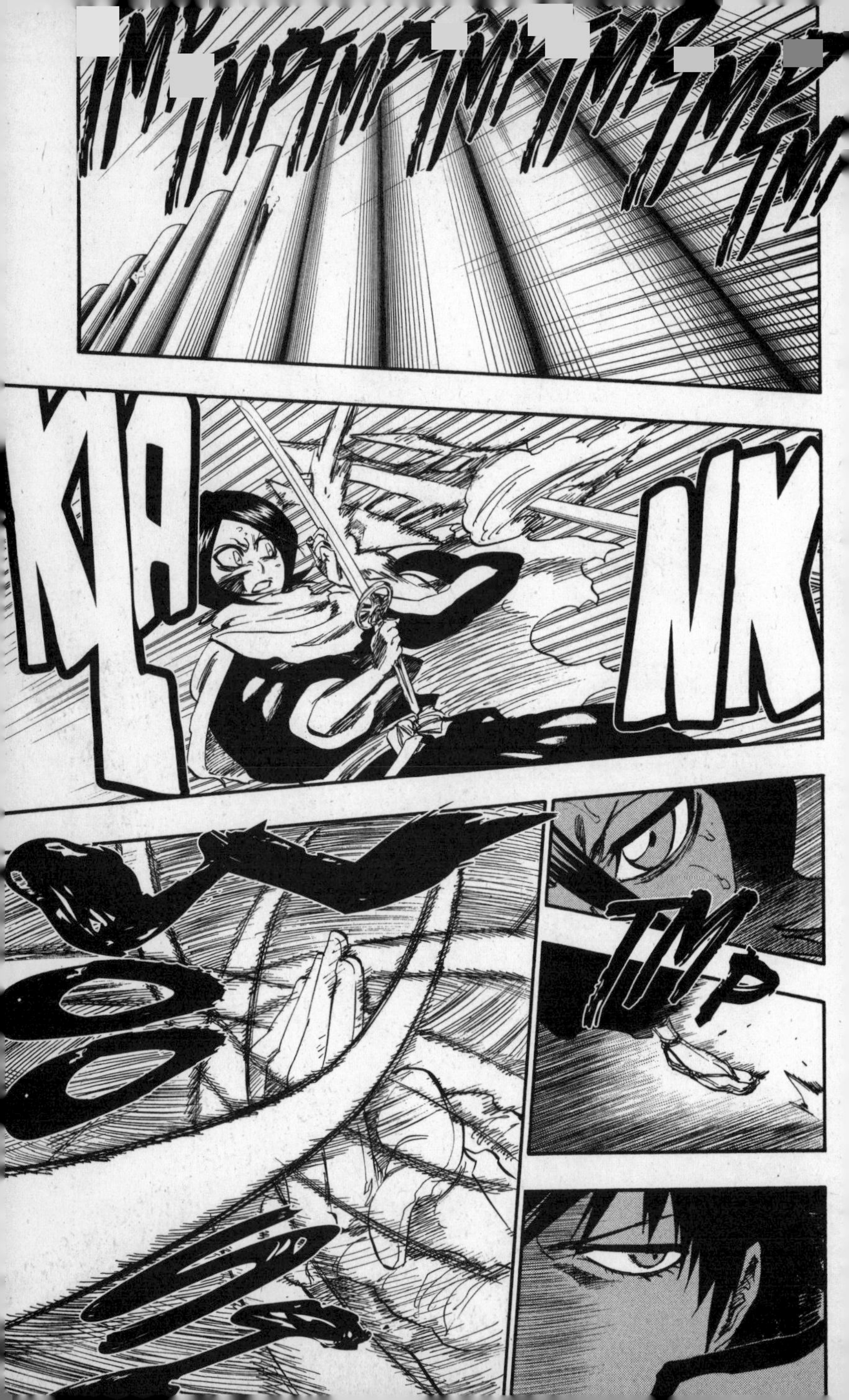
TMP TMP TMP TMP TMP TMP TMP
KRANK
TMP

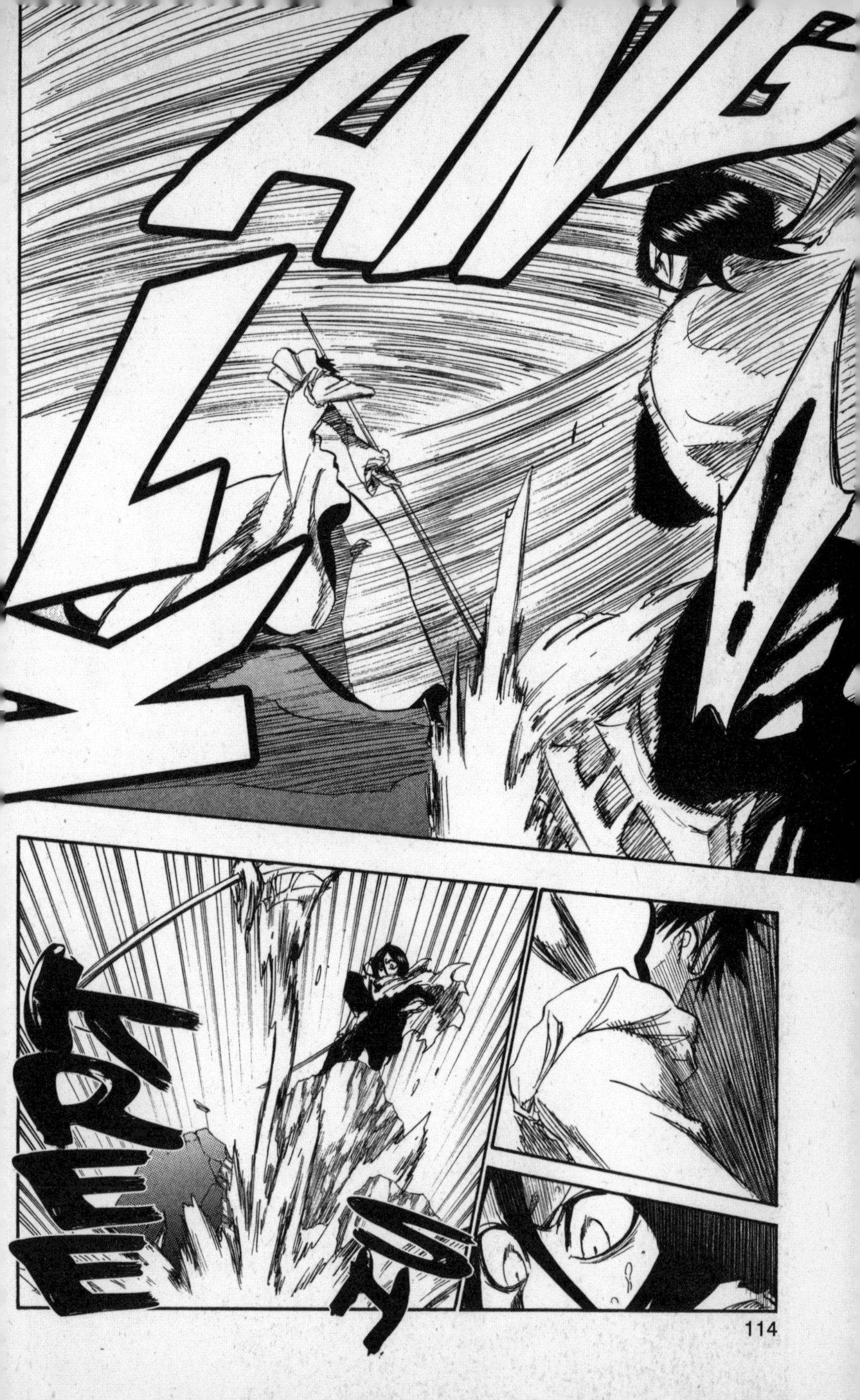
ZANG
KREE

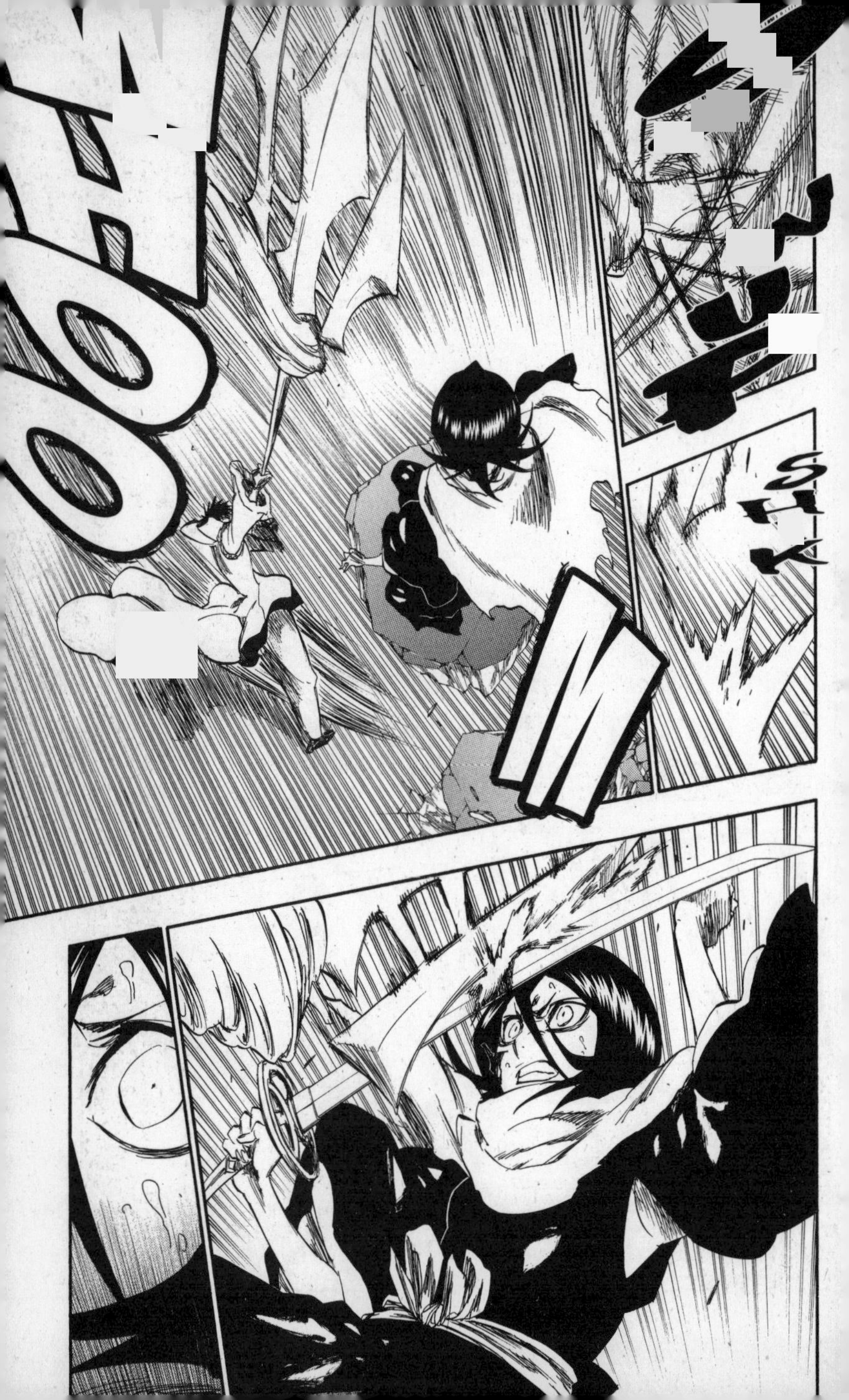
SHK

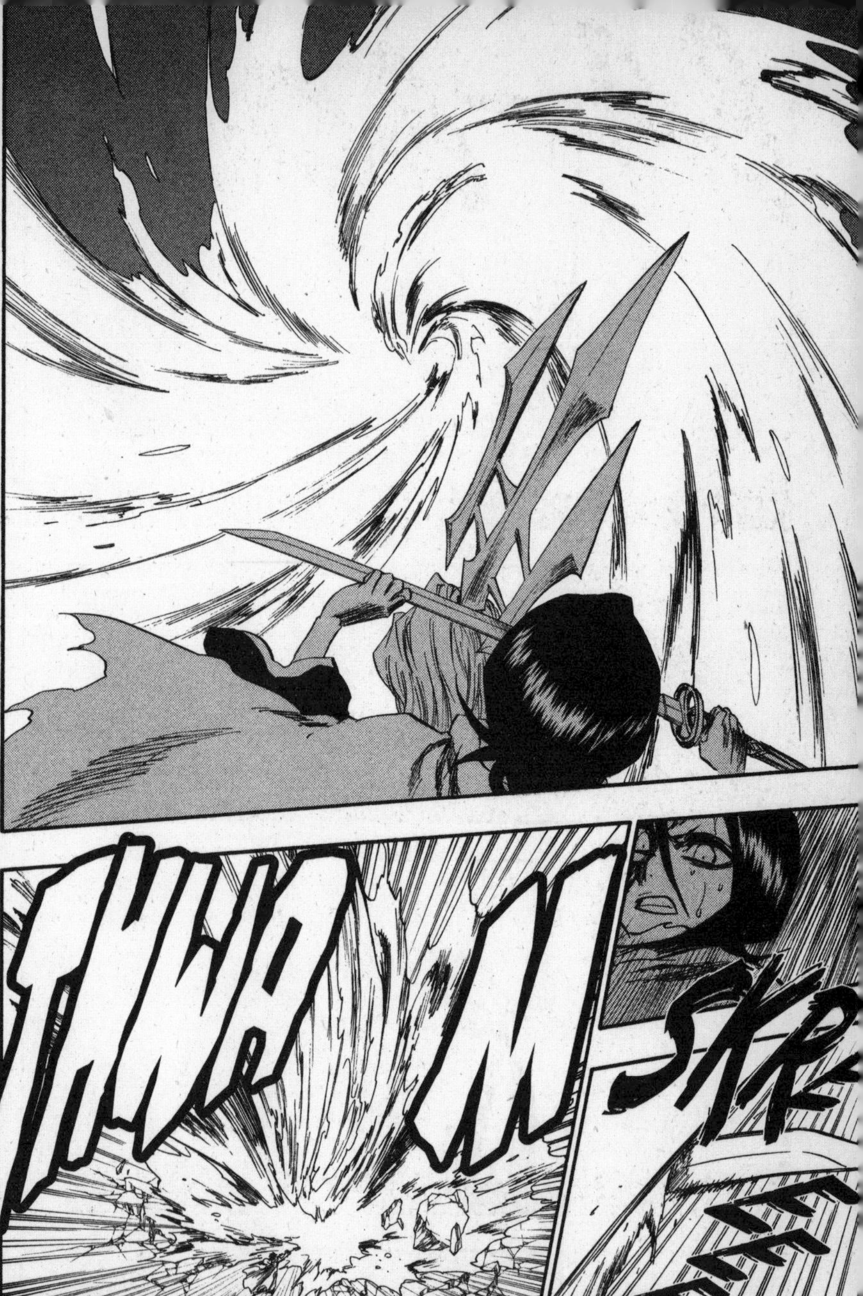
SKR
THWAM

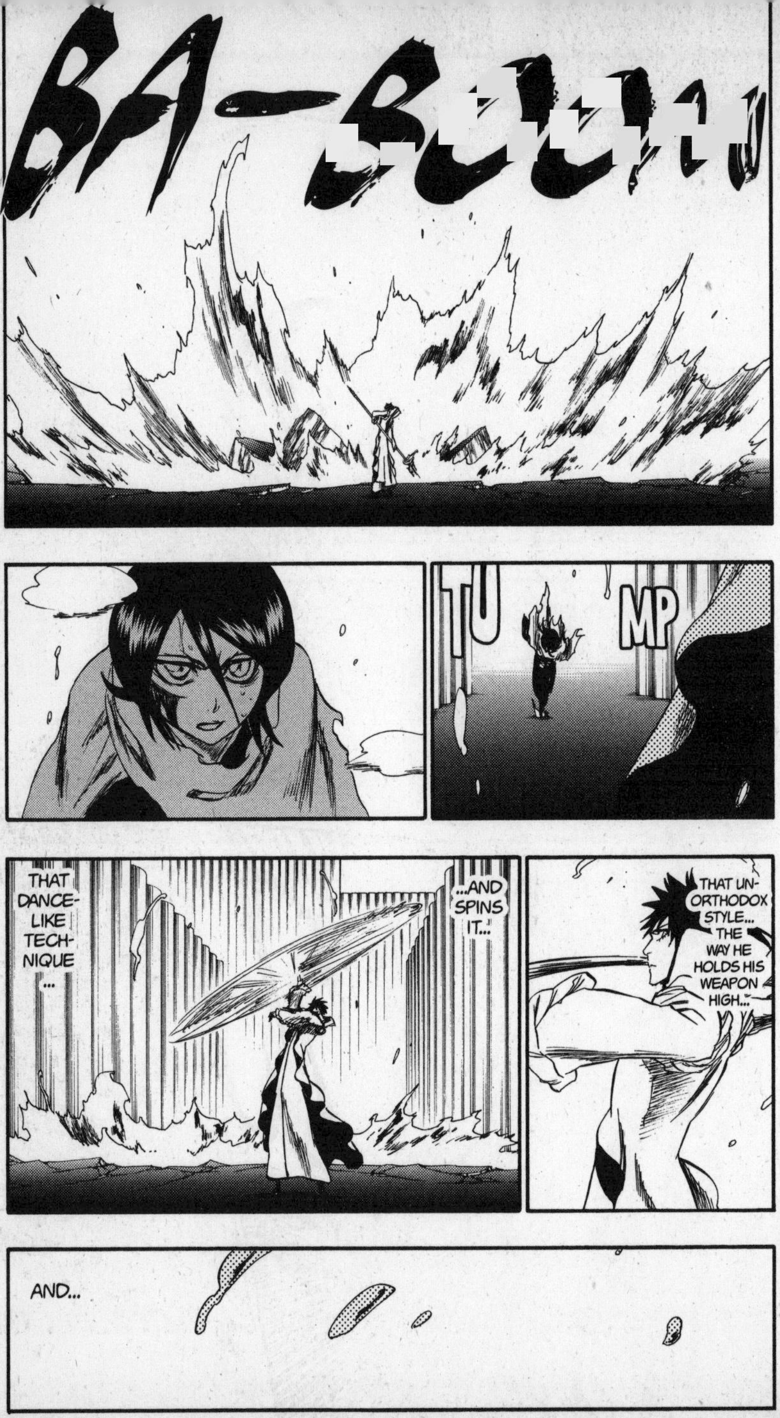

BA-BOOM
TUMP
THAT UNORTHODOX STYLE... THE WAY HE HOLDS HIS WEAPON HIGH...
...AND SPINS IT...
THAT DANCE-LIKE TECHNIQUE...
AND...

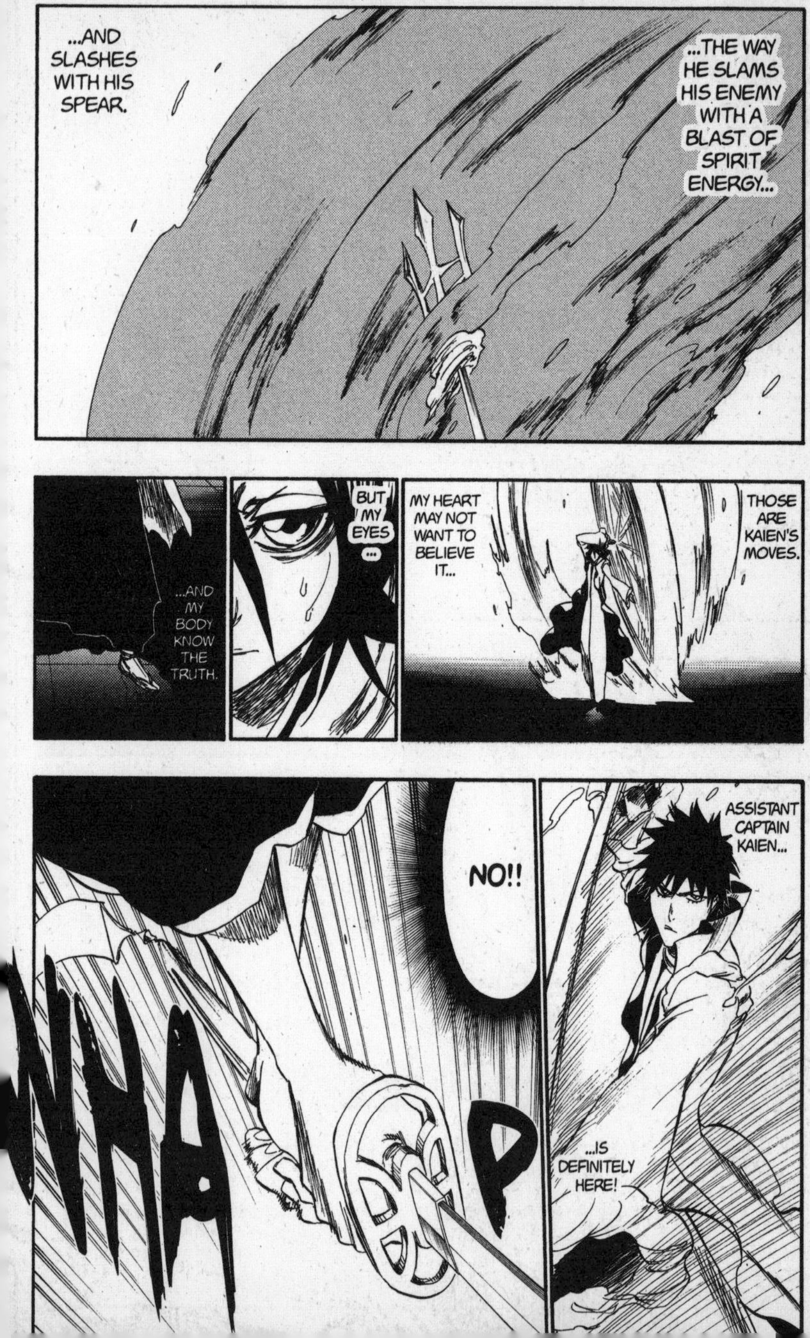
...THE WAY HE SLAMS HIS ENEMY WITH A BLAST OF SPIRIT ENERGY...
...AND SLASHES WITH HIS SPEAR.
THOSE ARE KAIEN'S MOVES.
MY HEART MAY NOT WANT TO BELIEVE IT...
BUT MY EYES...
...AND MY BODY KNOW THE TRUTH.
ASSISTANT CAPTAIN KAIEN...
...IS DEFINITELY HERE!
NO!!
WHAP

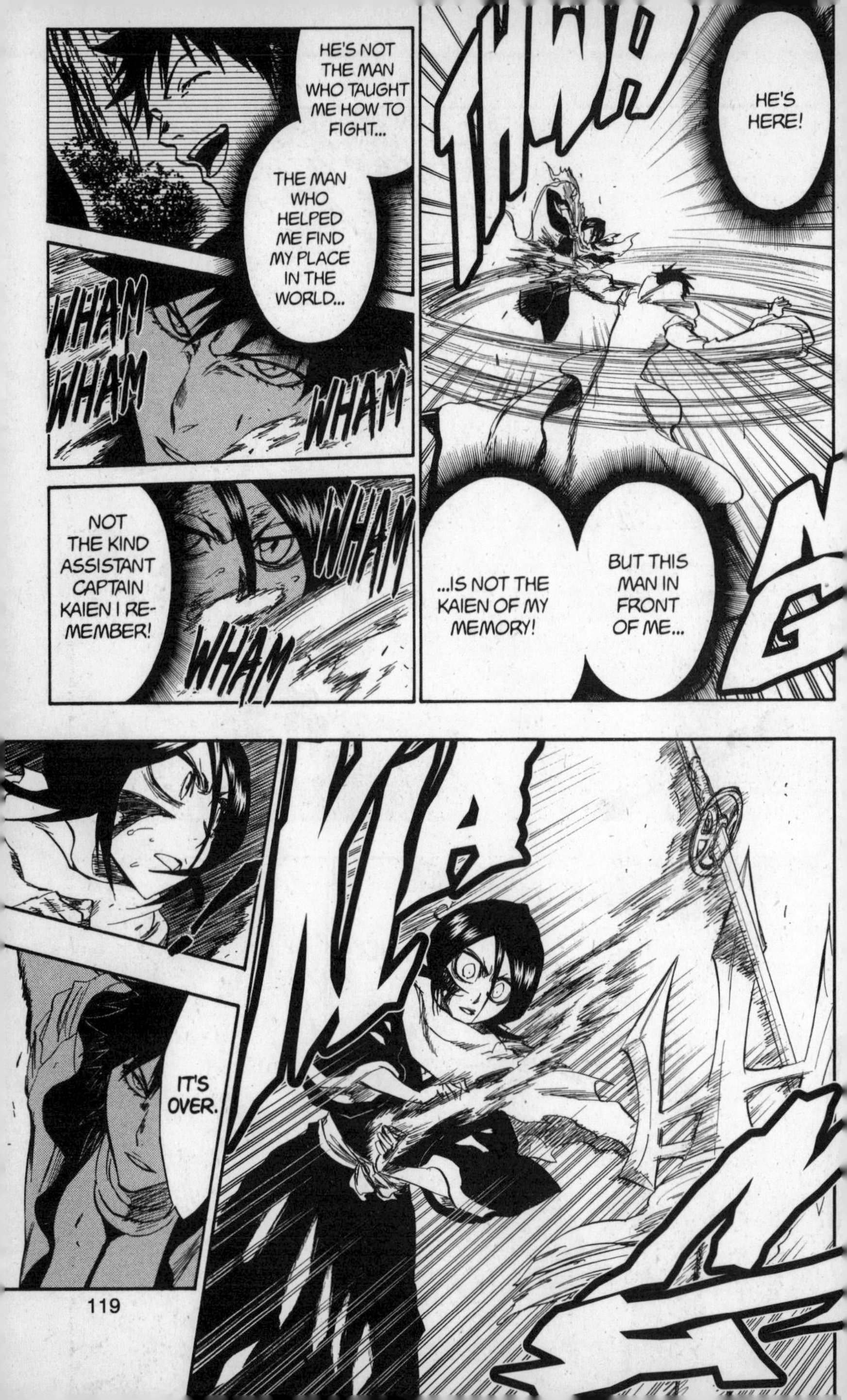
HE'S HERE!
BUT THIS MAN IN FRONT OF ME...
...IS NOT THE KAIEN OF MY MEMORY!
HE'S NOT THE MAN WHO TAUGHT ME HOW TO FIGHT...
THE MAN WHO HELPED ME FIND MY PLACE IN THE WORLD...
WHAM
WHAM WHAM
WHAM
WHAM
NOT THE KIND ASSISTANT CAPTAIN KAIEN I RE-MEMBER!
IT'S OVER.

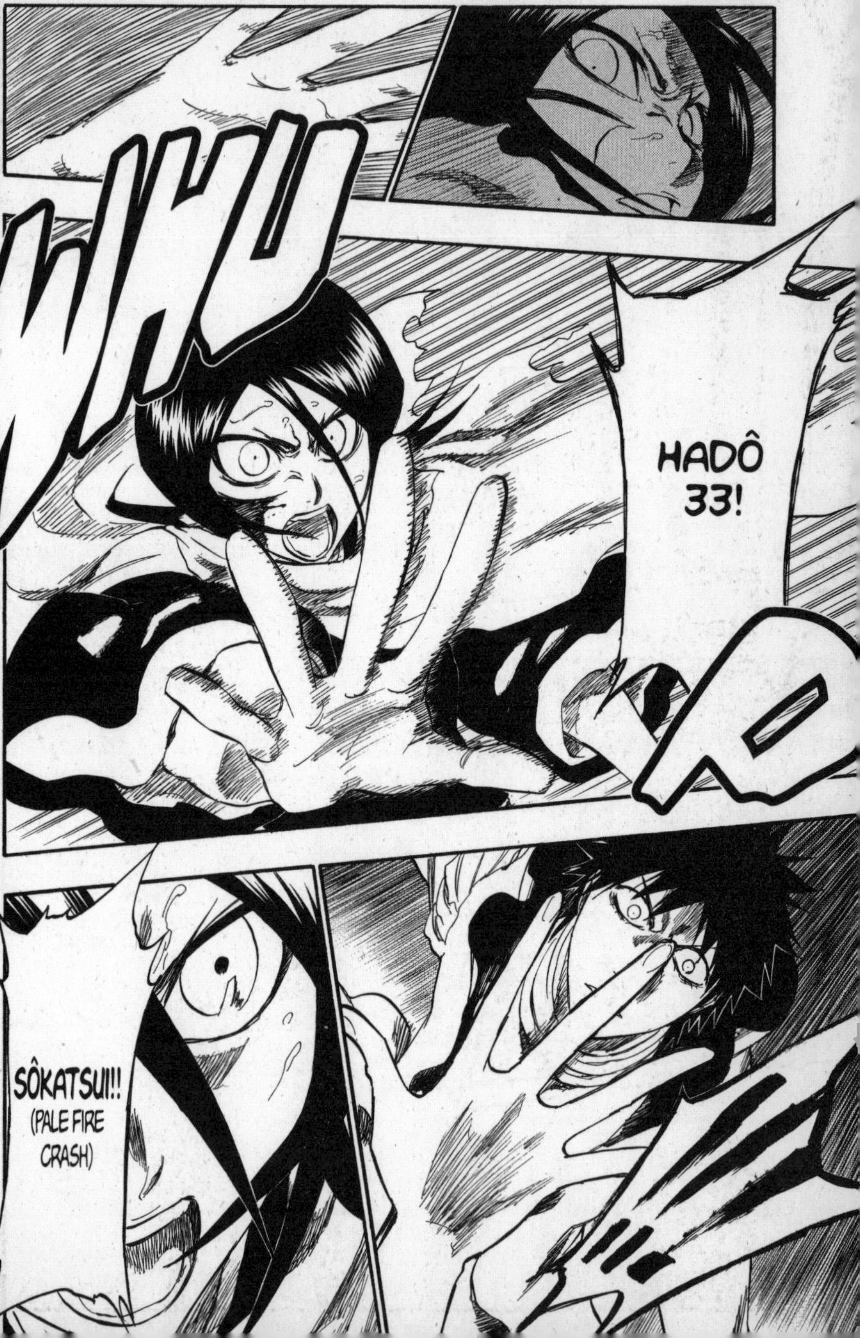
HADÔ 33!
SÔKATSUI!!
(PALE FIRE CRASH)

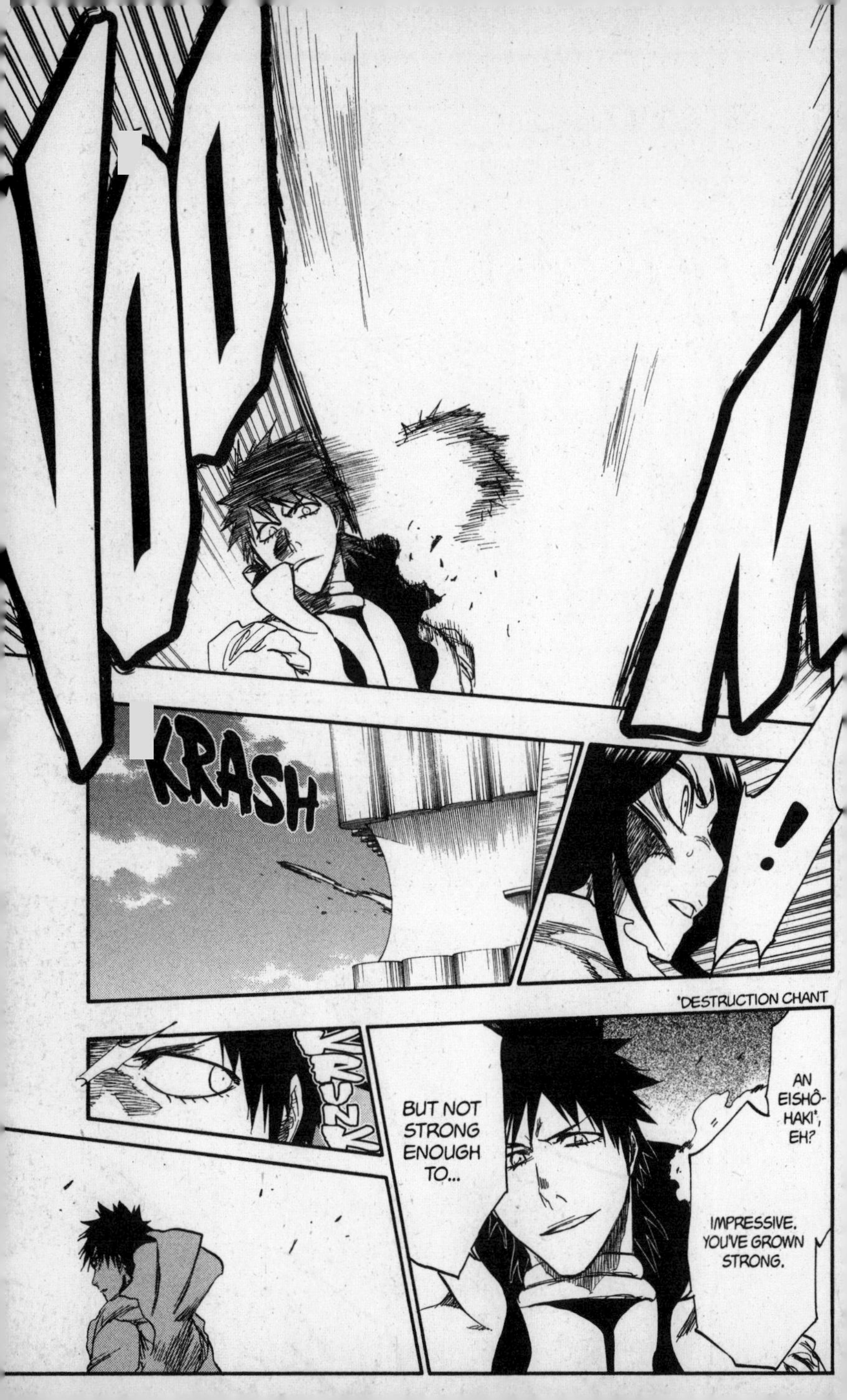
!
KRASH
AN EISHÔ-HAKI*, EH?
IMPRESSIVE. YOU'VE GROWN STRONG.
BUT NOT STRONG ENOUGH TO...

*DESTRUCTION CHANT

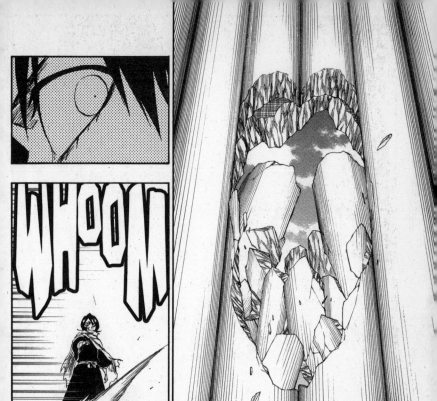

WHOOM

WHAT?

WHY IS HE RUNNING?

TMP

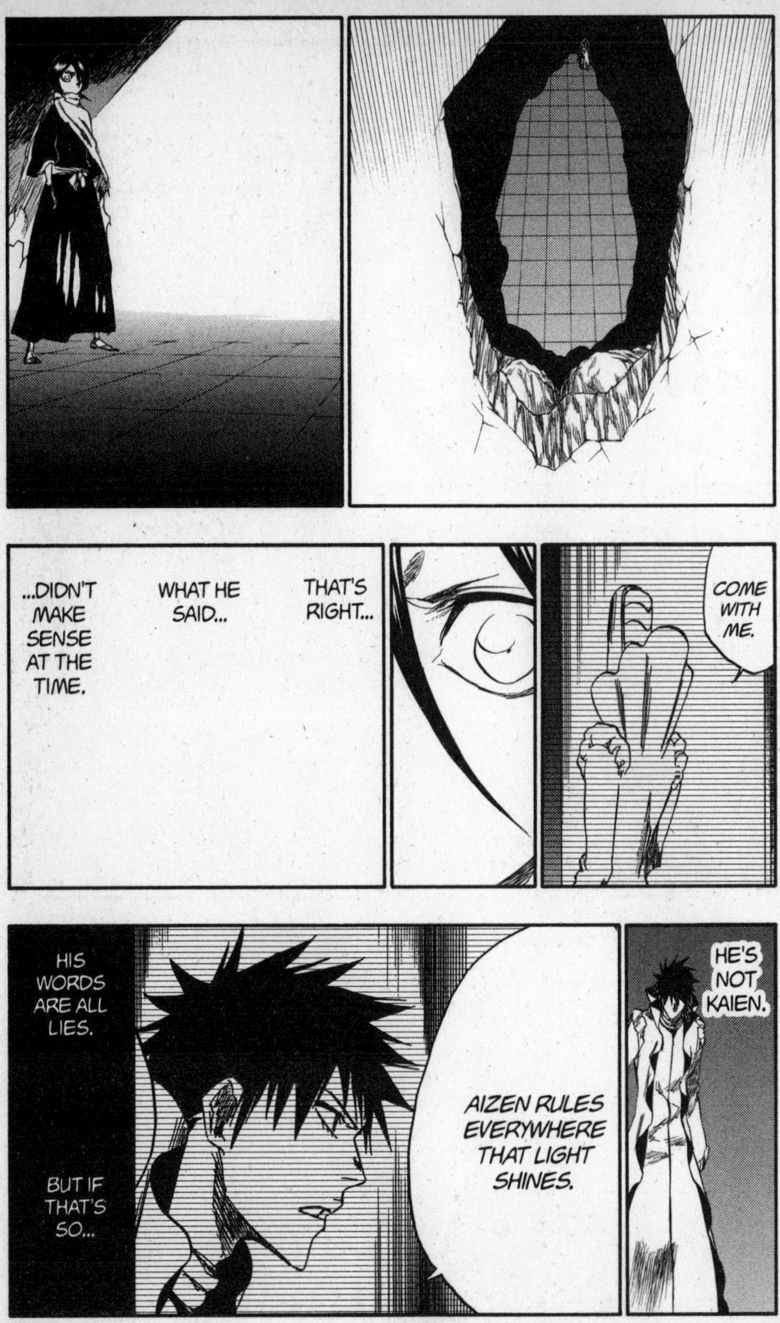
COME WITH ME.
THAT'S RIGHT...
WHAT HE SAID...
...DIDN'T MAKE SENSE AT THE TIME.
HE'S NOT KAIEN.
AIZEN RULES EVERYWHERE THAT LIGHT SHINES.
HIS WORDS ARE ALL LIES.
BUT IF THAT'S SO...

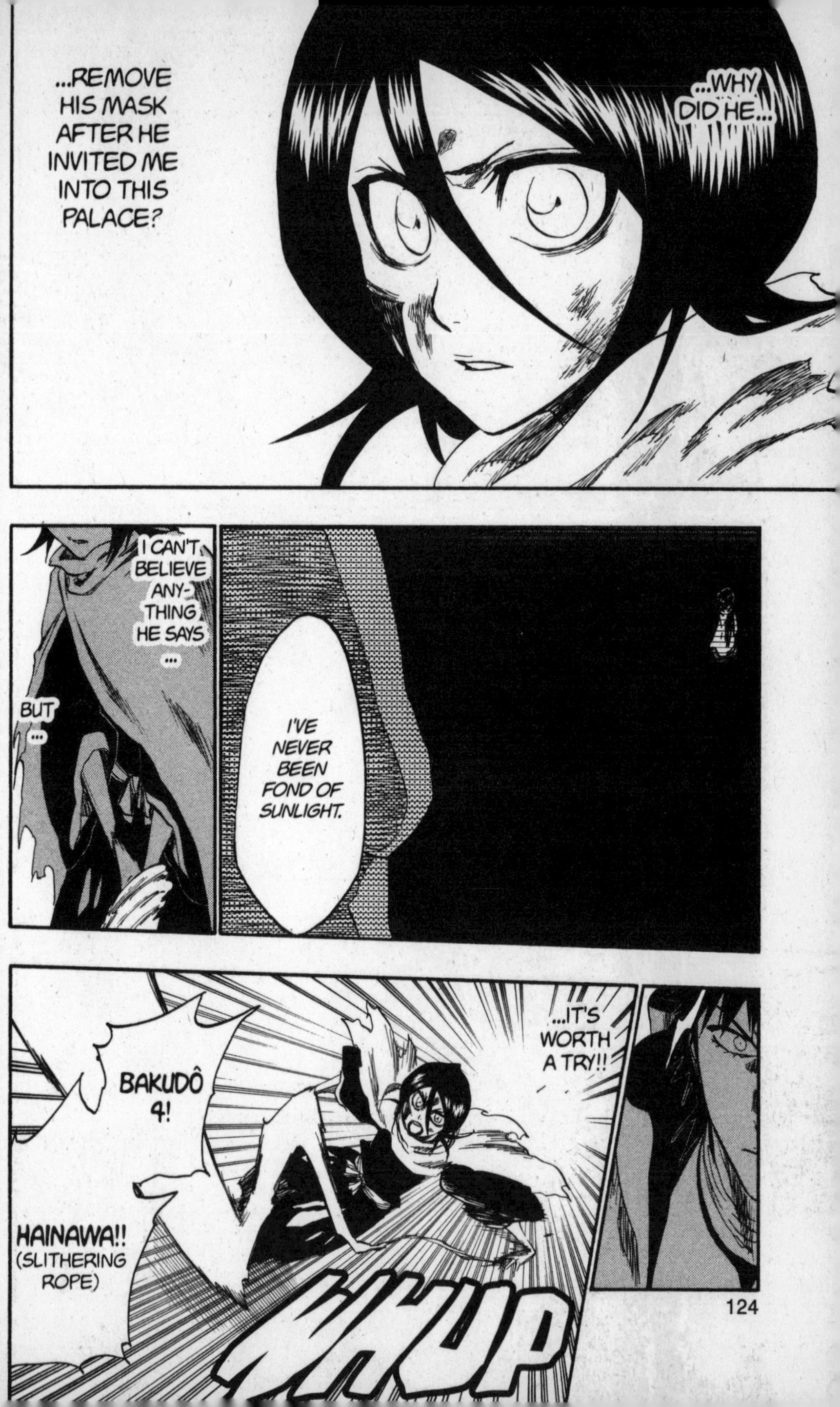
...WHY DID HE...
...REMOVE HIS MASK AFTER HE INVITED ME INTO THIS PALACE?
I'VE NEVER BEEN FOND OF SUNLIGHT.
I CAN'T BELIEVE ANYTHING HE SAYS...
BUT...
...IT'S WORTH A TRY!!
BAKUDÔ 4!
HAINAWA!! (SLITHERING ROPE)
WHUP

READ THIS WAY

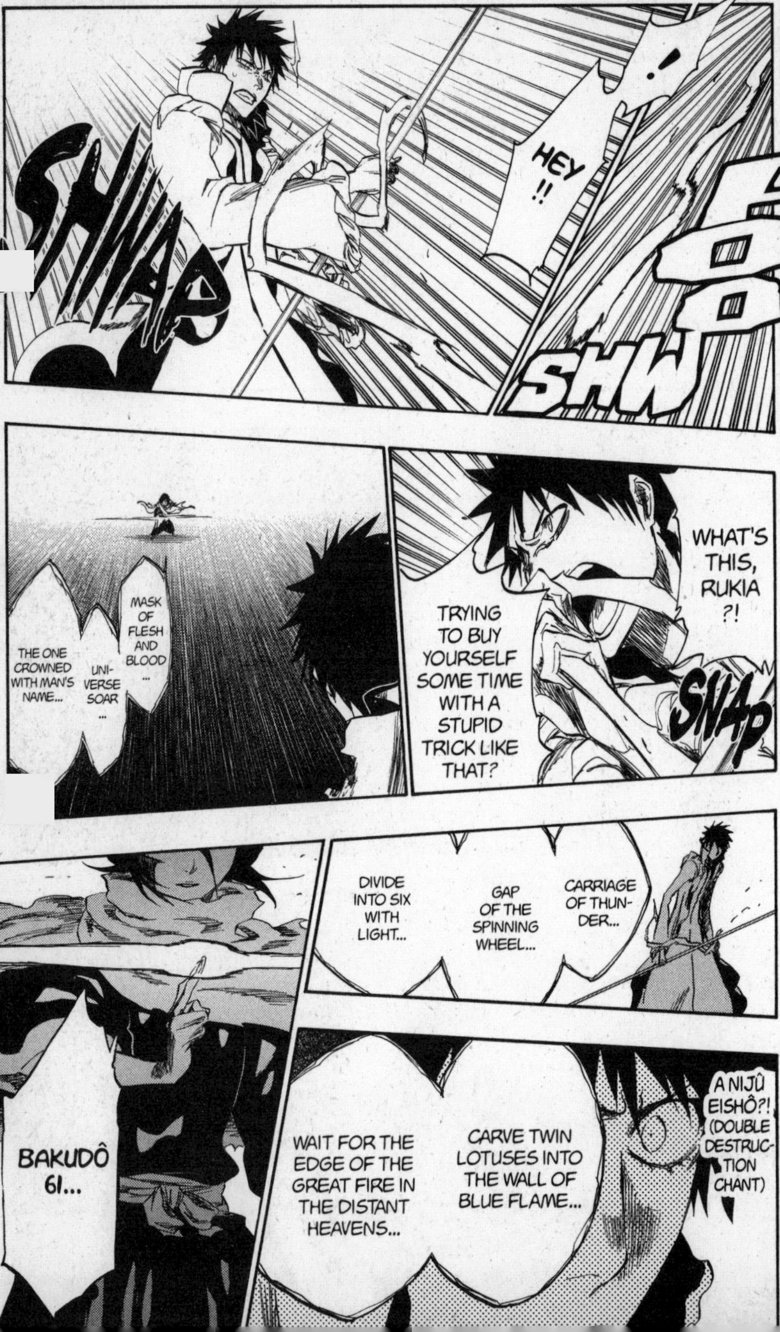

!
HEY!!
SHWAP
SHW
WHAT'S THIS, RUKIA?!
TRYING TO BUY YOURSELF SOME TIME WITH A STUPID TRICK LIKE THAT?
SNAp
MASK OF FLESH AND BLOOD...
UNI-VERSE SOAR...
THE ONE CROWNED WITH MAN'S NAME...
CARRIAGE OF THUN-DER...
GAP OF THE SPINNING WHEEL...
DIVIDE INTO SIX WITH LIGHT...
A NIJÛ EISHÔ?! (DOUBLE DESTRUC-TION CHANT)
CARVE TWIN LOTUSES INTO THE WALL OF BLUE FLAME...
WAIT FOR THE EDGE OF THE GREAT FIRE IN THE DISTANT HEAVENS...
BAKUDÔ 61...

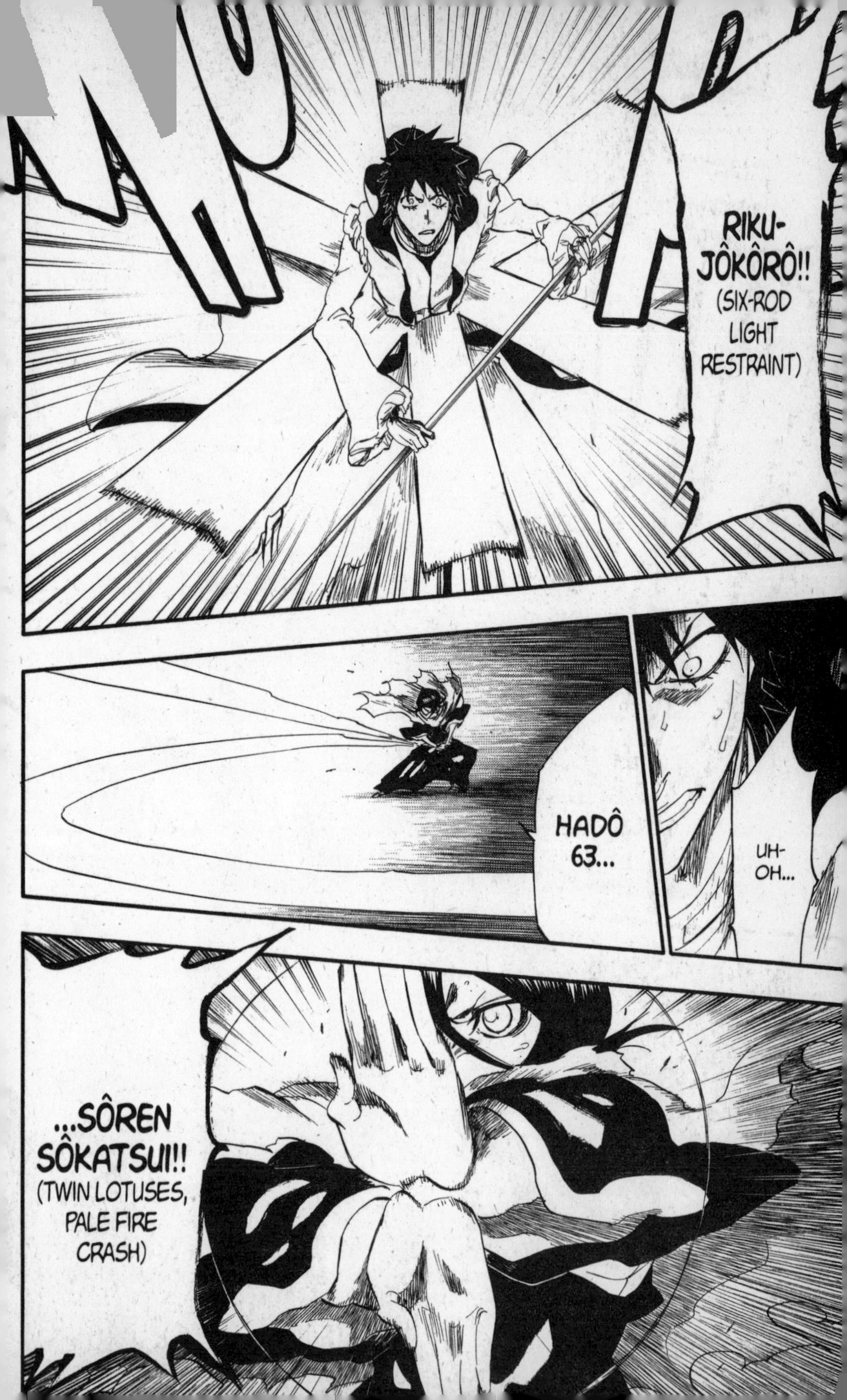
RIKU-
JÔKÔRÔ!!
(SIX-ROD
LIGHT
RESTRAINT)
UH-
OH...
HADÔ
63...
...SÔREN
SÔKATSUI!!
(TWIN LOTUSES,
PALE FIRE
CRASH)

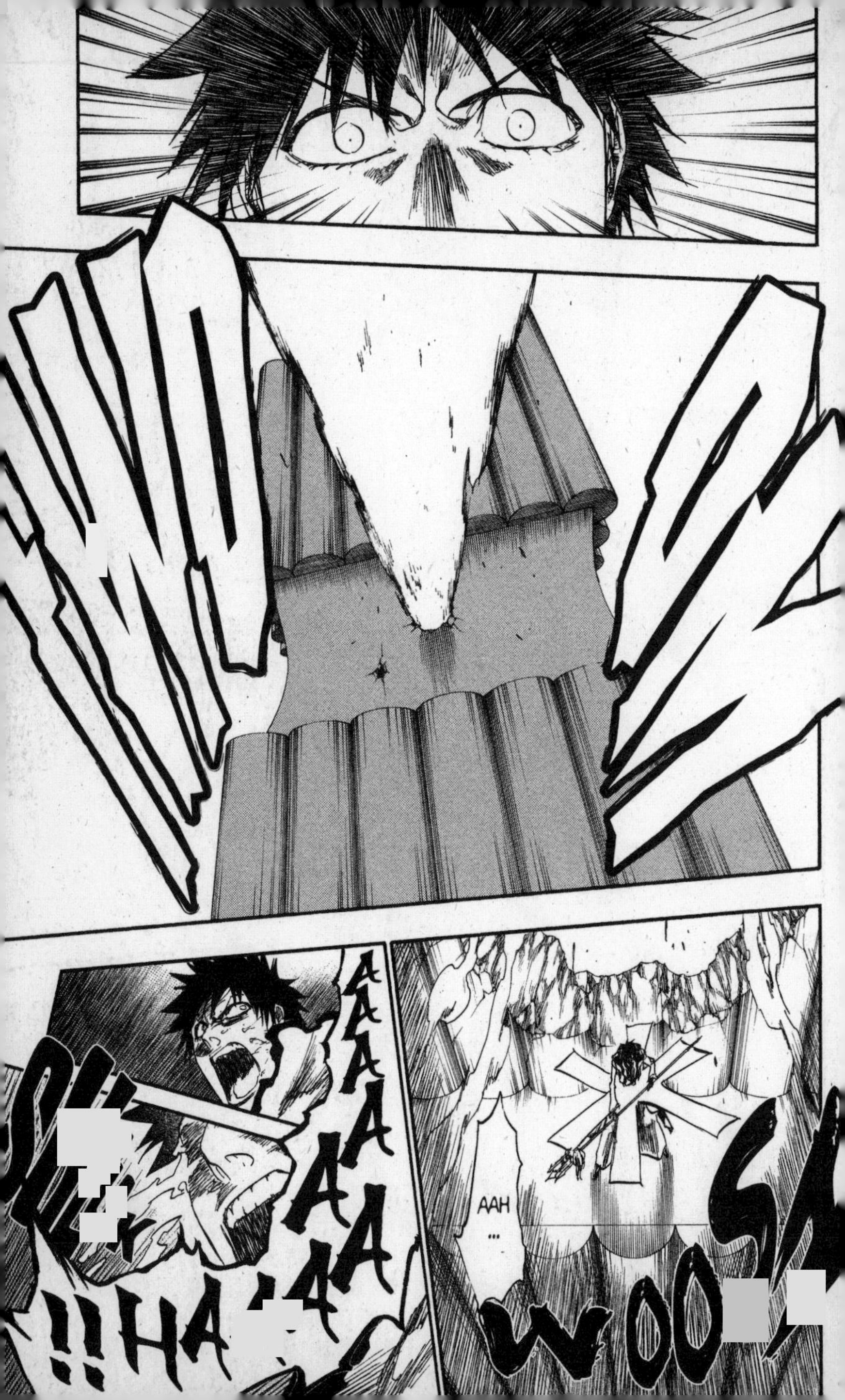
AAH ...
AAAAAAAA
!!!HA

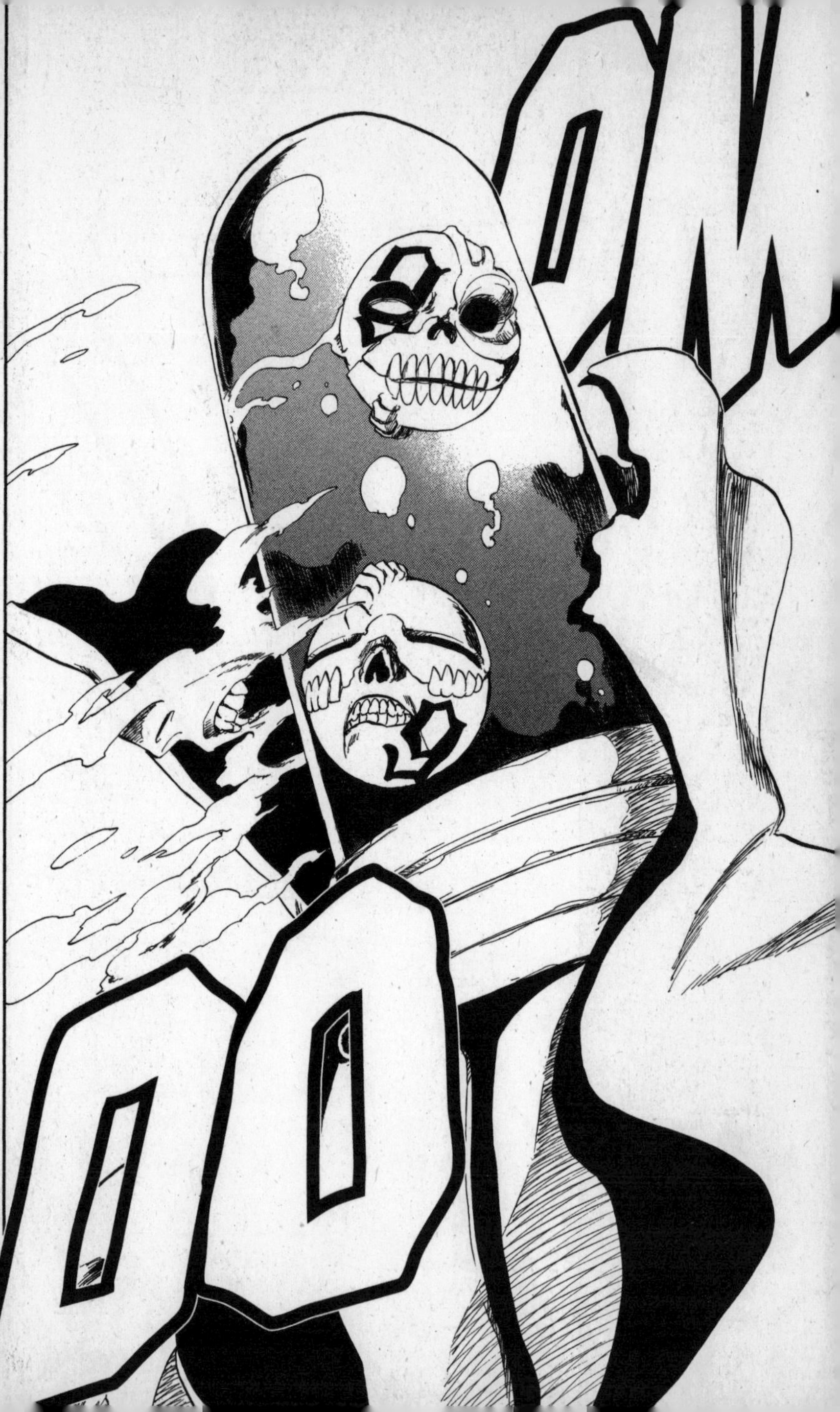
OOOM

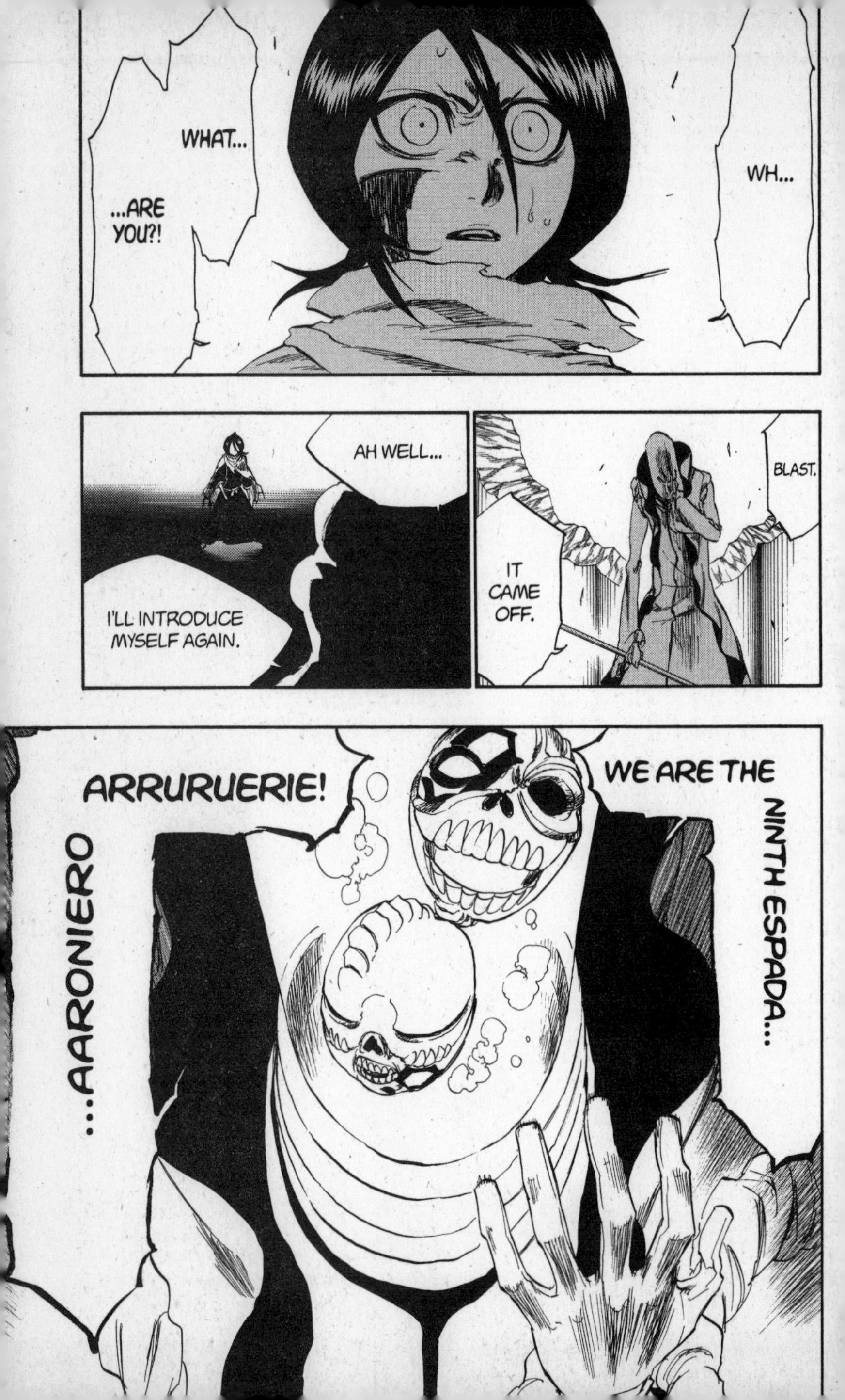
WH...
WHAT...
...ARE YOU?!
BLAST.
IT CAME OFF.
AH WELL...
I'LL INTRODUCE MYSELF AGAIN.
WE ARE THE NINTH ESPADA...
...AARONIERO
ARRURUERIE!

Keep on Hiding
From the Truth.

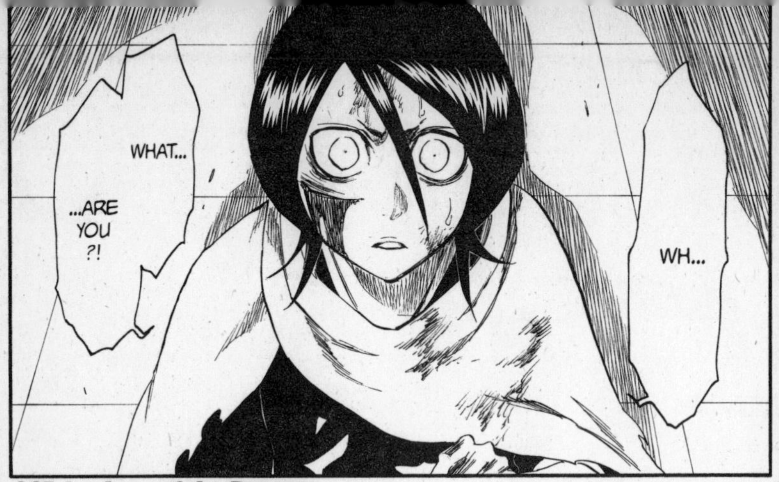
WH...
WHAT...
...ARE YOU ?!

267. Legions of the Regrets

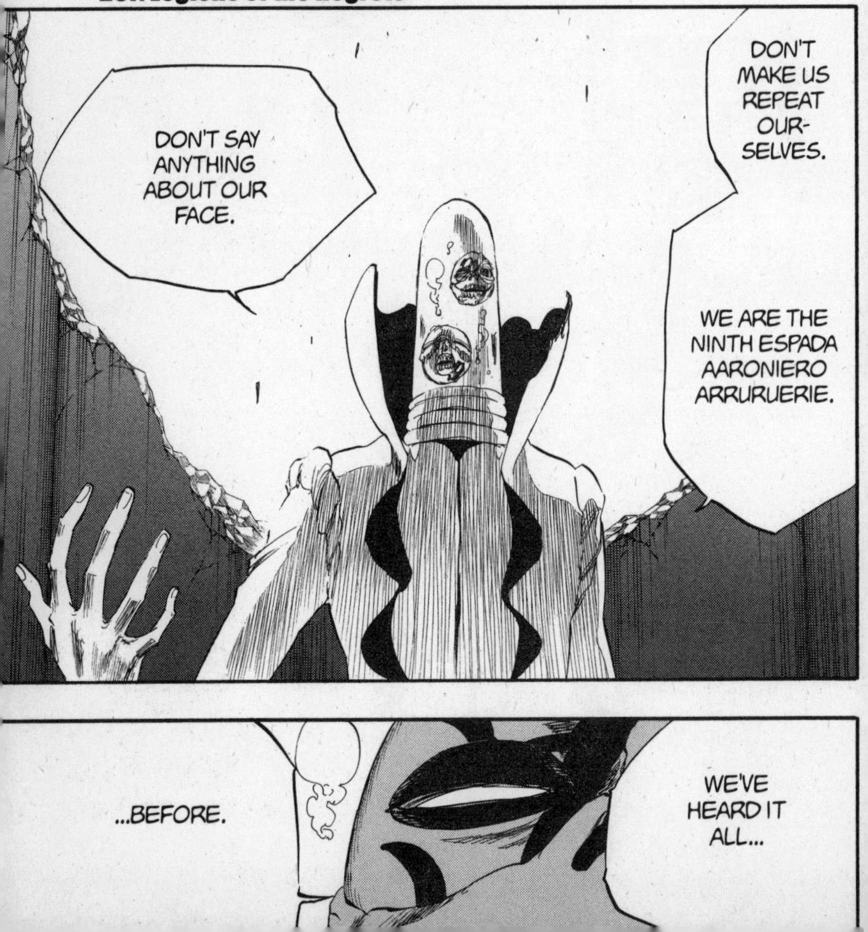
DON'T MAKE US REPEAT OUR-SELVES.
DON'T SAY ANYTHING ABOUT OUR FACE.
WE ARE THE NINTH ESPADA AARONIERO ARRURUERIE.
WE'VE HEARD IT ALL...
...BEFORE.

BLEACH 267. Legions of the Regrets

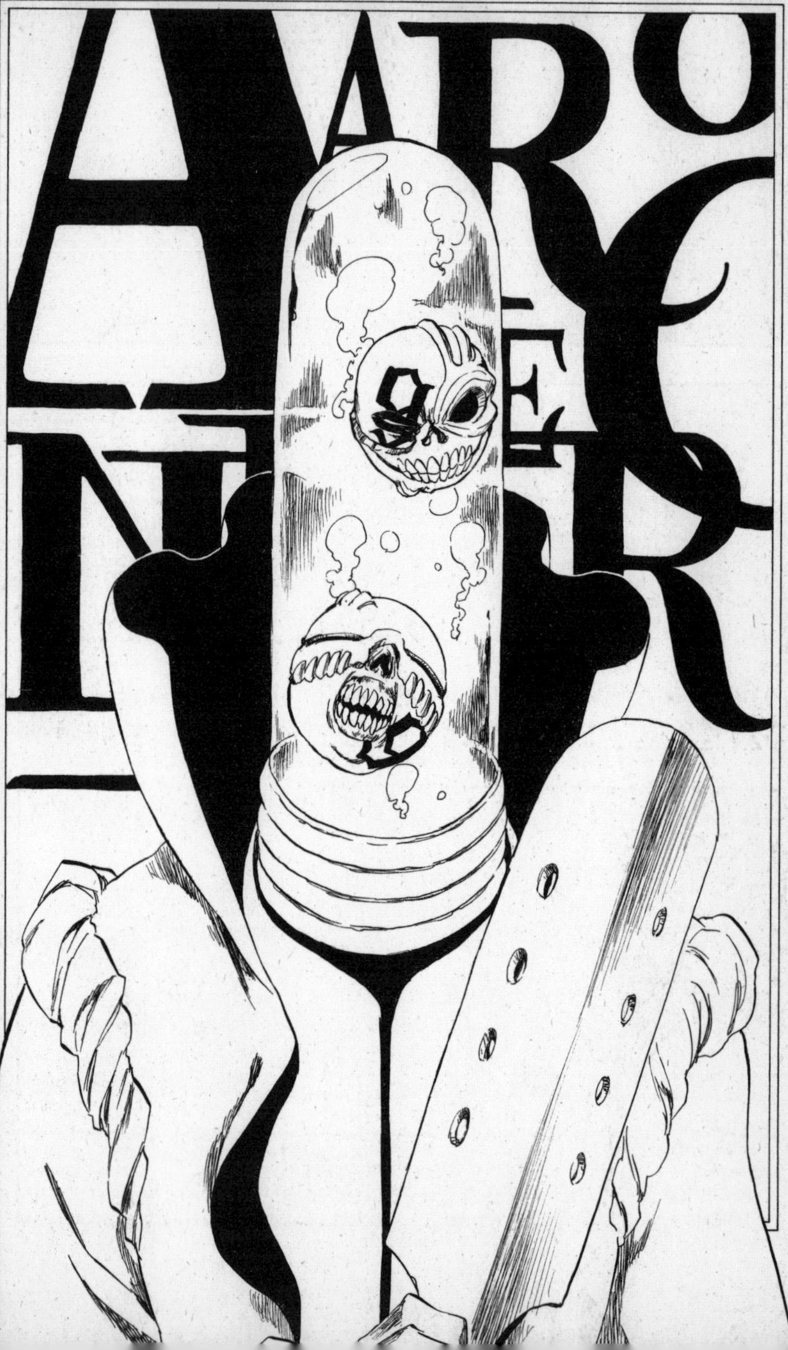

READ THIS WAY

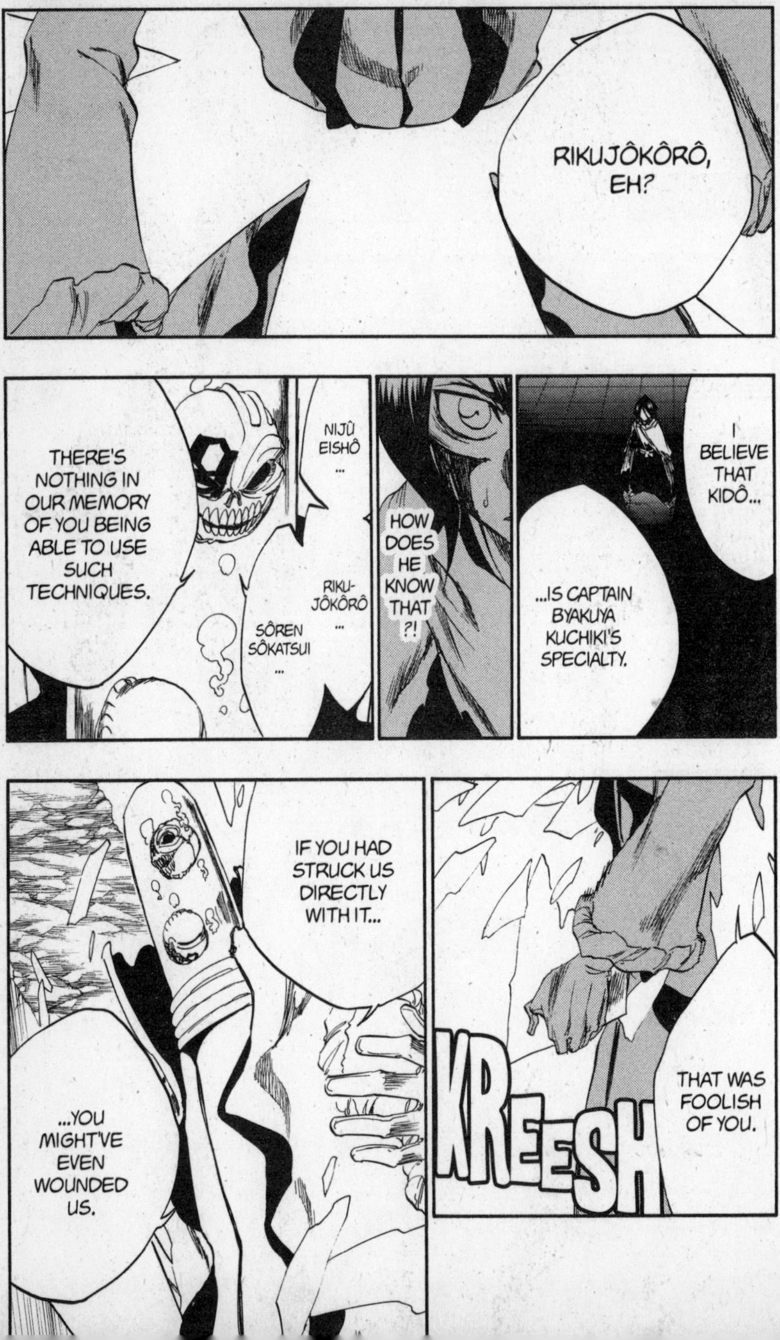
RIKUJÔKÔRÔ, EH?
I BELIEVE THAT KIDÔ...
...IS CAPTAIN BYAKUYA KUCHIKI'S SPECIALTY.
HOW DOES HE KNOW THAT?!
NIJÛ EISHÔ...
RIKUJÔKÔRÔ...
SÔREN SÔKATSUI...
THERE'S NOTHING IN OUR MEMORY OF YOU BEING ABLE TO USE SUCH TECHNIQUES.
KREESH
THAT WAS FOOLISH OF YOU.
IF YOU HAD STRUCK US DIRECTLY WITH IT...
...YOU MIGHT'VE EVEN WOUNDED US.

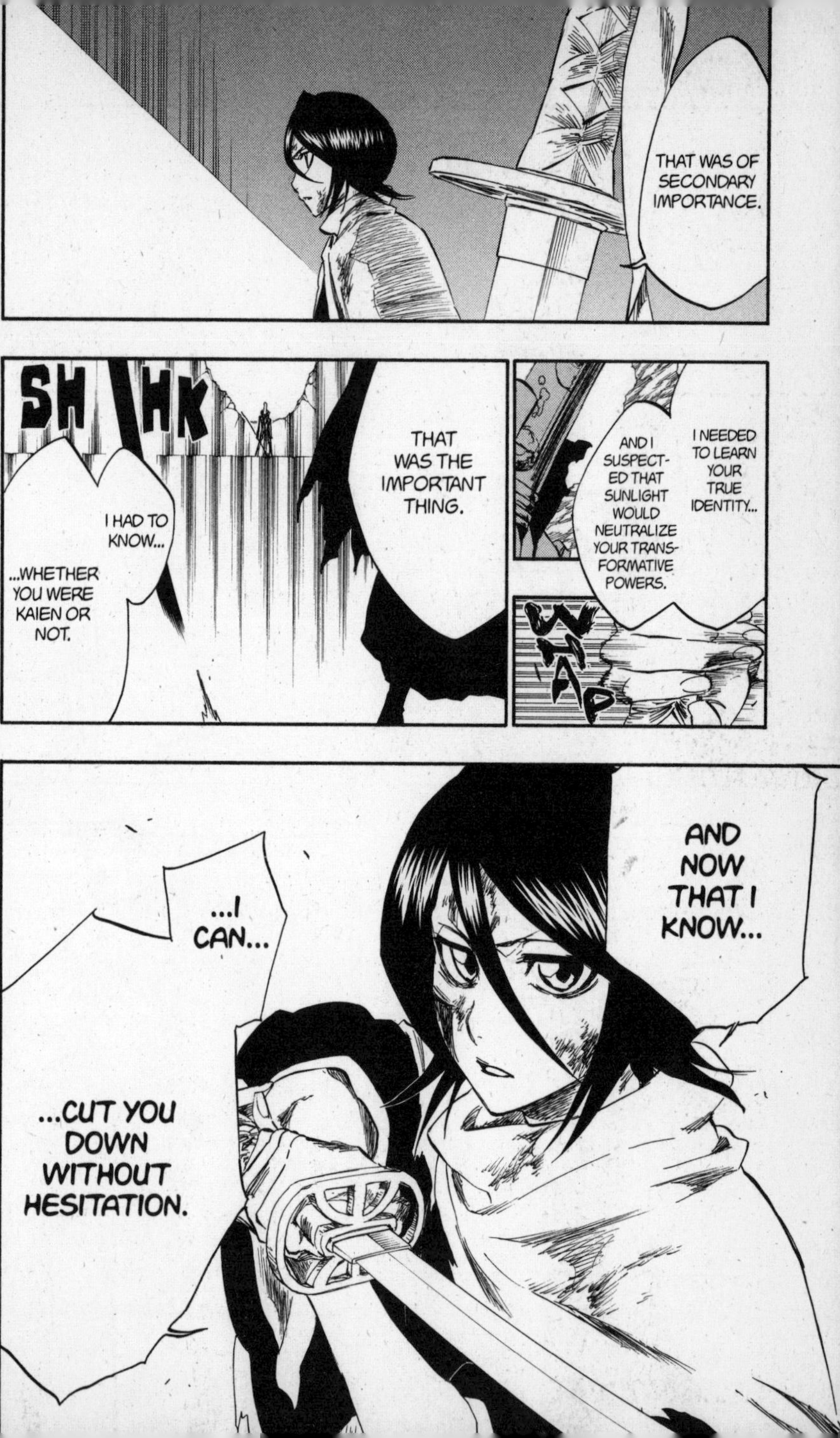
THAT WAS OF SECONDARY IMPORTANCE.
I NEEDED TO LEARN YOUR TRUE IDENTITY...
AND I SUSPECT-ED THAT SUNLIGHT WOULD NEUTRALIZE YOUR TRANS-FORMATIVE POWERS.
WHAP
THAT WAS THE IMPORTANT THING.
SHHK
I HAD TO KNOW...
...WHETHER YOU WERE KAIEN OR NOT.
AND NOW THAT I KNOW...
...I CAN...
...CUT YOU DOWN WITHOUT HESITATION.

READ THIS WAY

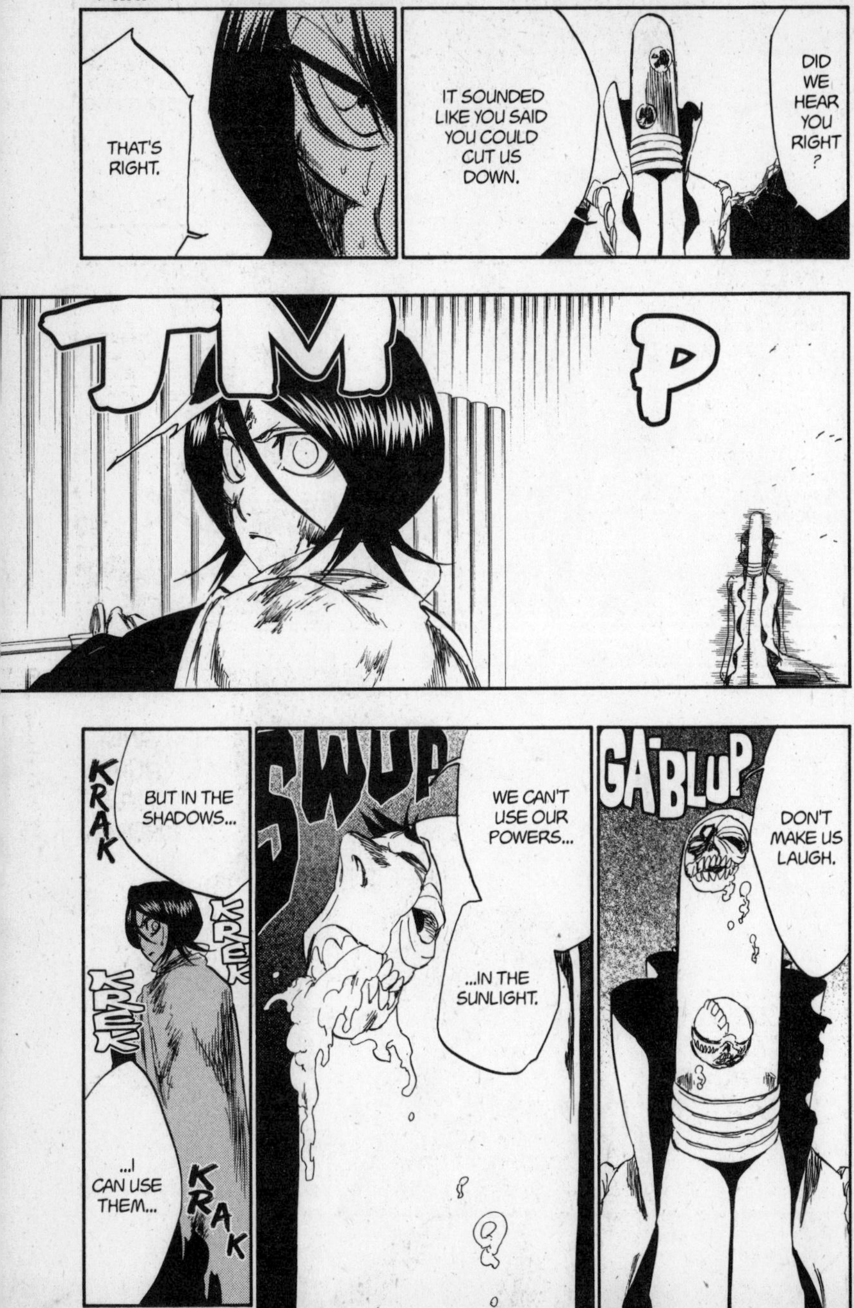
DID WE HEAR YOU RIGHT?
IT SOUNDED LIKE YOU SAID YOU COULD CUT US DOWN.
THAT'S RIGHT.
TMP
GA-BLUP
DON'T MAKE US LAUGH.
SWUP
WE CAN'T USE OUR POWERS...
...IN THE SUNLIGHT.
KRAK
BUT IN THE SHADOWS...
KREK
KREK
...I CAN USE THEM...
KRAK

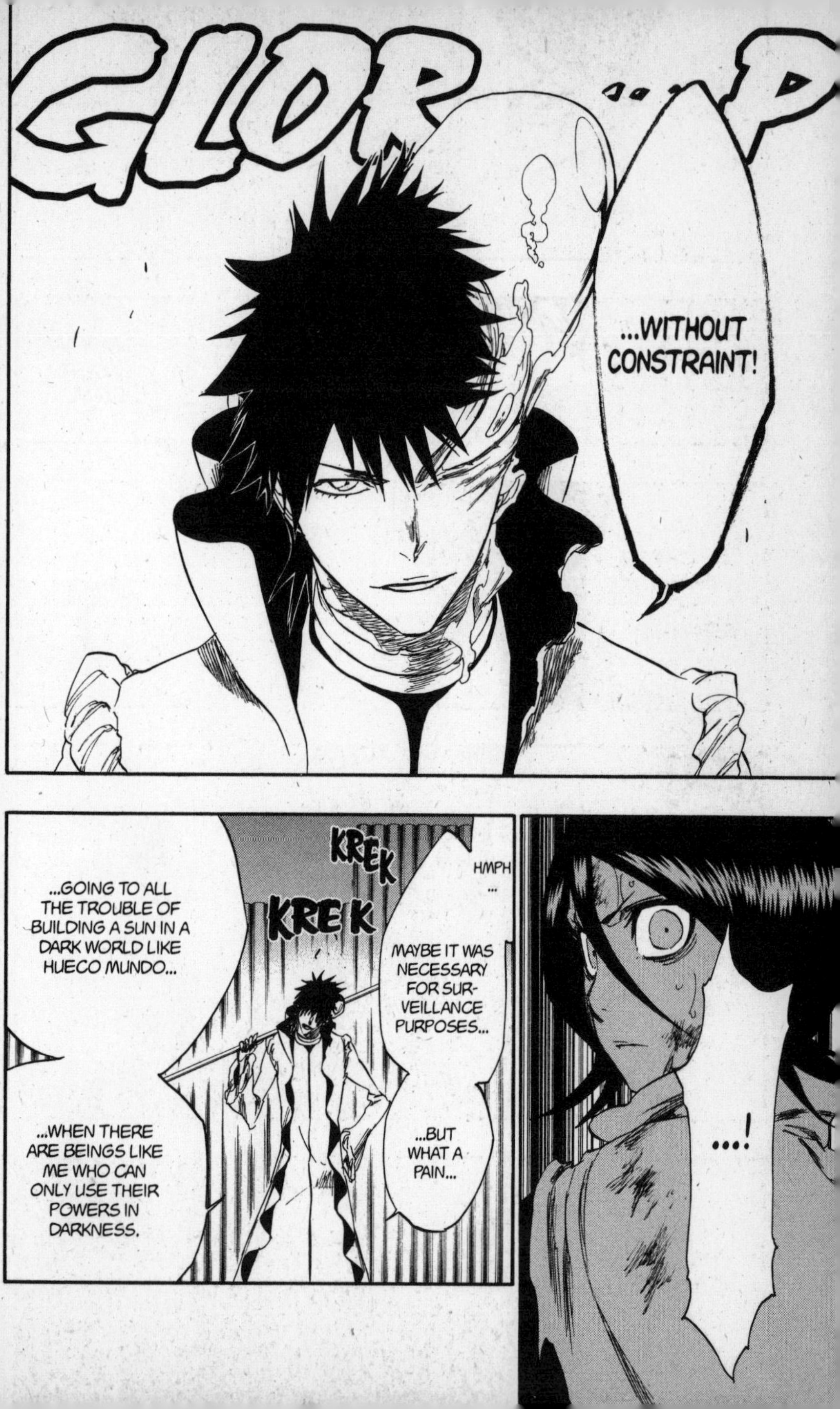
GLOR...P
...WITHOUT CONSTRAINT!
...!
HMPH ...
KREK
KRE K
MAYBE IT WAS NECESSARY FOR SUR-VEILLANCE PURPOSES...
...BUT WHAT A PAIN...
...GOING TO ALL THE TROUBLE OF BUILDING A SUN IN A DARK WORLD LIKE HUECO MUNDO...
...WHEN THERE ARE BEINGS LIKE ME WHO CAN ONLY USE THEIR POWERS IN DARKNESS.

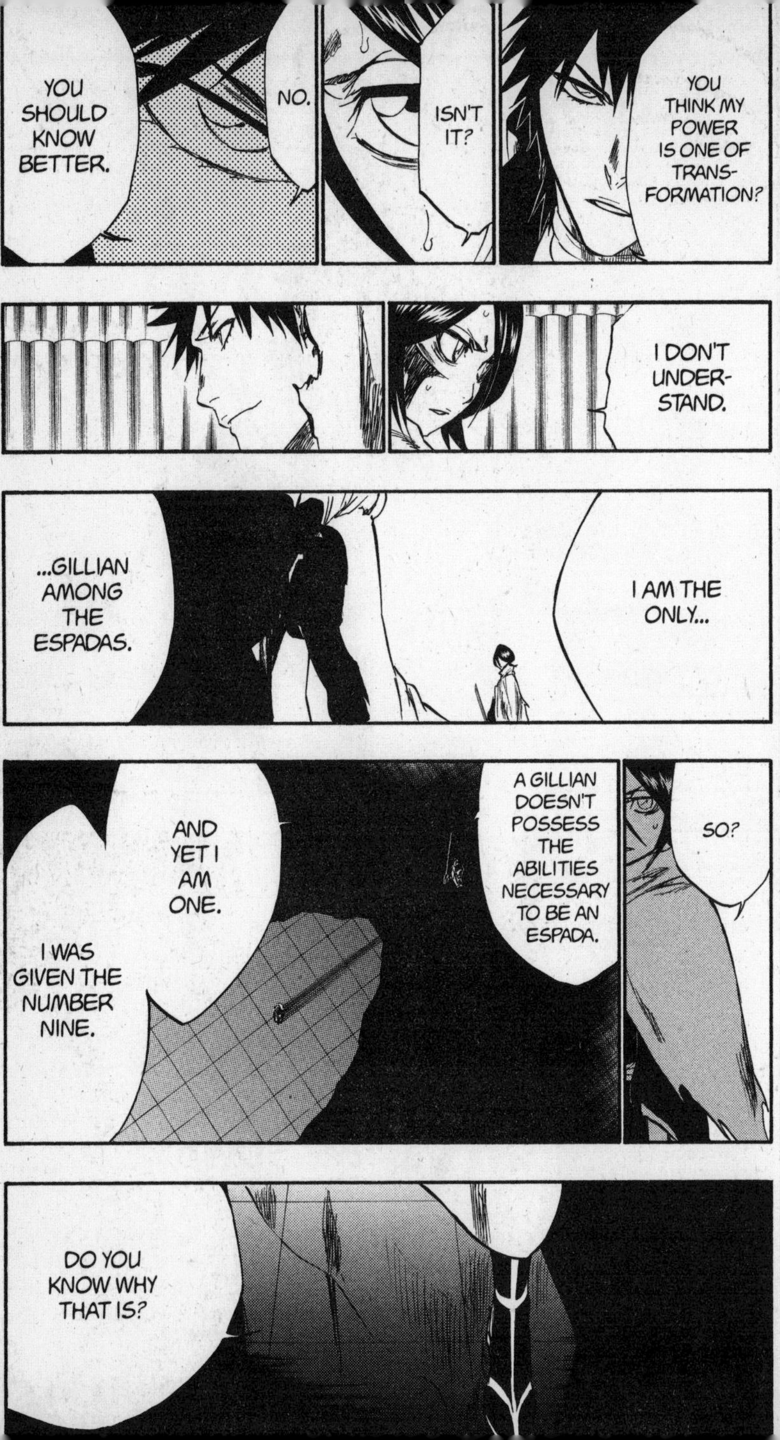
YOU THINK MY POWER IS ONE OF TRANS-FORMATION?
ISN'T IT?
NO.
YOU SHOULD KNOW BETTER.
I DON'T UNDER-STAND.
I AM THE ONLY...
...GILLIAN AMONG THE ESPADAS.
SO?
A GILLIAN DOESN'T POSSESS THE ABILITIES NECESSARY TO BE AN ESPADA.
AND YET I AM ONE.
I WAS GIVEN THE NUMBER NINE.
DO YOU KNOW WHY THAT IS?

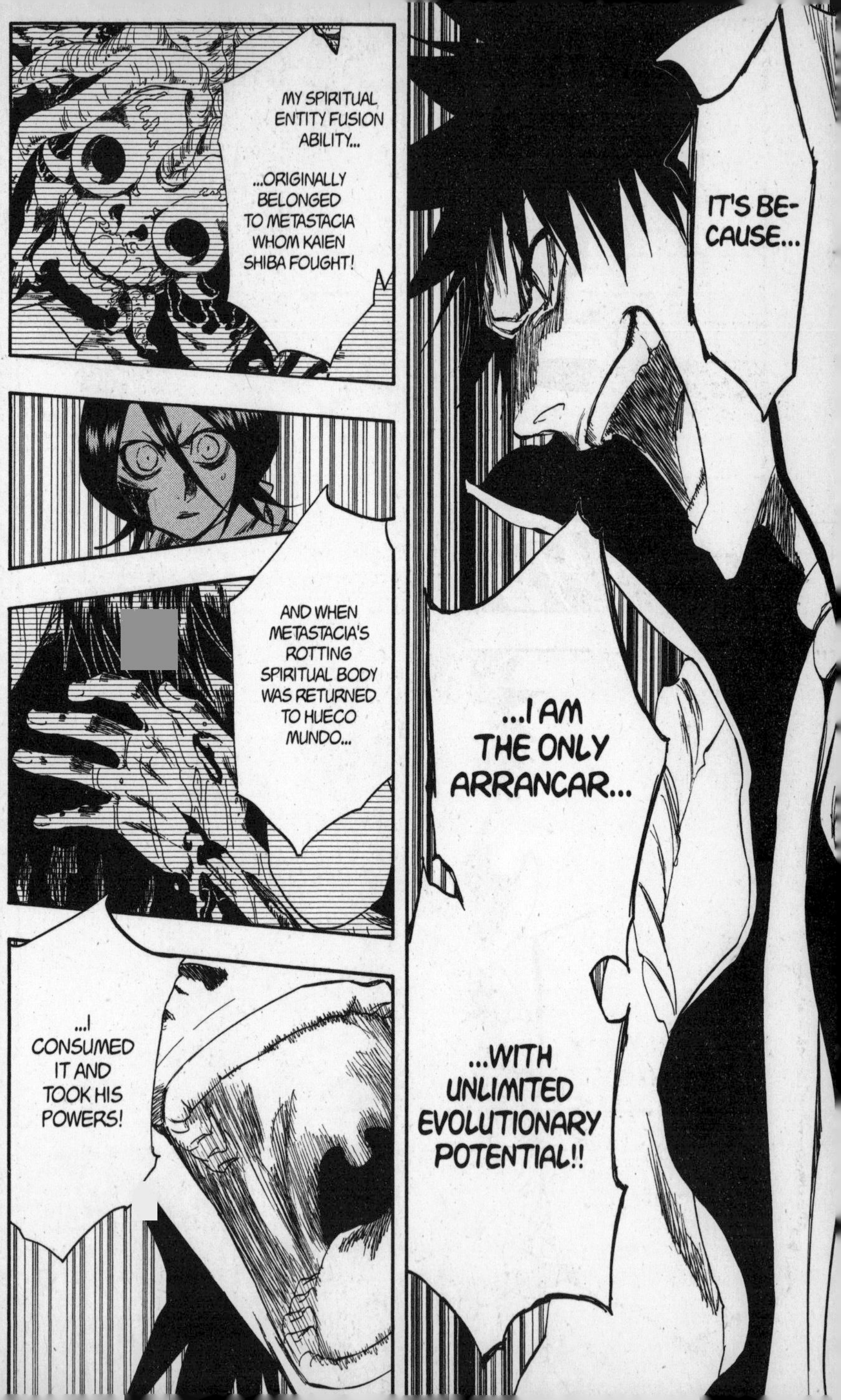
IT'S BE-CAUSE...
...I AM THE ONLY ARRANCAR...
...WITH UNLIMITED EVOLUTIONARY POTENTIAL!!
MY SPIRITUAL ENTITY FUSION ABILITY...
...ORIGINALLY BELONGED TO METASTACIA WHOM KAIEN SHIBA FOUGHT!
AND WHEN METASTACIA'S ROTTING SPIRITUAL BODY WAS RETURNED TO HUECO MUNDO...
...I CONSUMED IT AND TOOK HIS POWERS!

...ATE IT?!

YOU...

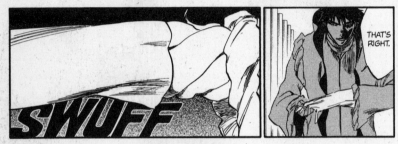

SWUFF

THAT'S RIGHT.

MY POWER IS CALLED GLOTONERÍA.

IT'S THE ABILITY TO CONSUME DEAD HOLLOWS AND TAKE THEIR SPIRIT ENERGY AND POWERS.

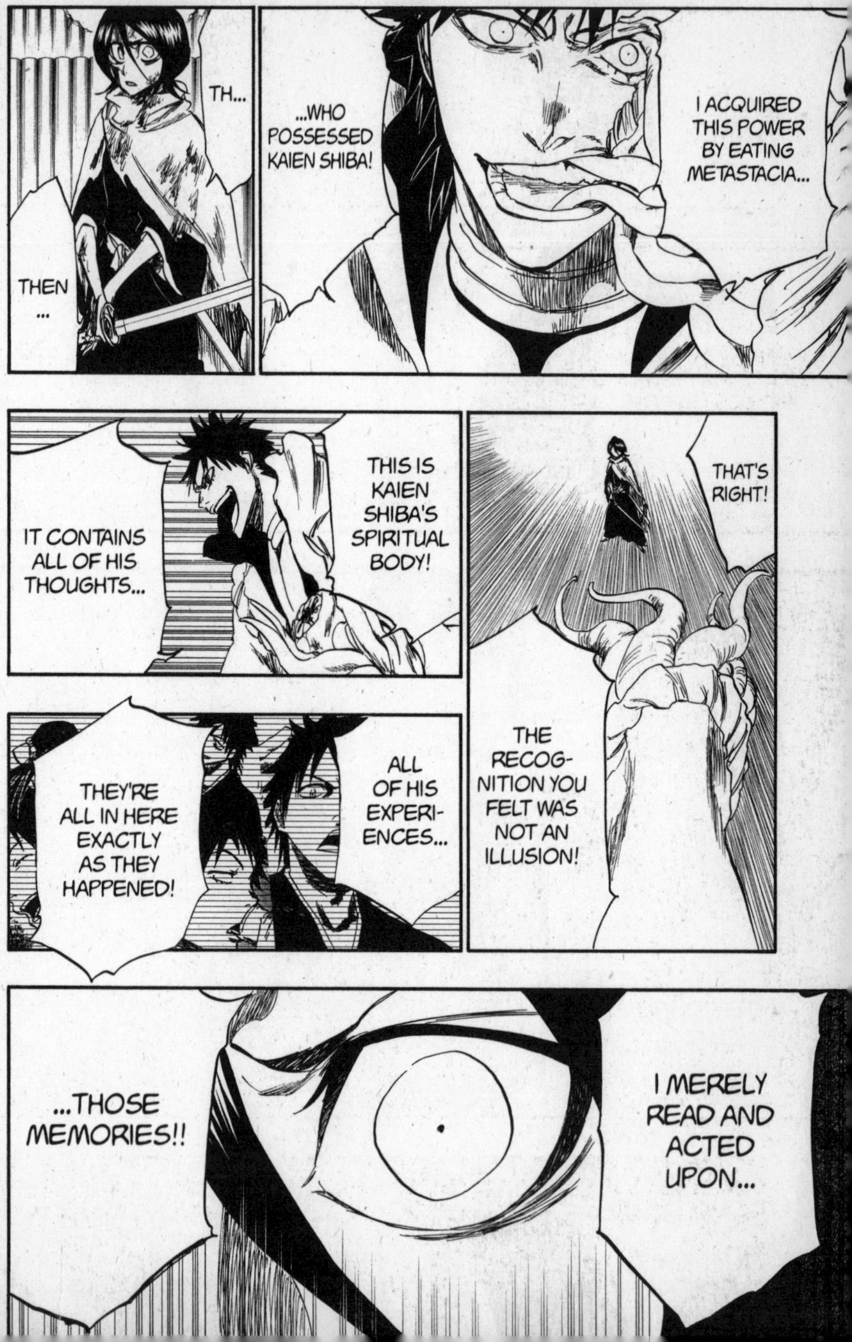
I ACQUIRED THIS POWER BY EATING METASTACIA...
...WHO POSSESSED KAIEN SHIBA!
TH...
THEN ...
THAT'S RIGHT!
THE RECOG-NITION YOU FELT WAS NOT AN ILLUSION!
THIS IS KAIEN SHIBA'S SPIRITUAL BODY!
IT CONTAINS ALL OF HIS THOUGHTS...
ALL OF HIS EXPERI-ENCES...
THEY'RE ALL IN HERE EXACTLY AS THEY HAPPENED!
I MERELY READ AND ACTED UPON...
...THOSE MEMORIES!!

READ THIS WAY

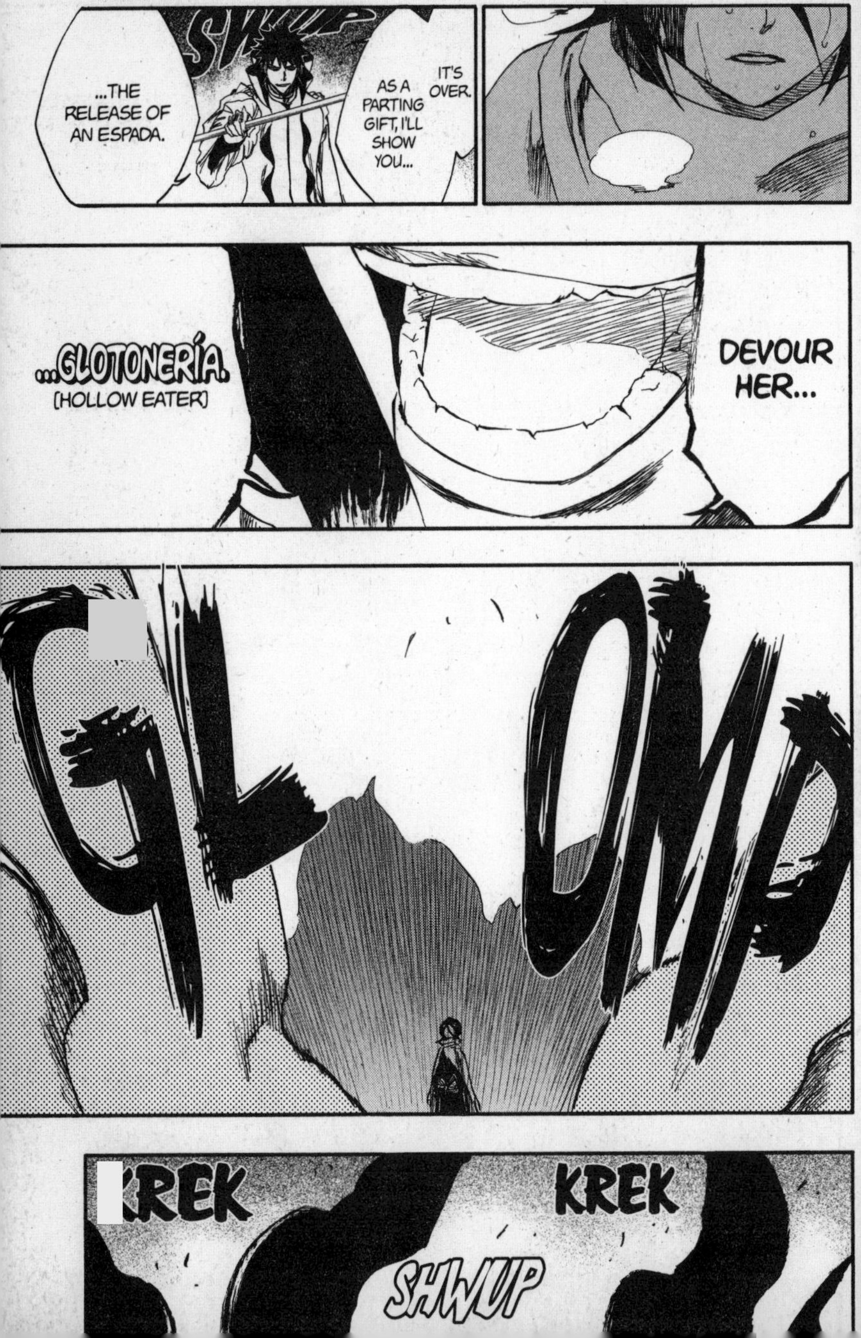
SHWUP
IT'S OVER.
AS A PARTING GIFT, I'LL SHOW YOU...
...THE RELEASE OF AN ESPADA.
DEVOUR HER...
...GLOTONERÍA.
[HOLLOW EATER]
GLOMP
KREK
KREK
SHWUP

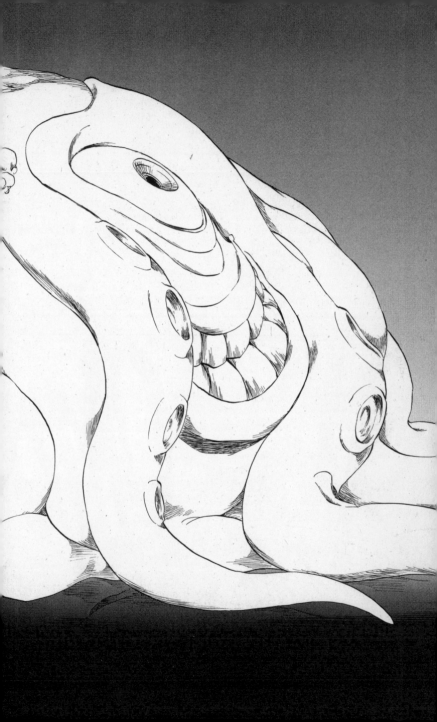

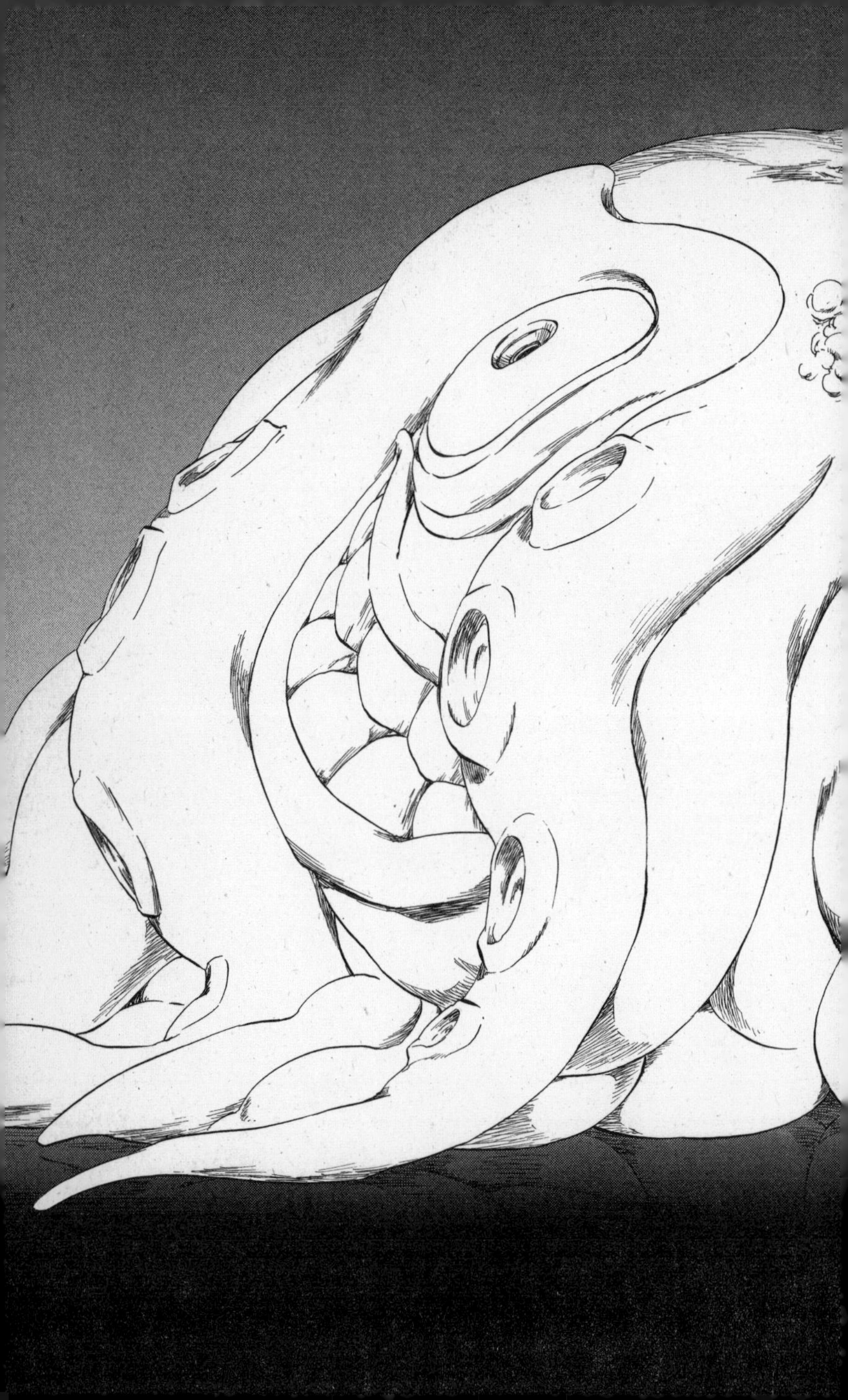

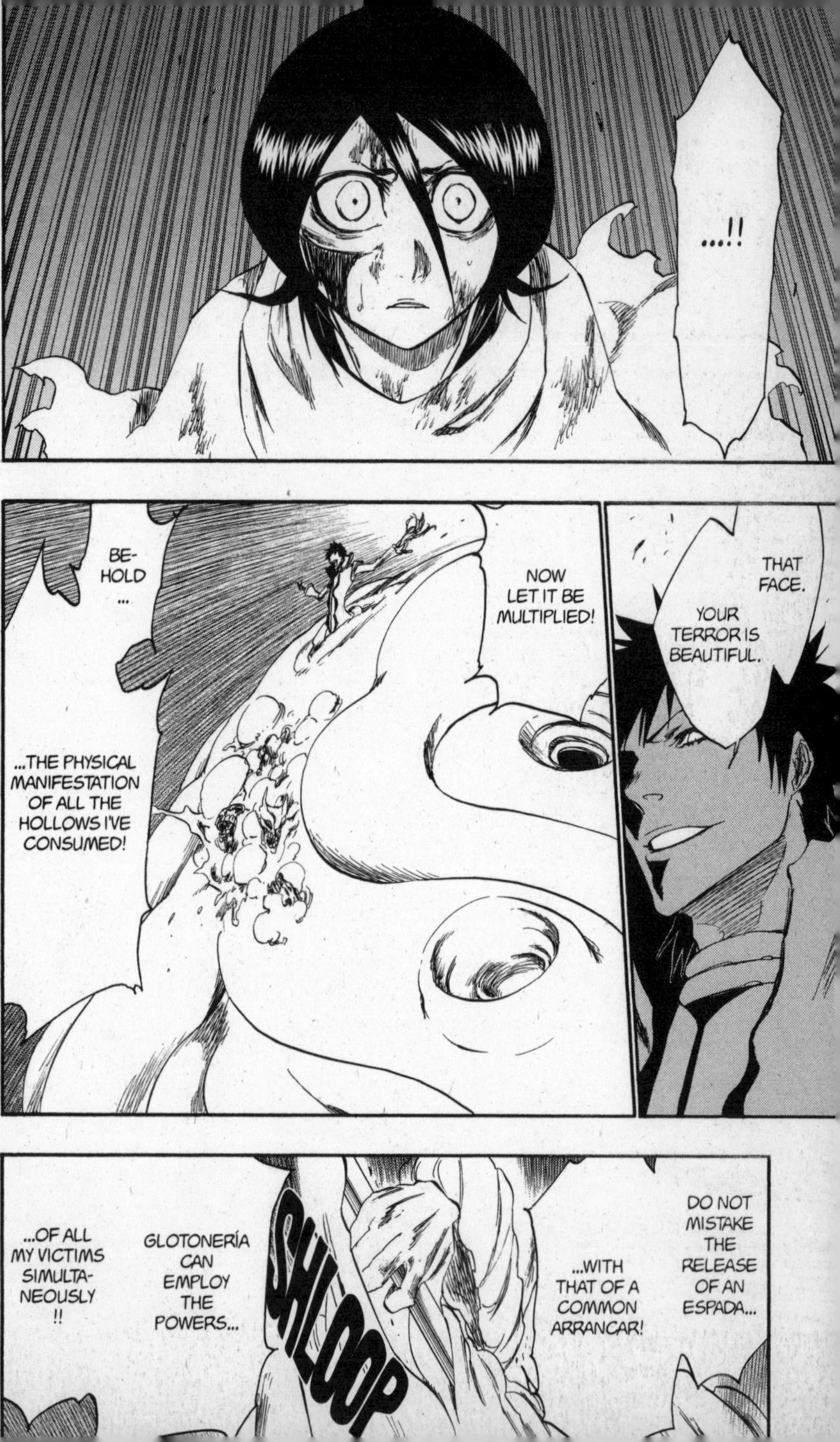
...!!
THAT FACE.
YOUR TERROR IS BEAUTIFUL.
NOW LET IT BE MULTIPLIED!
BE-HOLD ...
...THE PHYSICAL MANIFESTATION OF ALL THE HOLLOWS I'VE CONSUMED!
DO NOT MISTAKE THE RELEASE OF AN ESPADA...
...WITH THAT OF A COMMON ARRANCAR!
SHLOOP
GLOTONERÍA CAN EMPLOY THE POWERS...
...OF ALL MY VICTIMS SIMULTA-NEOUSLY !!

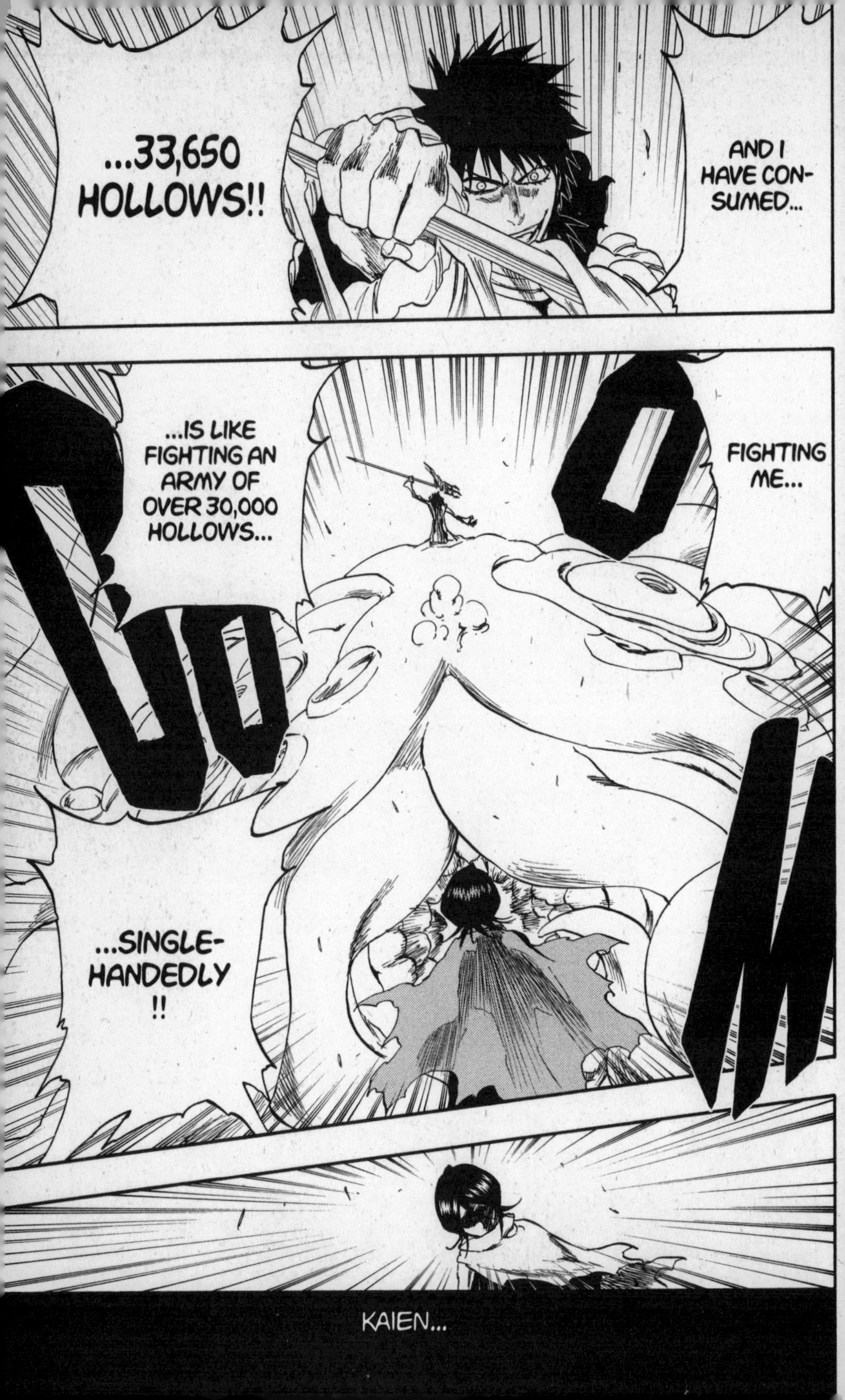
AND I HAVE CONSUMED...
...33,650 HOLLOWS!!
FIGHTING ME...
...IS LIKE FIGHTING AN ARMY OF OVER 30,000 HOLLOWS...
...SINGLE-HANDEDLY!!
KAIEN...

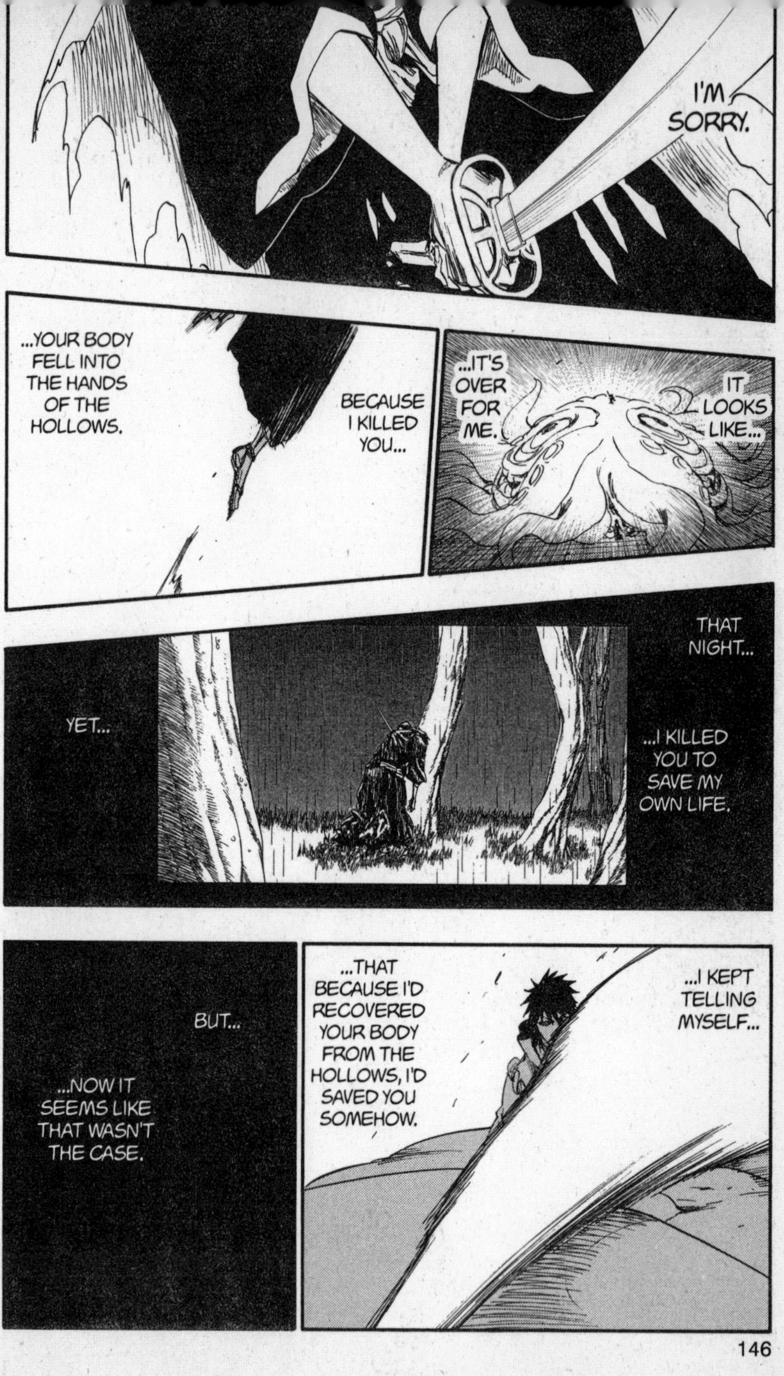
I'M SORRY.
IT LOOKS LIKE...
...IT'S OVER FOR ME.
BECAUSE I KILLED YOU...
...YOUR BODY FELL INTO THE HANDS OF THE HOLLOWS.
THAT NIGHT...
...I KILLED YOU TO SAVE MY OWN LIFE.
YET...
...I KEPT TELLING MYSELF...
...THAT BECAUSE I'D RECOVERED YOUR BODY FROM THE HOLLOWS, I'D SAVED YOU SOMEHOW.
BUT...
...NOW IT SEEMS LIKE THAT WASN'T THE CASE.

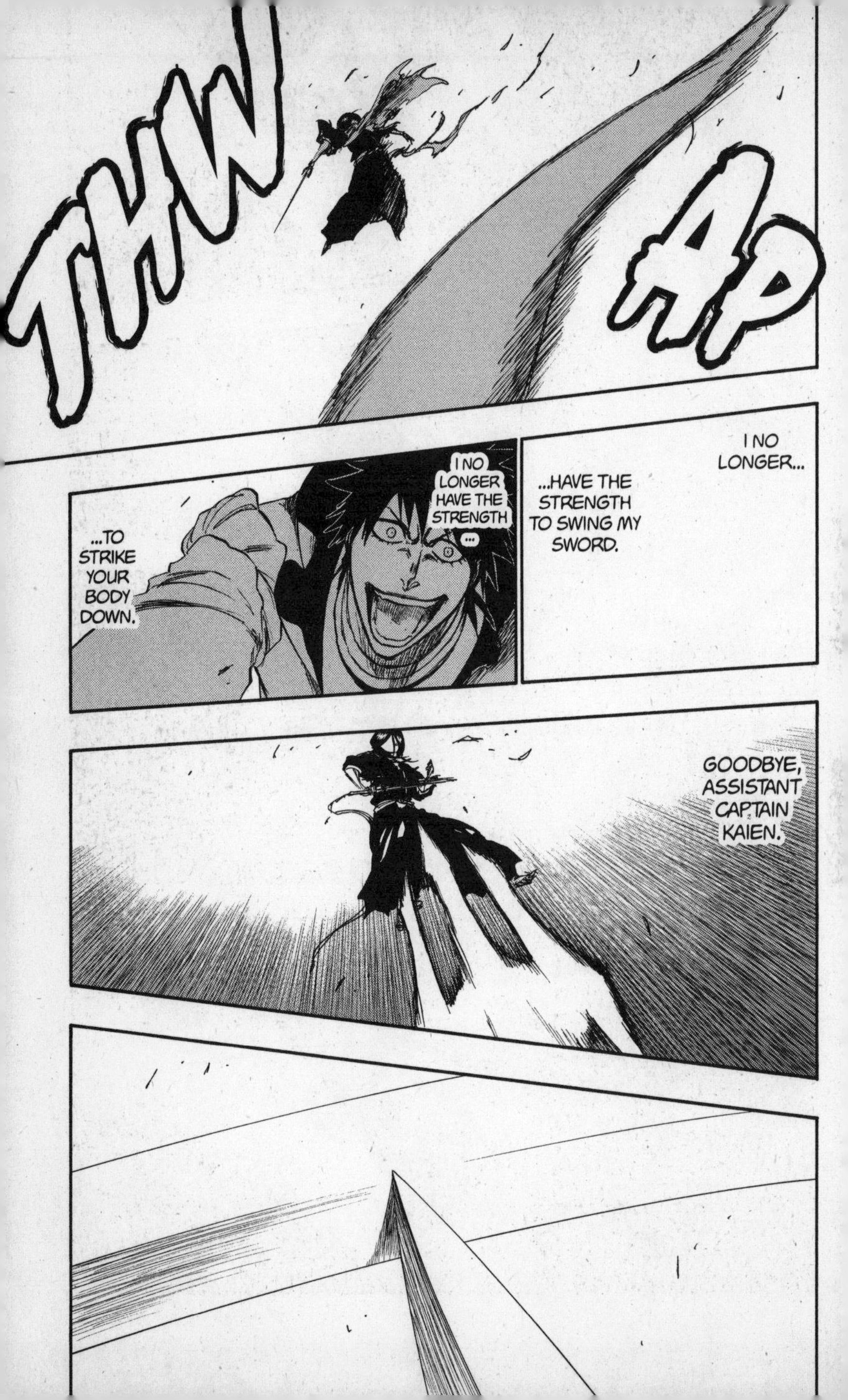
THWAP
I NO LONGER...
...HAVE THE STRENGTH TO SWING MY SWORD.
I NO LONGER HAVE THE STRENGTH ...
...TO STRIKE YOUR BODY DOWN.
GOODBYE, ASSISTANT CAPTAIN KAIEN.

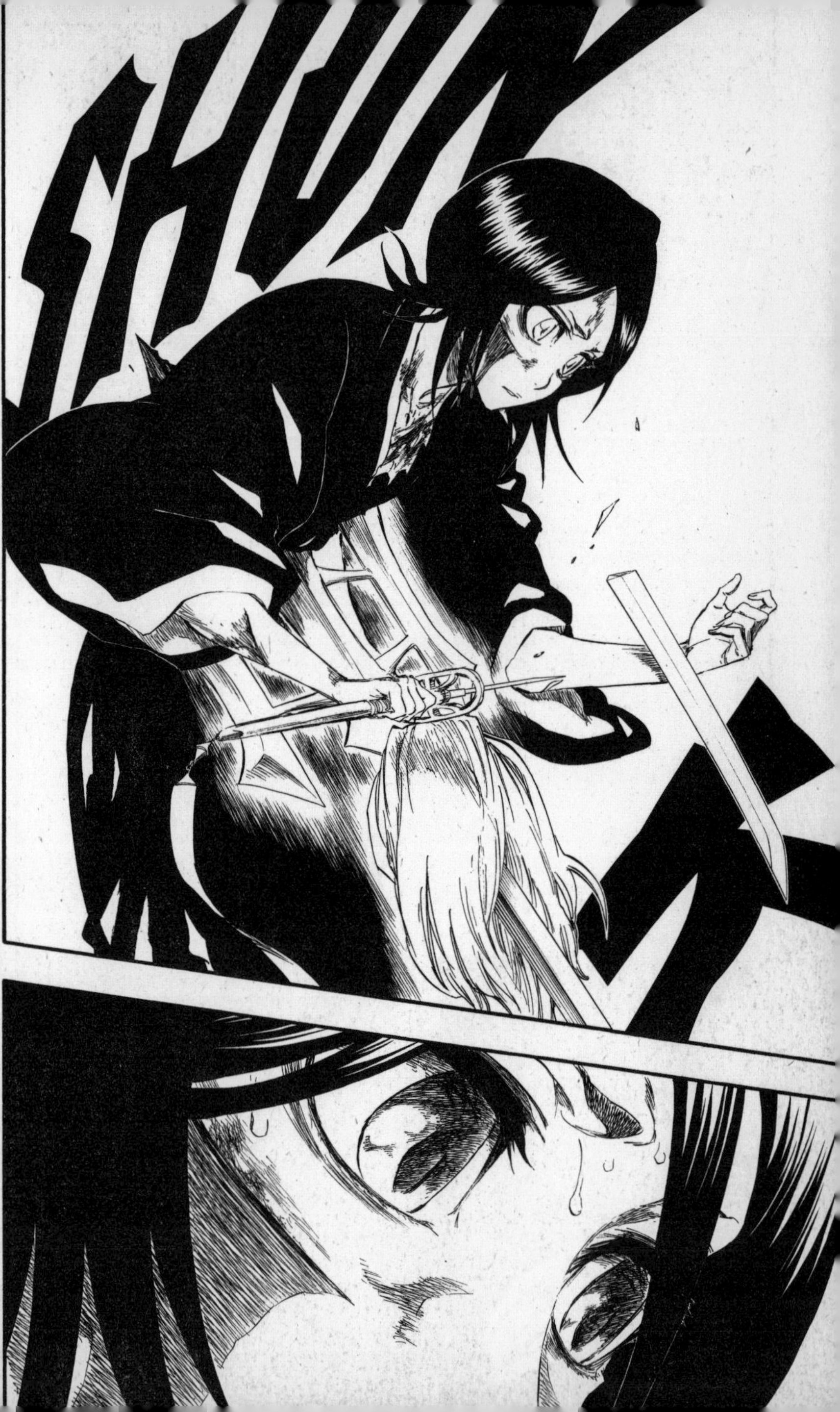
SHUNK

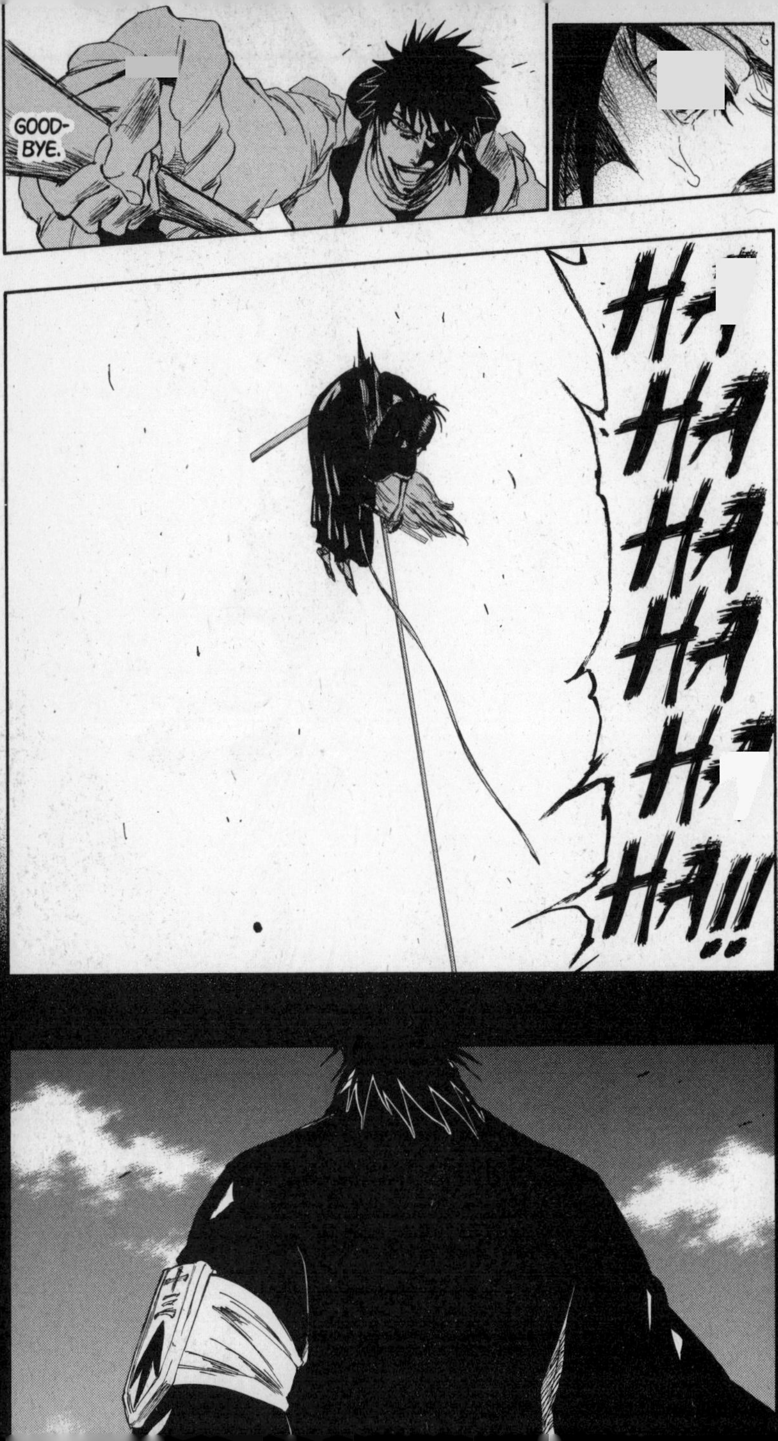
GOOD-BYE.
HA, HA HA HA HA HA!!

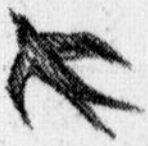

...what is your regret?

268. You Are Forbidden to Die

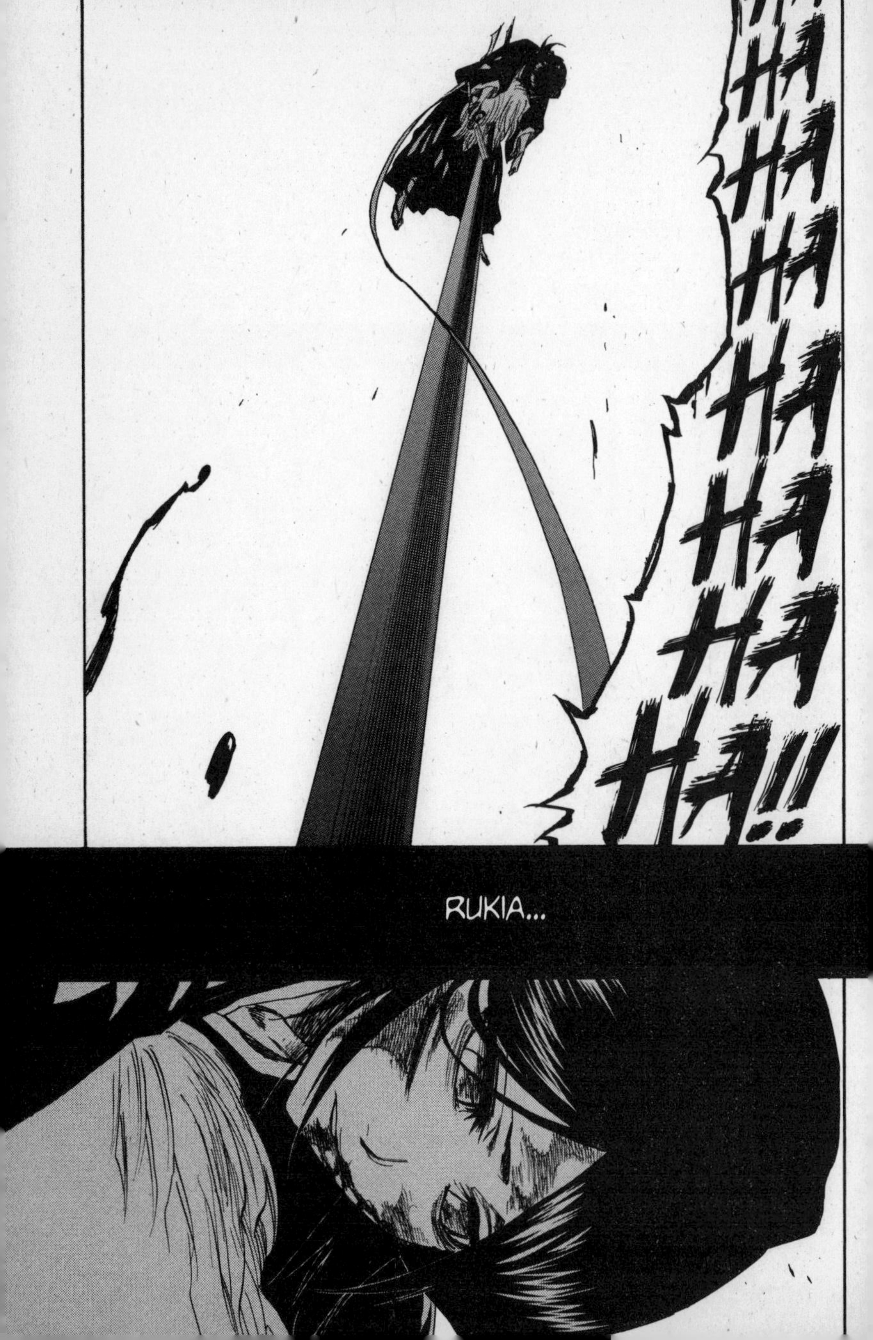
HAHAHAHAHAHAHAHAHAHAHAHAHAHAHAHAHAHAHAHAHAHAHAHAHAHA!!
RUKIA...

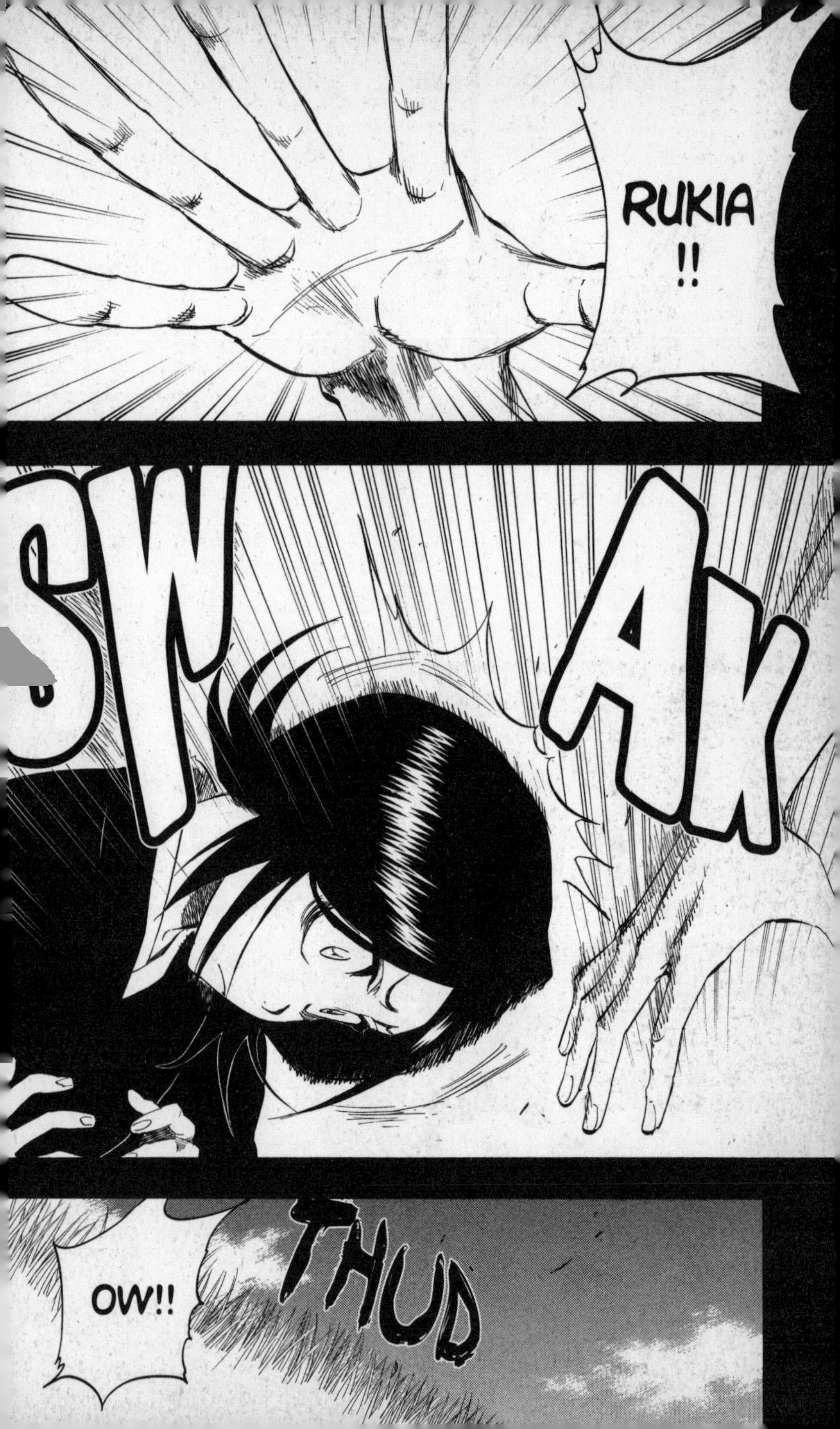
RUKIA !!
SWAK
OW!!
THUD

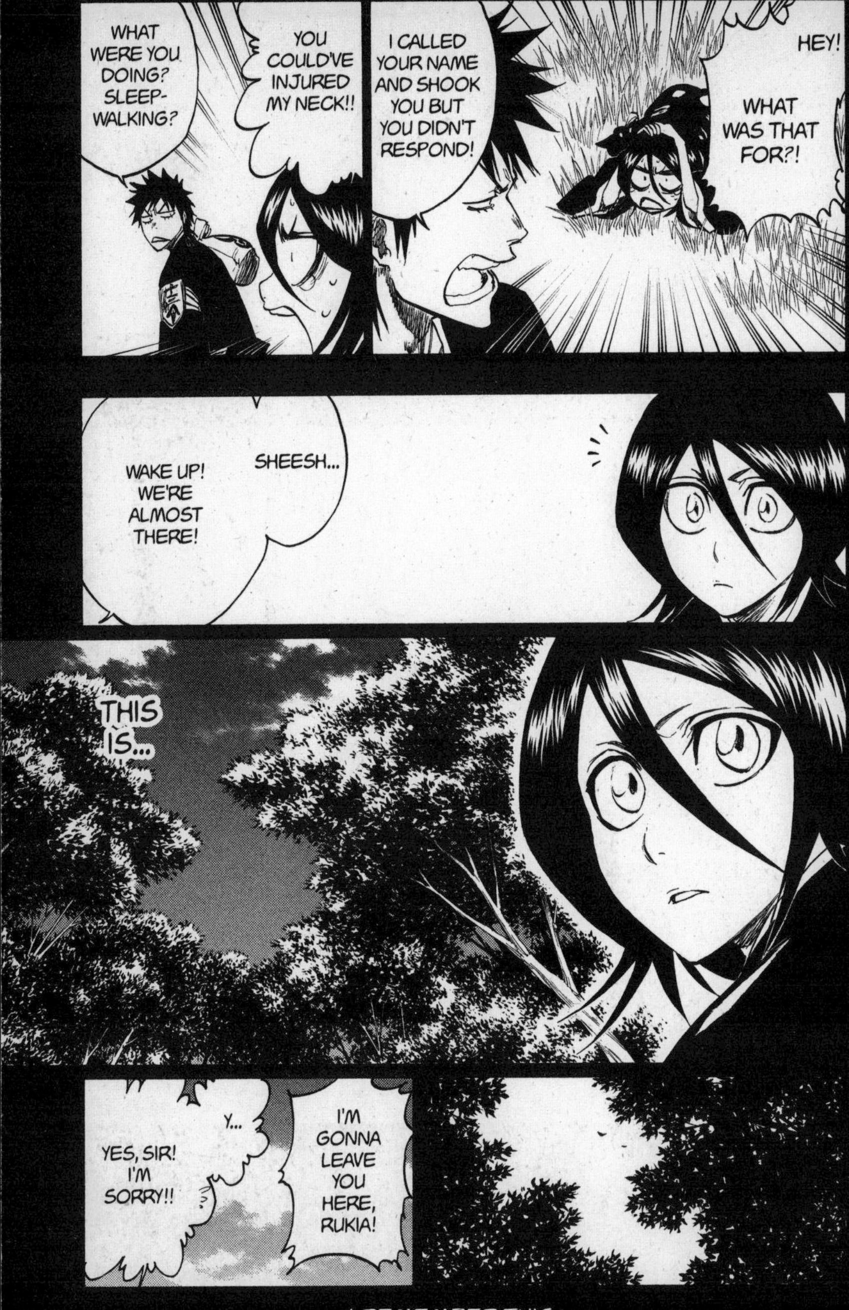
HEY!
WHAT WAS THAT FOR?!
I CALLED YOUR NAME AND SHOOK YOU BUT YOU DIDN'T RESPOND!
YOU COULD'VE INJURED MY NECK!!
WHAT WERE YOU DOING? SLEEP-WALKING?
SHEESH...
WAKE UP! WE'RE ALMOST THERE!
THIS IS...
I'M GONNA LEAVE YOU HERE, RUKIA!
Y...
YES, SIR! I'M SORRY!!

I REMEMBER THIS.

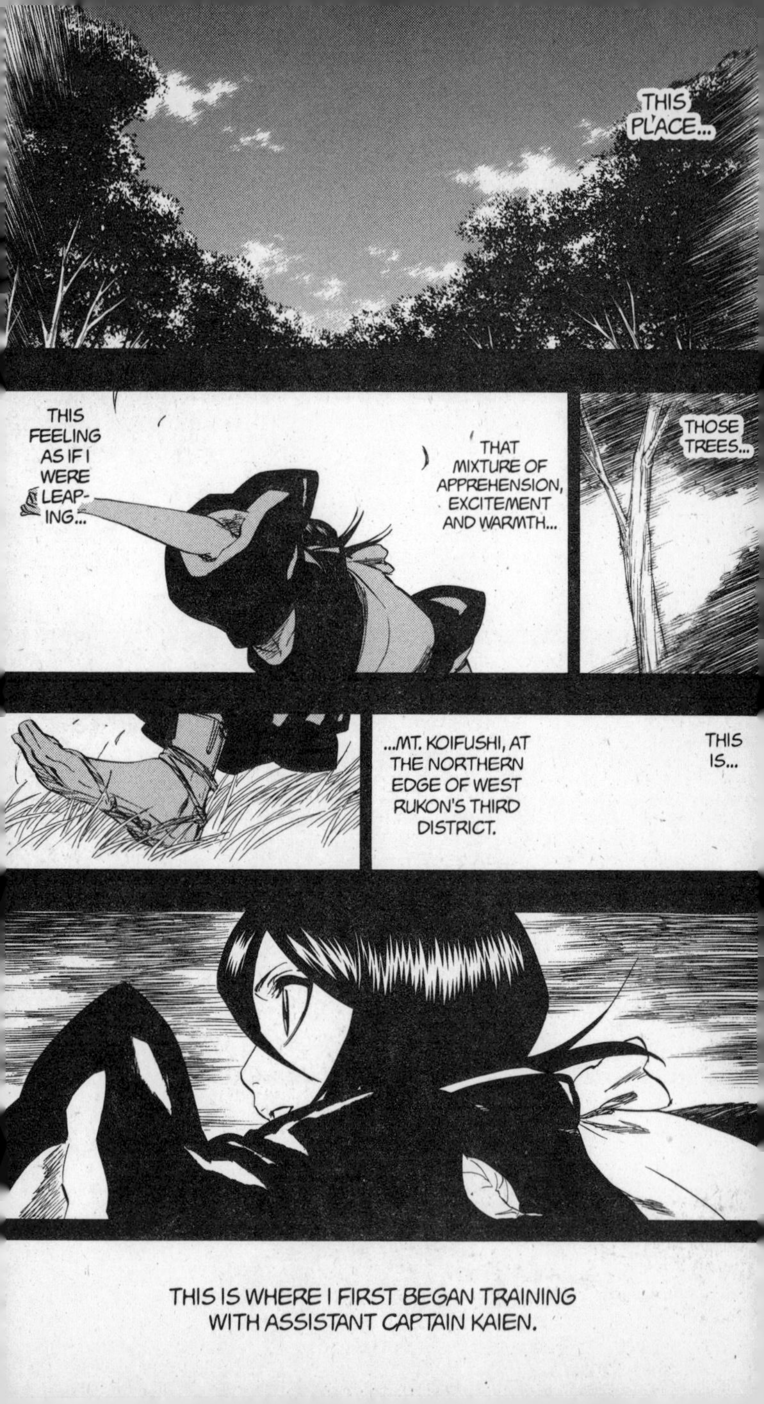
THIS PLACE...
THOSE TREES...
THAT MIXTURE OF APPREHENSION, EXCITEMENT AND WARMTH...
THIS FEELING AS IF I WERE LEAPING...
THIS IS...
...MT. KOIFUSHI, AT THE NORTHERN EDGE OF WEST RUKON'S THIRD DISTRICT.
THIS IS WHERE I FIRST BEGAN TRAINING WITH ASSISTANT CAPTAIN KAIEN.

BLEACH 268.

You Are Forbidden to Die

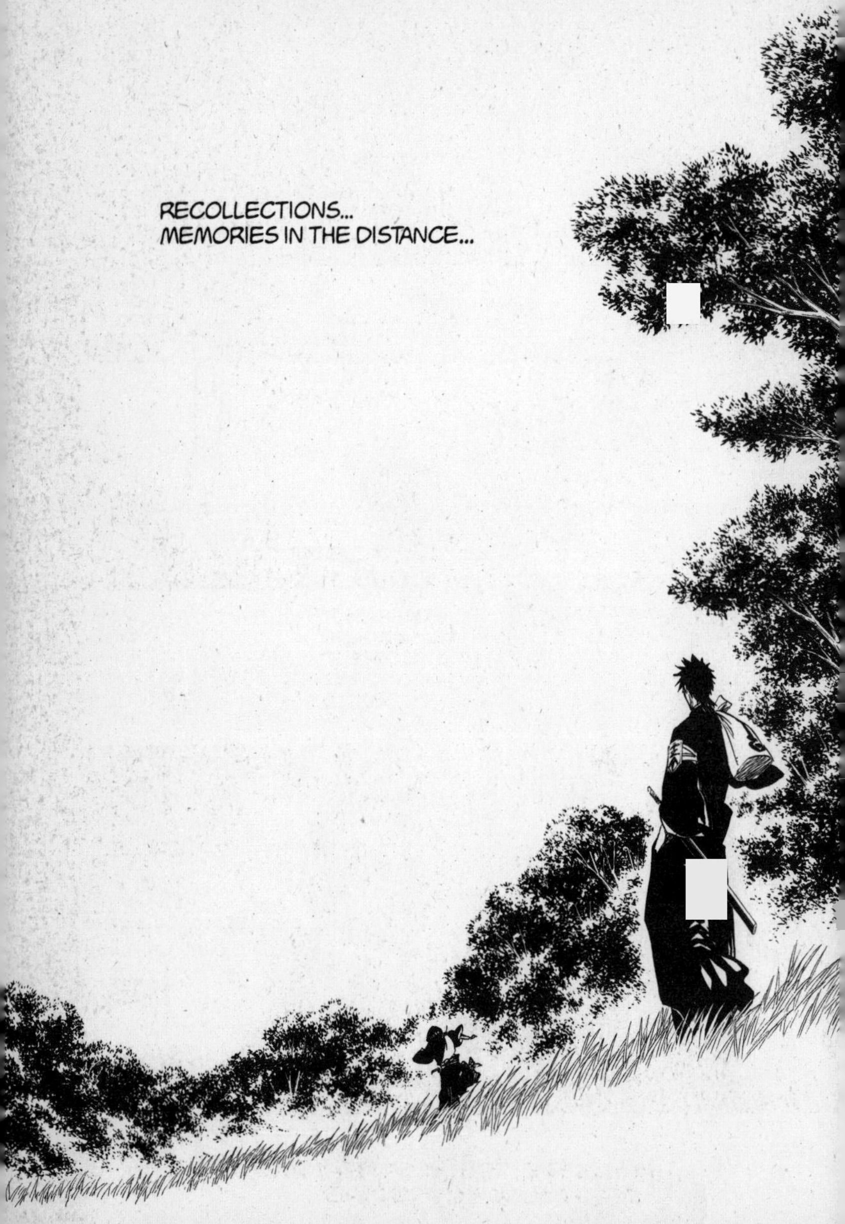
RECOLLECTIONS...
MEMORIES IN THE DISTANCE...

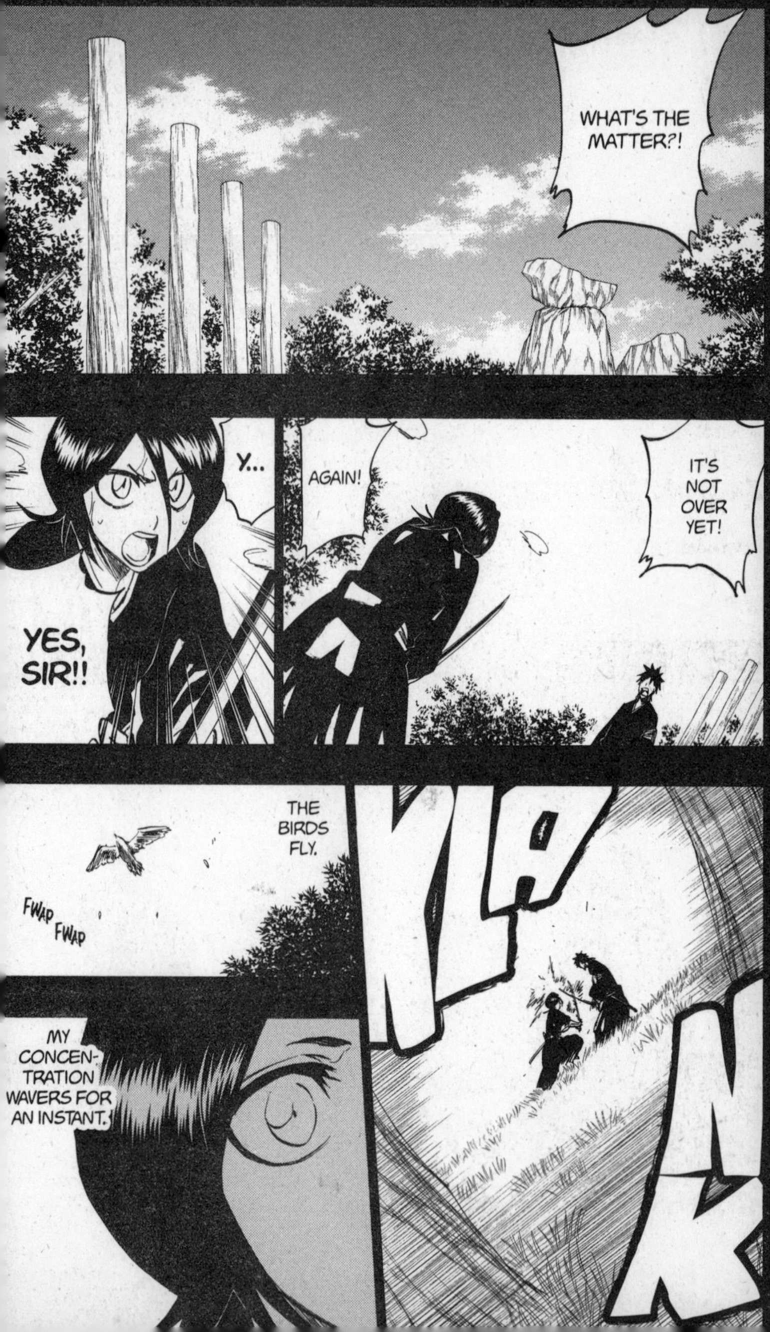
WHAT'S THE MATTER?!
IT'S NOT OVER YET!
AGAIN!
Y...
YES, SIR!!
THE BIRDS FLY.
FWAP FWAP
MY CONCENTRATION WAVERS FOR AN INSTANT.

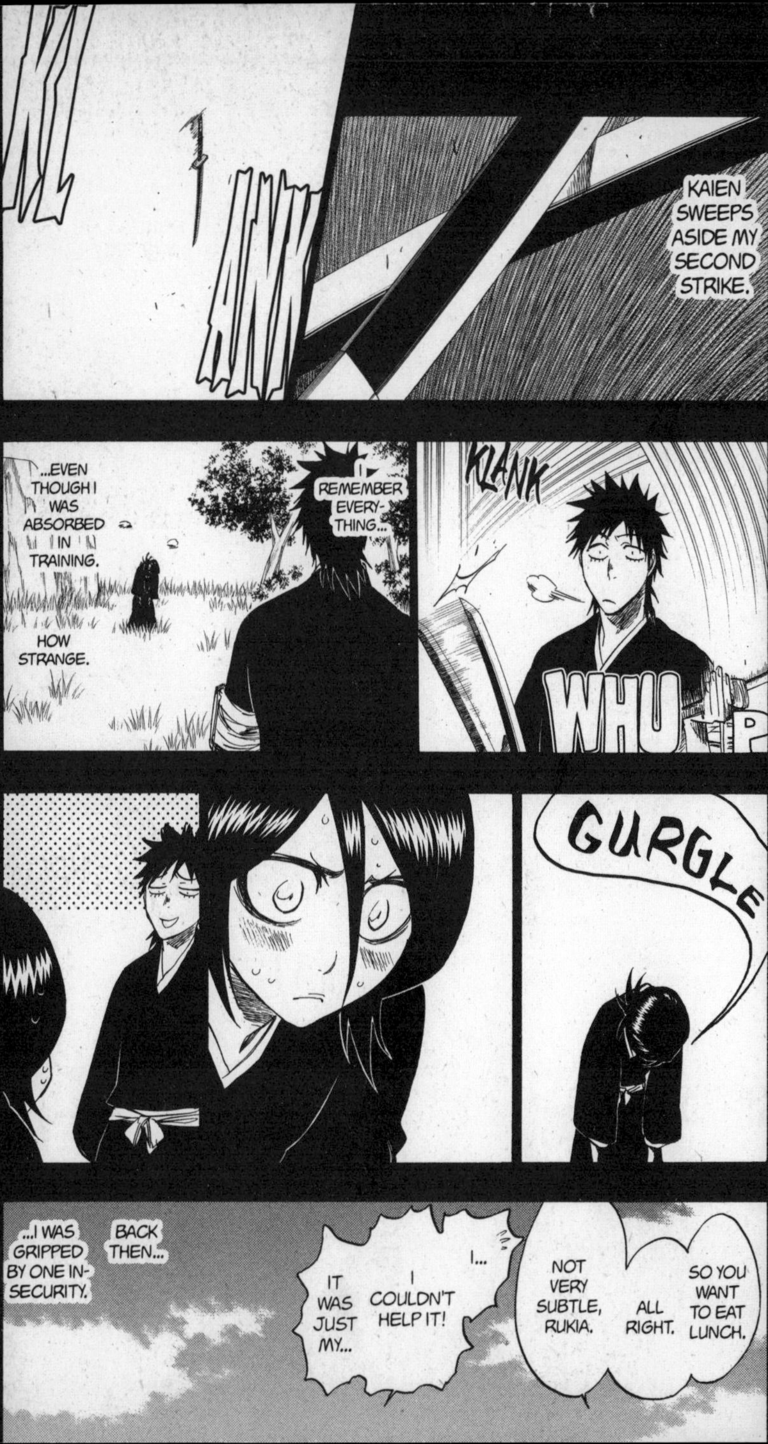
KAIEN SWEEPS ASIDE MY SECOND STRIKE.
KLANK
KLANK
WHUP
I REMEMBER EVERYTHING...
...EVEN THOUGH I WAS ABSORBED IN TRAINING.
HOW STRANGE.
GURGLE
SO YOU WANT TO EAT LUNCH.
ALL RIGHT.
NOT VERY SUBTLE, RUKIA.
I...
I COULDN'T HELP IT!
IT WAS JUST MY...
BACK THEN...
...I WAS GRIPPED BY ONE IN-SECURITY.

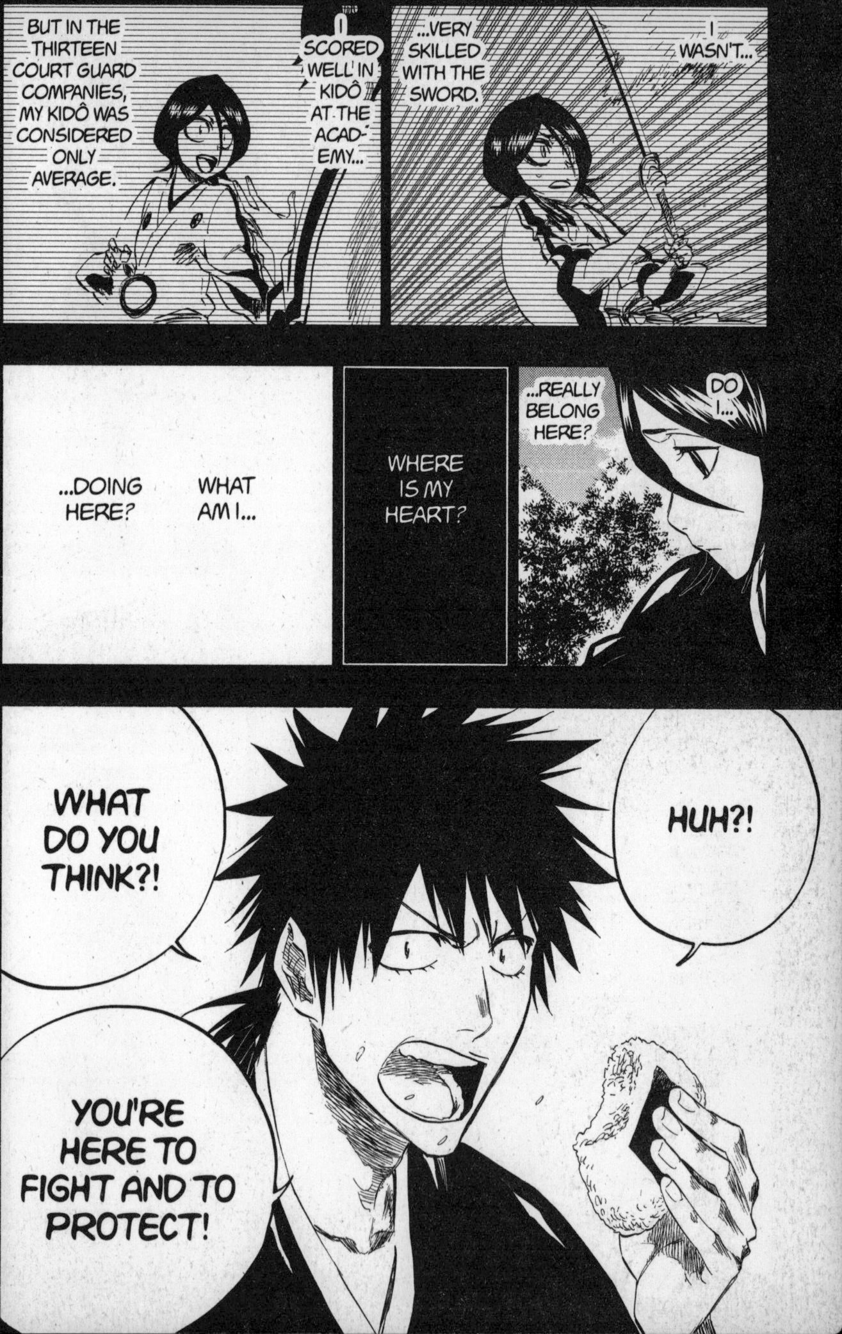
I WASN'T...
...VERY SKILLED WITH THE SWORD.
I SCORED WELL IN KIDÔ AT THE ACADEMY...
BUT IN THE THIRTEEN COURT GUARD COMPANIES, MY KIDÔ WAS CONSIDERED ONLY AVERAGE.
DO I...
...REALLY BELONG HERE?
WHERE IS MY HEART?
WHAT AM I...
...DOING HERE?
HUH?!
WHAT DO YOU THINK?!
YOU'RE HERE TO FIGHT AND TO PROTECT!

READ THIS WAY

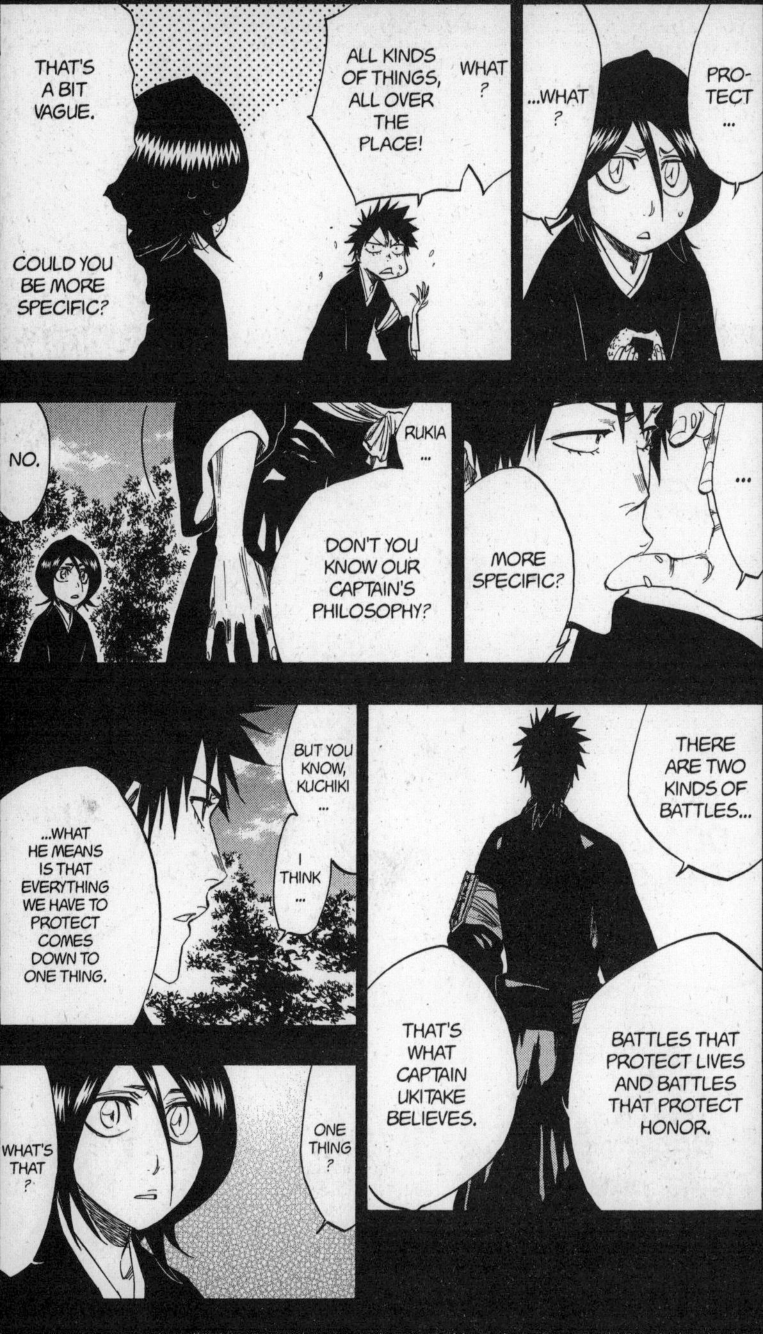
PRO-TECT ...
...WHAT?
WHAT?
ALL KINDS OF THINGS, ALL OVER THE PLACE!
THAT'S A BIT VAGUE.
COULD YOU BE MORE SPECIFIC?
...
MORE SPECIFIC?
RUKIA ...
DON'T YOU KNOW OUR CAPTAIN'S PHILOSOPHY?
NO.
THERE ARE TWO KINDS OF BATTLES...
BATTLES THAT PROTECT LIVES AND BATTLES THAT PROTECT HONOR.
THAT'S WHAT CAPTAIN UKITAKE BELIEVES.
BUT YOU KNOW, KUCHIKI ...
I THINK ...
...WHAT HE MEANS IS THAT EVERYTHING WE HAVE TO PROTECT COMES DOWN TO ONE THING.
ONE THING?
WHAT'S THAT?

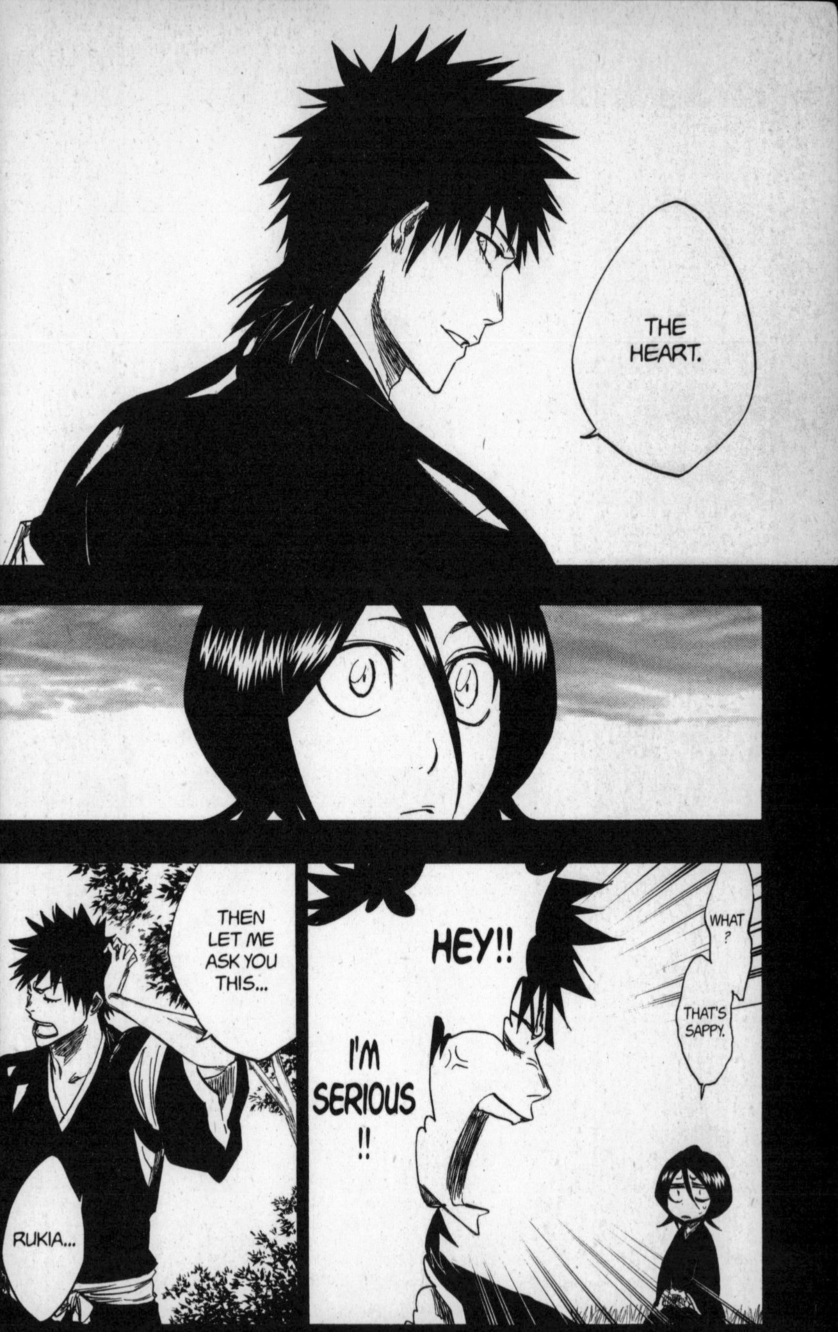
THE HEART.
WHAT?
THAT'S SAPPY.
HEY!!
I'M SERIOUS!!
THEN LET ME ASK YOU THIS...
RUKIA...

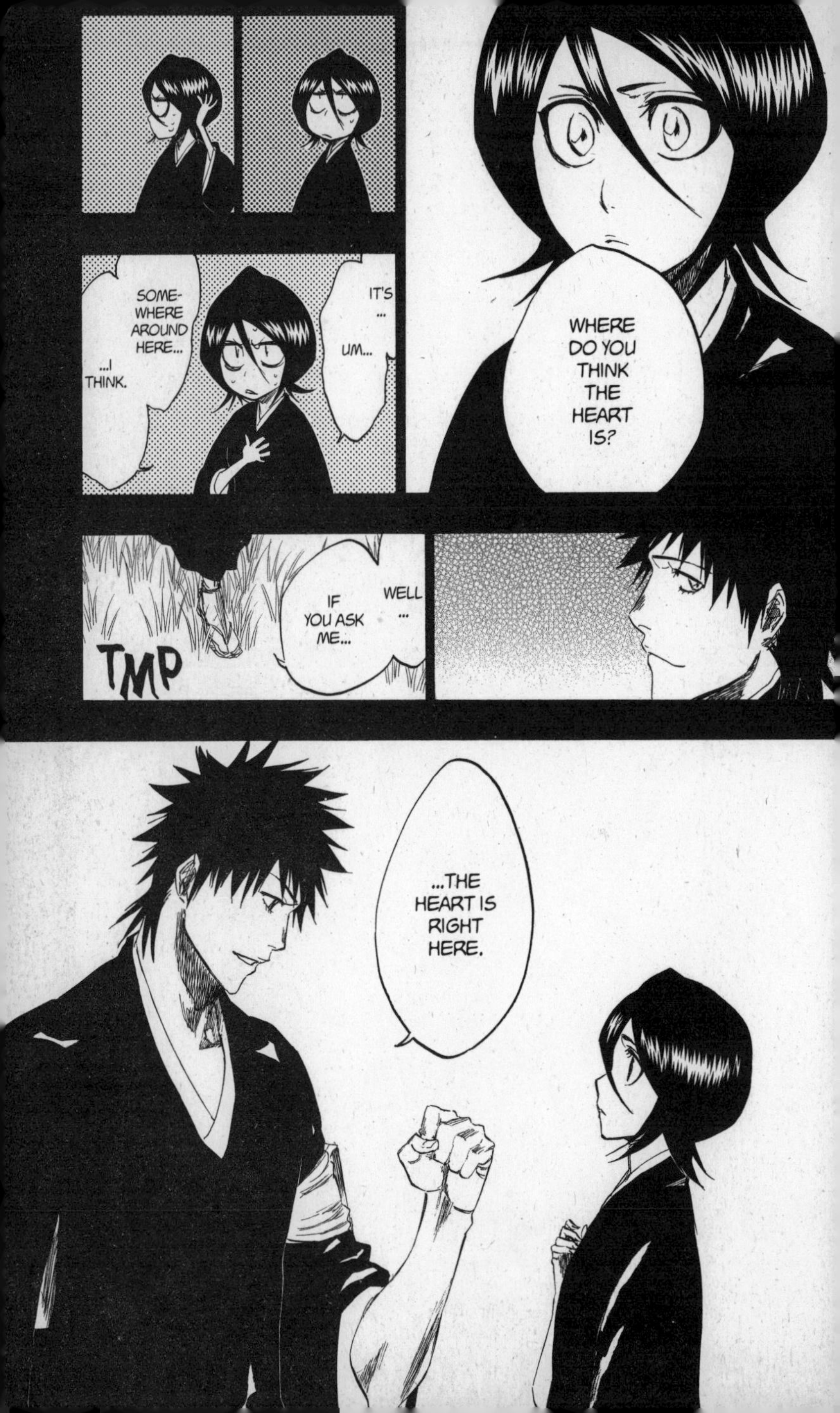
WHERE DO YOU THINK THE HEART IS?
IT'S ... UM...
SOME-WHERE AROUND HERE... ...I THINK.
WELL ... IF YOU ASK ME...
TMP
...THE HEART IS RIGHT HERE.

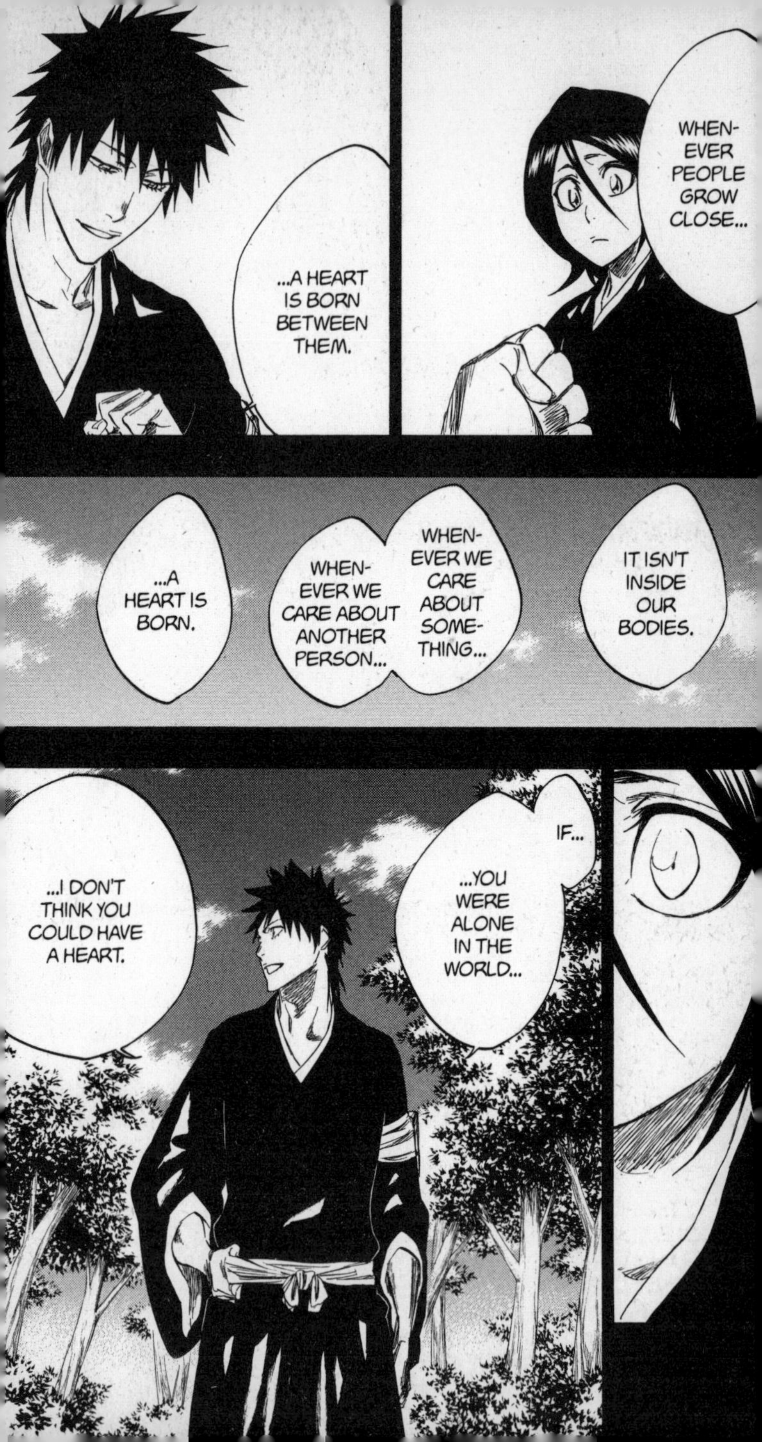
WHEN-EVER PEOPLE GROW CLOSE...
...A HEART IS BORN BETWEEN THEM.
IT ISN'T INSIDE OUR BODIES.
WHEN-EVER WE CARE ABOUT SOME-THING...
WHEN-EVER WE CARE ABOUT ANOTHER PERSON...
...A HEART IS BORN.
IF...
...YOU WERE ALONE IN THE WORLD...
...I DON'T THINK YOU COULD HAVE A HEART.

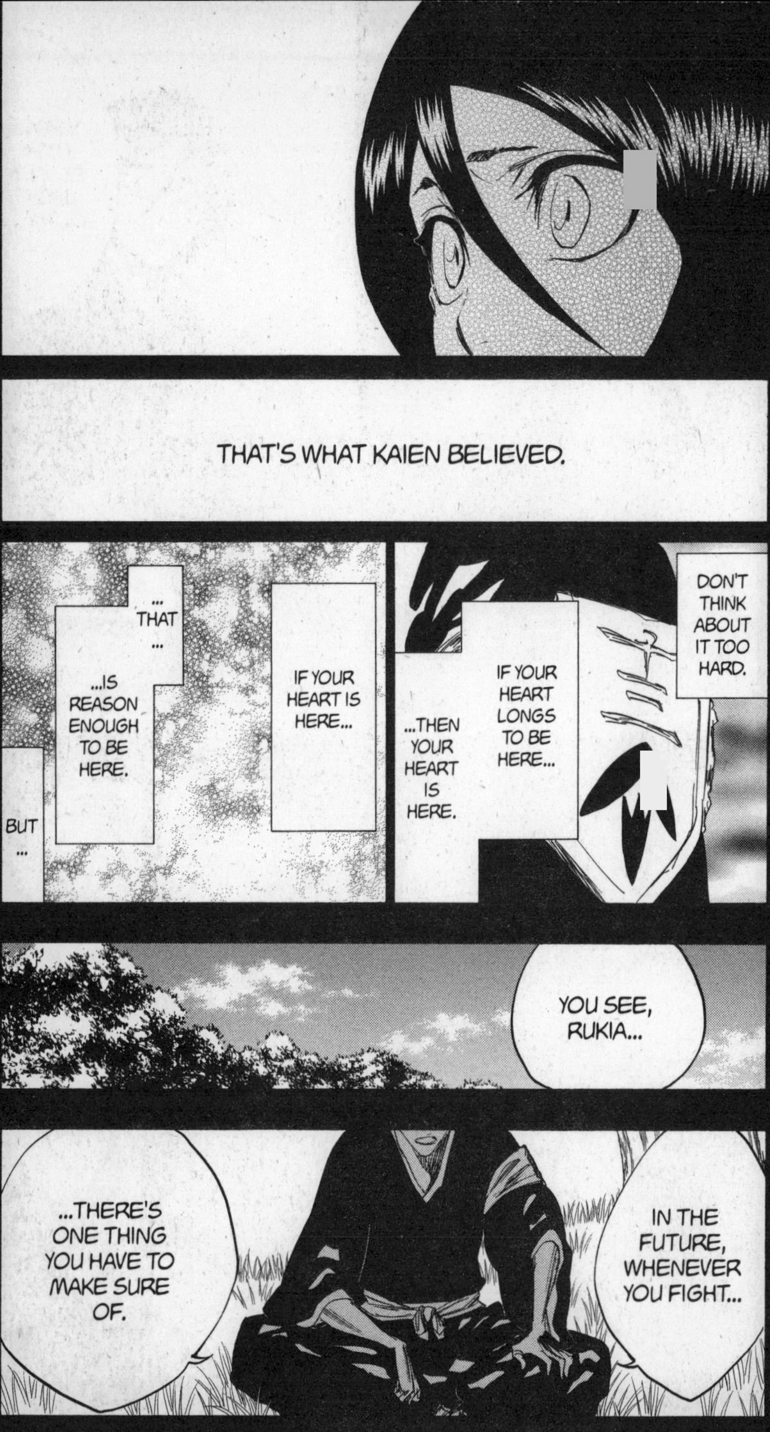
THAT'S WHAT KAIEN BELIEVED.
DON'T THINK ABOUT IT TOO HARD.
IF YOUR HEART LONGS TO BE HERE...
...THEN YOUR HEART IS HERE.
IF YOUR HEART IS HERE...
...THAT...
...IS REASON ENOUGH TO BE HERE.
BUT...
YOU SEE, RUKIA...
IN THE FUTURE, WHENEVER YOU FIGHT...
...THERE'S ONE THING YOU HAVE TO MAKE SURE OF.

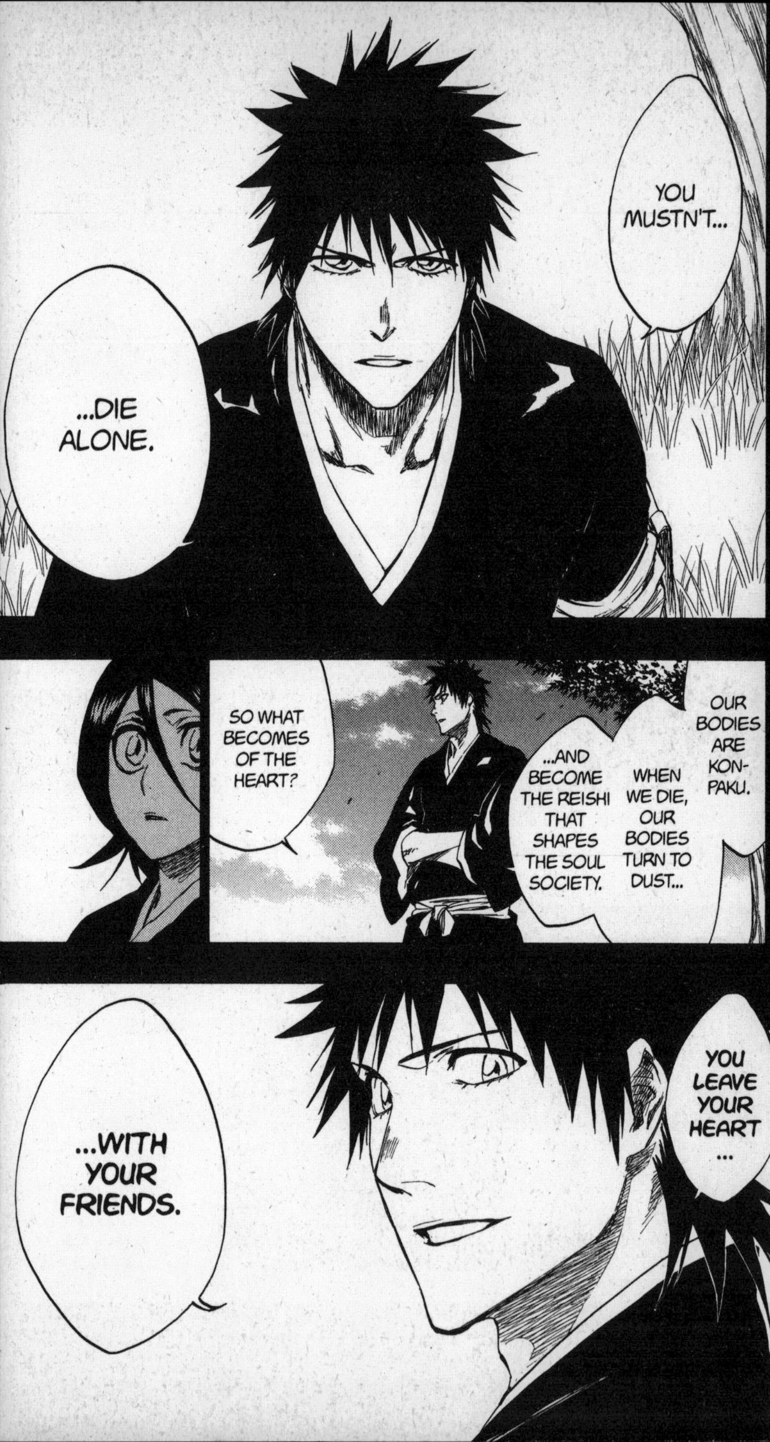
YOU MUSTN'T...
...DIE ALONE.
OUR BODIES ARE KON-PAKU.
WHEN WE DIE, OUR BODIES TURN TO DUST...
...AND BECOME THE REISHI THAT SHAPES THE SOUL SOCIETY.
SO WHAT BECOMES OF THE HEART?
YOU LEAVE YOUR HEART...
...WITH YOUR FRIENDS.

READ THIS WAY

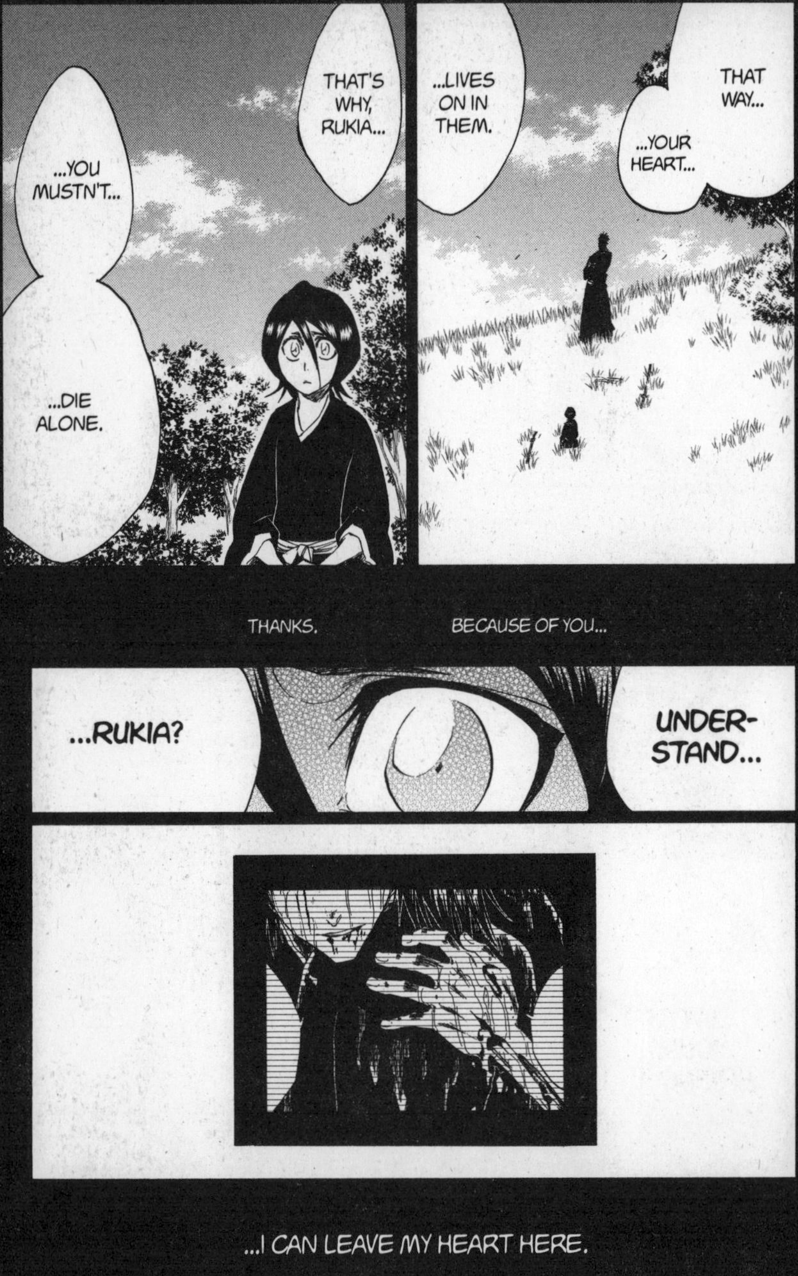
THAT WAY...
...YOUR HEART...
...LIVES ON IN THEM.
THAT'S WHY, RUKIA...
...YOU MUSTN'T...
...DIE ALONE.
BECAUSE OF YOU...
THANKS.
UNDER-STAND...
...RUKIA?
...I CAN LEAVE MY HEART HERE.

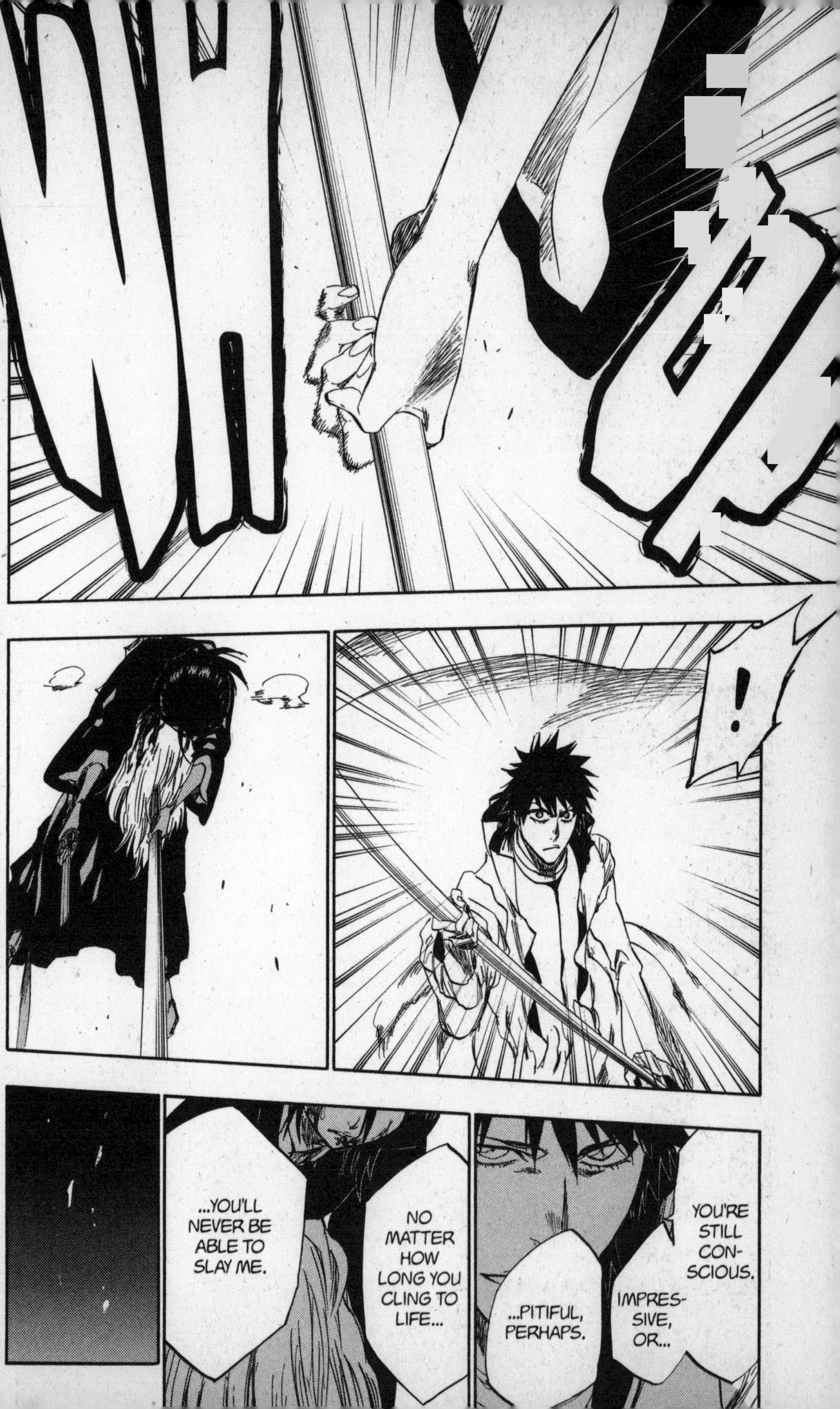
!
YOU'RE STILL CONSCIOUS.
IMPRESSIVE, OR...
...PITIFUL, PERHAPS.
NO MATTER HOW LONG YOU CLING TO LIFE...
...YOU'LL NEVER BE ABLE TO SLAY ME.

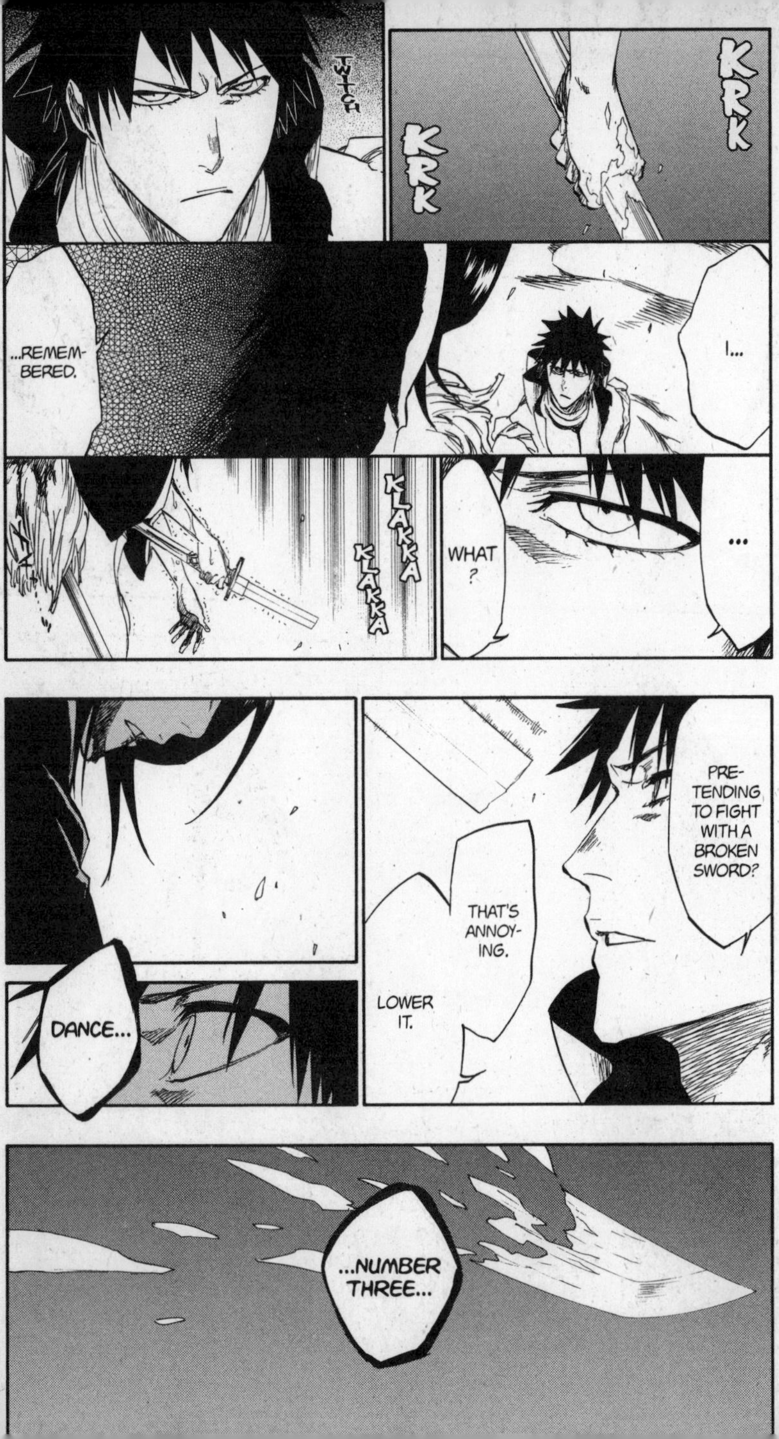
KRK
KRK
TWITCH
I...
...REMEM-
BERED.
...
WHAT
?
KLAKKA
KLAKKA
PRE-
TENDING
TO FIGHT
WITH A
BROKEN
SWORD?
THAT'S
ANNOY-
ING.
LOWER
IT.
DANCE...
...NUMBER
THREE...

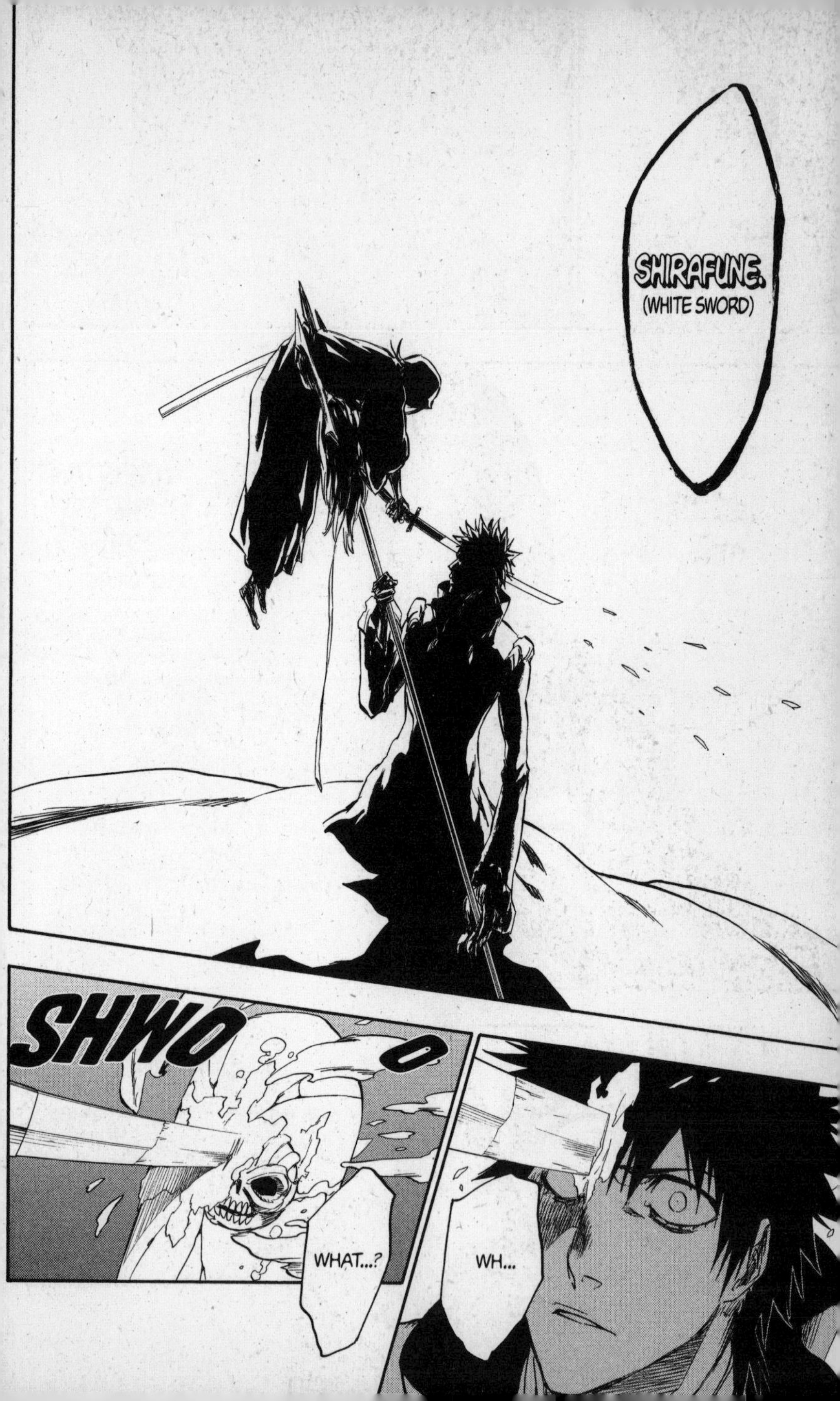
SHIRAFUNE.
(WHITE SWORD)
WH...
SHWO O
WHAT...?

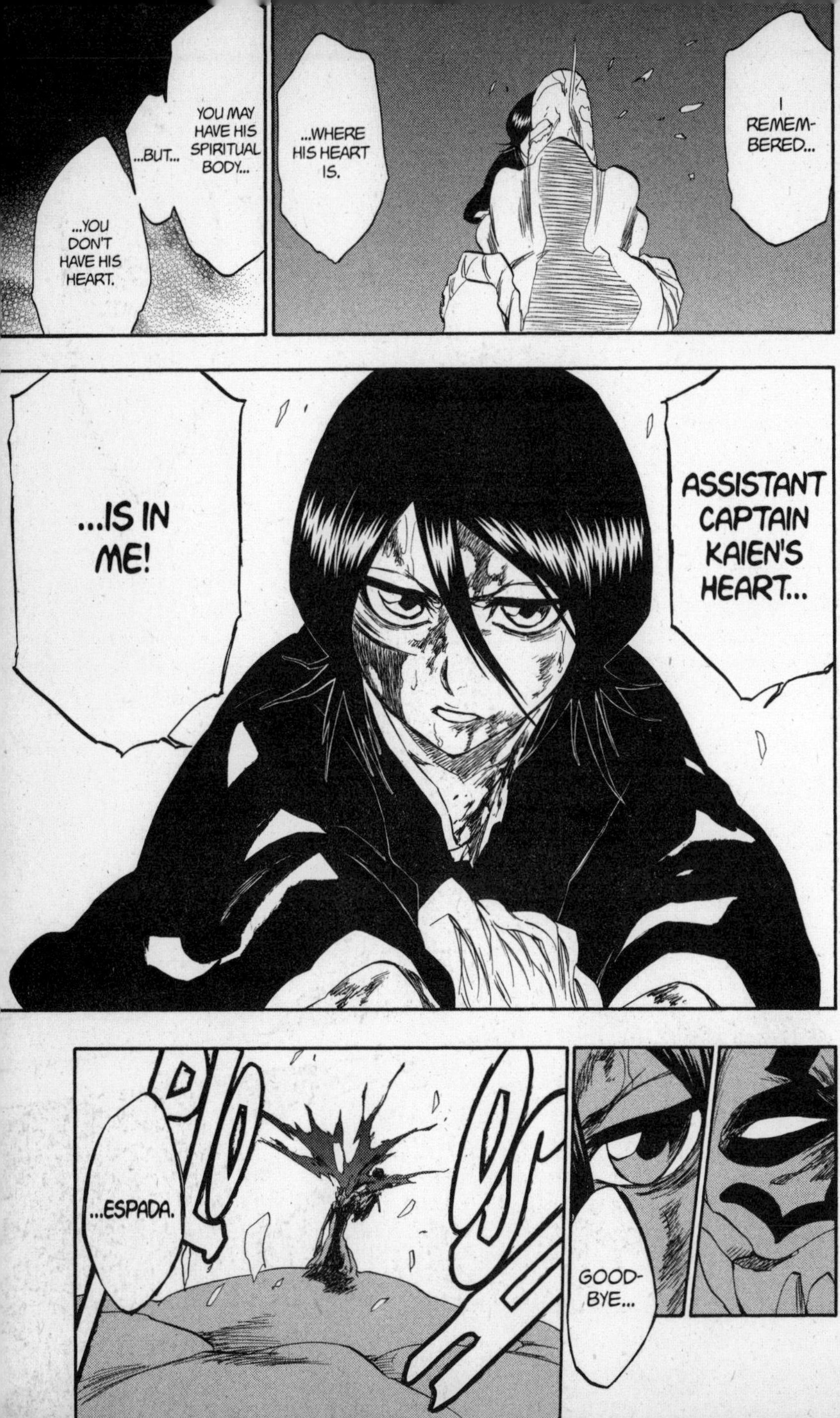
I REMEMBERED...
...WHERE HIS HEART IS.
YOU MAY HAVE HIS SPIRITUAL BODY...
...BUT...
...YOU DON'T HAVE HIS HEART.
ASSISTANT CAPTAIN KAIEN'S HEART...
...IS IN ME!
GOOD-BYE...
...ESPADA.

there is
no heart

without you.

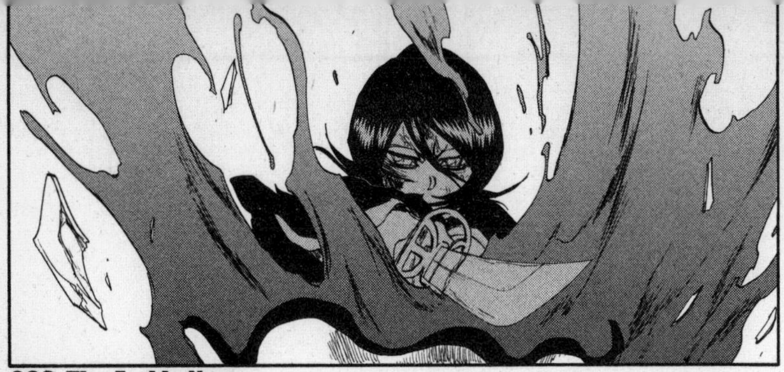

269. The End Is Near

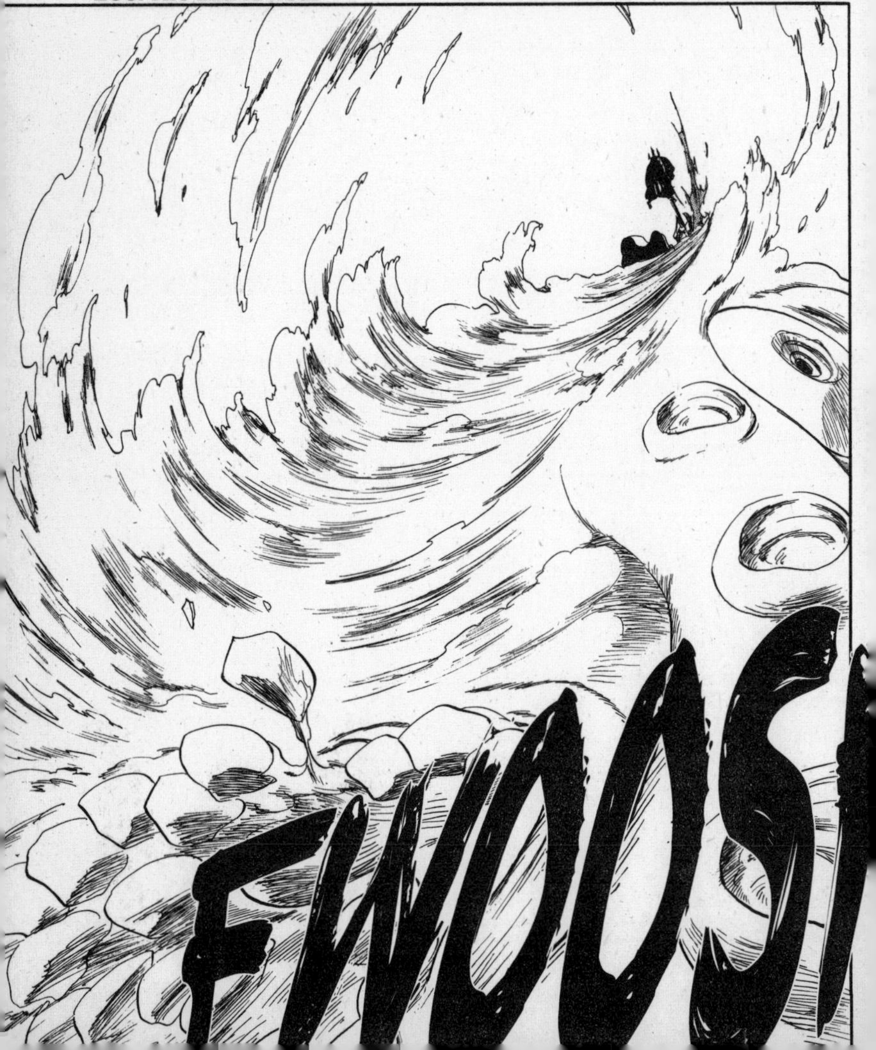
FWOOS

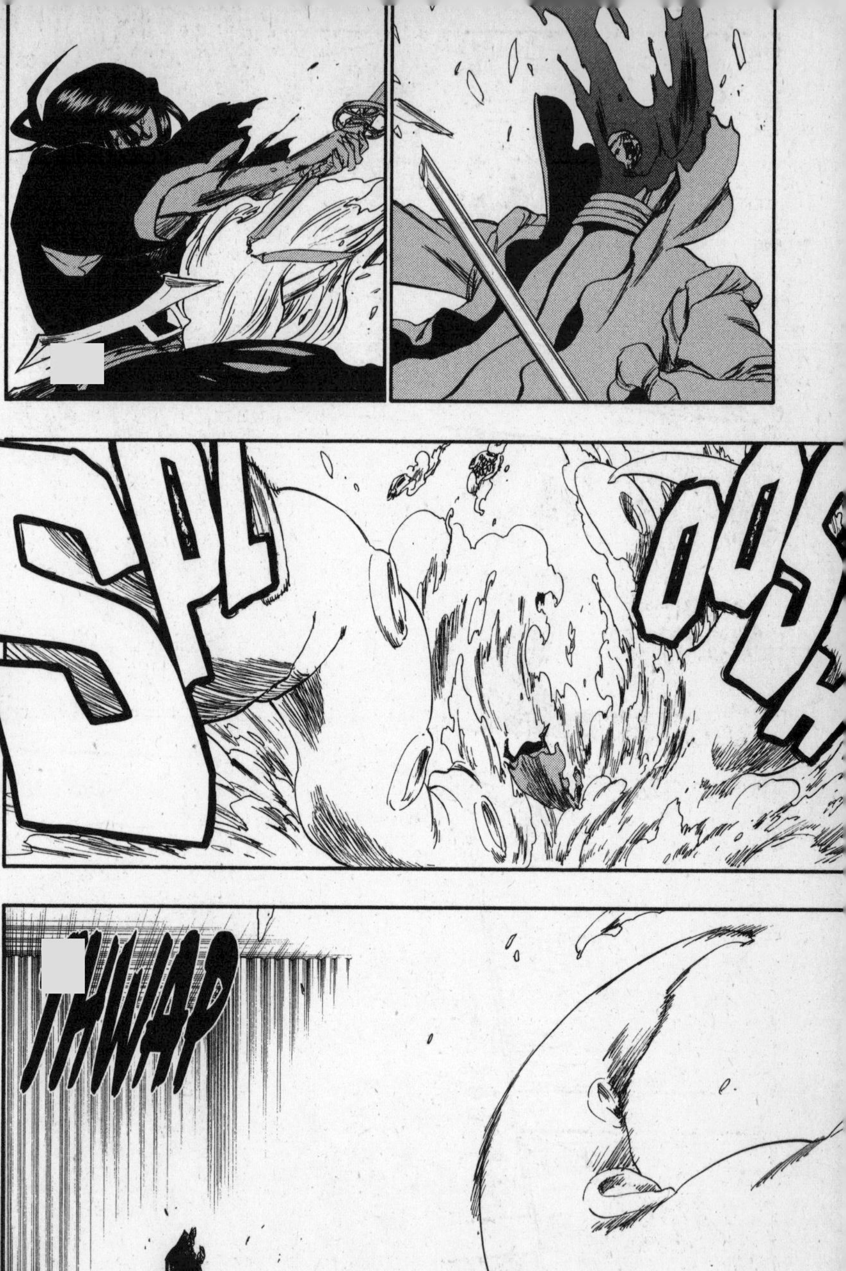
SPL
OOSH
THWAP

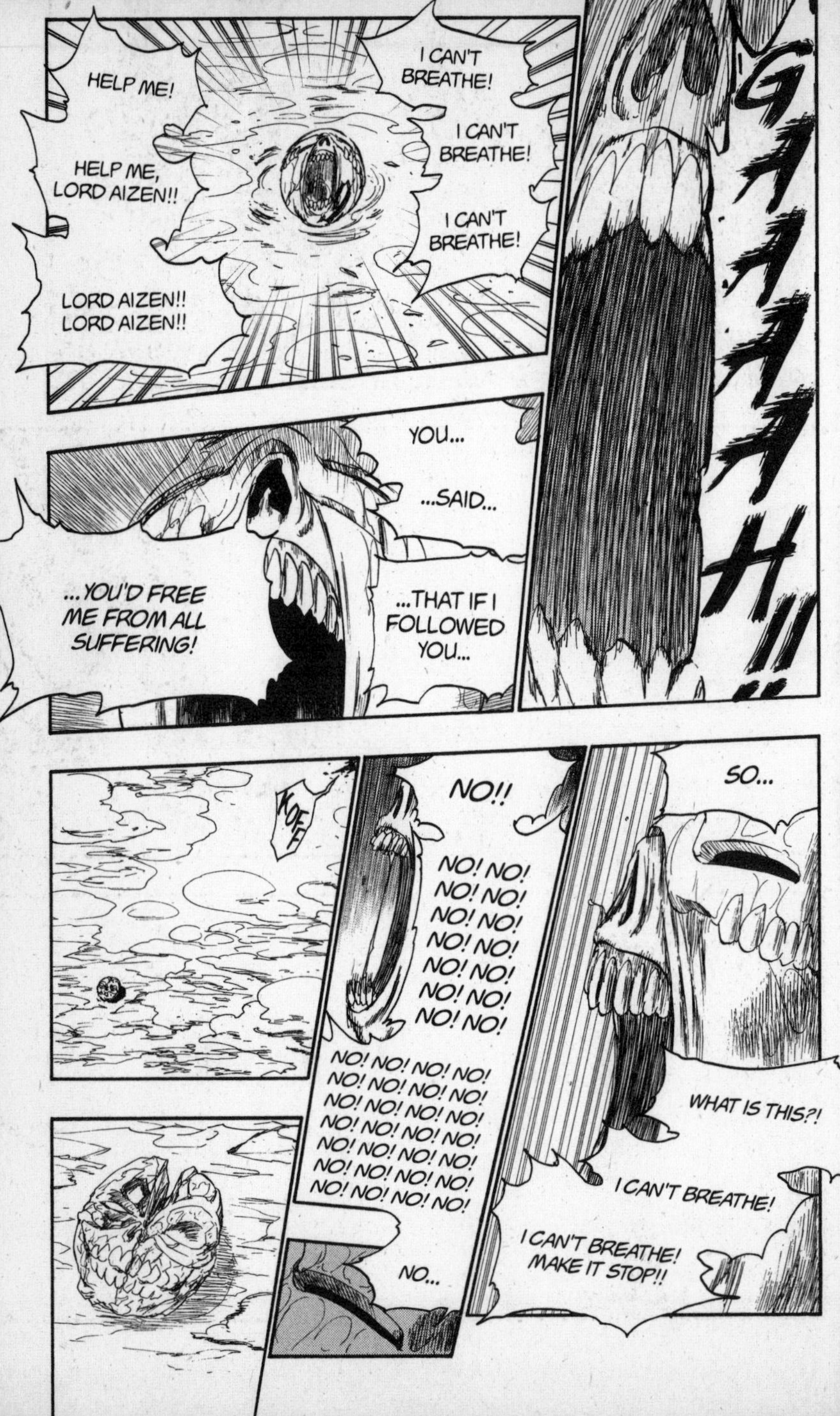
GAAAAAH!!
I CAN'T BREATHE!
I CAN'T BREATHE!
I CAN'T BREATHE!
HELP ME!
HELP ME, LORD AIZEN!!
LORD AIZEN!! LORD AIZEN!!
YOU...
...SAID...
...THAT IF I FOLLOWED YOU...
...YOU'D FREE ME FROM ALL SUFFERING!
SO...
WHAT IS THIS?!
I CAN'T BREATHE!
I CAN'T BREATHE! MAKE IT STOP!!
NO!!
NO! NO! NO! NO! NO! NO! NO! NO! NO! NO! NO! NO! NO! NO!
NO! NO! NO! NO! NO! NO! NO! NO! NO! NO! NO! NO! NO! NO! NO! NO! NO! NO! NO! NO! NO! NO! NO! NO! NO! NO! NO! NO!
NO...
KOFF

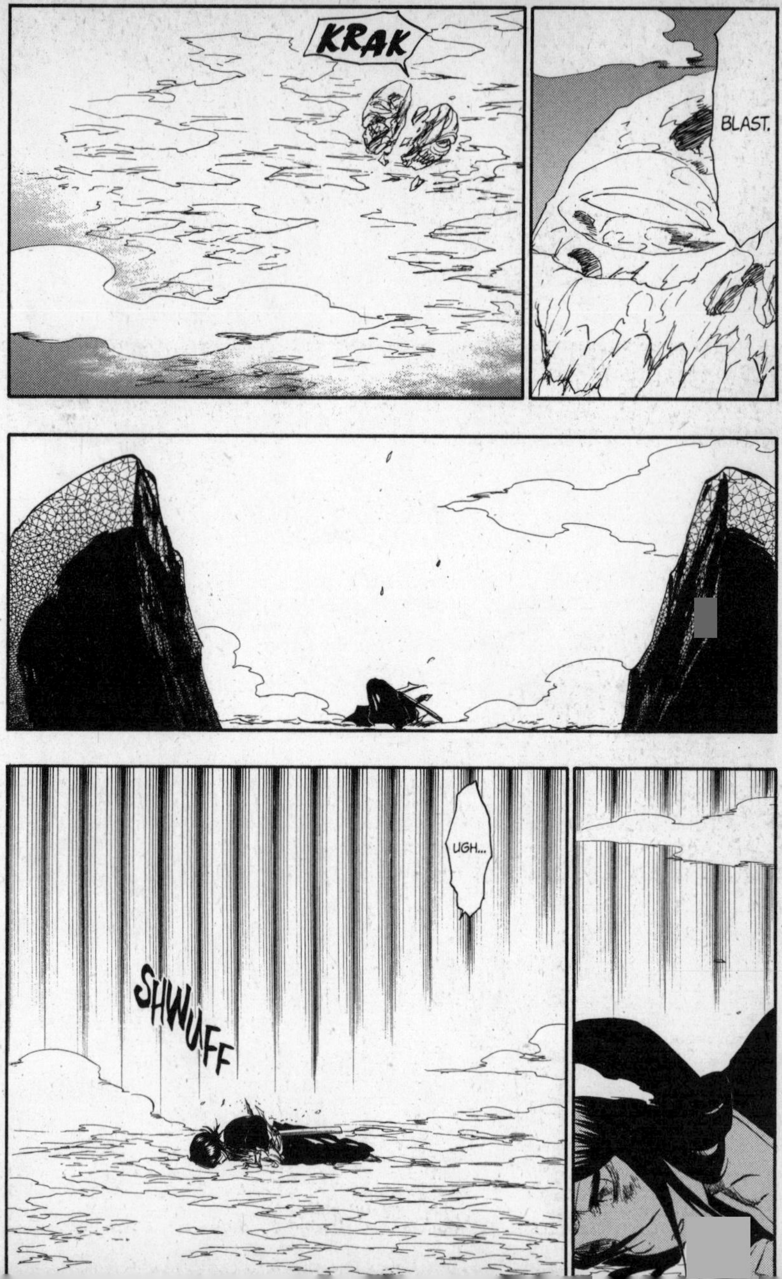
BLAST.
KRAK
UGH...
SHWUFF

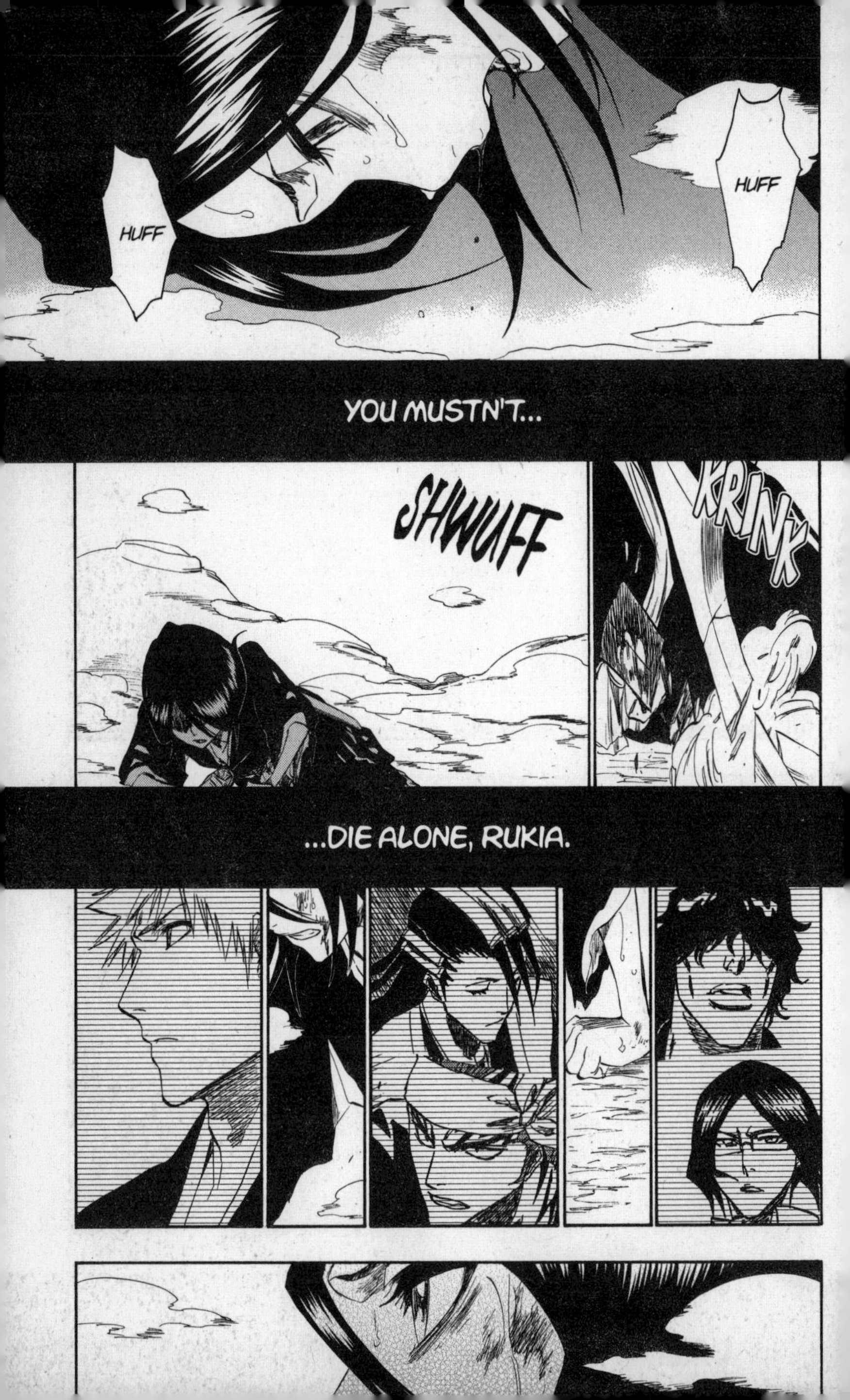
HUFF
HUFF
YOU MUSTN'T...
KRINK
SHWUFF
...DIE ALONE, RUKIA.

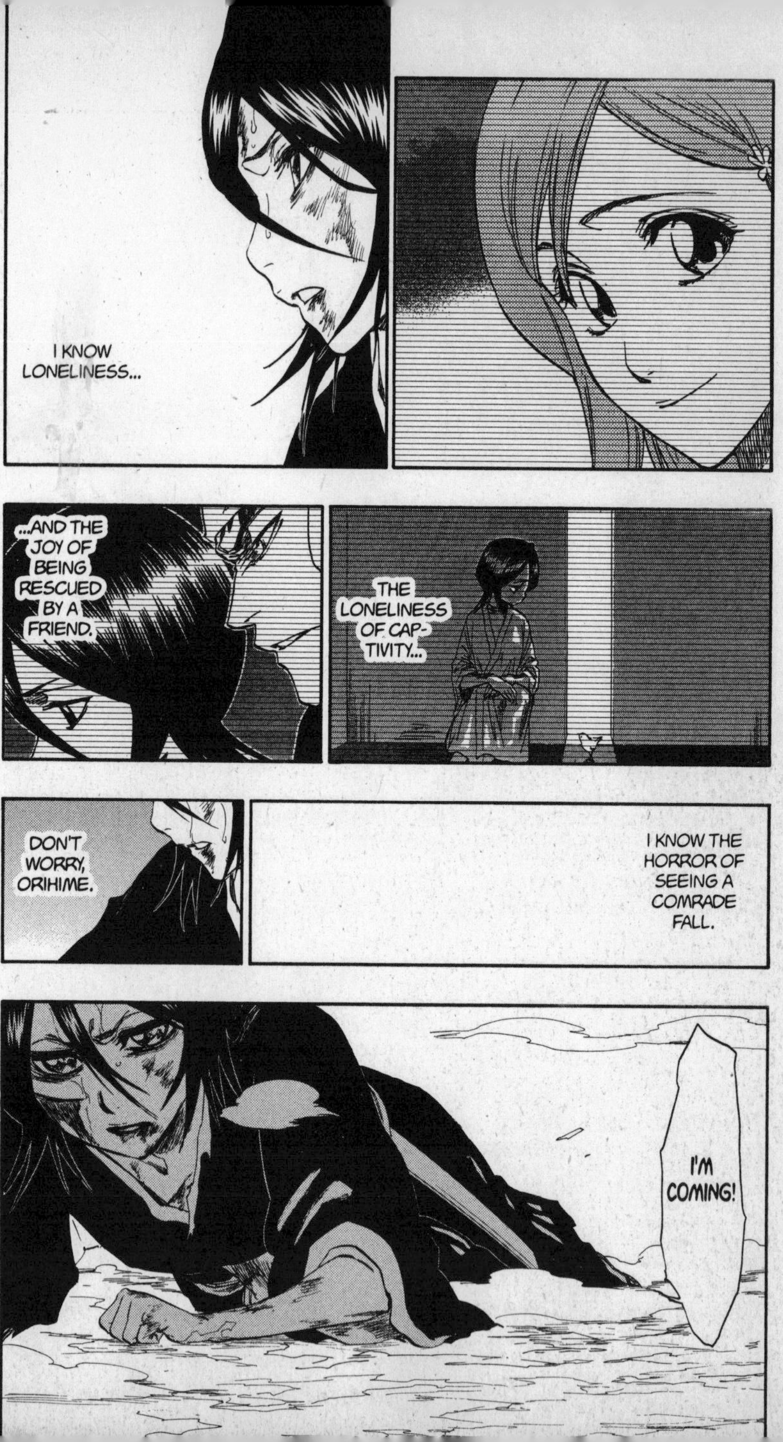
I KNOW LONELINESS...
THE LONELINESS OF CAP-TIVITY...
...AND THE JOY OF BEING RESCUED BY A FRIEND.
I KNOW THE HORROR OF SEEING A COMRADE FALL.
DON'T WORRY, ORIHIME.
I'M COMING!

THWUMP

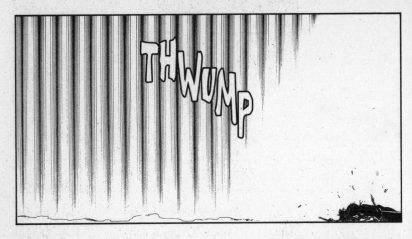

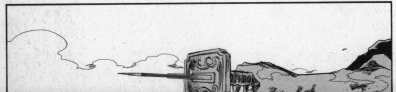

BLEACH 269.

The End Is Near

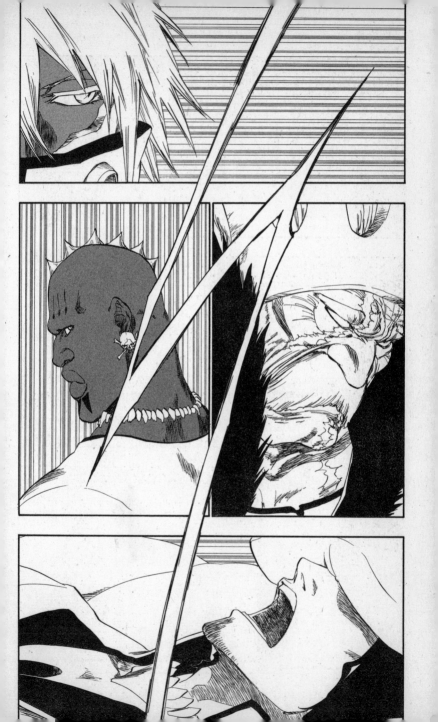

WHAT DO YOU WANT TO DO, HALIBEL ?!

AARO-NIERO, EH?

STUPID PUNK...

GETTING HIMSELF KILLED LIKE THAT.

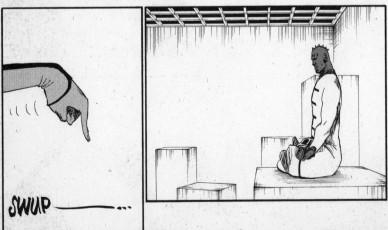

SWUP —————...

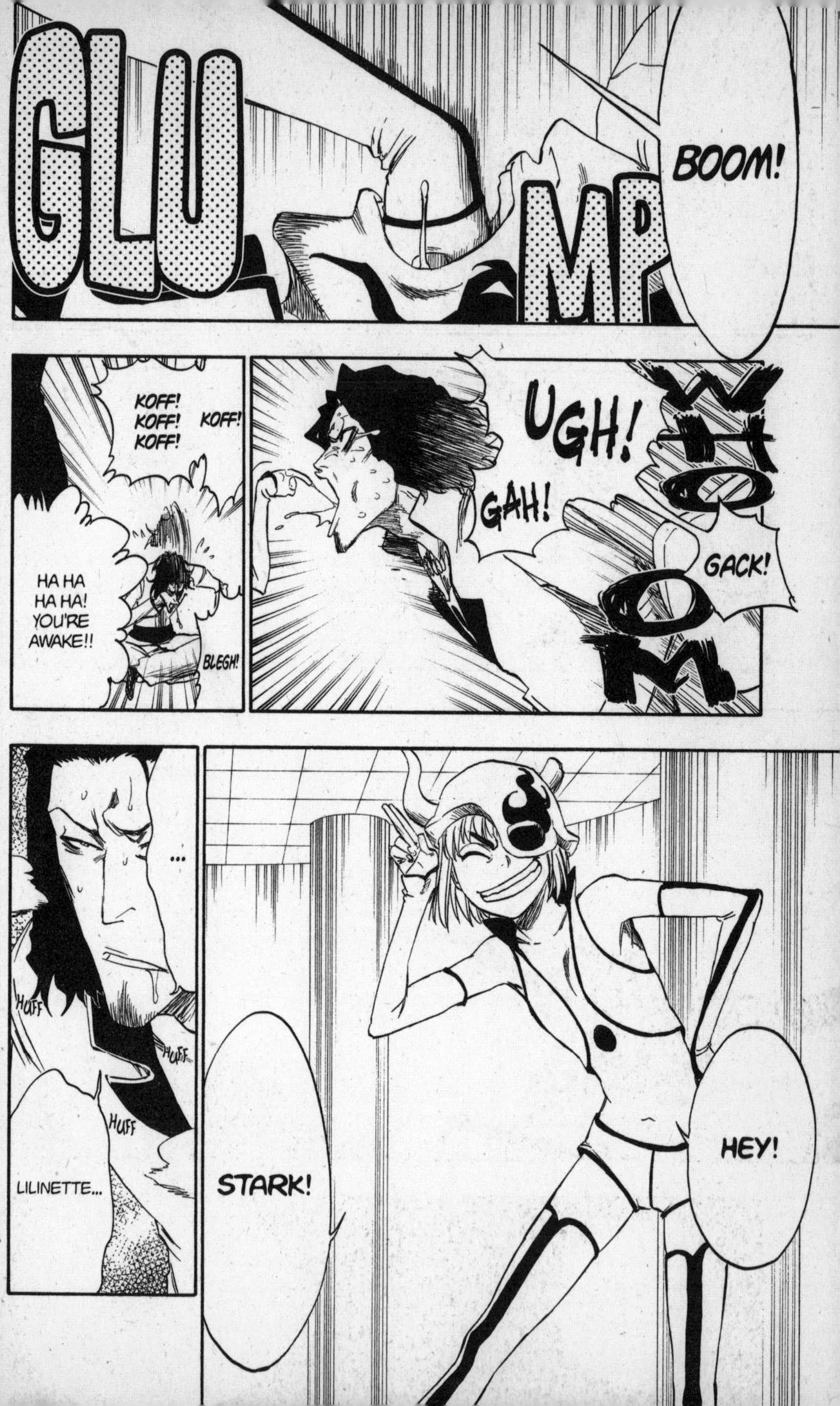
BOOM!
GLUMP
WHOOM
UGH!
GAH!
GACK!
KOFF!
KOFF! KOFF! KOFF!
HA HA HA HA! YOU'RE AWAKE!!
BLEGH!
HEY!
STARK!
...
HUFF
HUFF
HUFF
LILINETTE...

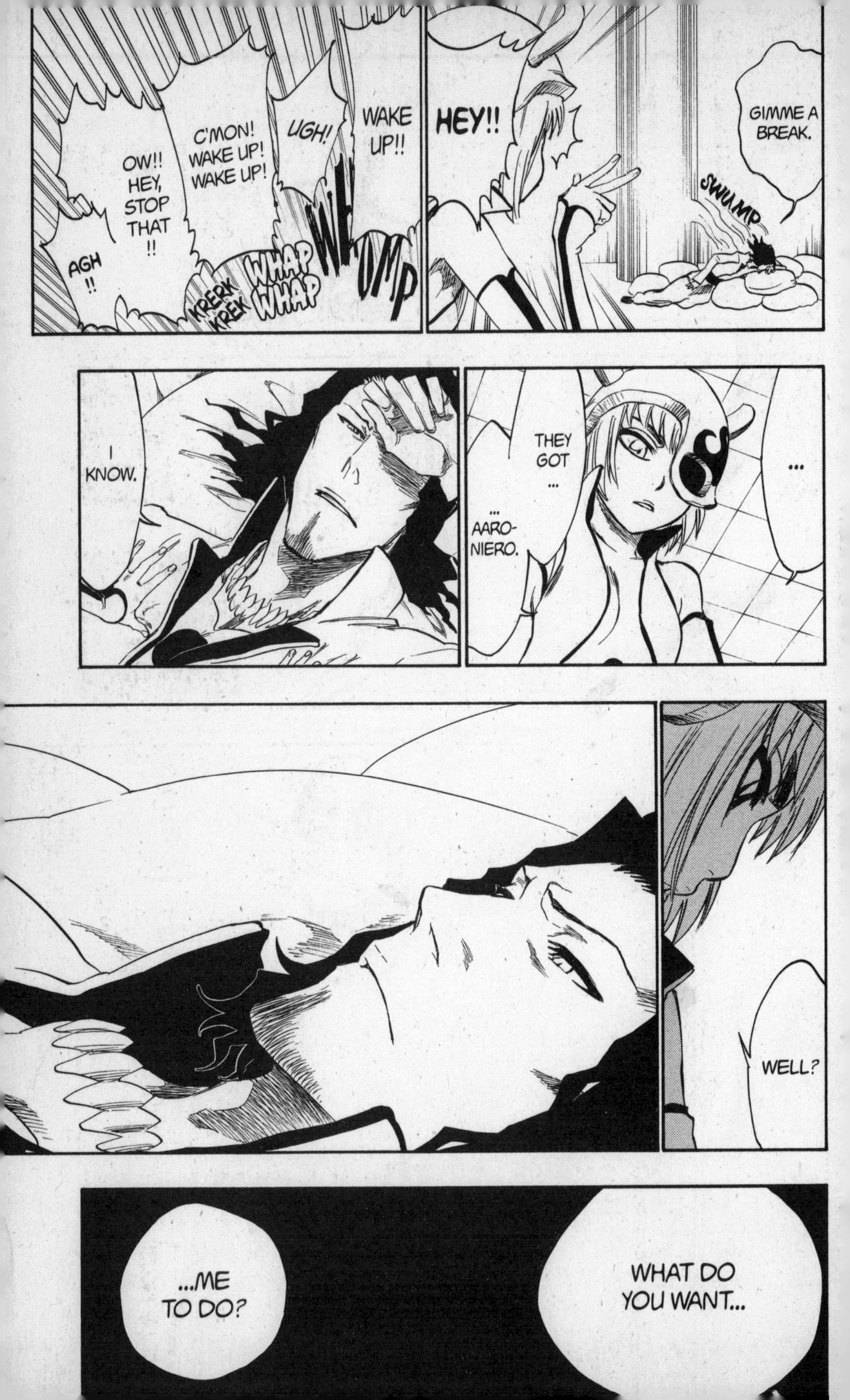
GIMME A BREAK.
SWUMP
HEY!!
WAKE UP!!
UGH!
C'MON! WAKE UP! WAKE UP!
WHAP WHAP
KRERK KREK
OW!! HEY, STOP THAT!!
AGH!!
...
THEY GOT ... ... AARO-NIERO.
I KNOW.
WELL?
WHAT DO YOU WANT...
...ME TO DO?

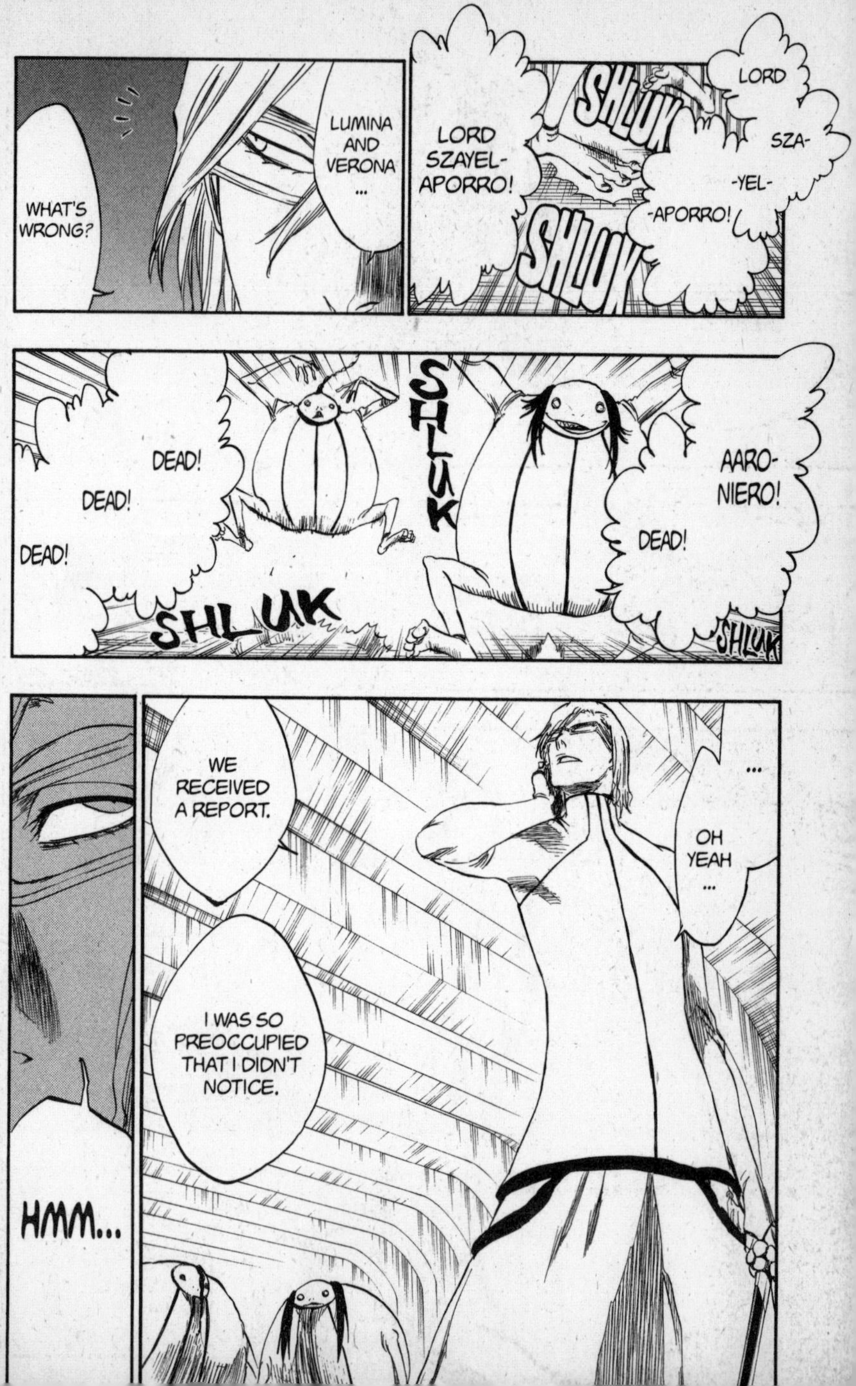
LORD SZA- -YEL- -APORRO!
SHLUK
LORD SZAYEL-APORRO!
SHLUK
LUMINA AND VERONA ...
WHAT'S WRONG?
AARO-NIERO!
DEAD!
SHLUK
SHLUK
DEAD!
DEAD!
DEAD!
SHLUK
... OH YEAH ...
WE RECEIVED A REPORT.
I WAS SO PREOCCUPIED THAT I DIDN'T NOTICE.
HMM...

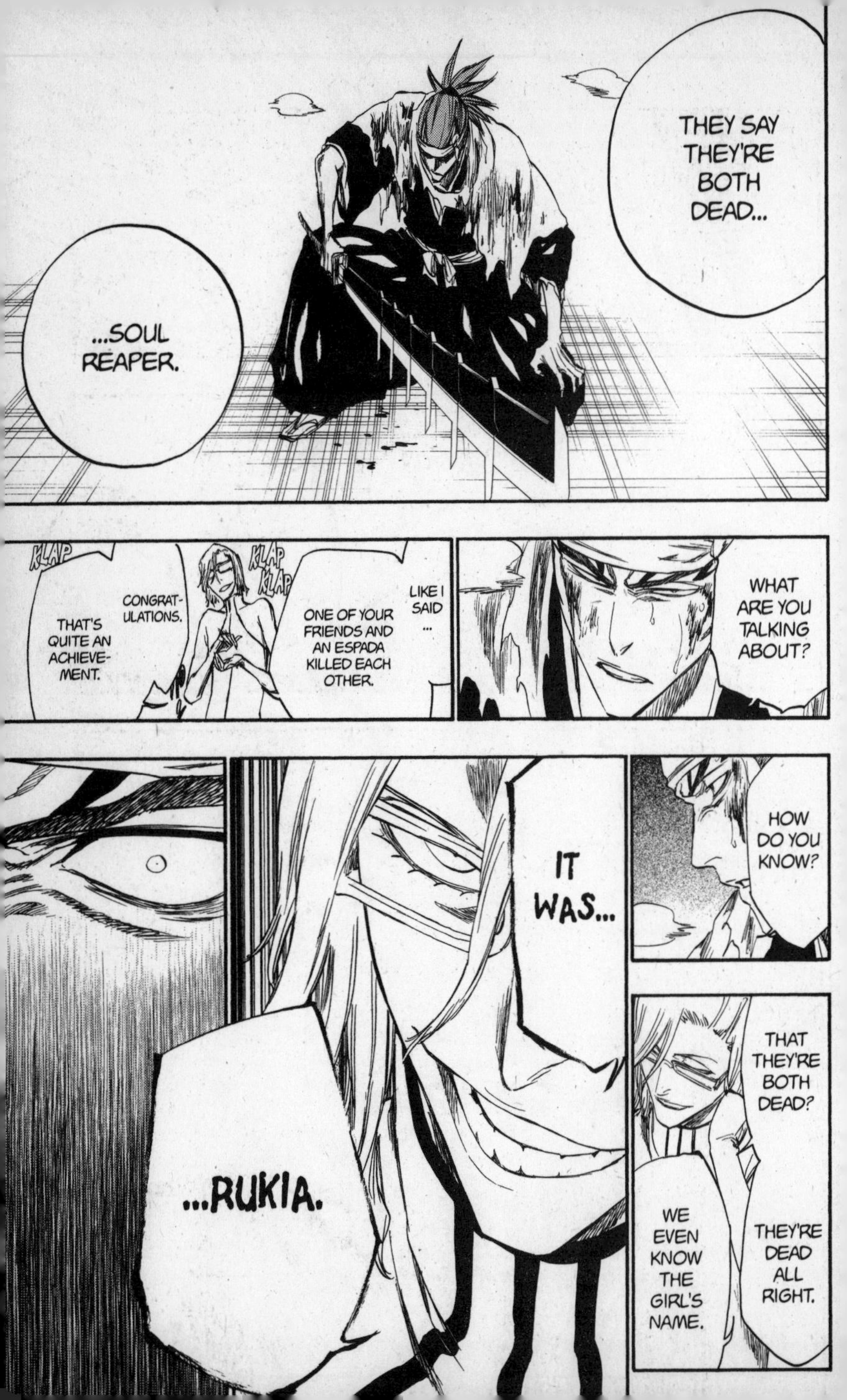
THEY SAY THEY'RE BOTH DEAD...
...SOUL REAPER.
WHAT ARE YOU TALKING ABOUT?
LIKE I SAID ...
ONE OF YOUR FRIENDS AND AN ESPADA KILLED EACH OTHER.
KLAP KLAP
CONGRAT-ULATIONS.
THAT'S QUITE AN ACHIEVE-MENT.
KLAP
HOW DO YOU KNOW?
THAT THEY'RE BOTH DEAD?
THEY'RE DEAD ALL RIGHT.
WE EVEN KNOW THE GIRL'S NAME.
IT WAS...
...RUKIA.

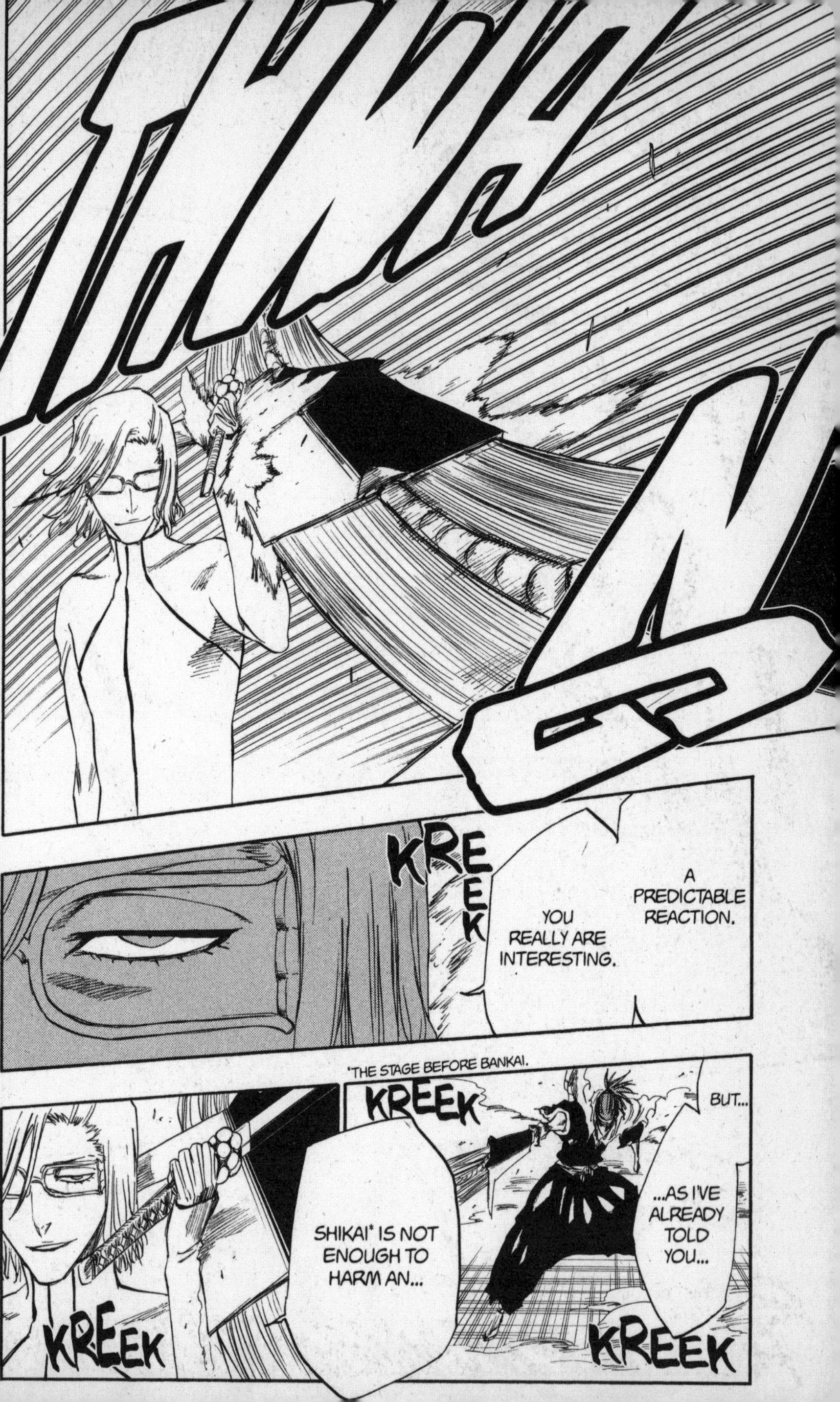
KREEEK
A PREDICTABLE REACTION.
YOU REALLY ARE INTERESTING.
*THE STAGE BEFORE BANKAI.
BUT...
KREEK
...AS I'VE ALREADY TOLD YOU...
KREEK
SHIKAI* IS NOT ENOUGH TO HARM AN...
KREEK

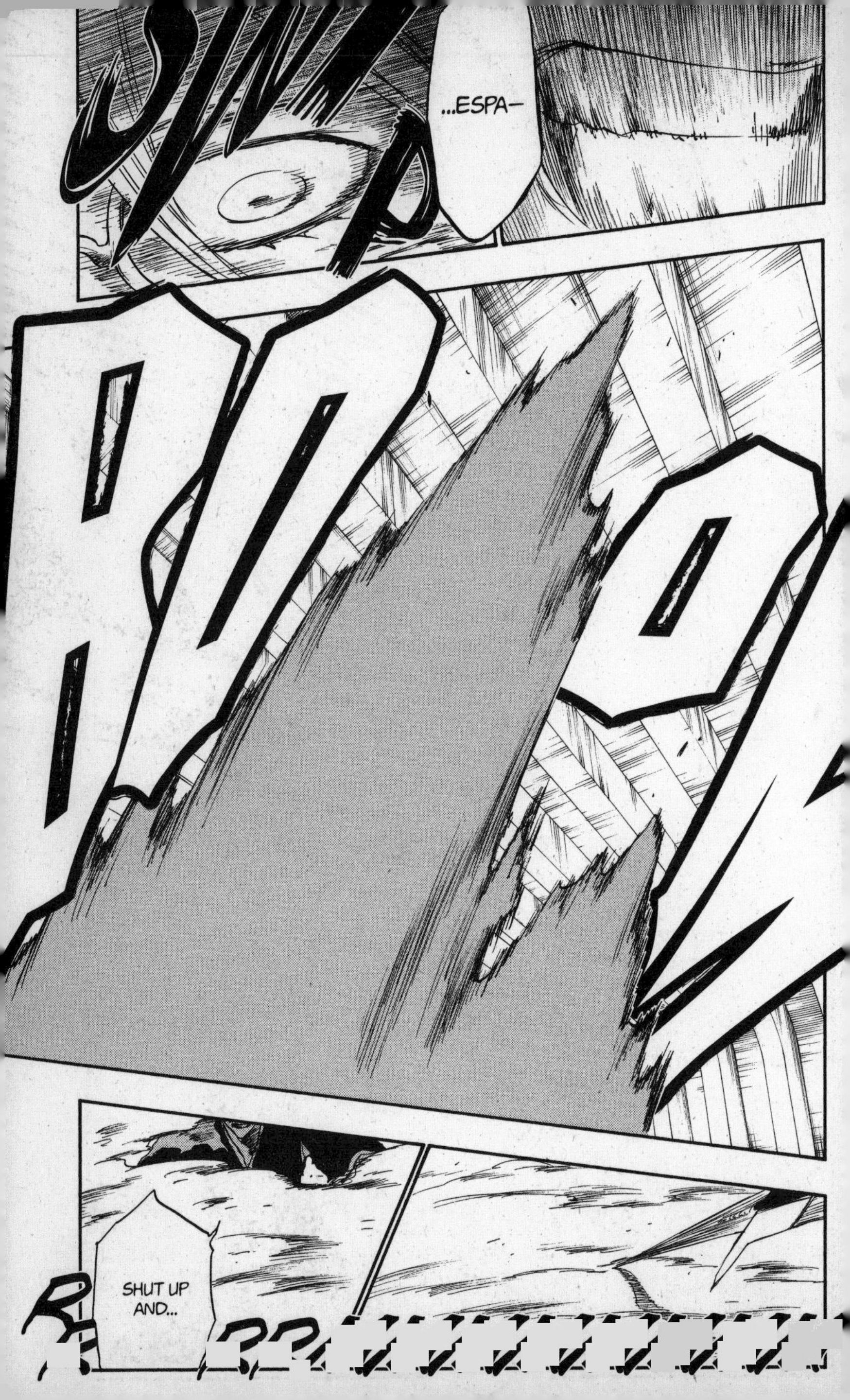
...ESPA–
SHUT UP AND...

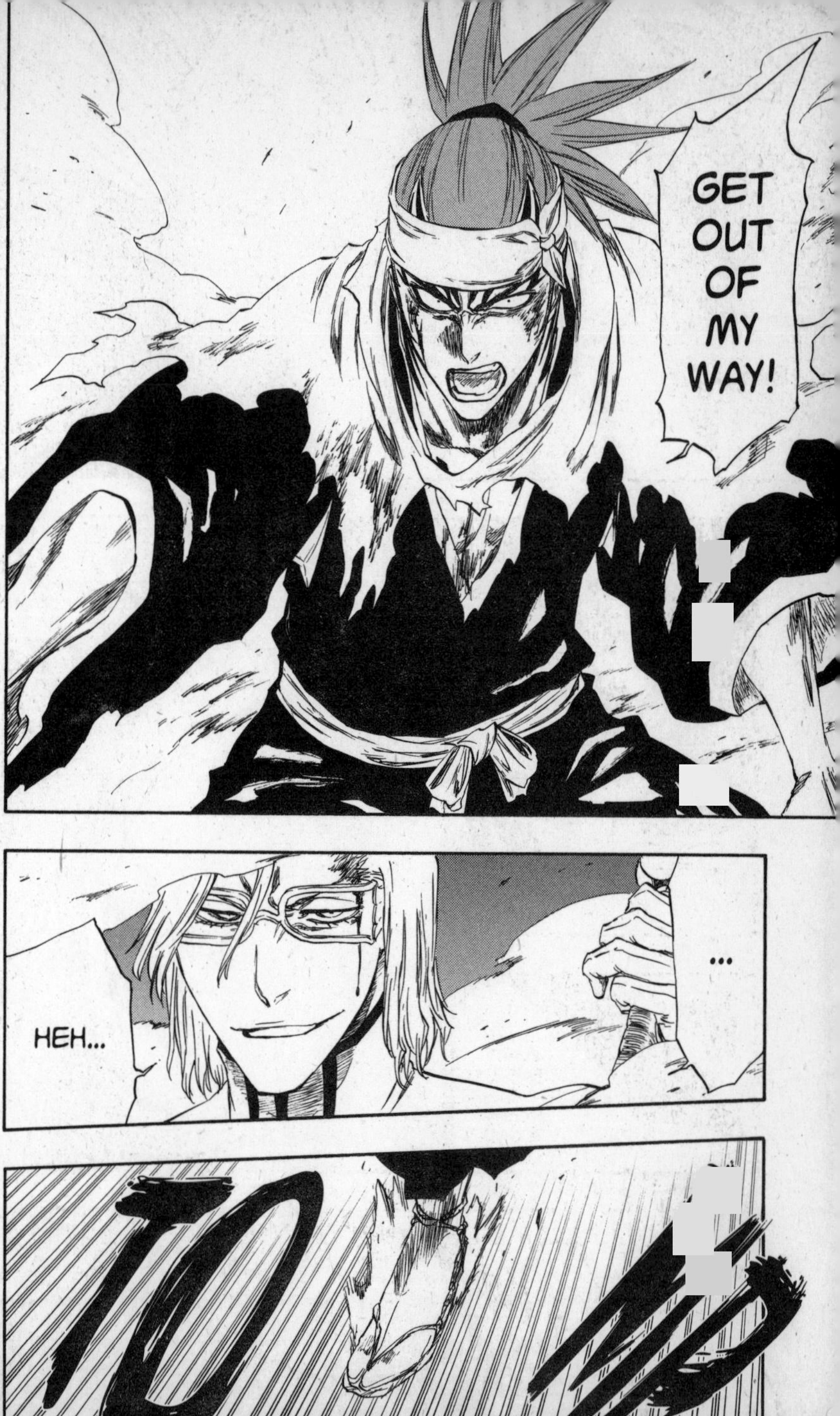
GET OUT OF MY WAY!
...
HEH...

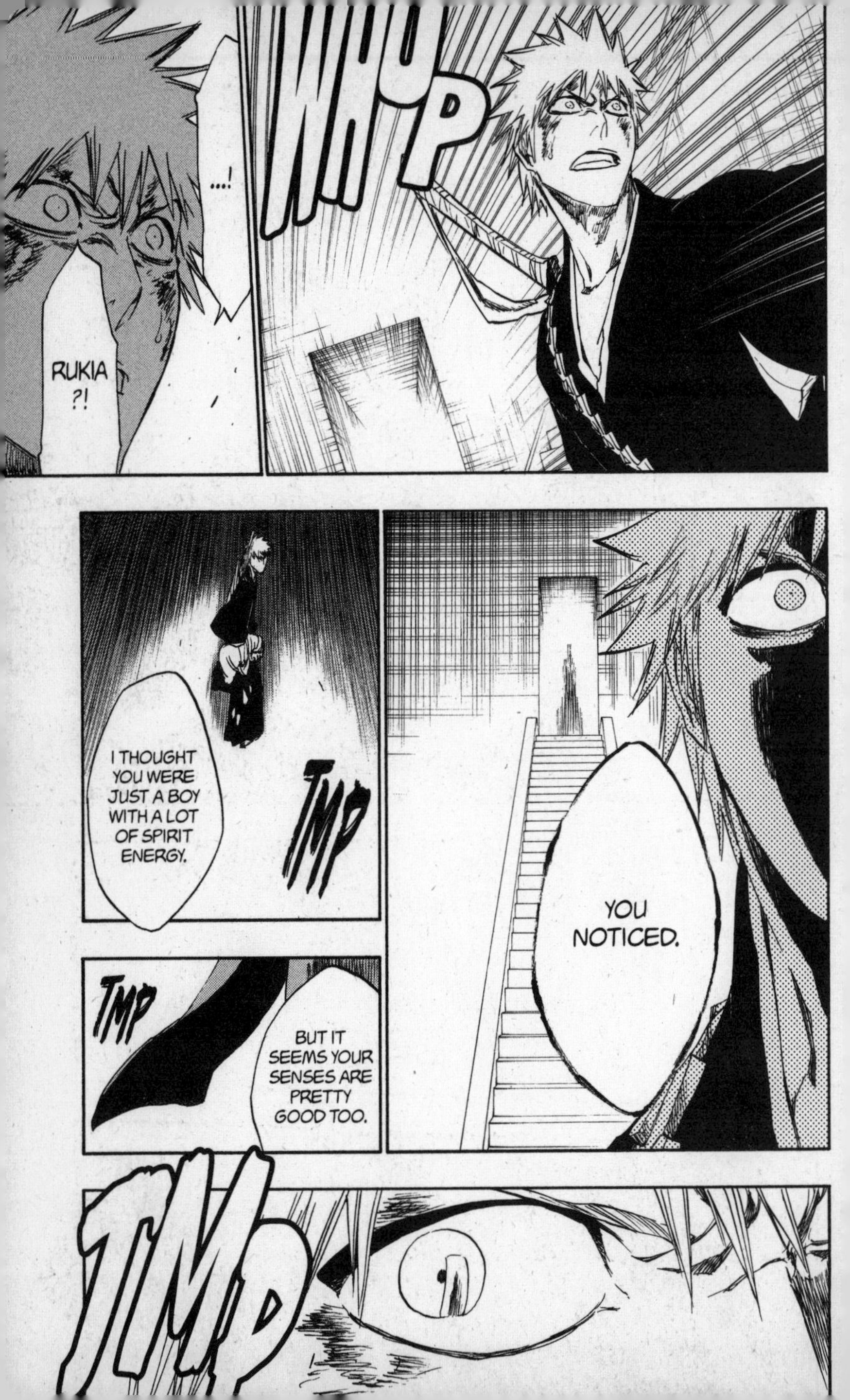
WHUP
...!
RUKIA ?!
YOU NOTICED.
I THOUGHT YOU WERE JUST A BOY WITH A LOT OF SPIRIT ENERGY.
TMP
BUT IT SEEMS YOUR SENSES ARE PRETTY GOOD TOO.
TMP
TMP

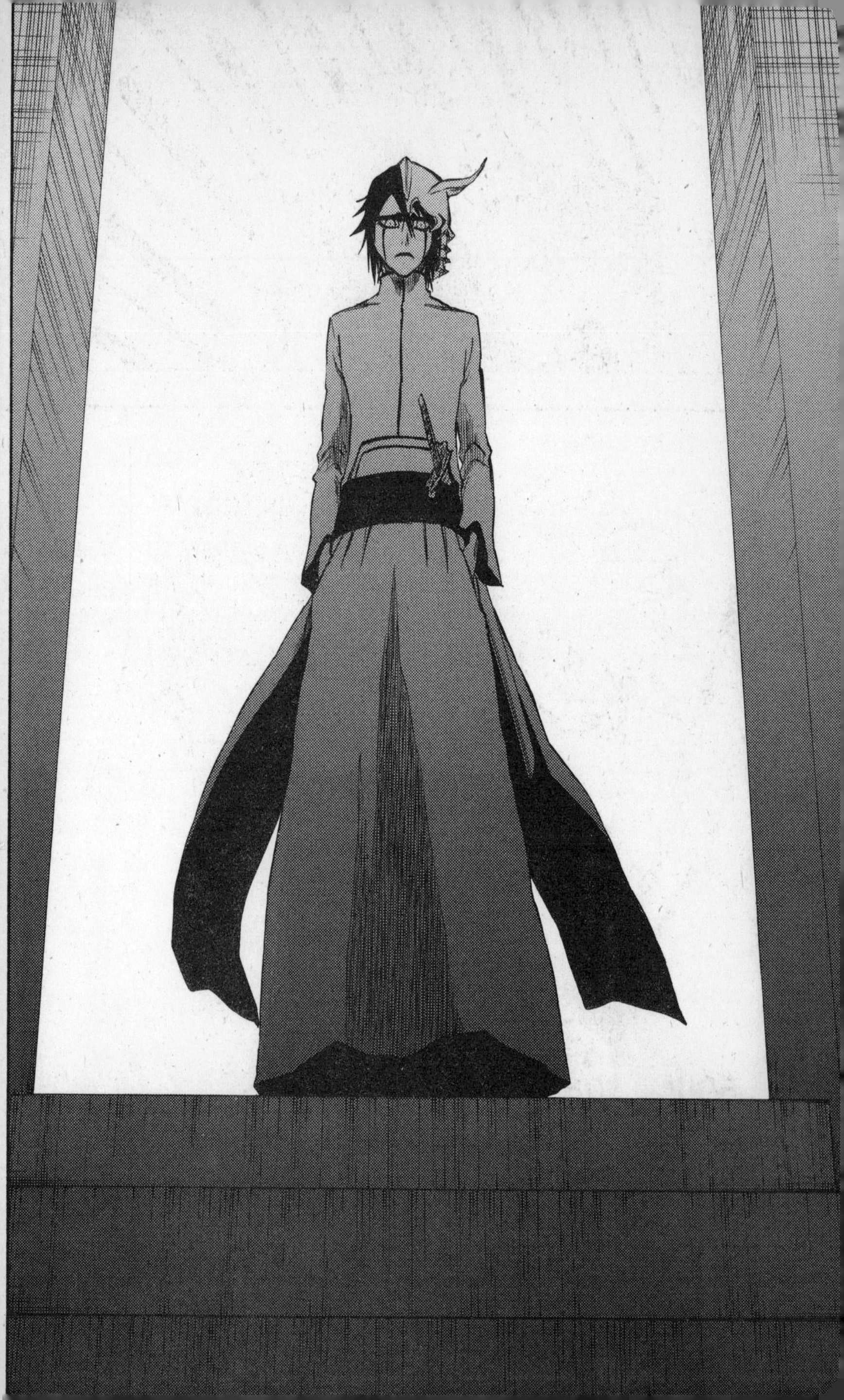

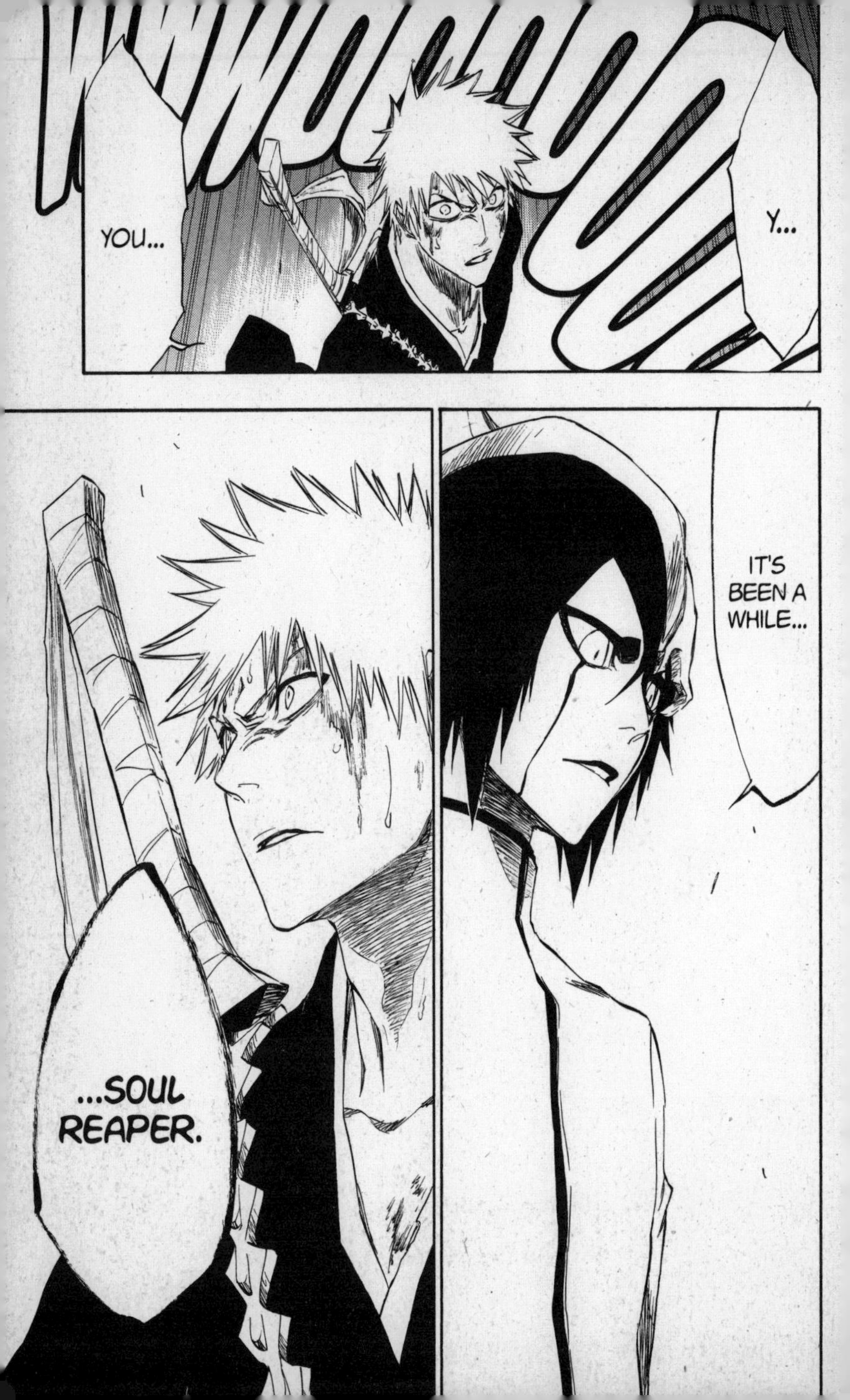
Y...
YOU...
IT'S BEEN A WHILE...
...SOUL REAPER.

CONTI
NUED
IN
BLEACH
31

Next Volume Preview

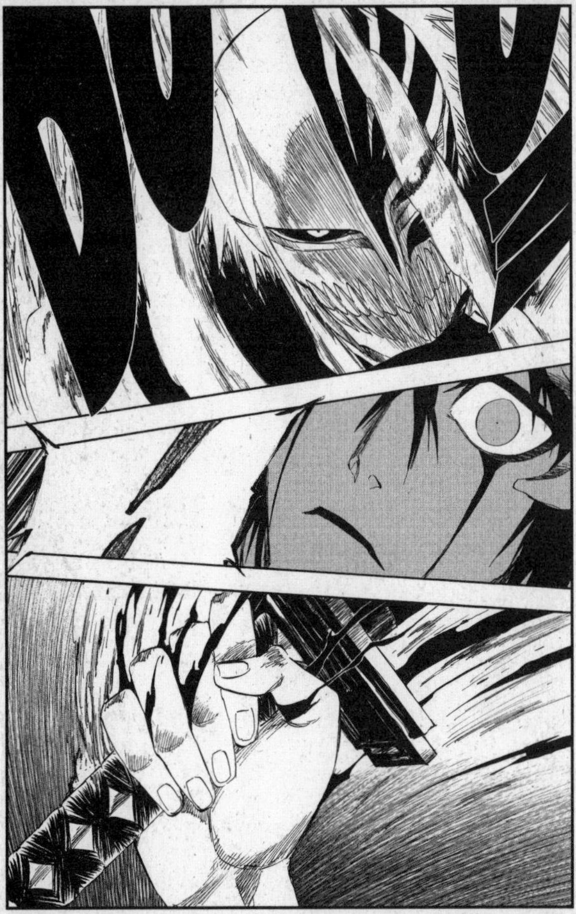

Ulquiorra goads Ichigo with news of Rukia's downfall and the truth about Orihime's abduction. Now Ichigo has all the motivation he needs to defeat his archenemy, but is he ready for this particular Espada?!

Read it first in SHONEN JUMP magazine!

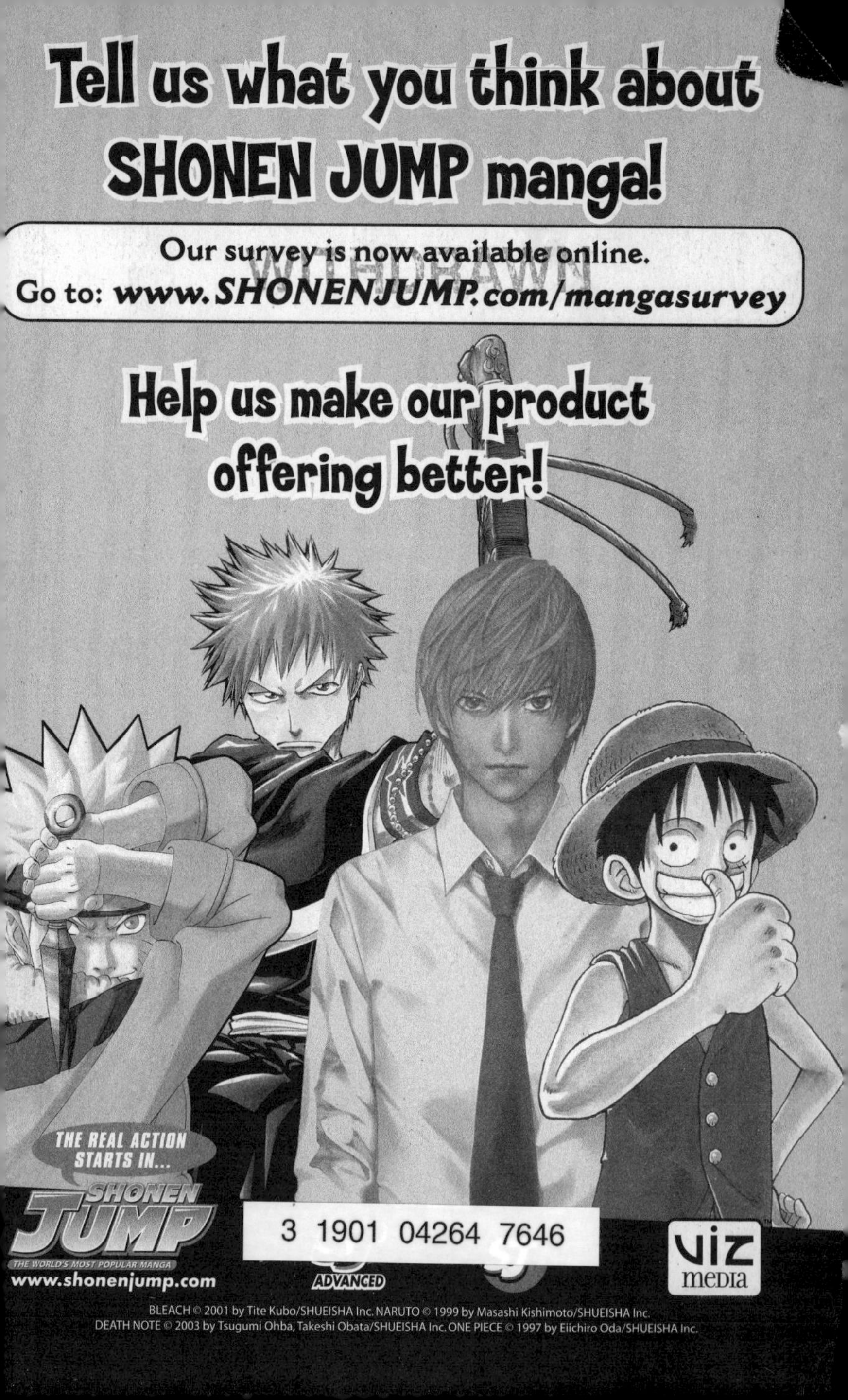
Tell us what you think about SHONEN JUMP manga!
Our survey is now available online.
Go to: www.SHONENJUMP.com/mangasurvey
Help us make our product offering better!
THE REAL ACTION STARTS IN...
SHONEN JUMP
THE WORLD'S MOST POPULAR MANGA
www.shonenjump.com
ADVANCED
3 1901 04264 7646
VIZ media
BLEACH © 2001 by Tite Kubo/SHUEISHA Inc. NARUTO © 1999 by Masashi Kishimoto/SHUEISHA Inc.
DEATH NOTE © 2003 by Tsugumi Ohba, Takeshi Obata/SHUEISHA Inc. ONE PIECE © 1997 by Eiichiro Oda/SHUEISHA Inc.